InfoPath 2013 Cookbook

121 Codeless Recipes for Beginners

S.Y.M. Wong-A-Ton

InfoPath 2013 Cookbook – 121 Codeless Recipes for Beginners

Copyright © 2013 by S.Y.M. Wong-A-Ton

Cover photo © by S.Y.M. Wong-A-Ton: Winter in New Zealand

To Sooch

Thank you for being uniquely you

Table of Contents

Introduction .... **vii**

    Who should read this book? viii

    How to use this book ix

    About the author x

    Support xi

Chapter 1: Form Template Design Basics **1**

    Form vs. form template 1

        1   Create a new form template 2

        2   Preview an InfoPath form 7

    Page layouts and layout tables 9

        3   Align labels and controls 14

    Controls 17

        4   Add a text box – method 1 19

        5   Add a text box – method 2 24

        6   Change a text box into a date picker 30

        7   Delete a control 33

        8   Bind a control to a different field 34

    Control and field properties 36

        9   Make a text box multi-line 37

        10   Make a text box mandatory 39

        11   Add a hidden field to a form 41

    Save and publish 42

        12   Publish an InfoPath form template 44

Chapter 2: Views **47**

What are views? 47

    13   Add a second view to a form template 48

    14   Make a view the default view 50

Read-only views 52

    15   Add a read-only view 53

Print views 54

    16   Add a print view 55

    17   Print data on a print view by overlaying text on an image 58

Chapter 3: Formulas 67

    18   Capitalize text in a text box 69

    19   Join text strings from two text boxes together 72

    20   Join two text strings and remove spaces if either text string is empty 75

Chapter 4: Rules 79

What are rules? 79

Types of rules 79

    21   Change the background color of a text box to red if it is blank 80

Action rules 86

    22   Set the value of a field 90

    23   Close a form when a button is clicked 94

    24   Switch to a read-only view when a button is clicked 95

Formatting rules 97

    25   Show a repeating table when a check box is selected 100

    26   Make a control read-only based on a condition 103

    27   Disable a button on a read-only view 106

    28   Enable a control when a check box is selected 108

Validation rules 109

    29   Make a field required based on a condition 110

    30   Check whether a number was entered 113

    31   Set a maximum length on text in a text box 115

Multiple conditions on rules 119

32   Show/hide sections based on a drop-down list box selection 119

Chapter 5: External Data Sources **127**

33   Get data from an XML file 128
34   Get data from a database table 133
35   Get data from a SharePoint list 136

Chapter 6: Submit Forms **139**

36   Enable a form to be submitted 139
37   Submit a form to a single destination using rules 145
38   Submit a form to multiple destinations using rules 150
39   Prevent form submission if a check box has not been selected 154
40   Submit form data to one Access database table 160
41   Submit form data to database tables with a one-to-many relationship 168

Read-only views and controls after submit 173
42   Switch to a read-only view on submit 173
43   Switch to a read-only view when a form is opened after submission 175
44   Make a control read-only upon submit 178

Chapter 7: Input Controls **181**

Text Boxes 181
45   Display the current time on a form when it opens 181
46   Calculate the sum of text boxes 186

Check Boxes and Option Buttons 189
47   Validate a check box 190
48   Toggle a check box on and off when a button is clicked 192
49   Make a field required based on the value of a check box 194
50   Select a check box to move text from one field to another 196
51   Select an option and have a text box appear on a different view 197

Drop-Down List Boxes 201
52   Populate a drop-down list box with static items 202
53   Populate a drop-down list box with data from a repeating table 205
54   Populate a drop-down list box with data from an XML file 207

55	Filter a drop-down list box based on the first character	213
56	Automatically select the first item in a drop-down list box	215
57	Clear the selected item in a drop-down list box	218
58	Count the amount of items in a drop-down list box	219
59	Check if an item exists in a drop-down list box	222
60	Populate a text box based on an item selected in a drop-down list box	226
61	Cascading drop-down list boxes using an XML file	231

Date Pickers and Date and Time Pickers ... **235**

62	Display the current date in a date picker	236
63	Extract the year from a date picker	238
64	Set the year of a date in a date picker using a drop-down list box	240
65	Display the month name for a selected date	242
66	Set a date picker to display the previous month in its calendar	245
67	Display the name of the day for a selected date	249
68	Force Sundays to be selected from a date picker	254
69	Display the time of a date and time picker in a drop-down list box	256
70	Add 7 days to a date in a date picker	268
71	Check whether a start date falls before an end date	270
72	Keep two date pickers within a 7-day date range from each other	272
73	Calculate a person's age based on a date of birth in a date picker	274
74	Calculate the difference in days between a date picker and today	276
75	Calculate the difference in days between two date pickers	280
76	Calculate the difference between two dates in a repeating table	284
77	Count the amount of holidays between two date pickers	290

Multiple-Section List Boxes ... **294**

78	Select one or more items by default in a multi-select list box	296
79	Limit a multi-select list box to a maximum of 3 selected items	298
80	Show or hide sections using a multiple-selection list box	304
81	Display items from a multiple-selection list box as multi-line text	310

Chapter 8: Objects ... **315**

Calculated Values ... **315**

| 82 | Dynamically change the label of a text box when an option is selected | 317 |

Buttons and Picture Buttons ... **319**

83	Change the label of a button when the button is clicked	322
84	Add line breaks to the label of a button	324
85	Enable a button by clicking on another button	326
86	Create a tabbed interface using buttons	328

File Attachments 333

87	Check if a file has been attached to a file attachment control	336
88	Clear a file attachment control	337
89	Make an attachment read-only – method 1	338
90	Make an attachment read-only – method 2	342
91	Add multiple files to a file attachment control	346

Chapter 9: Container Controls 347

Sections 347

92	Use sections to display error messages	348
93	Make a field mandatory when a specific choice section is selected	351

Repeating Tables and Repeating Sections 355

94	4 Ways to add a control to a repeating table	357
95	Remove the first empty row of a repeating table	363
96	Display a fixed amount of rows in a repeating table	365
97	Make an entire repeating table read-only	369
98	Make rows of a repeating table read-only by using check boxes	371
99	Count the number of rows in a repeating table – method 1	373
100	Count the number of rows in a repeating table – method 2	374
101	Count the number of rows changed in a repeating table	379
102	Count the number of occurrences of a word in a repeating table	384
103	Automatically number repeating table rows	387
104	Copy data from the previous row to a new row in a repeating table	389
105	Auto-populate a repeating table with week periods	392
106	Auto-populate a drop-down list box with past and future dates	395
107	Add a sum field to a repeating table	399
108	Add a running total sum to a repeating table	402
109	Calculate the average of all fields in 3 repeating tables	406
110	Hide the first row of a repeating table	409
111	Hide a row of a repeating table when a check box is selected	411
112	Highlight the last row of a repeating table	413

113   Highlight alternating rows in a repeating table 415
114   Limit the amount of rows added to a repeating table to a maximum ... 417
115   Change a green repeating table to red if it contains more than 3 rows 421
116   Shrinking drop-down list in a repeating table 424
117   Cascading drop-down list boxes in a repeating table 429
118   Export a repeating table's contents as a string 434
119   Export a repeating table's contents to a text box with line breaks 436
120   Copy data from a Secondary data source to the Main data source 439
121   Master/detail functionality with one master and two detail lists 442

Bonus Recipes **455**

Appendix **477**

Index **483**

Introduction

InfoPath 2013 is a desktop application that comes with the Microsoft Office Professional Plus 2013 suite of applications. When you install InfoPath 2013, an application that can display two interfaces, InfoPath Designer 2013 and InfoPath Filler 2013, is installed. InfoPath Designer 2013 is used to design InfoPath form templates, while InfoPath Filler 2013 can be used to fill out InfoPath forms.

InfoPath can be used to create electronic forms. Examples of electronic forms include: Leave request forms, travel expense forms, purchase order forms, etc. All forms are then stored on a computer instead of in a file cabinet as would be the case with paper-based forms.

InfoPath forms are meant to replace their paper-based counterparts, and like paper-based forms:

- InfoPath forms can be stored in a repository such as for example a database or SharePoint document library instead of a file cabinet.

- InfoPath forms can go from person to person via e-mail instead of snail mail.

- InfoPath forms can go from system to system (for example from an HR system to a storage system), and can forego manual entry or data transfer as would be the case with paper-based forms that must be manually entered into a system.

The main benefits of using InfoPath are:

1. Reduction of human errors. Data validation can be built into InfoPath forms, so that there is a smaller chance of human errors taking place when forms are being filled out. In addition, if the data from forms need to be entered into a system, they need not be manually entered, which significantly reduces typos and other errors.

2. Increase in productivity. A search system can be built around electronic forms to be able to find information quicker than when using paper-based forms.

3. Easy extraction of information. InfoPath forms are XML files, which are text files, and from which data can easily be extracted and read.

4. Easy passing and sharing of data between systems. InfoPath forms are XML files for which a structure can be defined and then used as a contract between systems. Systems can then pass these XML files between each other for data processing and automation.

If you are reading this book, I assume you have already installed InfoPath and have an idea what InfoPath could potentially do for your business, so want to learn how to best use it and do not need to be convinced of its benefits.

Who should read this book?

This book was written for Microsoft Office users who want to learn to use Microsoft InfoPath Designer 2013 without first going through countless pages of reference material about InfoPath before being able to design their first InfoPath form template. While this book was written for beginners who have no prior knowledge of InfoPath, it assumes that you are familiar with one or more other Microsoft Office products (such as Word or Excel) and that you are not a complete beginner using a computer and software products.

This book was also written specifically for beginners who are not necessarily programmers. While this book contains mathematical formulas, it does not contain any code instructions.

This book follows a practical approach. Almost each chapter first presents a short amount of theory explaining a few key concepts and then slowly builds your InfoPath design skills with step-by-step recipes (tutorials) that follow a logical sequence and increase in complexity as you progress through the book.

Almost every recipe has a discussion section that expands on the steps outlined in the recipe, offers additional information on what you have learned, or builds your knowledge and experience through additional questions and exercises.

You will not find everything you can do with InfoPath explained in this book, because this book is not meant to be used as a reference. You must see this book as a short course; a course that will quickly get you up and running with InfoPath 2013 and teach you how to design form templates using the most often used controls in InfoPath. Its goal is to make you feel comfortable enough to design InfoPath 2013 form templates while getting invaluable tips and tricks along the way as you learn, and enable you to explore InfoPath 2013 further on your own.

How to use this book

This book has been set up in cookbook-style with 121 recipes. Each recipe consists of 3 parts: A description of the problem, a step-by-step outline of the solution, and further discussion highlighting important parts of the recipe or expanding on what you have learned.

Chapters 1 through 4 are meant to give you a foundation for designing basic InfoPath 2013 form templates. They explain how to design form templates, work with views and formulas, and add controls and rules in InfoPath. You should not skip these chapters if you are an absolute beginner.

Chapters 5 and 6 are required if you want to design InfoPath form templates that get data from external data sources and if you want to set up forms to be submitted to a particular destination instead of just saving forms locally on disk.

Chapters 7, 8, and 9 present over 70 step-by-step recipes for working with several of the most popular controls in InfoPath.

Throughout this book you will find exercises and questions. Exercises have no answers, but are just tasks for you to carry out to explore InfoPath further. Questions have answers which you can find in the Appendix. For example, answer number 18-2 refers to recipe 18 and question number 2.

About the author

My name is S.Y.M. Wong-A-Ton and I have been a software developer since the start of my IT career back in 1997. The first Microsoft products I used as a developer were Visual Basic 4 and SQL Server 6.5. During my IT career I have developed as well as maintained and supported all types of applications ranging from desktop applications to web sites and web services. I have been a Microsoft Certified Professional since 1998 and have held the title of Microsoft Certified Solution Developer for almost as long as I have been in IT.

I was originally trained as a Geophysicist and co-wrote (as the main author) a scientific article while I was still a scientist. This article was published in 1997 in the Geophysical Research Letters of the American Geophysical Union.

I started exploring the first version of InfoPath in 2005 in my spare time and was hooked on it from day one. What I liked most about InfoPath was the simplicity with which I was able to quickly create electronic forms that were like small applications on their own; all this without writing a single line of code!

While exploring InfoPath, I started actively helping other InfoPath users, who were asking questions on the Internet, to come up with innovative solutions. And because the same questions were being asked frequently, I decided to start writing tutorials and articles about InfoPath on my web site "Enterprise Solutions", which evolved into what is known today as "BizSupportOnline" and can be visited at http://www.bizsupportonline.net.

Shortly after starting to share my knowledge about InfoPath with others, I received recognition from Microsoft in the form of the Microsoft Most

Valuable Professional (MVP) award, and have received this award every year since then, which as of writing has been 8 years in a row.

I hope you enjoy reading this book as much as I enjoyed writing it for you. In this book, I do not hold back anything I know about InfoPath. So I do hope you take away a lot from this book and that it achieves its purpose of getting you up and running with InfoPath 2013.

Support

Every effort has been made to ensure the accuracy of this book. Corrections for this book are provided at http://www.bizsupportonline.com.

If you have comments, questions, suggestions, improvements, or ideas about this book, please send them to bizsupportonline@gmail.com with "InfoPath 2013 Cookbook" in the subject line.

Chapter 1: Form Template Design Basics

Form vs. form template

The terms **form** and **form template** are used interchangeably when talking about InfoPath, but there is a difference between the two that you should understand.

An InfoPath form template forms the basis for an InfoPath form. This means that an InfoPath form cannot exist without first having an InfoPath form template. You use InfoPath Designer 2013 to create InfoPath form templates.

You can see an InfoPath form template as a blueprint to create one or more InfoPath forms. Let us take building a house as an analogy. Before you can build a house, you need a blueprint and all of the materials such as blocks, cement, wood, etc. before you can start building. And once you have created a blueprint, you can build several of the same type of houses using that blueprint. And last but not least, you can put furniture in the houses, and that furniture can differ per house.

In the world of InfoPath, the form template is the blueprint which consists of building materials such as views, layout tables, controls, rules, data sources, etc. The InfoPath form is the house, and you can create several of the same type of forms (houses) using the same form template (blueprint). The data you fill out each InfoPath form with can be seen as the furniture you put in the house. InfoPath forms can be filled out using either InfoPath Filler 2013 or a browser, depending on the type of form template you create.

InfoPath form templates are published to a particular location, and once published, can be used to create InfoPath forms. InfoPath form templates have an XSN file extension, while InfoPath forms are saved as XML files. InfoPath forms are always internally linked to the corresponding form template from which they were created. This also means that if you publish an InfoPath form template, use it to create InfoPath forms, and then delete or move it, you will not be able to open those InfoPath forms that are based on it anymore using InfoPath or a browser, because the forms will not be able to find their corresponding form template.

Tip:

> An InfoPath form cannot exist without an InfoPath form template. So never ever delete an InfoPath form template or move it once it has been published, because you will be unable to open any InfoPath forms that are based on that InfoPath form template.

When you use InfoPath Designer 2013, you use it to design InfoPath form templates and can also preview InfoPath forms with it. In preview mode InfoPath Designer 2013 becomes InfoPath Filler 2013, which is only used to fill out InfoPath forms.

The 4 most basic steps to design an InfoPath form template are:

1. Create a new form template.

2. Add views, page layouts, and layout tables to the form template.

3. Add controls to the form template.

4. Publish the form template.

In the recipes in this chapter you will explore each one of these steps.

1   Create a new form template

Problem

You have installed InfoPath Designer 2013 and want to create an InfoPath form template.

Solution

You can use one of the several default form templates provided by InfoPath 2013 to create and design an InfoPath form template.

To create a new **Blank Form** template in InfoPath 2013:

1. Open InfoPath Designer 2013.

2. On the **New** tab, click **Blank Form**, and then click **Design Form**, or double-click **Blank Form**.

InfoPath creates a new form template and switches to the **Home** tab.

Discussion

You can open InfoPath Designer 2013 via the shortcut that was created for it during installation or via the command prompt. To open InfoPath Designer 2013 via the command prompt:

1. Type **cmd** in the Windows search box and then click **cmd.exe** or **Command Prompt**.

2. Navigate to the directory where Microsoft Office was installed by entering for example the following into the **Command Prompt** window and pressing **Enter**:

```
cd "C:\Program Files (x86)\Microsoft Office\Office15"
```

The location specified above is the default location for a Microsoft Office installation. This location may be different on your computer.

3. To open InfoPath Designer 2013, type the following command into the **Command Prompt** window:

```
infopath.exe /design
```

4. To open InfoPath Filler 2013, type the following command into the **Command Prompt** window:

```
infopath.exe
```

When you open InfoPath Designer 2013, the first screen you are presented with is the **New** tab. Note that if you were already designing a form template in InfoPath, you can access the **New** tab by clicking on the **File** tab on the Ribbon in InfoPath Designer 2013.

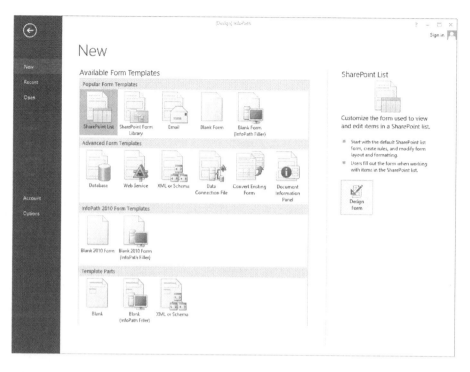

Figure 1. The New tab in InfoPath Designer 2013.

The type of form template you choose to create depends largely on what the InfoPath form is going to be used for, where you are going to publish the InfoPath form template, and how users are going to fill out forms.

Where filling out a form is concerned, you can create either a form that will be filled out using InfoPath Filler 2013, also known as an InfoPath Filler Form, or you can create a form that will be filled out through a browser, also known as a Web Browser Form. You must have access to a SharePoint Server for the latter type of forms.

InfoPath Filler Forms can be filled out only through InfoPath Filler 2013, while Web Browser Forms can be filled out using either a browser or InfoPath Filler 2013. If you are creating an InfoPath form template and are unsure which form template type to choose and have a SharePoint Server at your disposal, choosing a Web Browser Form will offer you more flexibility where filling out forms is concerned. The downside is that Web Browser Forms offer much less functionality than InfoPath Filler Forms, so you must assess whether you will be losing access to critical functionality (such as a few controls that are only available for InfoPath Filler Forms) before making your final decision. In any case, if you decide to first create a Web Browser Form and then later want to change this to an InfoPath Filler Form, you can always make the switch.

Throughout this book, you will be using mostly the **Blank Form** template to create form templates. The **Blank Form** template allows you to create an InfoPath form template that can be published to a SharePoint Server and create InfoPath forms that can be filled out either through a browser or Microsoft InfoPath Filler, so it results in a Web Browser Form being created.

To view the type of form template you have created, click **File ➤ Info ➤ Form Options**, and then on the **Form Options** dialog box, click **Compatibility** in the **Category** list, and then look at what has been selected in the **Form type** drop-down list box.

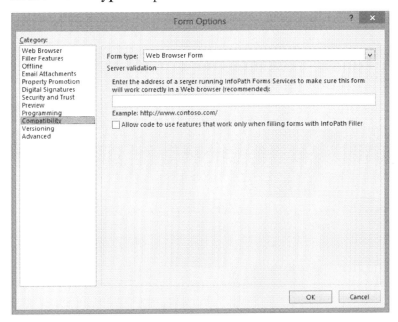

Figure 2. Compatibility category on the Form Options dialog box in InfoPath 2013.

You will see one of seven values in the **Form type** drop-down list box:

1. Web Browser Form
2. InfoPath Filler Form

3. Web Browser Form (InfoPath 2010)

4. InfoPath 2010 Filler Form

5. Web Browser Form (InfoPath 2007)

6. InfoPath 2007 Filler Form

7. InfoPath 2003 Filler Form

The 2003, 2007, and 2010 versions of form template types are provided so that you can create form templates that are compatible with InfoPath 2003, InfoPath 2007, SharePoint 2007, InfoPath 2010, and SharePoint 2010.

When you click **Blank Form** under **Popular Form Templates** on the **New** tab in InfoPath Designer 2013, you will see a brief description for the form template appear on the right-hand side of the screen and below that a **Design Form** button.

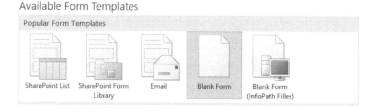

Figure 3. Blank Form template selected on the New tab in InfoPath Designer 2013.

Figure 4. Description for the Blank Form template in InfoPath 2013.

The description provides guidance as to what type of form template you are about to create. For example, the description for the **E-mail** form template says:

Design a form that can be distributed and submitted through e-mail.

- *Start with a built-in layout, add controls, create rules, and apply formatting.*
- *Users will fill out and submit the form in Microsoft Outlook.*

So the description tells you what the form template can be used for (Design a form that can be distributed and submitted through e-mail), how you can go about customizing it (Start with a built-in layout, add controls, create rules, and apply formatting), and how users can access and fill out the form (Users will fill out and submit the form in Microsoft Outlook).

Exercise

Click on each one of the available form templates on the **File ➤ New** tab and read their corresponding descriptions to familiarize yourself with the types of form templates you can create using InfoPath Designer 2013.

Questions

1. What can you create with InfoPath Designer 2013?
2. What can you create with InfoPath Filler 2013?
3. What is the difference between an InfoPath Filler Form and a Web Browser Form?

2   Preview an InfoPath form

Problem

You designed an InfoPath form template and want to see what forms that are based on this form template would look like and how they would function when you open them in InfoPath.

Solution

To see what an InfoPath form looks like at runtime and how it will work, you can preview it from within InfoPath Designer 2013.

To preview an InfoPath form:

1. In InfoPath, create a new **Blank Form** template.

2. Click **Home ➤ Form ➤ Preview**, press **F5**, or press **Ctrl+Shift+B** to preview the form.

Discussion

You can also save the InfoPath form template (XSN file) to disk and then double-click on the form template to fill out an InfoPath form (XML file) that uses that form template.

Whether you preview a form from within InfoPath Designer 2013 or double-click a form template to open and fill out a form, in both cases, InfoPath Filler 2013 is opened and used to preview, test, or fill out the form.

If you have previously saved an InfoPath form template to disk and want to open it from disk, right-click the XSN file, and then select **Design** from the context menu that appears. Selecting **Design** will open the form template in InfoPath Designer 2013, while selecting **Open** will open a form that is based on the form template in InfoPath Filler 2013.

Figure 5. Opening an InfoPath form template that has previously been saved to disk.

Note that you can also open an InfoPath form template via the command prompt. For example, if you saved an InfoPath form template named **OpenMe.xsn** in a directory called **C:\InfoPath**, then you would have to type the following in a command prompt window to open the form template in design mode:

```
infopath.exe /design "C:\InfoPath\OpenMe.xsn"
```

Exercise

When previewing a form in InfoPath Filler 2013, click on the save button and save the form locally on disk. When saving the form, you will see that you will be prompted to save the form as an **InfoPath Form (.xml)** file. Then open Notepad, select **File ➤ Open**, and browse to, select, and open the form you just saved. Remember to select **All Files (*.*)** as the file type to open in Notepad. What you will see in Notepad is a bunch of text, which is called XML.

This proves that InfoPath forms are just XML files that contain text. You can use this technique to view the data that is stored in your InfoPath forms without having to use InfoPath Filler 2013.

Question

1. What are the two ways you can preview an InfoPath form?

Page layouts and layout tables

When you create a new form template in InfoPath, InfoPath automatically creates the first view, which is called the **default view**, for you and adds a standard page layout to it. To see the view InfoPath created for you, select **Page Design ➤ Views ➤ View**.

Figure 6. View drop-down list box showing the default view created by InfoPath.

A view is a canvas on which you can place tables, text, and controls. You use views as the basis for designing your InfoPath form template.

If you do not like the standard page layout InfoPath adds when you create a **Blank Form** template, you can select it (by first clicking anywhere in the page layout table and then clicking on the small square in the upper left-hand corner of the page layout table), press **Delete** to delete it, and then add your own page layout.

Figure 7. Small square in the top left-hand corner of a page layout table in InfoPath 2013.

To add your own page layout, click **Page Design ➤ Page Layouts ➤ Page Layout Templates**, and then select one of the available page layouts from the drop-down menu that appears.

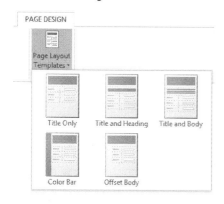

Figure 8. Page Layout Templates in InfoPath 2013.

Once you have a page layout on the view, you can refine the position of labels and controls by using layout tables. You can add a layout table with any number of rows and columns to lay out elements on a form. For layout tables you can choose from either predefined layout tables or custom tables.

To use one of the predefined layout tables, click on any of the layout tables on the **Insert** tab under the **Tables** group to add it to your form template.

Figure 9. Predefined layout tables in InfoPath 2013.

You can expand the list of layout tables by clicking on the drop-down arrow in the bottom right-hand corner of the list.

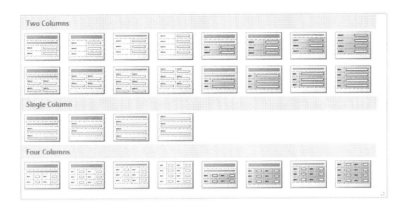

Figure 10. Expanded predefined layout tables list in InfoPath 2013.

To create a custom table you can use the **Custom Table** command on the **Insert** tab under the **Tables** group.

Custom
Table ▾

Figure 11. Custom Table command on the Insert tab under the Tables group.

You can add extra rows and columns to either a predefined layout table or a custom table by right-clicking in a table cell, selecting **Insert**, and then selecting **Columns to the Left**, **Columns to the Right**, **Rows Above**, or **Rows Below** from the context menu that appears.

Themes are sets of predefined colors and fonts you can use on page layouts and layout tables on your form. **Themes** are applied on a per view basis meaning that you can have two different themes applied to two different views, but all page layouts and layout tables on the same view get the same theme applied to them. To apply a theme to page layout and layout tables on a view, click on any of the themes that are located in the **Themes** list on the **Page Design** tab.

Note: Themes are not applied to custom tables, so if you want to make use of themes when designing an InfoPath form template, you must use the predefined layout tables and then apply the theme of your choice.

Tip:

To take advantage of themes in InfoPath you must use the predefined layout tables that are available on the **Insert** tab under the **Tables** group. While the **Custom Table** command on the **Insert** tab under the **Tables** group offers flexibility when creating layout tables, it is not associated with any theme that is available on the **Page Design** tab under the **Themes** group.

The following figure shows the relationship between views, page layouts, and layout tables in InfoPath.

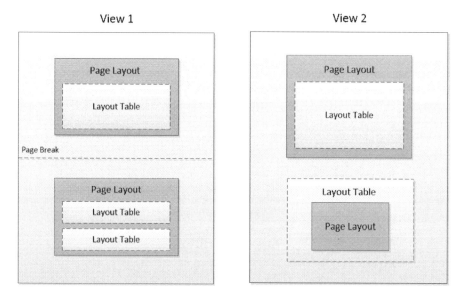

Figure 12. Relationship between views, page layouts, and layout tables.

An InfoPath form can consist of more than one view. In the example above, the form consists of two views: **View 1** and **View 2**.

You can place multiple page layouts on a view and a page layout can contain one or more layout tables. You can also place layout tables directly on a view and page layouts within layout tables. In the example above, **View 1** consists of two page layouts, while **View 2** has one page layout on the view and another one in a layout table.

You can place controls and text directly on a view, within a page layout, or within a layout table.

When printing a form, a view can span multiple pages when you add page breaks between the page layouts or layout tables on the view. **View 1** in the example above has a page break between its two page layouts.

To add a page break between page layouts or layout tables, click anywhere outside (so directly on the view) and below the page layout or layout table under which you want to add a page break, and then click **Insert ➤ Page Format ➤ Page Break** to add a page break. To delete a page break, select the page break on the view and then press **Delete**.

You can also add page breaks between views when creating views for printing purposes and for printing multiple views. You will learn more about print views later in recipe *16 Add a print view*.

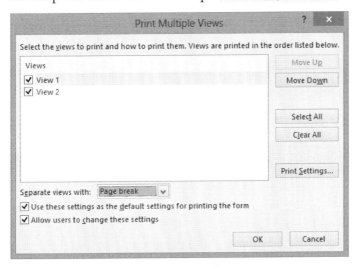

Figure 13. Separating views with page breaks when printing multiple views in InfoPath.

Note that page breaks are used only when printing forms and not when filling out forms. If you want to separate controls on multiple pages when filling out a form (either in the InfoPath Filler 2013 or a browser), you must use multiple views to do so. You will learn more about views in Chapter 2.

Tip:

> To see what a form would look like when you print it, you can use the **Print Preview** command, which is available via **File ➤ Print ➤ Print Preview**.

3   Align labels and controls

Problem

You have several labels and controls on an InfoPath form template and you want to align these labels and controls with each other.

Solution

You can use tables (layout tables or custom tables) to organize and align labels and controls in rows and columns of tables on an InfoPath form template.

To align labels and controls:

1. In InfoPath, create a new **Blank Form** template. InfoPath creates a default view with a standard page layout on it.

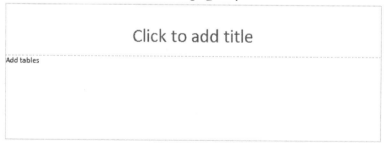

Figure 14. Default page layout added to a new Blank Form template in InfoPath 2013.

2. You can add layout tables inside the page layout. To do this, place the cursor inside the page layout, and then on the **Insert** tab under the **Tables** group, click on any of the layout tables to add one inside the standard page layout.

3. To add extra rows and columns to the layout table, right-click in the table cell to which you want to add a neighboring column or row, select **Insert** from the context menu that appears, and then select **Columns to the Left**, **Columns to the Right**, **Rows Above**, or **Rows Below** from the context menu that appears.

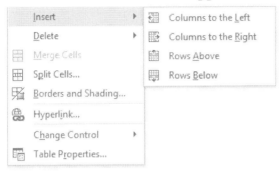

Figure 15. Insert table columns and rows context menu items.

4. If you want to merge cells, select the cells you want to merge by highlighting them, right-click the selection, and then select **Merge Cells** from the context menu that appears. If you want to split a cell in columns and rows, select **Split Cells** from the context menu.

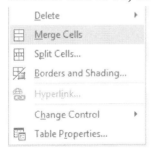

Figure 16. Merge Cells context menu item in InfoPath 2013.

5. To apply a theme to the page layout and layout table, on the **Page Design** tab under the **Themes** group, click on one of the available themes. Note: Themes cannot be applied to custom tables; only to predefined layout tables and page layouts.

6. To further position content within a cell, right-click in the cell, and select **Table Properties** from the context menu that appears.

7. On the **Table Properties** dialog box, use the **Table**, **Row**, **Column**, and **Cell** tabs to further configure the layout table as you wish.

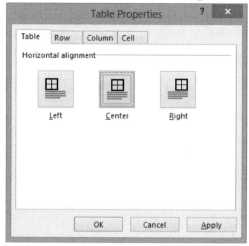

Figure 17. Table Properties dialog box in InfoPath 2013.

8. To design your form template, place controls or type text in the cells of the layout table.

Discussion

The steps outlined in the recipe above gave you a brief overview of laying out a form. For a step-by-step and concrete example of laying out controls on a form template, see recipe *17 Print data on a print view*.

Tip:

> To quickly add a row below the last row in a layout table, you can place the cursor in the right-most cell of the last row of the table, and then press **Tab** on your keyboard to add a new row below the last row.

Question

1. Can you add a page break between two custom tables that are located within a page layout? Tip: If you do not know the answer, try it out!

Controls

Controls are visual elements that allow you to interact with and enter data on an InfoPath form. InfoPath comes with three categories of controls:

1. Input
2. Objects
3. Containers

Input controls allow you to enter data on a form, objects allow you to interact with a form or add objects to it such as files, and containers are controls that can contain other controls.

You can open the **Controls** task pane to see the entire collection of controls that is available. To open the **Controls** task pane, click on the small arrow in the bottom right-hand corner of the **Controls** group on the **Home** tab on the Ribbon.

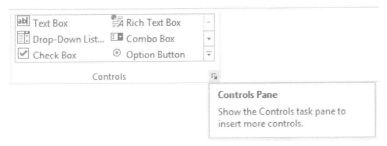

Figure 18. Arrow in the bottom right-hand corner of the Controls group.

You can also expand the controls section on the **Home** tab by clicking on the drop-down arrow in the bottom right-hand corner of the controls list box under the **Controls** group on the **Home** tab.

Figure 19. Controls task pane in InfoPath 2013.

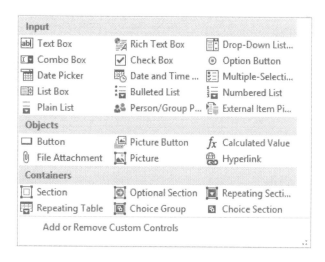

Figure 20. Expanded Controls group on the Home tab in InfoPath 2013.

The amount and types of controls you have available for designing your InfoPath form template depend on the type of form you are designing. If you are designing an InfoPath form that will be filled out only through InfoPath Filler, then you will have more controls available than if you are designing a form that will be filled out through a browser. The reason for this is that browser forms do not support the full set of controls that is available in InfoPath.

In the next recipe, you are going to add the most basic type of input control, a text box control, to a form template and then continue to explore how to use controls in InfoPath.

Exercise

In InfoPath, create a new **Blank Form** template, and then expand the **Controls** group on the **Home** tab to see the types of controls that are available for a Web Browser Form. Then click **File ➤ Info ➤ Form Options**. On the **Form Options** dialog box, select **Compatibility** in the **Category** list, select **InfoPath Filler Form** from the **Form type** drop-down list box, and then click **OK**. Expand the **Controls** group on the **Home** tab again to see the types of controls that are available for an InfoPath Filler Form. Which form type has the largest amount of controls available to it?

4   Add a text box – method 1

Problem

You want to allow users to enter text on an InfoPath form.

Solution

You can use a text box or a rich text box control in InfoPath to allow users to enter text on an InfoPath form.

To add a text box control to an InfoPath form template:

1.   In InfoPath, create a new **Blank Form** template.

2.   Click anywhere on the view of the form template, but preferably within a layout table or page layout, to place the cursor.

3. On the **Home** tab under the **Controls** group or on the **Controls** task pane, click **Text Box** to add a text box control to the view of the form template.

A text box should now appear wherever you last placed the cursor on the view.

Discussion

A text box control allows users to enter a text string into a field. It is one of the most basic controls you can add to an InfoPath form template.

There are two ways you can add any control to a form template:

1. By selecting the control from the **Controls** group on the **Home** tab on the Ribbon or from the **Controls** task pane. This action automatically creates a corresponding field for the control in the Main data source of the InfoPath form.

2. By first adding a field to the Main data source of a form template and then binding this field to a control on the InfoPath form.

We will get to what the *Main data source of an InfoPath form* is shortly.

In the solution described above, you used the first method to add a control (a text box in this case) to a form template. The second method for adding a text box (or any other control) to an InfoPath form template is discussed more in-depth in recipe *5 Add a text box – method 2*.

The terms **fields** and **controls** are terms that are used interchangeably when talking about InfoPath, but they represent two different things. The fact that they represent two different things becomes clear when you select a control and then look at the **Properties** group on the **Properties** tab. There you will see two commands: **Field Properties** and **Control Properties**.

Figure 21. Field Properties and Control Properties on the Properties tab in InfoPath 2013.

An InfoPath form in its most primitive form is an XML file that contains data, and this data is stored in XML elements. The XML elements in an InfoPath form are represented by fields and groups on the **Fields** task pane in InfoPath Designer 2013.

Fields and groups define the entire structure of an InfoPath form and allow data to be stored within an InfoPath form according to what is called an XML schema definition.

This brings us to the definition of the Main data source of an InfoPath form: The Main data source of an InfoPath form is the collection of fields and groups that define the structure of the form and in which data for the InfoPath form can be stored.

You can see what the structure of the Main data source of an InfoPath form looks like by looking at the **Fields** task pane in InfoPath Designer 2013. If the **Fields** task pane is not already open in InfoPath, you can open it via **Data ➤ Form Data ➤ Show Fields**.

Figure 22. The Show Fields command under the Form Data group on the Data tab.

Figure 23. Fields task pane in InfoPath Designer 2013.

In Figure 23, the Main data source of the InfoPath form consists of one group named **myFields** and a field named **field1**. The **myFields** group is a standard root group that InfoPath automatically creates when you do not base your form template on a custom XML schema. **field1** exists because of the text box you previously added to the form template; more on this later.

Without fields or groups in the Main data source of an InfoPath form, you cannot have data entry controls on a form, because fields allow data to be stored within an InfoPath form.

Controls, on the other hand, are visual elements that expose data that is stored in fields and groups of an InfoPath form. So controls have to be linked to fields or groups in the Main data source of a form to allow data to be stored within the form and/or to expose data that is stored within a form. The linking of a control to a field or group is called *binding*. Buttons are an exception to this rule, because they do not store any data, so you do not have to bind them to a field in the data source.

When you click on and select a control on the view of an InfoPath form template, you will see the field or group that control is bound to automatically highlight on the **Fields** task pane.

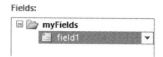

Figure 24. Highlighted field on the Fields task pane when a control is selected.

You can also see which field or group a control is bound to by looking at the binding information shown on the right-hand side of a control when you click on it to select it.

Figure 25. A Text Box control that is bound to a field named field1.

Not every field in the Main data source needs to be bound to a control on the view of a form template. Fields can exist in the Main data source without being exposed through controls on a form. Such fields are present in the Main data source but remain hidden from users and are therefore called *hidden fields* (also see recipe *11 Add a hidden field*). While users are unable to access hidden fields when filling out a form, such fields remain accessible through rules or code.

Technically speaking, you do not have to bind a control to a field, but practically speaking, if you do not bind a control to a field, you will not be able to store data for it in the InfoPath form. Always remember that controls function as a "gateway" to store data in the Main data source of an InfoPath form.

Important:

A control that you do not bind to a field is called an *unbound control*. Such controls cannot be used to store data in the Main data source of a form.

Exercise

Add a **Horizontal Repeating Table** control to a new InfoPath form template. What does the **Fields** task pane look like? Preview the form and interact with the control to see how it works.

Tip: If the control is missing and you do not know how to make it appear, go through the previous exercise (under the introductory section for *Controls*) again.

Question

1. What is the difference between fields and controls?

5   Add a text box – method 2

Problem

You want to allow users to enter text on an InfoPath form.

Solution

You can use a text box or a rich text box control in InfoPath to allow users to enter text on an InfoPath form.

To add a text box control to an InfoPath form template:

1. In InfoPath, create a new **Blank Form** template.

2. If the **Fields** task pane is not open, click **Data ➤ Form Data ➤ Show Fields**. This will open the **Fields** task pane.

3. On the **Fields** task pane, click to select the **myFields** group, and then click the drop-down arrow that appears on the right-hand side of the **myFields** group and select **Add** from the drop-down menu that appears.

4. On the **Add Field or Group** dialog box, type a name for the field (for example **firstName**) in the **Name** text box, leave **Field (element)** selected in the **Type** drop-down list box, leave **Text (string)** selected in the **Data type** drop-down list box, and click **OK**.

5. Drag the field you just created from the **Fields** task pane and drop it onto the view of the form template. InfoPath should automatically bind it to a **Text Box** control.

Discussion

As you saw in the solution above, a field has a name, a type, and a data type. To create a text box control, you first added a field that had the data type **Text (string)** to the Main data source of the form and then bound that field to a **Text Box** control on the view of the form template.

It is a best practice to give fields meaningful names, such as for example, **firstName** for a text field in which a person's first name will be stored, or **isSubmitted** for a **True/False (boolean)** field that represents a flag that indicates whether the form has been submitted or not. Always give fields names that describe the data that is being stored in them.

Note:

Field or group names cannot contain spaces or other special characters. They must begin with an alphabetic character or underscore (_), and can only contain alphanumeric characters, underscores, hyphens (-), and periods (.).

You can give a field a name on one of three ways:

1. Via the **Fields** task pane by double-clicking on the field and then entering a name on the **Field or Group Properties** dialog box.

Figure 26. Name text box on the Field or Group Properties dialog box of a field.

2. By right-clicking the control on the view of the form template, opening its **Properties** dialog box, and then entering a field name there.

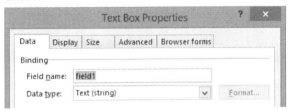

Figure 27. Field name text box on the Properties dialog box of a control.

3. By changing the **Name** field on the **Properties** tab under the **Properties** group on the Ribbon after you have selected the control

on the view of the form template.

Figure 28. Name text box under the Properties group on the Properties tab.

The **Field (element)** field type is suitable for most fields you create unless you want to create attributes on the XML elements contained in an InfoPath form, in which case you must select the **Field (attribute)** field type.

Other field and group types that are available in InfoPath are:

- Group

- Group (choice)

- Complete XML schema or XML document

In InfoPath, a group does not directly contain any data, but rather serves as a container for other groups and/or fields.

Note that you can make a group or field (element) repeating by selecting the **Repeating** check box on the **Add Field or Group** dialog box or on the **Field or Group Properties** dialog box.

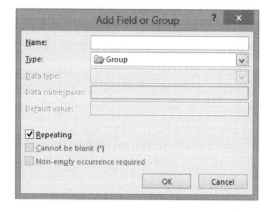

Figure 29. Repeating group settings on the Add Field or Group dialog box.

Repeating groups are used for binding to for example **Repeating Tables** or **Repeating Sections**. A repeating field can be used for binding to for example a **Multiple-Selection List Box** or a list (**Plain List**, **Bulleted List**, or **Numbered List**). You can recognize a repeating group or field on the **Fields** task pane by the blue square with a white downwards pointing arrow that appears on the group or field.

Figure 30. Icon for a repeating group in InfoPath.

Figure 31. Icon for a repeating field in InfoPath.

You can bind controls other than a **Text Box** control to a field that has the **Text (string)** data type assigned to it. For example, had you right-clicked (instead of left-clicked) the **firstName** field on the **Fields** task pane and then dragged-and-dropped it onto the view of the form template, InfoPath would have presented you with a context menu to choose a control from.

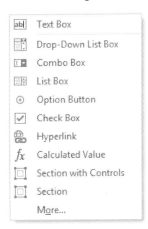

Figure 32. Context menu to select a control to bind to a Text (string) field.

You could have selected any of the controls listed in this context menu and bound that control to the **firstName** text field. As you can see, the top-most menu item is **Text Box**, which means that this is the default control that InfoPath will use to bind to the field if you do not specifically choose a control as is the case when you left-click a field on the **Fields** task pane and then drag-and-drop it onto the view of the form template.

When you dragged-and-dropped the field onto the view of the InfoPath form template, a label may have automatically been added for the control. InfoPath comes preconfigured to do this.

You can turn this feature off as follows:

1. Click **File ➤ Options**.
2. On the **InfoPath Options** dialog box on the **General** tab, click **More Options**.
3. On the **Options** dialog box, click the **Design** tab.
4. On the **Design** tab, deselect the **Create labels for controls automatically** check box.

If you prefer InfoPath to automatically create labels for you every time you add a field to the view of a form template, you can leave this feature turned on, of course.

Exercise

Click around on the **Options** dialog box to see what other options you can configure in InfoPath.

You may have also noticed that when you add any control to the form template, InfoPath automatically creates a corresponding field or group for it on the **Fields** task pane.

You can turn this feature off as follows:

1. Open the **Controls** task pane (see Figure 18).
2. At the bottom of the **Controls** task pane, deselect the **Automatically create data source** check box.

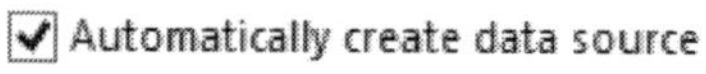

☑ Automatically create data source

Figure 33. Check box on the Controls task pane to automatically create fields.

I recommend that you leave this feature turned on until you are a bit more advanced and know what type of field or group is required in the Main data source for binding to a particular type of control.

Exercise

Add a second field named **lastName** under the **myFields** group. When you are on the **Add Field or Group** dialog box, take note of the rest of data types that are available in InfoPath to define fields.

The data types list consists of:

- Text (string)
- Rich Text (XHTML)
- Whole Number (integer)
- Decimal (double)
- True/False (boolean)
- Hyperlink (anyURI)
- Date (date)
- Time (time)
- Date and Time (dateTime)
- Picture or File Attachment (base64)
- Custom (complexType)

Exercise

Add any **Input** control to the form template by using the method described in recipe *4 Add a text box – method 1*. Once added, click on the control to select it, and then look at the data type InfoPath assigned to the field in the **Data Type** drop-down list box under the **Properties** group on the **Properties** tab on the Ribbon. Do this with as many controls as you can to familiarize yourself with the data type that can be used for each type of control.

Exercise

Try adding a group named **table** under the **myFields** group and then a repeating group named **row** under the **table** group, and then a text field named **column1** under the **row** repeating group. Then drag-and-drop the **row** repeating group onto the view of the form template, and see what happens. If you have done everything correctly, you should have been able to bind the **row** repeating group to a **Repeating Table**, **Repeating Section with Controls**, or **Repeating Section** control.

Note:

You may often hear the term *node* being used in relation to InfoPath as in *repeating group node*. *Node* is a term that is used in XML to refer to a node in the document tree. This can be an element node, an attribute node, or any other node type. In InfoPath, *node* is often used to refer to groups. So a *group* in the Main data source of an InfoPath form is the same thing as a *group node*, since groups are stored as XML elements. And because a field is stored as either an XML element or an XML attribute, it can also be called a *node*.

6   Change a text box into a date picker

Problem

You have a text box control on an InfoPath form and you want to change it into a date picker control.

Solution

You can change the data type of the field bound to the text box control into a date so that you can change the text box control into a date picker control.

To change a text box control into a date picker control:

1. In InfoPath, create a new **Blank Form** template.

2. Add a **Text Box** control to the view of the form template.

3. With the text box still selected, click **Properties ➤ Properties ➤ Field Properties**.

4. On the **Field or Group Properties** dialog box on the **Data** tab, change the **Data type** from **Text (string)** to **Date (date)**, and click **OK**.

5. Right-click the **Text Box** control and select **Change Control ➤ Date Picker** from the context menu that appears.

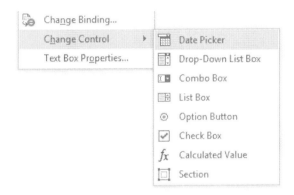

Figure 34. Change Control menu item on the context menu of a text box control.

6. Preview the form.

The text box should now have been converted into a date picker and you should be able to select and enter a date into the date picker control.

Discussion

You can change a control from one type to another by first changing the data type of the field that is bound to the control and then changing the control to the desired control. The data type of a field determines which controls can be bound to it and consequently also the list of controls that you will see appear when you want to change a control into another control.

Note that you could have also selected **Properties ➤ Modify ➤ Change Control ➤ Date Picker** on the Ribbon to change the text box into a date picker control.

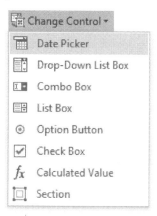

Figure 35. Changing a text box into a date picker via the Properties tab on the Ribbon.

Tip:

> To learn which data type you must assign to a field to be able to bind it to the type of control you want to bind it to, first add the type of control you want to use to the view of the form template, and then examine the data type of the field bound to that control. Do this for each type of control that is available in InfoPath and soon you will know which data type is required for each type of control.

Exercise

Try changing the **Date Picker** control into a **Rich Text Box** control. Hint: The data type of a **Rich Text Box** control is **Rich Text (XHTML)**.

7   Delete a control

Problem

You have a text box control on an InfoPath form and want to delete it.

Solution

You can delete a control by selecting it and pressing the **Delete** key on your keyboard. Deleting a control from the view of an InfoPath form template does not automatically also delete the field that the control is bound to in the Main data source of the form.

To delete the field that a control is bound to:

1. In InfoPath, on the **Fields** task pane, select the field you want to delete, click the drop-down arrow that appears on the right-hand side of the field, and select **Delete** from the drop-down menu that appears.

2. On the **Delete Field or Group** message box, click **Yes** to confirm the deletion of the field.

3. If you have not already deleted the control that was bound to the field, select it on the view of the form template, and press the **Delete** key on your keyboard, otherwise the control will remain unbound.

Discussion

As mentioned in the solution above, deleting a control from the view of an InfoPath form template does not automatically also delete the field bound to the control. This is also why you can delete a control (the visual part of data storage) in InfoPath, and still be able to save data in the Main data source of the form, because the field is still present in the Main data source of the InfoPath form as a hidden field (also see recipe *11 Add a hidden field to a form*).

Remember, fields are the most basic components of an InfoPath form template. They contain all of the form's data. Controls are just visual elements that expose the data stored in fields. And a control that is not bound to a field, cannot store data.

Tip:

When you are cleaning up an InfoPath form template and deleting controls from it, always remember to also delete the fields that the controls are bound to if you do not need the fields anymore, otherwise the fields will remain present in the Main data source of the form and unnecessarily take up space or if you have added rules to them, cause unexpected or unwanted behavior in your form. Note: You will learn what rules are in Chapter 4.

8   Bind a control to a different field

Problem

You have deleted a field that was previously bound to a text box control on an InfoPath form. This action left the text box control unbound, so you want to bind the text box control to another field in the Main data source of the form.

Solution

You can use the **Change Binding** command to change the binding of a control.

To unbind a control from a field:

1.   In InfoPath, create a new **Blank Form** template.

2.   Add a **Text Box** control to the view of the form template. This action will automatically create a field named **field1** on the **Fields** task pane if you did not turn off the **Automatically create data source** feature on the **Controls** task pane as described in the discussion section of recipe *5 Add a text box – method 2*.

3.   On the **Fields** task pane, click the drop-down arrow on the right-hand side of the field (**field1**), and select **Delete** from the drop-down menu that appears.

4. On the **Delete Field or Group** message box, click **Yes**.

5. Hover over the text box control on the form to verify that it is an unbound control. The text "Unbound (Control cannot store data)" should appear.

To bind a control to a different field:

1. In InfoPath, on the **Fields** task pane, right-click the **myFields** group, and select **Add** from the drop-down menu that appears.

2. On the **Add Field or Group** dialog box, type a name for the field (for example **firstName**) in the **Name** text box, leave **Field (element)** selected in the **Type** drop-down list box, leave **Text (string)** selected in the **Data type** drop-down list box, and click **OK**.

3. Click the unbound text box control to select it, and then click **Properties ➤ Properties ➤ Change Binding** on the Ribbon.

4. On the **Text Box Binding** dialog box, ensure that **Main** is selected in the **Data source** drop-down list box, select the **firstName** field, and click **OK**.

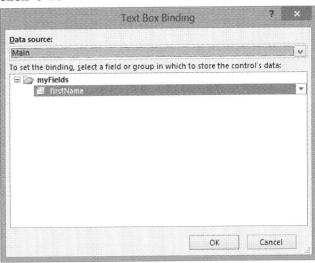

Figure 36. Text Box Binding dialog box in InfoPath 2013.

When you select the text box, the **firstName** field should now appear as the field the text box is bound to.

Figure 37. Text Box control bound to the firstName field.

Discussion

When a control on an InfoPath form is unbound, you will see the info text "Unbound (Control cannot store data)" appear when you hover over the control.

Figure 38. Info text for a control that is not bound to a field in the data source.

An unbound control exists on an InfoPath form, but is unable to store data in the Main data source of the form. You can see an unbound control as a "dummy" control that does not do anything. Note that the message InfoPath displays on an unbound control only provides additional information. It is not an error message, so you can ignore it if you wish. But just be aware that what the message states is true, so the control cannot and will not store data.

Control and field properties

Once you have added controls to a form template, you can set the values of properties of the controls to control how they behave. For example, you can change a text box from accepting only one line of text to accepting multiple lines of text.

Not all controls support the same types of properties. Control properties may differ between control types.

9   Make a text box multi-line

Problem

You have a text box on an InfoPath form and want the text box to be able to accept multiple lines of text.

Solution

You can set the **Multi-line** property of the text box to make it accept multiple lines of text.

To make a text box accept multiple lines of text:

1.   In InfoPath, create a new **Blank Form** template.

2.   Add a **Text Box** control to the view of the form template.

3.   Right-click the **Text Box** control, and select **Text Box Properties** from the context menu that appears.

4.   On the **Text Box Properties** dialog box, click the **Display** tab.

5.   On the **Text Box Properties** dialog box on the **Display** tab under **Options**, select the **Multi-line** check box, and click **OK**.

6.   Preview the form

When the form opens, type a text string in the text box and press **Enter** to add a new line. You should be able to type multiple lines of text in the text box.

Discussion

You can set properties of all controls in InfoPath. You can access the **Properties** dialog box of a control in one of two ways:

1.   Via the **Properties** tab under the **Control Tools** tab. These tabs appear when you select a control on a view of the form template. Click **Properties ➤ Properties ➤ Control Properties** to access the **Properties** dialog box for the selected control.

Figure 39. Properties tab in InfoPath Designer 2013.

Note that not all of the properties of a control are displayed on the **Properties** tab. To access more properties, you must open the **Properties** dialog box.

2. Via the context menu of a control. This menu appears when you right-click a control. You can then select the **Properties** menu item to open the **Properties** dialog box for the selected control.

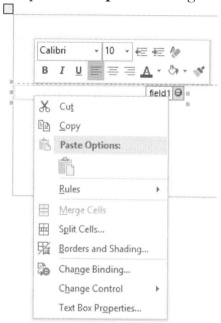

Figure 40. Context menu of a text box control in InfoPath 2013.

The settings that are available on the **Properties** dialog box differ per control. For example, while a text box control has a **Read-only** property, a drop-down list box control does not have one.

In addition, the tabs that are available on the **Properties** dialog box also differ per control. For example, while the **Properties** dialog box of a text box control has a **Display** tab, the **Properties** dialog box of a drop-down list box control does not have one.

Exercise

Take a moment to add a few controls to the view of the form template, open the **Properties** dialog box for each control, and study which settings are available on the tab pages of the **Properties** dialog box for each control.

Questions

1. Which displays a larger range of properties for a control? The **Properties** tab on the Ribbon or the **Properties** dialog for a control?

2. Which values can you select for the **Value when cleared** property of a check box control?

3. Can you make a check box read-only by setting a property of the check box?

10 Make a text box mandatory

Problem

You have a text box control on an InfoPath form, which you want to force users to always fill out.

Solution

If you require a user to always enter data in a particular control, you can make the field that is bound to the control required.

To make a field required:

1. In InfoPath, create a new **Blank Form** template.

2. Add a **Text Box** or any other type of control that can contain data to the view of the form template.

3. On the **Properties** tab under the **Modify** group, select the **Cannot Be Blank** check box. Alternatively, you can click **Properties ➤ Properties ➤ Field Properties** or **Properties ➤ Properties ➤ Control Properties**, and select the **Cannot be blank** check box on the **Data** tab of the control or field **Properties** dialog box.

4. Preview the form.

When the form opens, you should see a red asterisk (*) appear on the control that requires data to be entered, and when you hover over the control, the tooltip "Cannot be blank" should appear.

Discussion

When you select the **Cannot be blank** check box, you will see a red asterisk (*) appear behind the field name on the **Fields** task pane as an indication that the field must be filled out.

Figure 41. Red asterisk behind a required field on the Fields task pane in InfoPath 2013.

The method described in the solution above should be your preferred method for making fields required in InfoPath, unless you need to make a field required only when a certain condition is met, in which case you can use a **Validation** rule (see recipe *29 Make a field required based on a condition*).

Tip:

> If you are suddenly getting validation errors on an InfoPath form template you or someone else designed, always check the **Fields** task pane for red asterisks that indicate required fields. Because hidden fields (see recipe *11 Add a hidden field*) can be made required, this may result in unexpected validation errors when forms are being filled out or submitted.

11 Add a hidden field to a form

Problem

You have a field on an InfoPath form which you want to hide from users.

Solution

You can add a field to the Main data source of an InfoPath form without binding that field to a control. This will make the field hidden.

A second way of making a field hidden is by adding a control to the view of the form template and then deleting it. The latter action will not delete the field from the Main data source, so the field will effectively be hidden.

To create a hidden field in InfoPath (method 1):

1. In InfoPath, create a new **Blank Form** template.

2. On the **Fields** task pane, right-click the **myFields** group, and select **Add** from the drop-down menu that appears.

3. On the **Add Field or Group** dialog box, enter a name for the field, select the desired **Data type**, enter a **Default value** if necessary, and then click **OK**.

To create a hidden field in InfoPath (method 2):

1. In InfoPath, create a new **Blank Form** template.

2. Add a **Text Box** control or any other type of control that has the data type you want the hidden field to have, to the view of the form template. This step will automatically add a field to the Main data source of the InfoPath form if you did not turn off the **Automatically create data source** feature on the **Controls** task pane as described in the discussion section of recipe *5 Add a text box – method 2*.

3. Delete the control you just added from the view of the form template. This action will delete the control, but not the field that was bound to the control, from the Main data source, so will make the field hidden.

Discussion

Hidden fields are useful for storing data you do not want a user to see, but that you want to use to be able to manipulate the behavior of a form.

For example, if you want a user to be able to fill out a text box when she first opens the form, but not be able to modify the text anymore once she has submitted the form, you could add a hidden field to the form template to keep track of when the form has been submitted and then use the value of the hidden field to conditionally disable the text box when the user opens the submitted form (see for example recipe *43 Switch to a read-only view when a form is opened after submission*).

Tip:

> Never make a hidden field required. Because a user cannot access a hidden field through InfoPath Filler 2013 or a browser, she will not be able to set the value of a required hidden field unless you create a rule that sets the value of this field for her.

Save and publish

Technically speaking, once you have designed a form template and saved it to disk, it is ready to be used to create forms, that is, if you are the only one who is going to be using it from your own computer. This is called saving a form template.

If you want to allow other users to access and use your form template so that they too can create forms based on it, you must publish the form template to a publicly accessible location. This is called publishing a form template.

When you publish a form template to a particular location, the publish location is saved in all InfoPath forms (at the top of the file in what is called an XML Processing Instruction) that are created using that form template. You can find this publish location by opening a saved InfoPath form (XML file) in Notepad and looking at the text at the top of the file. The text for the XML Processing Instruction may look something like the following:

```
<?mso-infoPathSolution solutionVersion="1.0.0.17"
productVersion="15.0.0" PIVersion="1.0.0.0"
href="file:///C:\InfoPath\PublishedFormTemplate.xsn"
name="urn:schemas-microsoft-
com:office:infopath:PublishedFormTemplate:-myXSD-2013-03-04T19-59-
09" ?>
```

Every time a user opens a previously saved InfoPath form that is based on the published form template, the form will look for its corresponding form template at the publish location it has stored in its XML Processing Instruction. The **href** attribute in the XML Processing Instruction shown above points to the location where the InfoPath form will be looking for the form template that was used to create it.

If the form template has been moved or deleted from the publish location, the form will not be able to find the form template, so will not be able to be opened using InfoPath Filler 2013 or a browser. However, you can still open the InfoPath form in Notepad as was described in the exercise in recipe *2 Preview an InfoPath form*.

InfoPath Designer 2013 offers several locations you can publish a form template to, so that it can be shared among users. Two of the most popular locations are network location and SharePoint Server. The following recipe explains how to publish a form template to a network location.

12 Publish an InfoPath form template

Problem

You have designed an InfoPath form template and want to publish the form template so that other users on your network can use it to create forms.

Solution

To publish an InfoPath form template to a network location:

1. In InfoPath, create a new **Blank Form** template or use an existing form template.

2. Click **File ➤ Publish ➤ Network Location**.

Figure 42. Publish to Network Location command in InfoPath 2013.

3. If you have not already saved the form template, InfoPath will prompt you to save it. When a message box to save the form template appears, click **OK**, and then on the **Save As** dialog box, browse to a location, enter a name for the form template, and click **Save**. The **Publishing Wizard** should then appear in InfoPath.

4. On the **Publishing Wizard**, click **Browse**.

5. On the **Browse** dialog box, browse to the network location where you want to publish the form template, enter a **File name** for the form template, and click **OK**.

6. On the **Publishing Wizard**, accept the default name for the form template or type in a new name for the form template in the **Form template name** text box if you wish, and then click **Next**.

7. On the **Publishing Wizard**, you have the option to alter the location you entered in the previous step if all users who intend to fill out

InfoPath forms are unable to access the location you specified. You can specify a public URL or full network path. Specify a network path all form users have access to, and then click **Next**.

8. On the **Publishing Wizard**, click **Publish**.

9. On the **Publishing Wizard**, you can select the **Send the form to e-mail recipients** or the **Open this form template from the published location** check box if you wish before you click **Close**. The first option will allow you to send the form in an e-mail to a list of e-mail addresses you specify, and the second option will open a new form that is based on the published form template in InfoPath Filler 2013.

Users should now be able to go to the network location where you published the form template and double-click it to open and fill out an InfoPath form using InfoPath Filler 2013.

Discussion

If you do not have access to a SharePoint Server, but still want users in your organization to be able to share and fill out forms, you can publish your InfoPath form template to a location on a network or file share that is accessible by all users who need to fill out forms.

While publishing to a network location allows for sharing, users will have to have InfoPath Filler 2013 installed on their computers to be able to fill out forms. Filling out forms through a browser is only possible if you have a SharePoint Server with InfoPath Forms Services installed on it available.

InfoPath 2013 remembers where a previously published form template was published. Therefore, if you change a previously published form template and want to republish it, you can click **File ➤ Publish ➤ Quick Publish**, press **Ctrl+Shift+Q** on your keyboard, or click the small **Quick Publish** button on the Quick Access toolbar at the top of InfoPath Designer 2013.

Figure 43. Quick Publish command in InfoPath Designer 2013.

If you want to change a previously saved publish location to a new publish location, click **File ➤ Publish ➤ Network Location**, and republish the form template using the new location. The next time you use the **Quick Publish** button, InfoPath will publish the form template to the new publish location you last specified.

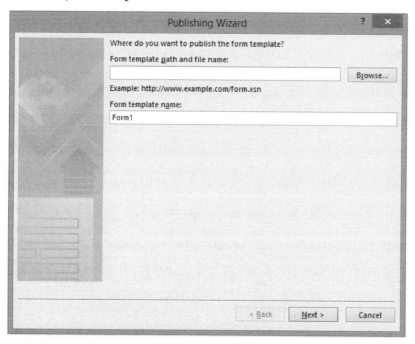

Figure 44. Publishing Wizard when publishing to a network location.

Exercise

Explore and read the descriptions of the publishing options that are available on the **File ➤ Publish** tab to familiarize yourself with them.

Questions

1. How many publishing commands are there on the **Publish** tab in InfoPath Designer 2013?

2. Is the **Quick Publish** command available for newly created InfoPath form templates that have never been published?

Chapter 2: Views

What are views?

A view is a canvas on which you can place page layouts, layout tables, text, and controls. You use views as the basis for designing an InfoPath form template.

An InfoPath form template can have one or more views. The default view is the first view that is displayed when a form opens; the startup view. When you create a new form template, one view is added to it by default, and this view automatically becomes the default view.

There can only be one default view at a time in an InfoPath form, but if you have multiple views in a form template, you can make another view the default view (see recipe *14 Make a view the default view*). You can see which view is the default view by an additional piece of text ("(default)") that is appended to the name of a view in the **View** drop-down list box under the **Views** group on the **Page Design** tab.

Figure 45. Default view as shown on the Page Design tab in InfoPath 2013.

Because a form template must always have at least one view, InfoPath will automatically create a new (default) view for you if you delete the last view of the form template.

Exercise

In InfoPath, create a new **Blank Form** template. Click **Page Design** ➤ **Views** ➤ **Delete** to delete **View 1**. When a message box appears, read what it says, and then click **Yes**. Is a view named **View 1** still present in the **View** drop-down list box under the **Views** group?

13 Add a second view to a form template

Problem

You have a form template that has one view and you want to add a second view to the form template.

Solution

You can use the **Page Design** tab to add a second view to an InfoPath form template.

To add a second view to a form template:

1. In InfoPath, create a new **Blank Form** template. InfoPath automatically creates a view named **View 1** and makes it the default view.

2. Click **Page Design ▶ Views ▶ New View** to open the **Add View** dialog box to add a second view to the form template.

3. On the **Add View** dialog box in the **New view name** text box, type a name for the view (for example **View 2**), and click **OK**.

View 2 should now appear as the current view in the **View** drop-down list box under the **Views** group on the **Page Design** tab.

Figure 46. A second view (View 2) as the currently selected view on the Page Design tab.

To switch back to **View 1** and make it the current view, select **View 1 (default)** from the **View** drop-down list box on the **Page Design** tab.

Discussion

Being able to add additional views to an InfoPath form template is an important action, because multiple views allow you to represent the same data in a form in different ways.

Remember we talked about the fact that the data of an InfoPath form resides in fields in the Main data source and that you use controls to visually expose this data? You can add to this that you can not only use controls to visually expose the data, but also place controls on different views to create different representations of the same data. Basically, you can have multiple controls (on the same or different views) pointing to the same field in the Main data source of a form to visually display the data in different ways.

For example, you can have a default view where a user can enter data, and when the user clicks a button, you switch to a second view and present the user with a read-only summary of the data she just entered. The second view would be called a read-only view (see recipe *15 Add a read-only view*).

You can also use multiple views to split very large forms into smaller, more palatable chunks of data to make the form easier for users to fill out. And with this concept, you can even use views to create wizard-like forms or tabbed interfaces (see recipe *86 Create a tabbed interface using buttons*) if you wish.

And finally, you can add additional views to a form template to create views that can be used specifically for printing a form (see recipe *16 Add a print view*). Here again you would be creating a different representation of the same data in a form.

In the solution above, you saw how to use the **View** drop-down list box on the **Page Design** tab to switch between views at design time; so when you are designing an InfoPath form template in InfoPath Designer 2013. You also have the ability to switch between views during runtime; so when you are filling out a form either in InfoPath Filler 2013 or a browser.

If you preview a form that has two views as in the solution above, you can use the **Current View** drop-down list box on the **Home** tab under the **Page Views** group to switch between **View 1** and **View 2**.

Figure 47. Current View drop-down list box on the Home tab in InfoPath Filler 2013.

If you do not want users to be able to use the **Current View** drop-down list box to switch between views, you can remove this option through the properties of the view.

To remove a view from the **Current View** drop-down list box in InfoPath Filler 2013 or a browser:

1. In InfoPath Designer 2013, click **Page Design**, and then select the name of the view you want to remove from the **Current View** drop-down list box in InfoPath Filler 2013 or a browser, from the **View** drop-down list box under the **Views** group.

2. Click **Page Design** ➤ **Views** ➤ **Properties**.

3. On the **View Properties** dialog box on the **General** tab, deselect the **Show on the View menu when filling out this form** check box, and click **OK**. Note that you cannot select the **Show on the View menu when filling out this form** check box if the form only has one view.

If your form template has two views and you remove one of them from the view menu, the **Current View** drop-down list box will not be shown. The **Current View** drop-down list box only appears if there is more than one view available to switch between in an InfoPath form.

You can delete a view in InfoPath Designer 2013 by first selecting the name of the view from the **View** drop-down list box under the **Views** group on the **Page Design** tab, and then clicking the **Delete** command under the **Views** group.

14 Make a view the default view

Problem

You have an InfoPath form template that has two views, **View 1** and **View 2**, where **View 1** is the default view. You want to make **View 2** the default view.

Solution

If you have multiple views in an InfoPath form, you can change the properties of one of the non-default views to make it the default view.

To make a non-default view the default view:

1. In InfoPath, create a new **Blank Form** template.

2. Add a view named **View 2** to the form template as described in recipe *13 Add a second view to a form template*.

3. Select **Page Design** ➤ **Views** ➤ **View** ➤ **View 2**. Note: A view automatically becomes the currently selected view immediately after you add it to the form template.

4. Click **Page Design** ➤ **Views** ➤ **Properties** to open the **View Properties** dialog box for **View 2**.

5. On the **View Properties** dialog box on the **General** tab, select the **Set as default view** check box, and click **OK**. The text **(default)** should now appear behind the **View 2** item in the **View** drop-down list box under the **Views** group on the **Page Design** tab, and should be gone from behind the **View 1** item in the **View** drop-down list box.

6. Preview the form.

The form should open with **View 2** as the first view being displayed.

Note: When previewing a form in InfoPath Designer 2013, InfoPath always starts up with the view that was last selected in the **View** drop-down list box under the **Views** group on the **Page Design** tab in design mode. So if you last selected **View 1** and then previewed the form, **View 1** would be shown as the startup view and not **View 2**, even if **View 2** is the default view.

To properly test the InfoPath form, save the form template to disk, and then open a new form by double-clicking the XSN file. This should open InfoPath Filler 2013 and display the correct default view you previously set.

Exercise

Open the **View Properties** dialog box of any view and on the **General** tab explore what you can configure for a view.

Questions

1. What is a default view?
2. How many default views can an InfoPath form have?
3. How can you hide a view from users?
4. Can you hide a view if it is the only view in the InfoPath form?
5. Suppose an InfoPath form has two views, **View 1** and **View 2**, where you have set **View 2** to be the default view. What happens when you delete **View 2**? Will there be no default views in the form?

Read-only views

Read-only views are views that make all of the controls, except for button controls, you place on the view, read-only. If you want to disable a button on a read-only view, you must either not put the button on the view (because it is not going to be used anyway) or use conditional formatting to disable it (see recipe *27 Disable a button on a read-only view*).

A read-only view is appropriate to use when you want to make all of the controls on a view read-only and also when controls do not offer a way to make them read-only.

If you want to have a mixture of read-only and non-read-only controls on a view, it is best not to make a view read-only, but to make the controls themselves read-only on an individual basis (see recipe *26 Make a control read-only based on a condition*), unless you have a large amount of controls, in which case you may want to split the controls up and place a few on read-only and others on non-read-only views.

15 Add a read-only view

Problem

You have an InfoPath form with a default view that is not read-only, and you want to create a second view to place controls on to make all of those controls read-only.

Solution

You can create a read-only view by selecting the **Read-only** check box for the view.

To add a read-only view to an InfoPath form:

1. In InfoPath, create a new **Blank Form** template.

2. Add any controls of your choice to the default view (**View 1**).

3. Click **Page Design ➤ Views ➤ New View**.

4. On the **Add View** dialog box, type a name in the text box (for example, **Read-Only View**), and click **OK**. InfoPath creates the new view and switches to it. You can see which view is currently being displayed on the canvas in InfoPath by looking at the **View** drop-down list box under the **Views** group on the **Page Design** tab.

Figure 48. Views group on the Page Design tab in InfoPath 2013.

5. Click **Page Design ➤ Views ➤ Properties** to open the **View Properties** dialog box for the **Read-Only View** view.

6. On the **View Properties** dialog box on the **General** tab under **View settings**, select the **Read-only** check box, and click **OK**.

7. Drag-and-drop existing fields (fields that you have already bound to controls on **View 1**) from the **Fields** task pane onto the read-only view to create read-only controls.

8. Preview the form.

Now when you open the InfoPath form, if **View 1** is not the view that comes up first (this depends on which view you had selected last in InfoPath Designer 2013), use the **Current View** drop-down list box on the **Home** tab to switch to **View 1**. Enter data into the controls on **View 1**, and then use the **Current View** drop-down list box to switch to the read-only view. On the read-only view, verify that the controls have indeed been made read-only, i.e. ensure that you cannot enter or change data that has been entered via **View 1**.

Tip:

> If you want to have two views that look similar, but one is read-only and the other is not, you can add a read-only view to the form template, then switch to the non-read-only view, press **Ctrl+A** to select all of the controls on the view, press **Ctrl+C** to copy all of the controls, switch back to the read-only view, and then press **Ctrl+V** to paste the controls on the read-only view. This is a quick and easy way to copy controls from one view to another.

Question

1. Are buttons that are placed on a read-only view disabled, so do they also become read-only?

Print views

A print view is a view that allows you to create a visual design that can be used specifically for printing data stored in a form.

You can create a print view and designate it to be the print view for one or more views that are used for filling out the form. If you do this, the print view will replace the non-print views when you print the form.

For example, if you have two views in a form, **View 1** and **View 2**, and you designate **View 2** to be the print view for **View 1**, then **View 2** will replace **View 1** when you print the form. So while users will have access to **View 1** when they are filling out the form, they will see **View 2** when they print the form.

16 Add a print view

Problem

You have several fields on an InfoPath form, but only want a selected few of those fields to appear on a separate view that you can use to print the form.

Solution

You can create a print view for the data in fields that you want to have printed on a form.

To add a print view to an InfoPath form template:

1. In InfoPath, create a new **Blank Form** template.

2. Add any controls of your choice to the default view (**View 1**).

3. Click **Page Design** ➤ **Views** ➤ **New View**.

4. On the **Add View** dialog box, type a name in the text box (for example, **Print View**), and click **OK**.

5. Typically, a print view is not meant to be selected by a user, so you may want to remove it from the **Current View** menu. To do this, click **Page Design** ➤ **Views** ➤ **Properties**, and then on the **View Properties** dialog box, deselect the **Show on the View menu when filling out this form** check box and click **OK**.

6. Add any fields, for which you want to print their data on the print view, to the print view. Remember to drag-and-drop existing fields from the **Fields** task pane onto the print view and not to add new fields or controls to the form template.

7. Select **Page Design ➤ Views ➤ View ➤ View 1 (default)**.

8. Click **Page Design ➤ Views ➤ Properties**.

9. On the **View Properties** dialog box, click the **Print Settings** tab.

10. On the **View Properties** dialog box on the **Print Settings** tab under the **Designate print view** section, select the print view you just created from the drop-down list box, and click **OK**. This should make InfoPath use the print view instead of **View 1** whenever you print **View 1**.

11. Repeat steps 7 through 10 for all of the views for which you want the print view to be used as the view for printing that view.

12. Ensure that **View 1 (default)** has been selected as the current view in the **Page Design ➤ Views ➤ View** drop-down list box and then preview the form.

When the form opens, enter some data, and then click **File ➤ Print ➤ Print Preview**. The view that appears should be the print view you created.

Discussion

InfoPath allows you to print more than one view when printing a form. You can set up which views should be printed by clicking the **Print Multiple Views** button on the **Print Settings** tab on the **View Properties** dialog box, and then selecting and configuring the views to print.

Print Multiple Views
Define print settings for multiple views in this form.
Print Multiple Views...

Figure 49. Print Multiple Views button on the Print Settings tab.

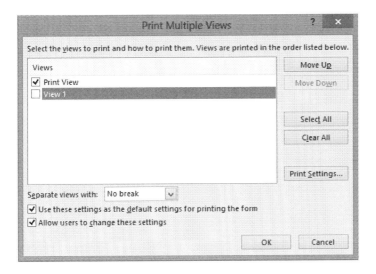

Figure 50. Print Multiple Views dialog box in InfoPath 2013.

Tip:

When creating a print view, you can bind text fields to **Calculated Value** controls instead of **Text Box** controls or **Drop-Down List Box** controls or any other type of control that has a border and stores just one value. Using a **Calculated Value** control will prevent unwanted borders from appearing around the data stored in the field bound to the control. You can also remove borders from a control through its **Borders and Shading** option.

Exercise

Take a moment to experiment with the different settings on the **Print Settings** tab of the **View Properties** dialog box and on the **Print Multiple Views** dialog box, and then use the **Print Preview** command to see how the form would be printed.

17 Print data on a print view by overlaying text on an image

Problem

You have an InfoPath form with a text box and a date picker on it, and you want to be able to print a name and a date on a certificate of completion image when you print the form.

Solution

You can create a print view for the form that has an image of the certificate of completion as its background, and then use page layout and layout tables to position controls that are bound to the same fields as the controls on the default view.

To print data on a print view by overlaying text on an image:

1. In InfoPath, create a new **Blank Form** template.

2. Add a **Text Box** control and a **Date Picker** control to the view of the form template. Name the text box **fullName** and the date picker **completionDate**.

3. Add a print view to the form template (see recipe *16 Add a print view*), name it **Print View**, and set it to be the print view for the default view (**View 1**). Remember to deselect the **Show on the View menu when filling out this form** check box on the **View Properties** dialog box, because you do not want the user to have access to this view unless she is printing the form.

4. Select **Page Design ➤ Views ➤ View ➤ Print View**, and then click **Page Design ➤ Views ➤ Properties**.

5. On the **View Properties** dialog box on the **General** tab under the **Background** section, click **Browse** to browse to and select the image that you want to use as the background image for the view.

6. On the **View Properties** dialog box on the **General** tab under the **Background** section, select **Upper Left** from the **Position** drop-down

list box, and click **OK**. This should place the image in the upper left-hand corner of the view. The form template should now resemble the following figure.

Figure 51. Page layout on top of background image of the print view.

From the image above, you can see that the page layout table is centered on the design canvas for the view, so you must change its position to align it with the background image and also make the background of the page layout transparent.

7.   Click anywhere inside the page layout table, then right-click the small square in the upper left-hand corner of the page layout table and select **Borders and Shading** from the context menu that appears.

8.   On the **Borders and Shading** dialog box on the **Borders** tab, click **None** under the **Presets** section to remove all of the borders.

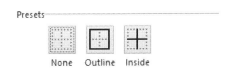

Figure 52. Presets section on the Borders tab of the Borders and Shading dialog box.

9.   On the **Borders and Shading** dialog box, click the **Shading** tab, select the **No color** option, and click **OK**.

10. Click anywhere inside the page layout table, then right-click the small square in the upper left-hand corner of the page layout table and select **Table Properties** from the context menu that appears.

11. On the **Table Properties** dialog box on the **Table** tab under the **Horizontal alignment** section, click **Left**, and then click **OK**.

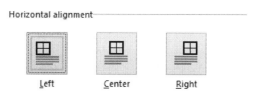

Figure 53. Horizontal alignment section on the Table Properties dialog box.

12. Resize the page layout table so that it covers the background image by hovering over either its right or bottom border, clicking and holding the mouse button down when the resize arrows appear, and then moving the mouse to make the table larger or smaller. The result is shown in the following figure. Please note that the borders of the page layout table have been made visible for clarity.

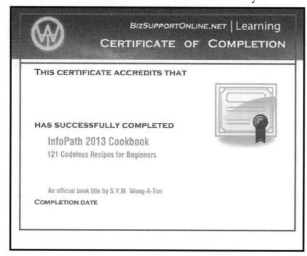

Figure 54. Transparent and resized page layout table on the background image.

13. Now you must divide the bottom cell of the page layout table to be able to perfectly align the controls you will place later on the form template.

To split the bottom cell of the page layout table in 4 rows and 2 columns, right-click inside the bottom cell, select **Split Cells** from the context menu that appears, and then on the **Split Cells** dialog box, type **2** for **Number of columns** and **4** for **Number of rows**, and then click **OK**.

14. Resize the rows and columns you just added. The result is shown in the following figure. Please note that the borders of the table have been made visible for clarity.

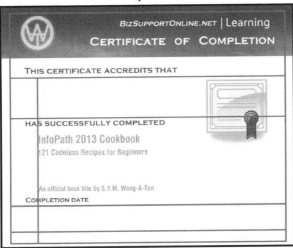

Figure 55. Page layout table with its cells split.

15. On the **Fields** task pane, right-click the **fullName** field, drag it to the view of the form template, drop it in row number 2 and column number 2 of the page layout table, and select **Calculated Value** from the context menu that appears when you drop it. A **Calculated Value** control does not have borders by default, so it is ideal to be used to display labels or text that does not need to be edited (read-only text), but just printed as is the case with print views.

16. With the calculated value control still selected, select **Home ➤ Format Text ➤ Arial Narrow** or any other font you want to use, and select **Home ➤ Format Text ➤ 18** as the font size.

17. Right-click the calculated value control you just added and select **Calculated Value Properties** from the context menu that appears.

18. On the **Calculated Value Properties** dialog box, click the **Size** tab, and type **0** for the **Top, Bottom, Left,** and **Right** paddings, type **20** for the **Top** and **Left** margins, type **0** for the **Bottom** and **Right** margins, and click **OK**. If you look closely at the canvas, the layout table does not start in the top left corner of the canvas in InfoPath Designer 2013 while there are no margins or paddings set on the page layout table. This is a visual design error that you must correct when printing. The background image however is placed nicely in the top left corner. The page layout table has an offset of approximately 20 pixels from the top and left borders of the canvas. When you print the form, this offset must be maintained for perfect alignment with the background image, which is why you must set this offset on the top and left margins of the controls.

19. Repeat steps 15 through 18 for the **completionDate** field, but place the field in row number 4 and column number 2, and make the font size **16** instead of **18**. The completed form should resemble the following figure. Please note that the borders of the table have been made visible for clarity.

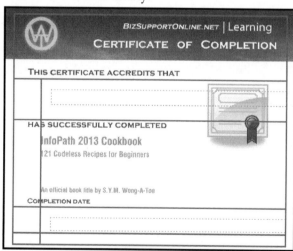

Figure 56. Completed print view with calculated value controls to display data.

20. Right-click the **completionDate** calculated value control and select **Calculated Value Properties** from the context menu that appears.

21. On the **Calculated Value Properties** dialog box on the **General** tab under the **Result** section, click **Format**.

22. On the **Date Format** dialog box, select your preferred date format (for example **14 March 2001**), and then click **OK**.

23. On the **Calculated Value Properties** dialog box, click **OK**.

24. Ensure that **View 1 (default)** is the currently selected view in the **View** drop-down list box on the **Page Design** tab, and then preview the form.

When the form opens, fill out the **fullName** and **completionDate** fields, and then click **File ➤ Print ➤ Print Preview** to display the **Print Preview** dialog box.

InfoPath should automatically use the print view you created for printing **View 1** (because you set it to do this in step 3) and the **Print Preview** dialog box should resemble the following figure.

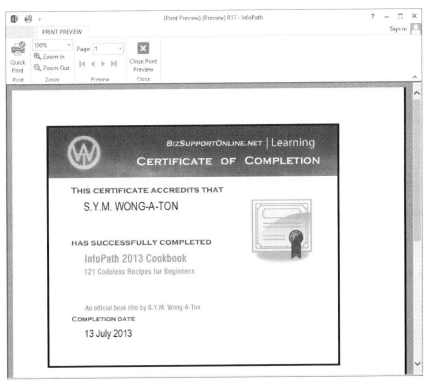

Figure 57. Print preview displaying the print view for View 1.

Had you made the page layout table's borders visible, then you would have seen that the page layout table moved up to the top left corner in the print view in print preview mode as shown in the following figure, which is why the correction of 20 pixels at the top and to the left of each calculated value control was necessary.

Figure 58. Completed InfoPath form with visible borders in the Print Preview window.

Discussion

Background images are set to print by default, but this setting can also be disabled. If it has been disabled, you can enable printing background images by clicking **File ➤ Options**, and then clicking **More Options** on the **InfoPath Options** dialog box. On the **Options** dialog box on the **General** tab, select the **Print background colors and pictures** check box, and then click **OK**. Click **OK** on the **InfoPath Options** dialog box to close it.

If the background image is not showing up in print preview mode after you have selected the **Print background colors and pictures** check box on the **Options** dialog box, ensure that the **Print Background Colors and Images** check box has been selected on the **Page Setup** dialog box of

Internet Explorer, which you can open by selecting **Page setup** from the **Print** menu in Internet Explorer.

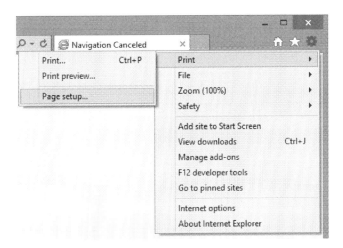

Figure 59. Print menu and Page setup menu item in Internet Explorer 10.

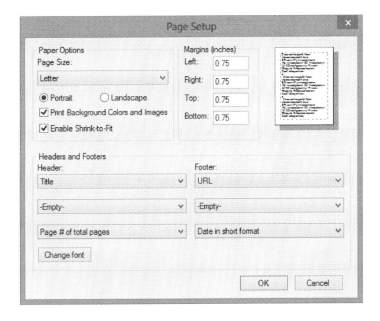

Figure 60. Page Setup dialog box in Internet Explorer 10 with the check box selected.

When creating a print view you generally want to use existing fields from the Main data source to add controls on the print view and design the view. Therefore, you must drag-and-drop existing fields from the **Fields** task pane onto the print view and not add new controls via **Home** ➤ **Controls** or the **Controls** task pane.

Tip:

> If you want to use a text box instead of a calculated value control to print text without getting the borders around the control, you can remove the borders through the **Borders and Shading** dialog box of the text box control, and then make the text box read-only through the **Text Box Properties** dialog box.

Chapter 3: Formulas

A formula is a calculation or an expression that can be used to calculate or construct the value of a field.

A formula can contain the values of fields, functions, or plain text. You can construct a formula for a field in InfoPath everywhere you see the formula button.

Figure 61. Button to open the Insert Formula dialog box in InfoPath.

The formula button opens the **Insert Formula** dialog box where you can construct a formula.

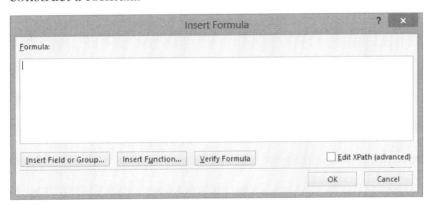

Figure 62. Insert Formula dialog box in InfoPath 2013.

On the **Insert Formula** dialog box, you can use the **Insert Field or Group** button to add the XPath expression for a field or group to a formula, you can use the **Insert Function** button to add a function to a formula, and you can type text into the **Formula** text box.

Note: XPath is used to navigate an XML document using paths to XML nodes. While you do not need to know XPath to be able to work with InfoPath on a basic level, it helps to know a little bit about it so that you can manually modify XPath expressions that InfoPath creates for you or just to understand what exactly is going on.

Once you are done constructing a formula, it is always recommended that you click the **Verify Formula** button to check whether your constructed formula contains any errors, and if it does, try to fix those errors.

On the **Insert Formula** dialog box, you will also see an **Edit XPath (advanced)** check box. InfoPath does not display the complete XPath expressions for fields by default, because XPath expressions can get very long and verbose. But if you want to see the full XPath expression for a field, you can select the **Edit XPath (advanced)** check box.

For example, if you add a text box named **field1** to your InfoPath form template and then click the **Insert Field or Group** button on the **Insert Formula** dialog box to select **field1**, you will see that InfoPath will display the field as

```
field1
```

in the **Formula** text box on the **Insert Formula** dialog box. And depending on which control or object you are adding the formula to, when you select the **Edit XPath (advanced)** check box, **field1** may appear as

```
my:field1
```

instead of

```
field1
```

When you get proficient at writing or manually modifying formulas and XPath expressions, you may want to use the **Edit XPath (advanced)** check box. A good example is when you want to manually add a filter to the XPath expression.

You will have ample opportunity to work with the **Insert Formula** dialog box as you progress through this book. This chapter only serves as a brief introduction to using the dialog box to insert formulas.

The following three recipes will demonstrate the use of functions, fields, and text in formulas.

Tip:

When adding a function to a formula through the **Insert Function** dialog box, when you click on the name of a function in the **Functions** list to select it, you will see a short description appear under the **Functions** list. Always use this description as guidance for how to use a particular function until you get familiar and comfortable using all available functions in InfoPath.

18 Capitalize text in a text box

Problem

You have a text box on an InfoPath form and want any text that is typed into this text box to be converted to uppercase (capitals) whenever the cursor moves off the text box.

Solution

You can use the **translate** function to convert lowercase characters to uppercase characters.

To capitalize text in a text box:

1. In InfoPath, create a new **Blank Form** template.

2. Add a **Text Box** control to the view of the form template.

3. Right-click the text box control and select **Text Box Properties** from the context menu that appears to open the **Text Box Properties** dialog box.

4. On the **Text Box Properties** dialog box on the **Data** tab under **Default Value**, click the formula button behind the **Value** text box.

5. On the **Insert Formula** dialog box, click **Insert Function**.

6. On the **Insert Function** dialog box, select **Text** in the **Categories** list, select **translate** in the **Functions** list, and click **OK**.

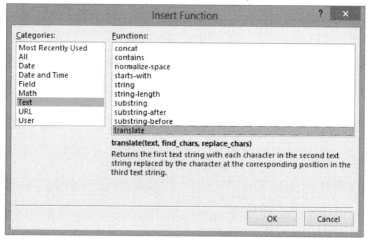

Figure 63. Insert Function dialog box in InfoPath 2013.

7. On the **Insert Formula** dialog box, double-click the first argument (the first text within the **translate** function that says "double click to insert field"). This should open the **Select a Field or Group** dialog box.

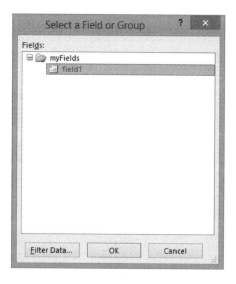

Figure 64. Select a Field or Group dialog box in InfoPath 2013.

8. On the **Select a Field or Group** dialog box, select the field bound to the text box (**field1**), and click **OK**.

9. On the **Insert Formula** dialog box, replace the second argument with "abcdefghijklmnopqrstuvwxyz", and the third argument with "ABCDEFGHIJKLMNOPQRSTUVWXYZ". The final formula should look like the following:

    ```
    translate(.,"abcdefghijklmnopqrstuvwxyz",
    "ABCDEFGHIJKLMNOPQRSTUVWXYZ")
    ```

10. Click **Verify Formula** to check whether the formula contains any errors and fix them if necessary, or click **OK** on the message box if there are no errors.

11. On the **Insert Formula** dialog box, click **OK**.

12. On the **Text Box Properties** dialog box, click **OK**.

13. Preview the form.

When the form opens, type a piece of text in the text box, and then press **Tab** to move off the text box. The text within the text box should have been converted to uppercase.

Discussion

The **translate** function takes 3 arguments and returns the first text string with each character in the second text string replaced by the character at the corresponding position in the third text string.

In the solution above, the characters being replaced are contained in the piece of text you type into the text box, and then all lowercase characters are replaced by corresponding uppercase characters.

For example, "c" is located on the third position in the text string containing the characters to replace. "c" would be replaced by "C", because "C" is located on the third position in the text string containing the characters to use as a replacement.

Exercise

Open the **Insert Function** dialog box via the **Insert Formula** dialog box, click on **All** in the **Categories** list, and then in the **Functions** list, sequentially go through each function and read its description below the **Functions** list box to familiarize yourself with the functions that are available in InfoPath.

Questions

1. What does the **now** function do?

2. What is the difference between the **now** and the **today** functions?

3. Which category of functions does the **sum** function fall under?

4. Which expression would you have to use in step 9 of the solution described above to remove all of the spaces in any piece of text that is typed into the text box?

19 Join text strings from two text boxes together

Problem

You have three text box controls on an InfoPath form. You want to enter text in the first two text box controls and have those two pieces of text joined together, be separated by a space, and placed into the third text box.

For example: Text box 1 contains the text "John", text box 2 contains the text "Doe", and you want the text "John Doe" to appear in text box 3.

Solution

You can use the **concat** function in InfoPath to join two or more strings together.

To join text strings from two text boxes together:

1. In InfoPath, create a new **Blank Form** template.

2. Add 3 **Text Box** controls to the view of the form template. The text box controls should get the names **field1**, **field2**, and **field3** by default.

3. Click the third text box to select it, and then on the Ribbon click **Properties ➤ Properties ➤ Default Value**. Note that you can set the default value of either the control itself or the field that the control is bound to. In this case, you are setting the default value of the field, not the control. Tip: Look at the title of the **Properties** dialog box (which says: "Field or Group Properties") and you will see that you are modifying properties of the field itself, not of the text box control. In recipe *18 Capitalize text in a text box*, you set the default value of the control, not of the field. Remember: If you set properties of a control, you are defining visual behavior of the form. If you set properties of a field, you are defining settings on the data source itself. Where the **Default Value** property is concerned, there is no difference between whether you set it on the control or on the field it is bound to.

4. On the **Field or Group Properties** dialog box on the **Data** tab under the **Default Value** section, click the formula button behind the **Value** text box.

5. On the **Insert Formula** dialog box, click **Insert Function**.

6. On the **Insert Function** dialog box, select **All** in the **Categories** list, then select **concat** in the **Functions** list, and click **OK**.

7. On the **Insert Formula** dialog box, double-click the first argument in the **concat** function where it says "double click to insert field".

8. On the **Select a Field or Group** dialog box, select **field1**, and click **OK**.

9. On the **Insert Formula** dialog box, replace the second argument in the **concat** function where it says "double click to insert field" with a space

    " "

10. On the **Insert Formula** dialog box, double-click the third argument in the **concat** function where it says "double click to insert field".

11. On the **Select a Field or Group** dialog box, select **field2**, and click **OK**.

12. On the **Insert Formula** dialog box, the formula should now say:

```
concat(field1, " ", field2)
```

Click **OK**.

13. On the **Field or Group Properties** dialog box, ensure that the **Refresh value when formula is recalculated** check box is selected, and then click **OK**. Selecting this check box ensures that the value of **field3** is recalculated whenever the value of either **field1** or **field2** changes.

14. Preview the form.

When the form opens, type text strings in the first and second text boxes, and then look at how the text in the third text box appears or changes.

Discussion

The **concat** function combines two or more fields or text strings into one text string, and is defined as follows:

```
concat(text1, text2, text3, text4, ...)
```

You must pass at least two fields or text strings as arguments to the **concat** function, otherwise InfoPath will display the error

Invalid number of arguments.

Be aware that the **concat** function accepts static text strings, InfoPath fields, or InfoPath functions as its arguments. For example, if you want to join the static text string "Name: " with the value of **field1**, you could use a formula such as:

```
concat("Name: ", field1)
```

The **concat** function can be used by itself or you can use its output as input for another function as demonstrated in recipe *20 Join two text strings and remove spaces if either text string is empty*.

Exercise

Change the formula you constructed and defined on **field3** into the following formula:

```
concat("The current date and time is: ", now())
```

and preview the form to see the result. This formula demonstrates how you can use a function (the **now** function) as input for another function (the **concat** function in this case).

Questions

1. Which category of functions does the **concat** function fall under?

2. Which formula would you have to use for the default value of **field3** if you wanted **field3** to display the following:

    ```
    Doe, John
    ```

    where "Doe" is a last name entered in **field2** and "John" is a first name entered in **field1**?

20 Join two text strings and remove spaces if either text string is empty

Problem

You have three text box controls on an InfoPath form. One for a first name, a second for a last name, and a third for a full name, which is composed by joining first and last names with a space between them.

If the first or second text box does not contain any text, you want the resulting text in the third text box not to be separated by a space.

For example: Text box 1 contains the text "John", text box 2 contains the text "Doe", and you want the text "John Doe" to appear in text box 3. But if text box 2 is empty and text box 1 contains the text "John", you want text box 3 to contain the text "John" instead of "John " (do you see that extra space behind the name?).

Solution

You can use the **concat** and **normalize-space** functions to join strings together and remove unwanted spaces from the resulting text string.

To join two text strings together and remove empty spaces if either text string is blank:

1. In InfoPath, create a new **Blank Form** template.

2. Add 3 **Text Box** controls to the view of the form template and name them **firstName**, **lastName**, and **fullName**, respectively.

3. Use the steps you learned in recipe *19 Join text strings from two text boxes together* to set the **Default Value** of **fullName** to be equal to the following formula:

    ```
    normalize-space(concat(firstName, " ", lastName))
    ```

    or

    ```
    normalize-space(concat(../my:firstName, " ", ../my:lastName))
    ```

    if you have the **Edit XPath (advanced)** check box selected on the **Insert Formula** dialog box.

4. Click **OK** when closing all dialog boxes.

5. Preview the form.

When the form opens, type a first name and a last name into the corresponding text boxes and see what appears in the text box for the full name. Then empty the last name text box and check whether there is an empty space behind the first name in the text box for the full name.

To see the difference in behavior when you do not use the **normalize-space** function, you should change the formula to the following formula:

```
concat(firstName, " ", lastName)
```

or use the form template you created in recipe *19 Join text strings from two text boxes together* to test the difference in behavior between the two solutions.

Discussion

The **normalize-space** function removes whitespace from a text string. You can use it to trim spaces from around a text string.

Exercise

Try to figure out what the **substring** function does and how you can use it. If you cannot figure it out, do not worry, because you will be using it in several recipes throughout this book.

Question

1. Which formula would you have to use for the default value of the **fullName** field to get a result such as for example

    ```
    John  DOE
    ```

    where "John" is entered into the **firstName** text box and "Doe" into the **lastName** text box. Hint: You must use the **translate** function.

Chapter 4: Rules

What are rules?

A rule in InfoPath is declarative logic that is executed in response to certain events and conditions. An example of a rule is the following: If a text box does not contain any text, so is blank, change its background color to red.

Types of rules

There are four types of rules in InfoPath:

1. Action
2. Formatting
3. Validation
4. Default Value

Action rules perform actions, such as for example setting the value of a field (see recipe *22 Set the value of a field*) or switching views (see recipe *24 Switch to a read-only view when a button is clicked*).

An Action rule

Figure 65. Icon and text for an Action rule on the Rules task pane in InfoPath 2013.

Formatting rules apply formatting to controls, such as for example when hiding a control or setting the background color of a control as demonstrated in recipe *21 Change the background color of a text box to red if it is blank*.

A Formatting rule

Figure 66. Icon and text for a Formatting rule on the Rules task pane in InfoPath 2013.

Validation rules validate whether the data entered in a field is what is expected, such as for example when checking whether a number is entered into a text box that should only accept numbers (see recipe *30 Check whether a number was entered*).

A Validation rule

Figure 67. Icon and text for a Validation rule on the Rules task pane in InfoPath 2013.

Default Value, while not officially called a "rule" in InfoPath, is similar to a **Set a field's value** action rule, but then without any conditions. And unlike a **Set a field's value** action where the value of a field is set by an action taking place elsewhere on the form, a default value is set by the field itself based on a formula that uses either its own value or the value of other fields on the form.

21 Change the background color of a text box to red if it is blank

Problem

You have a text box control on an InfoPath form and want its background color to change to red whenever there is no text in the text box.

Solution

You can use the **Add Rule** command in InfoPath to quickly add a rule with a condition to a control.

To change the background color of a text box to red if it is blank:

1.   In InfoPath, create a new **Blank Form** template.

2.   Add a **Text Box** control to the view of the form template.

3.   Click the text box to select it, and then select **Home ➤ Rules ➤ Add Rule ➤ Is Blank ➤ Bad**.

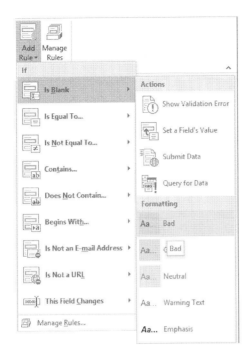

Figure 68. Adding a Formatting rule through the Add Rule command.

The **Rules** task pane should automatically open and InfoPath should create a **Formatting** rule as displayed in the following figure.

Figure 69. Rule details on the Rules task pane in InfoPath 2013.

4. Preview the form.

When the form opens, the background color of the text box should be red. As you type text in the text box, the text will also be red, because according to InfoPath, no change has taken place yet. Once you leave the text box, this will signal a change to InfoPath (that is, the value of the text box went from being blank to being something), so any rules you have set on the text box will then run. So when you are done typing, click or tab away from the text box. The background and foreground colors of the text box should return to their normal colors (black text on a white background).

Discussion

You can add a rule to an InfoPath form or control by clicking **Add Rule** or **Manage Rules** under the **Rules** group on the **Home** tab.

Figure 70. Add Rule and Manage Rules commands on the Home tab.

Add Rule allows you to quickly add rules with conditions, but does not allow you to add all types of rules. If you need to add a rule that is not available through the **Add Rule** command, you must use the **Manage Rules** command to open the **Rules** task pane and then add a rule from there.

On the **Rules** task pane, you will see a couple of things:

1. The name of the field or group you have added or are going to add a rule to is displayed just below the title bar of the **Rules** task pane. Always use this name to double-check whether you selected the correct group or field to add a rule to.

2. Rules that have been added to a field or group are listed below the name of the field or group on the **Rules** task pane. You can click on any rule listed here and select **Delete** from the drop-down menu that appears to delete the rule. You can also click the delete icon (black cross) behind the name of the field on the **Rules** task pane to delete

the rule you selected.

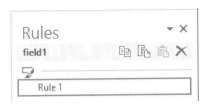

Figure 71. Rules task pane displaying a field's name and rule.

3. There is a **New** button on the **Rules** task pane with which you can add one of three types of rules (**Validation**, **Formatting**, or **Action**) to a field or group.

Figure 72. New button on the Rules task pane to add a rule.

4. There is a rule details section where you can change the name of the rule, add one or more conditions to the rule, change the rule type (if you initially added the wrong type of rule), and depending on the type of rule you selected, a section where you can add actions, define formatting, or enter a message.

You can get a quick overview of which rules have been defined in a form template by using the **Rule Inspector**, which you can open by clicking **Data ➤ Rules ➤ Rule Inspector**.

The **Rule Inspector** becomes a very useful tool to use when you are trying to debug a very complex form template that contains many rules that may be causing unexpected behavior.

Note that **Formatting** rules are not displayed on the **Rule Inspector**. Only rules that peform actions (**Action** rules, **Validation** rules, and **Default Values** containing calculations) can be found on the **Rule Inspector**.

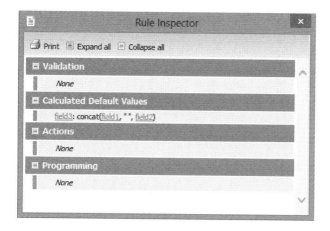

Figure 73. Rule Inspector in InfoPath 2013.

At the top of the **Rules** task pane, you will see a small toolbar with icons for commands with which you can copy a rule, paste a rule, delete a rule, and copy all rules. The first three commands are also available through the context menu of a rule.

Figure 74. Icons for commands to copy, paste, and delete rules via the Rules task pane.

The copy and paste commands are for copying and pasting rules between fields or groups, between form events such as the **Form Load** and **Form Submit** events, or between fields or groups and form events.

To copy and paste a rule:

1. On the **Rules** task pane, select the rule you want to copy.

2. Click the **Copy Rule** command.

3. Switch to the control, field, group, or form event you want to paste the rule on by either selecting the control, field, or group you want to paste the rule on, or by clicking **Data ➤ Rules ➤ Form Load** or **Data ➤ Rules ➤ Form Submit** if you are going to be pasting the rule on a form event.

4. Click the **Paste Rule** command to paste the rule.

To copy and/or paste all rules that have been defined on a field or group, you can make use of the **Copy All Rules** and **Paste All Rules** menu items that are accessible through the drop-down menu of a field or group on the **Fields** task pane.

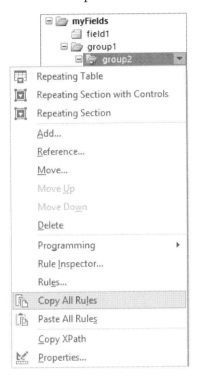

Figure 75. Copy All Rules and Paste All Rules menu items for a group.

While copying and pasting rules facilitate the process of transferring rules between fields, groups, controls, and form events, you must be careful using this functionality, since InfoPath may sometimes mess up field references used in rules that have been copied and pasted. So whenever you copy and paste a rule, always double-check whether the rule works as intended on the new control, field, group, or form event.

Exercise

Use the **Add Rule** command on the same text box you added in step 2 in the solution described above to show a validation error if the field is blank. Hint: You must perform the same action as in step 3, but then choose **Show Validation Error** from the drop-down menu.

On the **Rules** task pane, look at how InfoPath created the rule for you and which settings were used. Preview the form and then hover with the mouse pointer over the text box to see the error message appear as a tooltip. Also notice the red asterisk (*) that appears in the text box.

Questions

1. What are the four types of rules you can create in InfoPath?

2. Of these types of rules, which type(s) of rule(s) did you add in this recipe?

Action rules

Action rules perform actions, such as for example setting the value of a field (see recipe *22 Set the value of a field*) or switching views (see recipe *24 Switch to a read-only view when a button is clicked*).

Action rules can be defined for when:

- Buttons are clicked

- Values of fields change

- A form is opened (**Form Load**)

- A form is submitted (**Form Submit**)

You can set one or more conditions that determine when an **Action** rule should run.

An **Action** rule can contain one or more actions, but you can also create several **Action** rules with one action each. So when do you create one rule that contains multiple actions, and when do you create multiple rules that have one action each?

If you want to run a batch of actions under the same condition, then you should place all of the actions in one rule if possible, and add the condition to that rule. If you have several conditions under which actions should run, you must create several rules with the desired conditions and then add actions that should run under the condition for each rule.

Another reason for creating several **Action** rules instead of one **Action** rule with several actions is if you wanted to disable rules. Since you cannot disable individual actions in an **Action** rule, but only the rule as a whole, if you want to test actions by disabling rules, it is best to put each action in a rule or group the actions in such a way that you can disable a batch of actions as one rule.

To disable a rule, click the drop-down arrow on the right-hand side of the **Action** rule you want to disable, and then select **Disable** from the context menu that appears.

Figure 76. Disable menu item on the context menu of an Action rule.

Action rules run from top to bottom, one after the other. For example, if you have two **Action** rules (**Rule 1** and **Rule 2**) on a control without any conditions set on any of the rules, **Rule1** will run first and then **Rule 2** will run next. If both rules do the same thing, for example, set the value of the same field, the result of **Rule 2** will override that of **Rule 1**.

Figure 77. Two rules set on one field (field1).

Once a rule has run, you can prevent any other **Action** rules that have been added to a field from running by selecting the **Don't run remaining rules if the condition of this rule is met** check box on the **Rules** task pane. Selecting this check box will prevent any rules further down the chain from running.

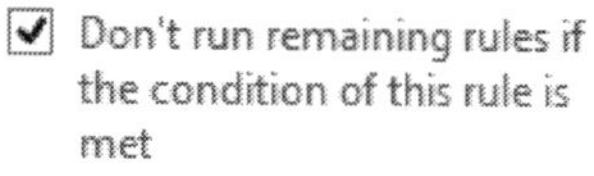

☑ Don't run remaining rules if the condition of this rule is met

Figure 78. Check box on a rule to prevent running other rules further down the chain.

A common question many who are new to InfoPath ask is: "To which control do I add the **Action** rule?" If there is one golden tip I can give you for **Action** rules, it is the following one.

Tip:

> You must always add **Action** rules to the source of the action. The source is defined as the field or control that drives the action (e.g. a button being clicked). The source determines what happens to the target, which receives the result of the action (e.g. the value of a field being set).

The following figure visually explains the statement above.

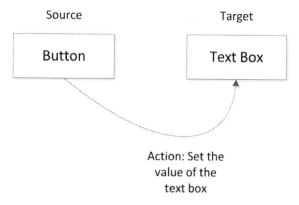

Figure 79. Action rule on a button setting the value of a text box.

In Figure 79, the **Action** rule should go on the button and not the text box.

While not officially called a rule in InfoPath, the simplest type of **Action** rule you can define in InfoPath is by setting the **Default Value** of a field or control to a formula. A **Default Value** calculation runs when the form opens or when the value of a field changes, and every time the formula is recalculated if you have selected that option.

A **Default Value** works slightly different than an **Action** rule. Because you cannot set conditions on a **Default Value**, it always runs. In addition, with **Action** rules you set the rule on the source, while with a **Default Value**, the target sets its own value which can be based on the value of another field (the source) or a formula.

It is good to know what kind of things you can do with each type of rule, so that if you are given the task to "disable a button" you know that you must add a **Formatting** rule to the button control and not an **Action** rule.

InfoPath offers the following actions you can use with **Action** rules:

- Set a field's value
- Switch views
- Query for data
- Submit data
- Close the form
- Send data to Web Part
- Change REST URL

Do not worry if you cannot memorize this list. As you continue to work with InfoPath, you will remember the types of rules you can add, and as you work through this book you will become familiar with several of the actions listed above.

22 Set the value of a field

Problem

You want to click a button on an InfoPath form and then have the text in a text box be set to "Hello InfoPath".

Solution

You can use an **Action** rule to set the value of a field.

To set the value of a field:

1. In InfoPath, create a new **Blank Form** template.

2. Add a **Text Box** control and a **Button** control to the view of the form template.

3. Click the button control to select it, and then select **Home ➤ Rules ➤ Add Rule ➤ When This Button Is Clicked ➤ Set a Field's Value**. This should open the **Rule Details** dialog box.

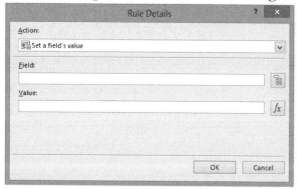

Figure 80. Rule Details dialog box in InfoPath 2013.

4. On the **Rule Details** dialog box, click the button behind the **Field** text box. This should open the **Select a Field or Group** dialog box where you can select a field for which its value must be set.

5. On the **Select a Field or Group** dialog box, select **field1** (which is bound to the text box control on the form), and click **OK**.

6. On the **Rule Details** dialog box, type the text **Hello InfoPath** (without any double quotes around it) in the **Value** text box, and click **OK**. The **Rules** task pane should automatically open if it was not already open.

7. If the **Rules** task pane is not open in InfoPath, click **Home ➤ Rules ➤ Manage Rules** to open it, and then select the button on the view of the form template to display any rules that have been added to the button on the **Rules** task pane. The details for the rule on the **Rules** task pane should resemble the following figure.

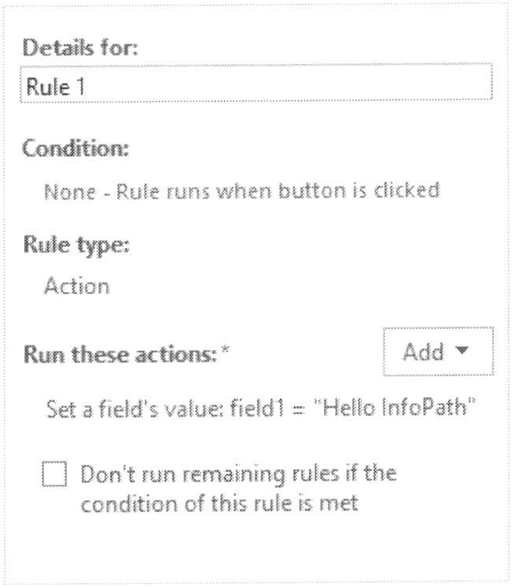

Details for:
Rule 1

Condition:
    None - Rule runs when button is clicked

Rule type:
    Action

Run these actions: *   Add ▼
    Set a field's value: field1 = "Hello InfoPath"

    ☐ Don't run remaining rules if the
        condition of this rule is met

Figure 81. Rules task pane with a rule on a button to set the value of a field.

8. Preview the form.

When the form opens, click the button. The text "Hello InfoPath" should appear in the text box.

Discussion

Let us dissect the logic for adding the rule in the solution described above.

The requirement for the recipe said: You want to click a button on an InfoPath form and then have the text in a text box be set to "Hello InfoPath".

The first question you should ask yourself when adding a rule is: What type of rule should I add? A **Default Value**, **Action**, **Formatting**, or **Validation** rule?

From reading the requirement above you know you want to take an action (click a button to set the value of a text box), which means that you have to add an **Action** rule; not set a **Default Value**, add a **Formatting** rule, or add a **Validation** rule.

Once you know you must add an **Action** rule, you must figure out what the source and what the target is.

From reading the requirement above you know that clicking the button is driving the action of setting the value of the text box, which means that the button is the source and the text box is the target.

Once you have identified the rule type to create (**Action**), the source (button), and the target (text box), you can go ahead and add the rule to the control, which in this case is the button.

In the solution described above, you used the **Add Rule** command on the **Home** tab to add an **Action** rule to the button. A second way of adding an **Action** rule to a button is to open the **Rules** task pane via **Home ➤ Rules ➤ Manage Rules**, and then on the **Rules** task pane click **New ➤ Action**.

In the solution described above, you could have also used the **Insert Formula** dialog box to set the value of the field. In step 6, instead of directly entering a static piece of text in the **Value** text box on the **Rule Details** dialog box, you could have clicked the formula button behind the **Value** text box to open the **Insert Formula** dialog box, and then on the **Insert Formula** dialog box, enter the static piece of text as follows:

```
"Hello InfoPath"
```

Unlike in step 6, you must use double quotes around the text to indicate that it is a static piece of text when you are using the **Insert Formula** dialog box. If you do not do this, InfoPath will display the following warning message when you click **Verify Formula** or **OK** to close the dialog box:

The formula contains one or more errors.

And when you click on the **Show Details** button on the warning message box, you would see the following message displayed:

```
Expected value type: end-of-string

Actual value: name
Hello -->InfoPath<--
```

InfoPath uses arrows (--> and <--) to indicate where it spotted an error.

```
Hello -->InfoPath<--
```

Note that this is just an indication; the error could be elsewhere. In addition, InfoPath is also saying that it is expecting the end of a string (**end-of-string**)

```
Expected value type: end-of-string
```

but that it found a **name**

```
Actual value: name
```

This should tell you that you should change or delete what InfoPath is pointing at, so the text **InfoPath** in this case, to make the formula work. But if you delete the text **InfoPath** and leave **Hello**, InfoPath will then display the next error, which is

```
"Hello" does not point to a valid location path of a field or
group.
```

For InfoPath to see the text **Hello** as a piece of text, you must put double quotes around the text **Hello**.

```
"Hello"
```

Exercise

Add a second text box named **field2** to the view of the form template. Select the button and then on the **Rules** task pane, delete the rule you added in step 3. With the button still selected, on the **Rules** task pane, click **New ➤ Action**. On the **Rules** task pane, behind the **Run these actions** label, click **Add ➤ Set a field's value**. This should open the same **Rule Details** dialog box you opened in step 3. Continue configuring the rule to set the value of **field1** to be equal to a piece of text that consists of the static piece of text "Hello" and whatever text is entered into **field2**. For example, if a user enters their name "John" in **field2**, the text in **field1** should say "Hello John". Hint: You must use the **concat** function in a formula.

23 Close a form when a button is clicked

Problem

You have a button on an InfoPath form and you want to be able to click the button to close the form.

Solution

You can add an **Action** rule with a **Close the form** action on the button to close the form when a user clicks the button.

To add a button with a rule that closes a form:

1. In InfoPath, create a new **Blank Form** template.

2. Add a **Button** control to the view of the form template.

3. With the button still selected, click **Home ➤ Rules ➤ Manage Rules** to open the **Rules** task pane.

4. On the **Rules** task pane, click **New ➤ Action**.

5. On the **Rules** task pane behind **Run these actions**, click **Add ➤ Close the form**.

6. On the **Rule Details** dialog box, click **OK**.

7. Preview the form.

When the form opens, click the button. The form should close.

Discussion

Let us dissect the logic for adding the rule in the solution described above.

You want to close a form by clicking a button. Because closing a form is an action in InfoPath, you know you must add an **Action** rule.

You want to close a form by clicking a button. From this you know that clicking the button should take place first, so the button is the source. Then you must close the form. This makes the form the target.

Having gone through the thought process above, you know you must create an **Action** rule on the button (the source) with an action to close the form (the target).

Note:

> You could have also used the **Add Rule** command under the **Rules** group on the **Home** tab to add a **Close the form** action to the button.

24 Switch to a read-only view when a button is clicked

Problem

You added a read-only view to an InfoPath form template. Now you want to have the form switch to the read-only view when a button is clicked.

Solution

From going through the previous two recipes, you should now know that when someone says: "I want to be able to switch to another view when a button is clicked", you must add a **Switch views** action to a rule on a button.

Before you continue, review these questions and answers:

1. What is the action the user wants to perform? Answer: The user wants to switch to another view, so I must add an **Action** rule that switches views.

2. I must add an **Action** rule, so what is the source? Answer: The button, because that drives switching views. So I must add the rule to the button.

3. Does this rule depend on the value of another field? Is there a condition that must be met before this rule can run? Answer: No, so I must add an action that is unrestricted, so there is no condition that has to be set on the rule.

This is the kind of thought process you must try to develop whenever you want to have something happen on an InfoPath form. Now let us walk through the steps for making this solution work.

To switch to a read-only view when a button is clicked:

1. In InfoPath, create a new **Blank Form** template.

2. Add a read-only view to the form template as described in recipe *15 Add a read-only view*.

3. Switch back to the default view, and add a **Button** control to it.

4. With the button still selected, select **Home ➤ Rules ➤ Add Rule ➤ When This Button Is Clicked ➤ Switch Views**.

5. On the **Rule Details** dialog box, select the read-only view from the **View** drop-down list box, and then click **OK**.

6. Preview the form.

When the form opens, click the button on the default view. The read-only view should appear.

Discussion

Typically when you add a **Switch Views** button to an InfoPath form, you may not want users to be able to select a view from the **Current View** drop-down list box. You can prevent users from switching views by removing a view's name from the menu as you already saw in the discussion section of recipe *13 Add a second view to a form template*.

Switching views does not have to be restricted to button controls. You can also add a **Switch views** action to a rule that runs when the form opens. You could use this technique for example with a condition to check whether the form has already been submitted, and if it has been, switch to the read-only view when the form is opened after it has been submitted (see recipe *43 Switch to a read-only view when a form is opened after submission*).

Another example would be to submit a form using rules, and then add a rule to switch to the read-only view immediately after the form has been submitted without closing the form (see recipe *42 Switch to a read-only view on submit*).

Formatting rules

Formatting rules apply formatting to controls, such as for example when hiding a control or setting the background color of a control as demonstrated in recipe *21 Change the background color of a text box to red if it is blank*. **Formatting** rules can be applied to controls, but not to form events (load and submit).

InfoPath offers the following formatting options you can use with **Formatting** rules:

- Hide this control
- Disable this control
- Don't allow users to insert or delete this control
- Change the style or color of the font for this control
- Change the background color of this control

You can set one or more conditions that determine when a **Formatting** rule should run.

The difference between **Action** and **Formatting** rules is that you are forced to set a condition on a **Formatting** rule, while this is not the case for **Action** rules. So a **Formatting** rule always runs under a specified condition.

Another difference is that unlike **Action** rules, a **Formatting** rule can only apply one type of formatting to a control at a time. In the case of **Action** rules, all of the rules run from top to bottom unless you stop them by selecting a check box. This is not the case for **Formatting** rules.

So while you can add multiple **Formatting** rules that have the same condition and different or the same type of formatting to a control, if the condition of the first **Formatting** rule defined on the control is met, its formatting will be applied to the control and all other **Formatting** rules further down the chain will be ignored.

So you should always add only one **Formatting** rule to a control or if you want to add multiple **Formatting** rules ensure that the conditions of all of the **Formatting** rules on the control are mutually exclusive.

To answer the question "To which control do I add the **Formatting** rule?" I can give you the following tip.

Tip:

> You must always set **Formatting** rules on the target. The target is defined as the control that receives the results (e.g. setting the color of the font for the control) based on a condition (e.g. if the field is blank). Conditions can be based on the value of the target itself, the value of another field, a static value, or a formula.

The following figure visually explains the previous statement.

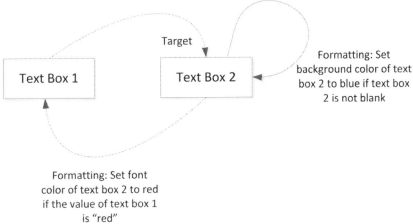

Figure 82. Formatting rules on text box 2 setting colors based on conditions.

In the example in Figure 82, you want to add two **Formatting** rules to text box 2.

The first **Formatting** rule depends on the value of text box 1. This **Formatting** rule says that the font color of text box 2 should be set to red if "red' is typed into text box 1. So text box 1 is driving the action of setting the font color of text box 2. This makes text box 1 the source and text box 2 the target. Setting the font color falls under formatting, so you must add a **Formatting** rule to the target (text box 2), with a condition that is based on the value of the source (text box 1).

The second **Formatting** rule depends on the value of text box 2 itself. This **Formatting** rule says that the background color of text box 2 should be set to blue if text box 2 is not blank. So text box 2 is driving the action of setting its own background color. This makes text box 2 both the source and the target. Setting the background color falls under formatting, so you must add a **Formatting** rule to the target (text box 2) with a condition that is based on the value of the source (text box 2).

Because you want to set two **Formatting** rules on the same control (text box 2), you must make sure that the conditions of the two rules are mutually exclusive. And if you map out the logic, you will see that you must add 4 **Formatting** rules instead of 2 to make the rules mutually exclusive as listed in the following table.

Rule	Conditions	Formatting to Apply
1	Text box 1 = "red" and Text box 2 is not blank	Font Color = Red Background Color = Blue
2	Text box 1 = "red" and Text box 2 is blank	Font Color = Red Background Color = White
3	Text box 1 ≠ "red" and Text box 2 is not blank	Font Color = Black Background Color = Blue
4	Text box 1 ≠ "red" and Text box 2 is blank	Font Color = Black Background Color = White

Table 1. Creating mutually exclusive Formatting rules in InfoPath.

You will learn more about conditions in recipes to come.

25 Show a repeating table when a check box is selected

Problem

You have a check box on an InfoPath form and want to show a repeating table whenever the check box is selected.

Solution

You can use conditional formatting (a **Formatting** rule with conditions) on a section control that contains the repeating table to show or hide the repeating table when the check box is selected or deselected.

To show a repeating table when a check box is selected:

1. In InfoPath, create a new **Blank Form** template.

2. Add a **Check Box** control to the view of the form template and name it **showTable**.

3. Add a **Section** control to the view of the form template, then click anywhere within the section control, and add a **Repeating Table** control within the section control. You can accept the default of 3 columns for the repeating table control.

4. Click on the section control (the label that says "Section") to select it, and then click **Home ➤ Rules ➤ Manage Rules** to open the **Rules** task pane. A second way to select the section control would be to, on the **Fields** task pane, click on the group node (**group1**) that the section control is bound to in the Main data source of the form.

5. On the **Rules** task pane, ensure that **group1** (which is bound to the section control) is listed at the top of the **Rules** task pane, and then click **New ➤ Formatting** to add a **Formatting** rule to **group1**.

6. On the **Rules** task pane under **Formatting**, select the **Hide this control** check box. This will hide the section control with the repeating table in it.

7. On the **Rules** task pane under **Condition**, click the text that says **None** to add a condition.

8. On the **Condition** dialog box, select **showTable** from the first drop-down list box, leave **is equal to** selected in the second drop-down list box, select **FALSE** from the third drop-down list box, and click **OK**. This condition will allow the section control containing the repeating table to be hidden when the value of **showTable** is equal to **FALSE**, so when the check box has not been selected. The following condition should now appear on the **Rules** task pane under **Condition**:

    ```
    showTable = FALSE
    ```

    instead of the text

    ```
    None
    ```

9. Preview the form.

When the form opens, the repeating table should be invisible. Select the check box. The repeating table should appear.

Discussion

Let us dissect the logic for adding the rule in the solution described above.

You want to show a repeating table. Because showing and hiding falls under formatting in InfoPath, you know you must add a **Formatting** rule.

You want to show a repeating table by selecting a check box. From this you know that the value of the check box will drive visibility of the repeating table. So the check box is the source and the repeating table is the target.

But because you can only hide fields or rows in a repeating table and not the entire repeating table itself, and you want to show or hide the entire table, you must create a container for the repeating table.

Section controls are ideal containers to use, because when they are invisible, they give up their space. So for example, if you had a text box right below the section control and you made the section control hidden, the text box would automatically move up to take up the space of the section control.

You can place any type of control within a section control. In this case, you want to place the repeating table within the section control, and then make the section control become the target for formatting instead of the repeating table.

Having gone through the thought process above, you now know that you must add a **Formatting** rule to the section control (the target) with a formatting of "hide this control" and a condition that checks whether the value of the check box (the source) is equal to FALSE (the value of the check box when it is deselected).

In other words, the section control should be shown when the check box is selected. If you reverse this logic it means that the section control should be hidden when the check box is deselected. In the solution described above, you used the latter logic to set up the **Formatting** rule.

26 Make a control read-only based on a condition

Problem

You have a date picker and a button on an InfoPath form and want to make the date picker read-only when the button is clicked.

Solution

You can use a **Formatting** rule to make a control read-only and then add a condition to the rule to apply the formatting only when the condition is met.

To make a control read-only based on a condition:

1. In InfoPath, create a new **Blank Form** template.

2. Add a **Date Picker** control and a **Button** control to the view of the form template.

3. Add a hidden field named **isReadOnly** to the Main data source of the form (see recipe *11 Add a hidden field*). You will use this hidden field to make the date picker read-only. If the hidden field has a value of "lock" then the date picker should be read-only, otherwise you should be able to select a date. The button will be used to set the value of the hidden field.

4. Click the button to select it, and then select **Home ➤ Rules ➤ Add Rule ➤ When This Button Is Clicked ➤ Set a Field's Value**.

5. On the **Rule Details** dialog box, click the button behind the **Field** text box.

6. On the **Select a Field or Group** dialog box, select **isReadOnly**, and click **OK**.

7. On the **Rule Details** dialog box, type the text **lock** (without any double quotes around it) in the **Value** text box, and click **OK**. The action on the **Rules** task pane for the button should now say:

```
Set a field's value: isReadOnly = "lock"
```

8. Click the date picker to select it. The **Rules** task pane should switch to display the rules for the date picker.

9. On the **Rules** task pane, click **New ➤ Formatting** to add a **Formatting** rule to the date picker.

10. On the **Rules** task pane under **Condition**, click the text **None**.

11. On the **Condition** dialog box, select **isReadOnly** from the first drop-down list box, leave **is equal to** selected in the second drop-down list box, select **Type text** from the third drop-down list box (this will change the drop-down list box into a text box), type **lock** (without any double quotes around it) in the text box, and then click **OK**. The condition on the **Rules** task pane should now say:

    ```
    isReadOnly = "lock"
    ```

    This condition allows the **Formatting** rule to run only when the value of the **isReadOnly** hidden field has been set to the text **lock**.

12. On the **Rules** task pane under **Formatting**, select the **Disable this control** check box. This will make the date picker read-only if the condition has been met.

13. Preview the form.

When the form opens, enter a date in the date picker and then click the button. After clicking the button, try to change the date in the date picker by either typing a date or clicking on the calendar button of the date picker to select a date. You should not be able to modify the date in the date picker anymore.

Discussion

In the solution described above you had to use a **Formatting** rule to make a date picker control read-only. Unlike a text box control, which has a **Read-Only** property that you can set at design time, many controls in InfoPath do not have such a property. The date picker is such a control.

So to make controls that do not have a **Read-Only** property read-only, you must use a **Formatting** rule with a formatting of **Disable this control**.

Another situation in which you may want to use such a **Formatting** rule is if you wanted to make a control read-only based on a condition. The **Read-Only** property of a text box is not accessible at runtime through rules, so if you wanted to make a text box control read-only based on a condition, you would have to use a **Formatting** rule to achieve this.

And finally, there are controls on which you cannot set conditional formatting (for example file attachment controls on web browser forms). In such cases you will have to get creative or change your form design in such a way to achieve the results you are after. For two examples of how you could make a file attachment control read-only, see recipe *89 Make an attachment read-only – method 1* and recipe *90 Make an attachment read-only – method 2.*

If you do not want to make a control read-only based on a condition, but rather always make the control read-only similar to the **Read-Only** property of a text box control, see the discussion section of recipe *27 Disable a button on a read-only view.*

Exercise

Try making the date picker read-only when a check box is selected instead of when a button is clicked. Hint: The check box control should replace the hidden field. If you cannot figure it out, see recipe *28 Enable a control when a check box is selected.*

Questions

1. Does a **Picture** control have a **Read-Only** property?

2. Does a **Combo Box** have a **Read-Only** property?

3. How would you go about making a group of controls read-only based on a condition without having to individually make the controls read-only?

27 Disable a button on a read-only view

Problem

You want to permanently display a button on a read-only view of an InfoPath form as disabled.

Solution

You can permanently disable a button by using a **Formatting** rule that has a condition that makes the rule always run.

To disable a button on a read-only view:

1. In InfoPath, create a new **Blank Form** template.

2. Add a read-only view to the form template (see recipe *15 Add a read-only view*).

3. Add a **Button** control to the read-only view.

4. With the button still selected, click **Home ➤ Rules ➤ Manage Rules** to open the **Rules** task pane.

5. On the **Rules** task pane, click **New ➤ Formatting** to add a **Formatting** rule to the button.

6. On the **Rules** task pane under **Condition**, click the text **None**.

7. On the **Condition** dialog box, select **The expression** from the first drop-down list box. A text box to enter an expression should appear. Replace all of the text in the text box with the following expression:

   ```
   true()
   ```

   which represents the **true** function, and click **OK**. This condition will always return a value equal to **TRUE**, so will always be met, so the rule will always run.

8. On the **Rules** task pane under **Formatting**, select the **Disable this control** check box.

9. Preview the form.

When the form opens, the button on the read-only view should be shown as dimmed, so disabled.

Discussion

If you require the button to only be disabled on the read-only view when the read-only view is displayed, you must implement a solution similar to the solution described in recipe *26 Make a control read-only based on a condition* to keep track of when the read-only view is displayed (for example by using a **Switch views** action) and then set a **Formatting** rule on the button based on the value of the field that is tracking switching to the read-only view.

In the solution described above you made a **Formatting** rule always run by adding a condition to it that said:

```
true()
```

While the **true** function returns a value equal to **TRUE** in InfoPath, you could have also used any expression that returns a value equal to **TRUE**, such as for example the following expression:

```
1 = 1
```

In the solution described above you also learned how to use an expression to return the value for a condition by selecting **The expression** on the **Condition** dialog box. Ordinarily, whenever you select **The expression** from the first drop-down list box on the **Condition** dialog box, you are forced to know the exact expression you want to type into the text box and do not get any help from InfoPath to construct it. So while I knew I had to type in

```
true()
```

to return a value equal to **TRUE**, you as a beginner would not know this. So in recipe *31 Set a maximum length on text in a text box* I will show you a way to cheat when constructing expressions for conditions in InfoPath.

Tip:

> Because buttons do not display data visually such as text boxes, it is recommended that you delete them from a read-only view rather than disable them, unless they have a specific purpose such as switching back to a non-read-only view or submitting the form.

28 Enable a control when a check box is selected

Problem

You have a date picker control on an InfoPath form that you want to enable whenever a check box is selected.

Solution

You can add a **Formatting** rule to the date picker to enable it based on a condition that the check box should be selected for the rule to run.

To enable a control when a check box is selected:

1. In InfoPath, create a new **Blank Form** template.

2. Add a **Check Box** control and a **Date Picker** control to the view of the form template. Name the check box control **isEnabled**.

3. Add a **Formatting** rule to the date picker control with a condition that says:

   ```
   isEnabled = FALSE
   ```

   and with a formatting of **Disable this control**. This rule will disable the date picker when the **isEnabled** check box is deselected, so will enable the date picker when the check box is selected.

4. Preview the form.

When the form opens, the date picker should be disabled and you should not be able to enter or select a date. Select the check box. The date picker should now be enabled and you should be able to enter or select a date.

Discussion

You can use conditional formatting to enable or disable any input control. To see the list of input controls in InfoPath, expand the list of controls under the **Controls** group on the **Home** tab or open the **Controls** task pane by clicking on the arrow in the bottom right-hand corner of the **Controls** group on the **Home** tab on the Ribbon. The controls are listed in categories with the **Input** group of controls being the first.

From the controls that fall under the **Objects** category, you can enable or disable any control, except for the **Calculated Value** control, the **Vertical Label** control, the **Signature Line** control, and the **File Attachment** control when it is placed on a web browser form. If you want to disable a file attachment control based on a condition, see recipe *89 Make an attachment read-only – method 1* and recipe *90 Make an attachment read-only – method 2*.

And finally, you cannot disable **Containers**, but you are able to hide and show them.

Question

1. Since you cannot disable container controls, such as for example a **Repeating Table** control, how would you go about making an entire repeating table read-only?

Validation rules

Validation rules validate whether the data entered in a field is what is expected such as for example when checking whether a number is entered into a text box that should only accept numbers (see recipe *30 Check whether a number was entered*).

Validation rules can only be applied to fields, and not to form events (load and submit).

Validation rules behave very much like **Formatting** rules with the only difference that you do not apply formatting to a control, but rather display a message for the control if its value is invalid.

You can have more than one **Validation** rule on a field and can set one or more conditions that determine when a **Validation** rule should run, but like **Formatting** rules, if you add multiple **Validation** rules, you should always add rules that have mutually exclusive conditions.

To answer the question "To which control do I add the **Validation** rule?" I can give you the following tip.

Tip:

> You must always set **Validation** rules on the target. The target is defined as the field that should be validated based on a condition (e.g. if the field is blank). Conditions can be based on the value of the target itself, the value of another field, a static value, or a formula.

29 Make a field required based on a condition

Problem

You have a drop-down list box control on an InfoPath form and want to force users to select an item from it when they have typed a piece of text into a text box elsewhere on the form.

Solution

In recipe *10 Make a text box mandatory* you learned about the preferred way for making fields required when there are no conditions for a field to be mandatory. However, you must use a **Validation** rule if you want a field to be required based on a condition.

In this solution, you will use a **Validation** rule with a condition that checks whether a text box is not empty and if it is not, require the value of a drop-down list box not to be equal to an empty string.

To make a drop-down list box required if a text box contains text:

1. In InfoPath, create a new **Blank Form** template.

2. Add a **Drop-Down List Box** control and a **Text Box** control to the view of the form template. Name the drop-down list box **title** and the text box **lastName**.

3. Right-click the drop-down list box and select **Drop-Down List Box Properties** from the context menu that appears.

4. On the **Drop-Down List Box Properties** dialog box on the **Data** tab under **List box choices**, ensure that the **Enter choices manually** option is selected and click **Add**.

5. On the **Add Choice** dialog box, type the text **Mr** in both the **Value** and the **Display name** text boxes, and click **OK**. With this you have added a static item to the drop-down list box.

6. Repeat the previous step to add the following items to the list box: **Mrs**, **Ms**, **Miss**, and **Sir**. Click **OK** to close the **Drop-Down List Box Properties** dialog box when you are done.

7. Click the **Drop-Down List Box** to select it, and then click **Home ➤ Rules ➤ Manage Rules** to open the **Rules** task pane.

8. On the **Rules** task pane, click **New ➤ Validation** to add a **Validation** rule to the drop-down list box.

9. On the **Rules** task pane under **Condition**, click the text **None**.

10. On the **Condition** dialog box, select **lastName** from the first drop-down list box, select **is not blank** from the second drop-down list box, and click **And**. Note that clicking **And** should add a second line where you can specify a second expression for the condition.

11. On the **Condition** dialog box, select **title** from the first drop-down list box for the second expression, select **is blank** from the second drop-down list box for the second expression, and click **OK**. The final

condition on the **Rules** task pane should say:

```
lastName is not blank
and
title is blank
```

which means that if the **lastName** field (bound to the text box) contains text and the **title** field (bound to the drop-down list box) is empty (no item has been selected from the drop-down list box), then a message must be displayed to the user to select an item from the **title** drop-down list box.

12. On the **Rules** task pane, enter a message such as for example "You must select a title" in the **ScreenTip** text box.

13. Preview the form.

When the form opens, type text into the text box, and then move away from the text box by clicking elsewhere on the form. A red asterisk should appear in the drop-down list box as an indication that it is a required field. And if you hover over the drop-down list box, you should see the message you typed in earlier for the **ScreenTip** appear. Select a title from the drop-down list box. The red asterisk should disappear.

Discussion

Had you enabled submission of the form and clicked on the **Submit** button, the following message would have been shown and prevented you from submitting the form until you selected an item from the drop-down list box:

InfoPath cannot submit the form, because it contains validation errors. Errors are marked with either a red asterisk (required fields) or a red, dashed border (invalid values).

Exercise

Try making a text box required when a check box is selected. Hint: If you cannot figure it out, see recipe *49 Make a field required based on the value of a check box*.

30 Check whether a number was entered

Problem

You have a text box on an InfoPath form in which users are allowed to enter numbers. You want to be able to check whether a number was entered into the text box when the user navigates away from the text box.

Solution

You can add a **Validation** rule that uses a regular expression on the text box to check whether a number was entered into the text box.

To check whether a number was entered into a text box control:

1. In InfoPath, create a new **Blank Form** template.

2. Add a **Text Box** control to the view of the form template.

3. Click the text box to select it, and then click **Home ➤ Rules ➤ Manage Rules** to open the **Rules** task pane.

4. On the **Rules** task pane, click **New ➤ Validation**.

5. On the **Rules** task pane under **Condition**, click the text **None**.

6. On the **Condition** dialog box, select **field1** from the first drop-down list box, select **does not match pattern** from the second drop-down list box, and select **Select a pattern** from the third drop-down list box.

7. On the **Data Entry Pattern** dialog box, type the following regular expression in the **Custom pattern** text box:

    ```
    [\-\+]?[0-9]*\.?[0-9]+
    ```

    and click **OK**.

8. On the **Condition** dialog box, click **OK**.

9. On the **Rules** task pane, type in a **ScreenTip** message for the **Validation** rule, for example, "Invalid number".

10. Preview the form.

When the form opens, type a piece of text in the text box. A red dashed border should appear around the text box and when you hover over the text box, you should see the **ScreenTip** message you entered earlier. Now enter a valid number in the text box and move or tab away from the text box. The red dashed border should disappear.

Discussion

If you have a field in which only numbers should be entered, it is recommended to set the **Data type** of that field to **Whole Number (integer)** or **Decimal (double)** instead of leaving the data type of the field set to **Text (string)** and then adding a **Validation** rule to the field as you have done in the solution described above.

By setting the data type of a field to a numeric data type, InfoPath will automatically validate any data entered into that field. The added benefit of setting the data type to a numeric data type as a way of automatically validating data is that you can then use the **Format** button on the **Properties** dialog box of the control bound to the field to set the appearance of the number, for example by setting the amount of decimal places that should be displayed, setting whether to use digit grouping or not, and how negative numbers should be displayed.

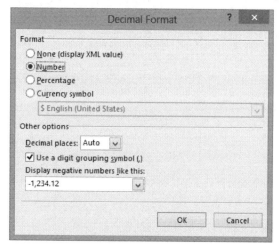

Figure 83. Decimal Format dialog box in InfoPath 2013.

In the solution above, you used a regular expression to validate data. While the explanation of how regular expressions work and are constructed is beyond the scope of this book, just be aware that you can use them in InfoPath as expressions for conditions on rules, and that you can use the Internet to find regular expression patterns for use in InfoPath.

31 Set a maximum length on text in a text box

Problem

You have a text box on an InfoPath form and want to prevent users from typing more than 10 characters into the text box.

Solution

You can set the **Limit text box to** property of a text box to be equal to a number of characters or you can use the **string-length** function in a **Validation** rule to check the length of a text string typed into a text box and then display an error message if the length exceeds the maximum allowable length.

To set a maximum length on text in a text box (method 1):

1. In InfoPath, create a new **Blank Form** template.

2. Add a **Text Box** control to the view of the form template.

3. Right-click the text box control and select **Text Box Properties** from the context menu that appears.

4. On the **Text Box Properties** dialog box, click the **Display** tab, select the **Limit text box to** check box, enter an amount of characters in the counter text box behind the **Limit text box to** check box, and then click **OK**. Note: The **Limit text box to** check box is disabled when the **Multi-line** check box is selected.

5. Preview the form.

When the form opens, start typing text into the text box. As soon as you have entered the amount of characters you specified as the limit for the text box, you should not be able to enter more text into the text box.

To set a maximum length on text in a text box (method 2):

1. In InfoPath, create a new **Blank Form** template.

2. Add a **Text Box** control to the view of the form template.

3. With the text box control still selected, click **Home ➤ Rules ➤ Manage Rules** to open the **Rules** task pane.

4. On the **Rules** task pane, click **New ➤ Validation** to add a **Validation** rule to the text box.

5. On the **Rules** task pane under **Condition**, click the text **None**.

6. On the **Condition** dialog box, select **Use a formula** from the third drop-down list box. This should open the **Insert Formula** dialog box.

7. On the **Insert Formula** dialog box, type

    ```
    string-length()
    ```

    or insert this function by clicking **Insert Function**, selecting **string-length** from the **Functions** list on the **Insert Function** dialog box, and then clicking **OK**.

8. Place the cursor between the brackets of the function and click **Insert Field or Group**.

9. On the **Select a Field or Group** dialog box, select **field1** (which is bound to the text box to evaluate), and click **OK**. The final formula should look like the following:

    ```
    string-length(.)
    ```

    This formula returns the amount of characters in the text string typed into the text box (**field1**).

10. On the **Insert Formula** dialog box, click **OK**.

11. On the **Condition** dialog box, select **The expression** from the first drop-down list box. The expression in the text box now looks like the following:

```
. = string-length(.)
```

12. On the **Condition** dialog box in the text box, delete everything in front of and including the equal sign (InfoPath added this to the expression when you selected **The expression** from the first drop-down list box), and add a comparison that checks whether the string length is greater than 10 as follows:

```
string-length(.) > 10
```

and click **OK**. This expression evaluates to **TRUE** when the amount of characters typed into the text box is greater than 10.

13. On the **Rules** task pane in the **ScreenTip** text box, type "Only 10 characters maximum allowed".

14. Preview the form.

When the form opens, type a text string that has more than 10 characters (spaces and line breaks are also counted as characters) in the text box. A red dashed border should appear around the text box when you tab away from the field, and when you hover over the text box you should see the error message appear. Now delete a few of the characters until the text string is less than 10 characters long. The red dashed border should disappear.

Discussion

While you can set the **Limit text box to** property of a text box to restrict the amount of text entered into a text box, this property is not enabled for multi-line text boxes. In such cases, you could resort to data validation to check the length of a text string typed into a text box.

You can use the **string-length** function to check the length of a text string. The **string-length** function accepts one argument (the text string to evaluate) and returns the number of characters in a text string.

In this recipe you also learned a technique to construct an expression to use with the **The expression** option on the **Condition** dialog box. The **Use a formula** option in the third drop-down list box on the **Condition** dialog box is a handy feature to use when you want to construct a formula for use as an expression, but do not know how to manually construct it.

Had you selected **The expression** from the first drop-down list box immediately after you opened the **Condition** dialog box, you would have been forced to know the exact expression to type into the text box for the expression. By using the **Use a formula** option in the third drop-down list box (this option is available if a field has been selected in the first drop-down list box), you can cheat your way to constructing an expression that can be used with the **The expression** option on the **Condition** dialog box.

Note that if you have selected **The expression** from the first drop-down list box and want to construct an expression using the **Use a formula** option, you must first select a field in the first drop-down list box on the **Condition** dialog box so that the third drop-down list box that contains the **Use a formula** option appears.

In step 12 of the solution described above, you used the **is greater than** comparison operator to complete the expression. The following table lists comparison operators you can use in expressions in InfoPath.

Comparison Operator	Meaning
=	Is equal to
!=	Is not equal to
<	Is less than
>	Is greater than
<=	Is less than or equal to
>=	Is greater than or equal to

Table 2. Comparison operators that can be used in expressions in InfoPath.

Question

1. The **string-length** function also counts spaces as characters. What would the formula in step 9 of the solution described above have to be for the **string-length** function not to count spaces?
Hint: Remember the **translate** function from recipe *18 Capitalize text in a text box*?

Multiple conditions on rules

In previous recipes, you have already seen how to add a condition to a rule. All types of rules, except for default values, can have conditions added to them. Conditions are optional for **Action** rules and mandatory for **Formatting** and **Validation** rules.

In InfoPath, you can add only one condition to a rule. If you want to add multiple conditions to a rule, you must add multiple expressions to the condition for the rule, and join these expressions together using the "and" or "or" Boolean operators. The following recipe shows and explains how.

32 Show/hide sections based on a drop-down list box selection

Problem

You have one drop-down list box and two section controls on an InfoPath form and you want to show each section control depending on the item that is selected in the drop-down list box.

Solution

You can use multiple expressions in a condition on a **Formatting** rule to show or hide sections based on the selected item in a drop-down list box.

To show or hide sections based on the selected item in a drop-down list box:

1. In InfoPath, create a new **Blank Form** template.

2. Add a **Drop-Down List Box** control and two **Section** controls to the view of the form template. Ensure that the sections are placed one under the other and that there are no blank lines between them. Name the drop-down list box **selectColor**.

3. Right-click the drop-down list box and select **Drop-Down List Box Properties** from the context menu that appears.

4. On the **Drop-Down List Box Properties** dialog box on the **Data** tab, leave the **Enter choices manually** option selected, and click **Add**.

5. On the **Add Choice** dialog box, type **1** in the **Value** text box, type **Red** in the **Display name** text box, and click **OK**. Repeat this step to add a second choice that has a value of **2** and a display name of **Blue**.

6. On the **Drop-Down List Box Properties** dialog box, click **OK**. With this you have added two static items to the drop-down list box.

7. Right-click the first section and select **Borders and Shading** from the drop-down menu that appears.

8. On the **Borders and Shading** dialog box, click the **Shading** tab, select the **Color** option, select a red color from the color picker, and click **OK**.

9. Right-click the second section and select **Borders and Shading** from the drop-down menu that appears.

10. On the **Borders and Shading** dialog box, click the **Shading** tab, select the **Color** option, select a blue color from the color picker, and click **OK**.

11. Click the first section to select it, and then click **Home ➤ Rules ➤ Manage Rules** to open the **Rules** task pane.

12. On the **Rules** task pane, ensure that **group1** is listed under the title bar. If it is not, click the title of the first section control again to select it or click **group1** in the Main data source of the form on the **Fields** task pane.

13. On the **Rules** task pane, click **New ➤ Formatting** to add a **Formatting** rule to **group1**.

14. On the **Rules** task pane under **Formatting**, select the **Hide this control** check box.

15. On the **Rules** task pane under **Condition**, click the text **None**.

16. On the **Condition** dialog box, select **selectColor** from the first drop-down list box, leave **is equal to** selected in the second drop-down list box, select **Type text** from the third drop-down list box, and type **2** in the text box.

17. On the **Condition** dialog box, click **And** to add a second expression, and select **or** from the drop-down list box.

18. On the **Condition** dialog box on the second row, select **selectColor** from the first drop-down list box, select **is blank** from the second drop-down list box, and click **OK**. The **Condition** on the **Rules** task pane should now say:

```
selectColor = "2"
or
selectColor is blank
```

What this condition does is allow the rule to run to hide the first section if the item **Blue**, which has a value equal to **2**, is selected from the **selectColor** drop-down list box (`selectColor = "2"`) or if no item has been selected from the drop-down list box (`selectColor is blank`).

19. Click the second section to select it, and then repeat the steps 12 through 18 for the second section (**group2**), but add two expressions that say:

```
selectColor = "1"
or
selectColor is blank
```

What this condition does is allow the rule to run to hide the second section if the item **Red**, which has a value equal to **1**, is selected from the **selectColor** drop-down list box (`selectColor = "1"`) or if no item has been selected from the drop-down list box (`selectColor is blank`).

20. Preview the form.

When the form opens, the drop-down list box should not have an item selected in it, so both sections should be hidden (invisible). When you select **Red** from the drop-down list box, the red section should appear. And when you select **Blue** from the drop-down list box, the blue section should appear.

Discussion

In the solution described above, you saw how to add multiple conditions on a rule by adding multiple expressions to the condition on the rule.

After adding the first expression, you can add a second expression by clicking the **And** button behind the third drop-down list box on the **Condition** dialog box. Once you click the **And** button, a drop-down list box should appear from which you can select either **and** or **or** to join the two expressions together.

To delete an expression for a condition you have previously added, click the **Delete** button on the **Condition** dialog box behind the expression you want to delete.

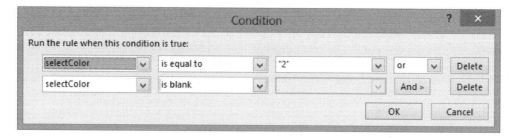

Figure 84. Condition dialog box for a condition with multiple expressions.

InfoPath allows you to add up to a maximum of five rows of expressions on the **Condition** dialog box. But if you require more than five expressions for a condition, you can add additional expressions as follows:

1. For an existing condition, on the first row of expressions, select **The expression** from the first drop-down list box. If we take the solution described above, the following expression for the condition on the first section would then appear:

    ```
    ../my:selectColor = "2"
    ```

2. For an existing condition, on the second row of expressions, select
    The expression from the first drop-down list box. If we take the
    solution described above, the following expression for the condition
    on the first section would then appear:

    ```
    ../my:selectColor = ""
    ```

3. Join the two previous expressions together with an "or" operator by
    copying the text for the second expression, typing **or** behind the text
    for the first expression, and then pasting the text for the second
    expression you copied in the text box for the first expression. The
    complete expression for the condition for the first section would
    then look like the following:

    ```
    ../my:selectColor = "2" or ../my:selectColor = ""
    ```

4. Delete the second row of expressions or use it to add another new
    expression to the condition.

5. Continue adding expressions until you hit the maximum of five or
    continue combining the text for expressions to suit your needs.

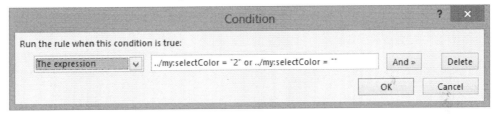

Figure 85. Condition dialog box for a condition that combines two expressions.

You can make use of any of the Boolean operators listed in the following
table when using the **The expression** option on the **Condition** dialog box
to join expressions together.

Boolean Operator	Function
and	Joins two expressions together by stating that both expressions must be TRUE for the result of the combination of expressions to evaluate to TRUE.

or	Joins two expressions together by stating that either one of the expressions can be TRUE for the result of the combination of expressions to evaluate to TRUE.
not	Negates the result of an expression, meaning that the opposite of the expression must be true for the final expression to evaluate to TRUE.
()	Groups expressions.

Table 3. Boolean operators that can be used in expressions for conditions in InfoPath.

Remember that the result of a condition must always evaluate to either **TRUE** or **FALSE**. Whether you use one or multiple expressions to construct a condition so that it evaluates to either **TRUE** or **FALSE** is irrelevant. The final result of the condition is what InfoPath uses to run an action, apply formatting, or validate a field.

Tip:

When joining expressions together using a combination of "or" and "and" operators, it is recommended to use brackets to group and separate **and**-expressions from **or**-expressions to avoid having to guess what takes precedence. For example, if you have the following expression:

```
a = "2" or a = "" and b = "1"
```

group the expressions as follows:

```
(a = "2" or a = "") and b = "1"
```

or as follows:

```
a = "2" or (a = "" and b = "1")
```

depending on the logic you want to implement. In the first expression
`( (a = "2" or a = "") and b = "1" )`

```
a = "2" or a = ""
```

will be evaluated before its result is added to

```
b = "1"
```

using an "and" operator. Likewise, in the second expression (`a = "2"`
`or (a = "" and b = "1")`)

```
a = "" and b = "1"
```

will be evaluated before its result is added to

```
a = "2"
```

using an "or" operator. This will ensure that the Boolean logic is clear
and that the final expression does not result in unexpected behavior.

Chapter 5: External Data Sources

InfoPath allows you to connect to external data sources such as for example XML files, databases, SharePoint lists and libraries, and Web Services to retrieve data.

Once you have set up a connection to retrieve data from an external data source, this data source becomes what is called a *Secondary data source* of the InfoPath form.

InfoPath form templates may contain the structure (XML schema) for Secondary data sources, and while you may choose to include data from Secondary data sources in form templates, this data will never be stored in InfoPath forms that are based on those form templates.

Important:

> If you want to permanently store data in an InfoPath form, always create fields in the Main data source of the InfoPath form to store this data in. Data in Secondary data sources is never stored in an InfoPath form.

Secondary data sources can be used in InfoPath to populate drop-down list boxes, look up data (for example, look up the name of the manager of an employee), or used as a temporary storage location while a user is filling out a form.

You must add **Receive data** connections to an InfoPath form template to be able to connect to external data sources for data retrieval. Commands with which you can add data connections to an InfoPath form template to retrieve data from external data sources are located under the **Get External Data** group on the **Data** tab in InfoPath 2013.

Figure 86. Commands under the Get External Data group on the Data tab in InfoPath.

33 Get data from an XML file

Problem

You have an XML file that contains data you want to use in an InfoPath form.

Solution

You can add a **Receive data** connection to the XML file to the form template to be able to retrieve data from that XML file and use it within the InfoPath form.

Suppose you have an XML file named **LineBreak.xml** with the following contents:

```
<break>
  <value>&#xD;</value>
</break>
```

To get data from an XML file:

1. In InfoPath, create a new **Blank Form** template.

2. Select **Data ➤ Get External Data ➤ From Other Sources ➤ From XML File**.

Figure 87. From XML File command in InfoPath 2013.

3. On the **Data Connection Wizard**, click **Browse**.

4. On the **Open** dialog box, browse to and select the **LineBreak.xml** file, and then click **Open**.

5. On the **Data Connection Wizard**, click **Next**.

6. On the **Data Connection Wizard**, read the text that is displayed, and then click **Next**.

7. On the **Data Connection Wizard**, enter a name for the data connection (for example **LineBreak**), leave the **Automatically retrieve data when form is opened** check box selected, and click **Finish**.

With this you have added a Secondary data source for an XML file to the form template. If you look in the drop-down list box on the **Fields** task pane, you should see **LineBreak (Secondary)** listed.

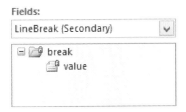

Figure 88. Secondary data source for the XML file on the Fields task pane.

Now you can use the Secondary data source to get data from the XML file and then use the data in your InfoPath form for example to add a line break to the text on a button (see recipe *84 Add line breaks to the label of a button*).

Discussion

While you used the **From Other Sources** ➤ **From XML File** command under the **Get External Data** group on the **Data** tab to add a data connection that retrieves data, you could have also added a data connection to the InfoPath form template via the **Data Connections** dialog box.

To open the **Data Connections** dialog box and add a **Receive data** connection to an XML file:

1. Click **Data** ➤ **Get External Data** ➤ **Data Connections**.

2. On the **Data Connections** dialog box, click **Add**.

3. When the **Data Connection Wizard** opens, select the **Create a new connection to** option, select the **Receive data** option, and click **Next**.

4. On the second screen of the **Data Connection Wizard**, select **XML document** and click **Next**. After this you will be on the same screen as you were in step 3 of the solution described above, so can continue adding the connection by following the rest of the steps in the solution described above.

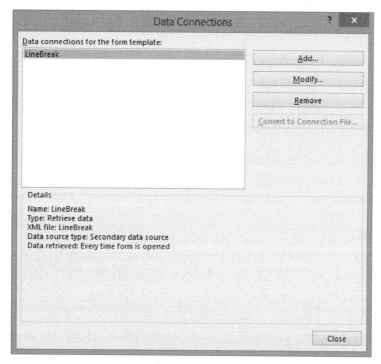

Figure 89. Data Connections dialog box in InfoPath 2013.

The data connection you added previously (**LineBreak**) should be listed on the **Data Connections** dialog box. At the bottom of the **Data Connections** dialog box you can see more details for the data connection, such as for example that its type is **Retrieve data**, that it is a **Secondary data source**, that it connects to an XML file, and when data is retrieved.

In InfoPath you can create two types of data connections: **Receive** and **Submit** data connections. **Receive data** connections are used to retrieve data into InfoPath and **Submit data** connections are used to submit InfoPath data to a particular destination.

If you are adding an XML file as a Secondary data source to an InfoPath form, you can choose to **Include the data as a resource file in the form**

template. This option is selected by default in InfoPath if you are adding a data connection to an XML file to a Web Browser Form, because a Web Browser Form does not have access to the local computer or the network location where the original XML file might be located.

Once the XML file has been added as a resource file to the form template, you can find that XML file by opening the **Resource Files** dialog box via **Data ➤ Form Data ➤ Resource Files**.

Figure 90. Resource Files command under the Form Data group on the Data tab.

Figure 91. Resource Files dialog box in InfoPath 2013.

Resource files are files that exist in a form template (XSN file) and are useful when you require data to be available in the form template when a form has no connectivity to the Internet or elsewhere.

While you can add resource files to an InfoPath form template through the **Resource Files** dialog box, they will not be of much use to you unless you connect them to a Secondary data source, because you cannot directly access resource files from within InfoPath unless you are using them as for example images on **Picture Button** controls.

In step 3 of the solution above, you clicked **Browse** to add an XML file as a resource file to the form template. Had you already previously added a resource file to the form template via the **Resource Files** dialog box, then you could have clicked on the **Resource Files** button on the **Data Connection Wizard** in step 3 of the solution to select that existing XML file, instead of browsing to and selecting a new XML file. This is how you can also add a **Receive data** connection to an XML file to be able to create a Secondary data source for an existing XML resource file.

In the solution described above you selected the **Automatically retrieve data when form is opened** check box when creating the data connection. Because the XML file contained very little data it was okay to select this check box in this case. On the other hand, if the XML file contained a very large amount of data and you selected this check box, the form would have taken a very long time to load.

So whenever Secondary data sources have a chance of containing a large amount of data, it is best not to select the check box to automatically retrieve data when the form is opened, but to:

1. Only retrieve the data when the user really needs it by using a **Query for data** action in a rule on a button; or

2. Filter the data before it is retrieved into InfoPath so that it only loads the data that is absolutely required by the user.

Taking the two aforementioned precautions should speed up the initial load time of InfoPath forms.

Exercise

Open the **Data Connections** dialog box and click **Remove** to delete the data connection you previously added for the XML file. Close the dialog box. Open the **Resource Files** dialog box. Did InfoPath also delete the resource file that InfoPath added when you created the data connection?

34 Get data from a database table

Problem

You have an Access database table that contains data you want to use on an InfoPath form.

Solution

You can add a **Receive data** connection to the Access database to the form template to be able to read data from a table within the database and use the data within the InfoPath form.

Suppose you have an Access database named **RunningShoes.accdb**, which has a table named **Brand** and a second table named **Model**.

Brand has two columns:

1. BrandID (autonumber; primary key)
2. BrandName (text)

Model has three columns:

1. ModelID (autonumber; primary key)
2. ModelName (text)
3. BrandID (number; foreign key related to the BrandID column in **Brand**)

To get data from the **Brand** database table:

1. In InfoPath, create a new **Blank Form (InfoPath Filler)** template.

2. Click **Data ➤ From Other Sources ➤ From Database**.

Figure 92. From Database command in InfoPath 2013.

3. On the **Data Connection Wizard**, click **Select Database**.

4. On the **Select Data Source** dialog box, browse to and select the **RunningShoes.accdb** database file, and then click **Open**. After you select the Access database, the **Select Table** dialog box should appear.

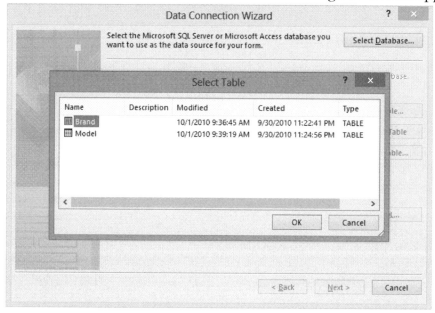

Figure 93. Select Table dialog box in InfoPath 2013.

5. On the **Select Table** dialog box, select **Brand**, and click **OK**.

6. On the **Data Connection Wizard**, click **Next**.

7. On the **Data Connection Wizard**, click **Next** again. Note: If you want to store the data from the database in the form template for offline use, you can select the **Store a copy of the data in the form template** check box, before clicking **Next**. It is not recommended to select this check box if the database contains sensitive information.

8. On the **Data Connection Wizard**, name the data connection **Brand**, leave the **Automatically retrieve data when form is opened** check box selected, and click **Finish**. See the discussion section of recipe *33 Get data from an XML file* for when to and when not to select the **Automatically retrieve data when form is opened** check box.

With this you have added a Secondary data source for an Access database table to the form template. If you look in the drop-down list box on the **Fields** task pane, you should see **Brand (Secondary)** listed.

Figure 94. Secondary data source for the database table on the Fields task pane.

Discussion

You can also use the technique described in the solution above to retrieve data from a SQL Server database. In this recipe you started out creating an **InfoPath Filler Form** template, because you cannot connect a **Web Browser Form** template to an Access database. You will see the following message appear if the InfoPath form template you are adding the database connection to is a **Web Browser Form** template, so for example if you created a new **Blank Form** template instead of a new **Blank Form (InfoPath Filler)** template.

Figure 95. Access database connections are not supported in Web Browser Forms.

Tip:

You can see what kind of form template you have open in InfoPath Designer 2013 by going to **File ➤ Info ➤ Form Options**, selecting **Compatibility** in the **Category** list on the **Form Options** dialog box, and then checking the currently selected form type in the **Form type** drop-down list box.

Questions

1. When you create a **Blank Form** template, what kind of database or databases are you allowed to select? Hint: Try adding a **Receive data** connection to a database via the **Data Connections** dialog box.

2. When you create a **Blank Form (InfoPath Filler)** template, what kind of database or databases are you allowed to select? Hint: Try adding a **Receive data** connection to a database via the **Data Connections** dialog box.

3. Based on the results from the previous two questions, what kind of databases does InfoPath support? For example, can you connect an InfoPath form directly to an Oracle database?

35 Get data from a SharePoint list

Problem

You have a SharePoint list that contains data you want to display on an InfoPath form.

Solution

You can add a **Receive data** connection to the SharePoint list to the form template to be able to read data from the SharePoint list and display the data on the InfoPath form.

Suppose you have a SharePoint list named **OfficeApplications** that contains the following data:

Title	Color
Word	Blue
Excel	Green
Access	Red
PowerPoint	Orange
OneNote	Purple
InfoPath	Purple
Publisher	Blue

To get data from a SharePoint list:

1. In InfoPath, create a new **Blank Form** template.

2. Click **Data ➤ Get External Data ➤ From SharePoint List**.

Figure 96. From SharePoint List command in InfoPath 2013.

3. On the **Data Connection Wizard**, enter the URL to the SharePoint site where the SharePoint list you want to connect to is located, and click **Next**.

4. On the **Data Connection Wizard**, select the SharePoint list you want to connect to (**OfficeApplications** in this case) from the **Select a list or library** list box, and click **Next**.

5. On the **Data Connection Wizard**, select any fields (for example, **Title** and **Color**) from the SharePoint list that you want to display or use on the InfoPath form, and click **Next**.

6. On the **Data Connection Wizard**, click **Next**.

7. On the **Data Connection Wizard**, enter a name for the data connection (for example **OfficeApplications**), leave the **Automatically retrieve data when form is opened** check box selected, and click **Finish**. See the discussion section of recipe *33 Get data from an XML file* for when to and when not to select the **Automatically retrieve data when form is opened** check box.

With this you have added a Secondary data source for a SharePoint list to the form template. If you look in the drop-down list box on the **Fields** task pane, you should see **OfficeApplications (Secondary)** listed.

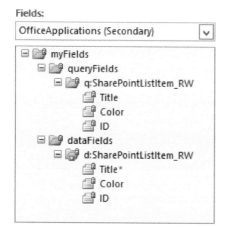

Figure 97. Secondary data source for the SharePoint list on the Fields task pane.

Now you can use the data connection to the SharePoint list to get data from the SharePoint list and use it in your InfoPath form for example to populate a drop-down list box. Note that any data you retrieve from a SharePoint list will eventually be located in fields and groups under the **dataFields** group. So you would have to bind those fields and groups to controls on the InfoPath form to be able to display data. Fields under the **queryFields** group of a Secondary data source for a SharePoint list are only used to set up a query or filter to retrieve specific data from the SharePoint list.

Chapter 6: Submit Forms

Submitting a form means sending it to a particular destination for it to be stored or processed. You can submit an InfoPath form to one of six destinations:

1. To an e-mail address or list of e-mail addresses.
2. To a SharePoint Library.
3. To a Web Service.
4. To a SharePoint Server Connection.
5. To a web server (HTTP).
6. To a hosting environment, such as an ASP.NET page or a hosting application.

All submit destinations have one thing in common: The InfoPath form is sent to someone or somewhere (to a person, to a SharePoint site, to a database, etc.) and stored there, and is not stored locally on disk.

You must add **Submit data** connections to an InfoPath form template to be able to submit data to a particular destination. Commands with which you can add data connections to an InfoPath form template to submit data are located under the **Submit Form** group on the **Data** tab in InfoPath 2013.

Figure 98. Commands under the Submit Form group on the Data tab in InfoPath.

36 Enable a form to be submitted

Problem

You have an InfoPath form which you want to enable to be submitted and for which you want the **Submit** command to appear on the Ribbon.

Solution

You can enable a form to be submitted and have the **Submit** command appear on the Ribbon by setting options on the **Submit Options** dialog box. In this recipe, you will not be sending the form to a particular destination (person, SharePoint list, database, etc.), but rather simulate a submit by switching to another view when the form is submitted.

To enable a form to be submitted:

1. In InfoPath, create a new **Blank Form** template.

2. Add a second view named **Form Submitted View** to the form template as described in recipe *13 Add a second view to a form template*, and type the static piece of text "The form has been submitted" directly on the view.

3. Switch back to **View 1** (the default view).

4. If you preview this form as it currently is, you will see that the **Submit** command is nowhere to be found on the Ribbon, which means that the form has not been enabled to be submitted.

5. Click **Data ➤ Submit Form ➤ Submit Options** to open the **Submit Options** dialog box. As you can see, the **Allow users to submit this form** check box is deselected, which is why the **Submit** command is not present on the Ribbon.

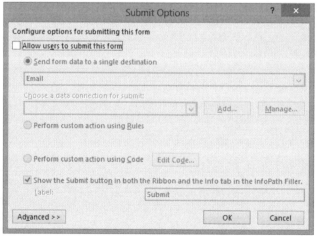

Figure 99. Submit Options dialog box without submit configured in InfoPath 2013.

On the **Submit Options** dialog box, select the **Allow users to submit this form** check box, select the **Perform custom action using Rules** option, click **Advanced**, select **Leave the form open** in the **After submit** drop-down list box, and then click **OK**. When you close the **Submit Options** dialog box, the **Rules** task pane should appear, because you selected the **Perform custom action using Rules** option. At the top of the **Rules** task pane, you should see the form event name **Form Submit** listed.

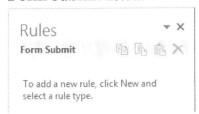

Figure 100. Rules task pane for the Form Submit event in InfoPath 2013.

You should also see that the **Form Submit** command under the **Rules** group on the **Data** tab has been toggled on, which also means that if you ever want to access the rules that have been added to the **Form Submit** event of a form, you can click the **Form Submit** command under the **Rules** group on the **Data** tab to open the **Rules** task pane and access the rules for that event.

Figure 101. Form Submit command under the Rules group on the Data tab.

The **Form Submit** event is the event that takes place when a user submits a form. You can run rules or code during the **Form Submit** event. The intention is for you to simulate submitting the form through rules and then once the form has been submitted, have it remain open and display the **Form Submitted View** view.

6. On the **Rules** task pane, click **New ➤ Action** to add an **Action** rule to the **Form Submit** event.

7. On the **Rules** task pane, click **Add ➤ Switch views**.

8. On the **Rule Details** dialog box, select **Form Submitted View** from the **View** drop-down list box, and click **OK**. With this you have configured a rule to run when the form is submitted and have the form switch to display the **Form Submitted View** view.

9. Preview the form.

When the form opens, the **Submit** command should now be present on the **Home** tab on the Ribbon.

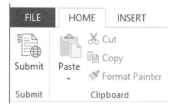

Figure 102. Submit command on the Home tab in InfoPath Filler 2013.

Click the **Submit** command. The **Form Submitted View** should appear.

Discussion

There are four ways you can enable an InfoPath form to be submitted:

1. Via the **Submit Options** dialog box, configure the form to be submitted to one specific destination, or add a submit data connection to the form template and then set that data connection to be the default submit connection for the form. The latter should automatically configure the form to be submitted to one specific destination (see recipe *37 Submit a form to a single destination using rules*).

2. Via the **Submit Options** dialog box, configure the form to be submitted by running rules in the **Form Submit** event. You have the option to configure the form to be submitted to one or more destinations (see recipe *38 Submit a form to multiple destinations using rules*).

3. Add one or more submit data connections to the form template without setting any of them to be the default submit connection, and

then use **Action** rules on controls to call those submit data connections. This method does not require you to enable the form to be submitted via the **Submit Options** dialog box and also does not have the **Submit** command appear on the Ribbon unless you have set one of the submit data connections to be the default submit connection.

4. Create a form template that comes with a submit data connection such as for example a **Database** form template (see recipe *40 Submit form data to one Access database table* and recipe *41 Submit form data to database tables with a one-to-many relationship*).

In the solution described above, you learned how to enable a form to be submitted through rules that run during the **Form Submit** event and have the **Submit** command appear on the Ribbon. The **Submit** command is configured to appear by default, but you can also configure it to not appear on the Ribbon by deselecting the **Show the Submit button in both the Ribbon and the Info tab in the InfoPath Filler** check box on the **Submit Options** dialog box.

Note that the form was not sent to a destination (person, SharePoint site, database, etc.), but that a different view was displayed once the submit had taken place. You will be sending the form to one or several destinations in recipes to come.

If you want to use a normal button or picture button instead of the **Submit** command on the Ribbon to submit a form, you can do so as follows:

1. Follow the steps in the solution described above.

2. Add a **Button** or **Picture Button** control to the view of the form template.

3. Click the button to select it, and then select **Submit** from the **Action** drop-down list box under the **Button** group on the **Properties** tab.

Figure 103. Action drop-down list box on the Properties tab on the Ribbon.

The **Submit** button action on a normal button or picture button allows you to run the same functionality as you would have otherwise run by clicking the **Submit** command on the Ribbon. Note that clicking the **Submit Actions** command under the **Button** group on the **Properties** tab will open the **Submit Options** dialog box, which means that you can also access and configure the form submit options from this location.

4. Preview the form.

When the form opens, you can test it as you have previously tested it. Clicking the button or picture button should work the same way as clicking the **Submit** command on the Ribbon.

You can also use a normal button or picture button to submit an InfoPath form (method 3 listed at the beginning of this discussion section) without first configuring submit options by just having the button run **Action** rules with **Submit data** actions that call submit data connections you have added to a form template (see the discussion section of recipe *38 Submit a form to multiple destinations using rules*). Note that you must leave the **Action** property of the button set to **Rules and Custom Code** for such a solution to work. Changing the **Action** property of a button to **Submit** is only required if you want that button to perform the same action as the **Submit** command on the Ribbon would perform.

Exercise

Create a new **Blank Form** template, and then click **File ➤ Info ➤ Form Options**. On the **Form Options** dialog box, ensure that **Web Browser** is selected in the **Category** list. Is the **Submit** check box enabled? This **Submit** check box also enables the **Submit** command to appear on the Ribbon when forms are opened in a web browser. Click on the text that says: "Submit is not configured…" Read the instructions on the message box that appears. Now open the **Form Options** dialog box for the form template you created in the solution described above and verify that the **Submit** check box is enabled and that it has been selected.

Exercise

Open the **Submit Options** dialog box again, and explore the options present on it. For example, click on the **Advanced** button and explore what kind of things you can do if form submission fails or succeeds, and what you can do after submitting the form.

37 Submit a form to a single destination using rules

Problem

You have an InfoPath form which you want to submit (send) to a list of people via e-mail.

Solution

You can enable submit on the InfoPath form and then create an e-mail submit data connection to submit the form to a list of e-mail addresses.

To submit an InfoPath form to a single destination (here: a list of e-mail addresses) using rules:

1. In InfoPath, create a new **Blank Form** template.

2. Add 4 **Text Box** controls to the view of the form template, and name them **managerEmail**, **employeeEmail**, **subject**, and **notes**, respectively.

3. Click **Data** ➤ **Submit Form** ➤ **To E-mail**.

Figure 104. To Email command highlighted under the Submit Form group.

4. On the **Data Connection Wizard**, click the formula button behind the **To** text box.

5. On the **Insert Formula** dialog box, construct a formula similar to the following:

```
concat(managerEmail, "; ", employeeEmail)
```

and click **OK**. What this formula does is concatenate two e-mail addresses with a semi-colon separating them.

6. On the **Data Connection Wizard**, type an e-mail address (e.g. **someone@somewhere.com**) in the **Cc** text box. As you can see, you can also type in a static e-mail address to send the form to.

7. On the **Data Connection Wizard**, click the formula button behind the **Subject** text box.

8. On the **Insert Formula** dialog box, click **Insert Field or Group**.

9. On the **Select a Field or Group** dialog box, select the **subject** field, and click **OK**. Here you are using the value of a form field as the subject for the e-mail. You could have also typed in a static piece of text in the **Subject** text box instead of using the value of a form field. The latter applies to almost all of the text boxes on the **Data Connection Wizard**.

10. On the **Insert Formula** dialog box, click **OK**.

11. On the **Data Connection Wizard**, click **Next**.

12. On the **Data Connection Wizard**, select the **Send only the active view of the form and no attachment** option. You could also choose to send the form as an attachment in the e-mail and even attach the form template to the e-mail so that users are able open the form if you have not published the form template to a shared (network) location. By selecting the option to send only the active view, you must ensure that you publish the form template to a network location after you are done designing the form template. Read the descriptive text on the **Data Connection Wizard** and then click **Next**.

13. On the **Data Connection Wizard**, accept the default data connection name of **Email Submit**, leave the **Set as the default submit connection** check box selected, and click **Finish**.

14. Now that you have created the submit data connection, you must enable the form to be submitted. Click **Data ➤ Submit Form ➤ Submit Options**.

15. On the **Submit Options** dialog box you should see that the **Allow users to submit this form** check box has already been selected for you and that the **Send form data to a single destination** option has been set to **Email** using the **Email Submit** data connection you created in the previous steps. Had these options not automatically been selected for you, you could have selected and set them yourself. In addition, you could have also created the submit data connection via the **Submit Options** dialog box by clicking the **Add** button that is located behind the **Choose a data connection for submit** drop-down list box on the **Submit Options** dialog box.

16. On the **Submit Options** dialog box, click **OK**.

17. Preview the form.

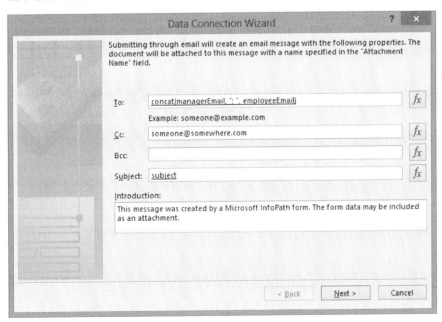

Figure 105. Configurations on the Data Connection Wizard in InfoPath 2013.

When the form opens, type e-mail addresses into the **managerEmail** and **employeeEmail** text boxes, a subject line into the **subject** text box, and some notes in the **notes** field if you wish, and then click **Submit**. InfoPath should open a **Message** dialog box.

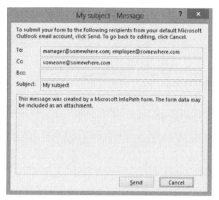

Figure 106. Message dialog box to submit an InfoPath form to a list of e-mail recipients.

Click **Send** to send the e-mail. Once the message has been sent, the e-mail recipients (**manager@somewhere.com**, **employee@somewhere.com**, and **someone@somewhere.com**) should be able to open the e-mail in Outlook and see the current view with the data you entered in InfoPath.

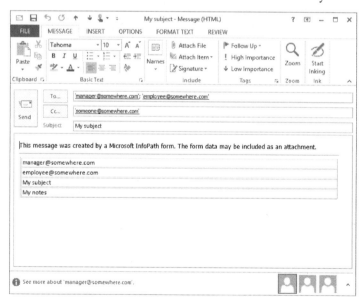

Figure 107. E-mail message in Outlook 2013 displaying the view of the InfoPath form.

Discussion

Submitting an InfoPath 2013 form to one or more e-mail addresses requires users to have Microsoft Outlook 2013 installed on their computers.

You cannot prevent the **Message** dialog box from appearing before sending an e-mail from InfoPath. This dialog box not only serves as a confirmation that you do indeed want to send the e-mail, but also to prevent e-mail messages from accidentally being sent or the e-mail functionality in InfoPath from being abused by sending spam e-mails.

In step 13 of the solution described above, you left the **Set as the default submit connection** check box selected on the last screen of the **Data Connection Wizard**. Because an InfoPath form can be submitted to one or more destinations, you can add one or more submit data connections to a form template. However, a form template can only have one of those submit data connections as its default submit connection at any given point in time. The submit data connection for which you have selected its **Set as the default submit connection** check box on the **Data Connection Wizard**, will become the default submit connection of the form. And once you have selected the **Set as the default submit connection** check box on the **Data Connection Wizard**, the form template will automatically be configured to be submitted to a single destination. You saw this in step 15 when you opened the **Submit Options** dialog box. Had you not selected the **Set as the default submit connection** check box on the **Data Connection Wizard**, then you would have had to set up the submit options yourself as you will do in the next recipe.

Also note that if you intend to submit a form to multiple destinations using rules, you should deselect the **Set as the default submit connection** check box on the **Data Connection Wizard** for all submit data connections you add to a form template. In any case, if you forget to do this, and later choose to submit a form using rules via the **Submit Options** dialog box, InfoPath will automatically change the submit data connection you specified as the default submit connection by deselecting the **Set as the default submit connection** check box for that specific submit data connection.

38 Submit a form to multiple destinations using rules

Problem

You have an InfoPath form which you want to submit to two different SharePoint form libraries.

Solution

You can use **Action** rules to submit an InfoPath form to more than one destination.

To submit an InfoPath form to multiple destinations (for example two SharePoint form libraries) using rules:

1. In SharePoint, create two form libraries and name them **TwoLibs1** and **TwoLibs2**, respectively.

2. In InfoPath, create a new **Blank Form** template.

3. Click **Data ➤ Submit Form ➤ To SharePoint Library**.

4. On the **Data Connection Wizard**, type the URL to the **TwoLibs1** SharePoint form library you created earlier, for example

    ```
    http://servername/TwoLibs1/
    ```

    where **servername** is the name of the SharePoint server and top-level site in a site collection and **TwoLibs1** is the name of the first form library.

5. On the **Data Connection Wizard**, click the formula button behind the **File name** text box.

6. On the **Insert Formula** dialog box, construct a formula similar to the following:

    ```
    concat("TwoLibs1_", now())
    ```

    and then click **OK**. This formula generates a unique name for the InfoPath form by appending the date and time to the text

"TwoLibs1_". Note: You must do this to prevent error messages from appearing when you try to submit a form that has a name that already exists in the SharePoint form library. The chance of two people submitting a form at exactly the same time is small. However, you could select the **Allow overwrite if file exists** check box to prevent such error messages from taking place, but I recommend not doing this just in case two people do happen to submit a form at exactly the same time. It is best to have the submission fail rather than to overwrite someone else's form. Another option is to include the user name in the form name by using a formula such as:

```
concat("TwoLibs1_", userName(), "_", now())
```

because a combination of user name and date/time should be guaranteed to be unique.

7. On the **Data Connection Wizard**, click **Next**.

8. On the **Data Connection Wizard**, type **TwoLibs1 SharePoint Library Submit** as the name for the data connection, deselect the **Set as the default submit connection** check box, and click **Finish**.

9. Click **Data ➤ Submit Form ➤ To SharePoint Library**, and repeat steps 4 through 8 to add a data connection to submit the form to the **TwoLibs2** SharePoint form library. Remember to replace "TwoLibs1" with "TwoLibs2" in the formula you use for constructing the name of the form, and name the data connection **TwoLibs2 SharePoint Library Submit**.

10. Click **Data ➤ Submit Form ➤ Submit Options**.

11. On the **Submit Options** dialog box, select the **Allow users to submit this form** check box, select the **Perform custom action using Rules** option, and click **OK**. This should open the **Rules** task pane to define actions for the **Form Submit** event.

12. On the **Rules** task pane, InfoPath should have already added a submit action for the first data connection (**TwoLibs1 SharePoint Library Submit**) you created, so click **New ➤ Action** to add a rule for the **TwoLibs2 SharePoint Library Submit** data connection.

13. On the **Rules** task pane with **Rule2** selected, click **Add ➤ Submit data**.

14. On the **Rule Details** dialog box, select **TwoLibs2 SharePoint Library Submit** from the **Data connection** drop-down list box, and click **OK**.

15. Save the form template to a location on disk.

16. Click **File ➤ Publish ➤ SharePoint Server** to start publishing the form template to SharePoint.

17. On the **Publishing Wizard**, enter the URL to the SharePoint site where the two form libraries are located, and click **Next**.

18. On the **Publishing Wizard**, leave the **Enable this form to be filled out by using a browser** check box selected, leave the **Form Library** option selected, and click **Next**.

19. On the **Publishing Wizard**, select the **Update the form template in an existing form library** option, select **TwoLibs1** from the **Form library to update** list, and click **Next**.

20. On the **Publishing Wizard**, click **Next**.

21. On the **Publishing Wizard**, click **Publish**.

22. On the **Publishing Wizard**, click **Close**.

23. In SharePoint, navigate to the **TwoLibs1** form library and click **new document** to test the form.

When the form opens, click **Submit** to submit the form. A new form named "TwoLibs1_[datetimevalue]" should have been created in the **TwoLibs1** SharePoint form library. Navigate to the **TwoLibs2** SharePoint form library. A new form named "TwoLibs2_[datetimevalue]" should have also been created in the **TwoLibs2** SharePoint form library. Note that the datetime value should be the same (except for perhaps a second or so difference) as that for the form in the **TwoLibs1** SharePoint form library and that the contents of the two forms in the two form libraries should also be the same, because it is one and the same form that has been submitted to two different SharePoint form libraries.

Discussion

In the solution described above, you enabled the **Submit** command on the Ribbon and used the **Form Submit** event to run rules that submitted a form to two different SharePoint form libraries. If you do not want to submit the form during the **Form Submit** event and/or do not want to enable the **Submit** command on the Ribbon, you could use a normal button or picture button to submit the form as follows:

1. Follow steps 1 through 9 of the solution described above.

2. Add a **Button** or **Picture Button** control to the view of the form template. Note that the **Action** property of a button or picture button is set to **Rules and Custom Code** by default. Leave this setting as is.

3. Click the button to select it, and then click **Home ➤ Rules ➤ Manage Rules** to open the **Rules** task pane.

4. On the **Rules** task pane, click **New ➤ Action** to add a rule for the **TwoLibs1 SharePoint Library Submit** data connection.

5. On the **Rules** task pane with **Rule1** selected, click **Add ➤ Submit data**.

6. On the **Rule Details** dialog box, select **TwoLibs1 SharePoint Library Submit** from the **Data connection** drop-down list box, and click **OK**.

7. Repeat steps 4 through 6 to add a **Submit data** action rule for the **TwoLibs2 SharePoint Library Submit** data connection.

8. On the **Rules** task pane, click **New ➤ Action**.

9. On the **Rules** task pane, click **Add ➤ Close the form**.

10. On the **Rule Details** dialog box, click **OK**. This rule should close the form once the form has been submitted to the two SharePoint form libraries.

11. Continue with step 15 of the solution described above.

The solution described in this recipe is not limited to submitting to two data connections, neither to only SharePoint form libraries. You can add any number of data connections to submit a form to as well as mix up the types of submit destinations.

If you do not have a SharePoint Server available, you could try creating two e-mail submit data connections (see recipe *37 Submit a form to a single destination using rules*) instead of two SharePoint form library submit connections, and configure the form to be submitted through rules using those two e-mail submit data connections.

Note that for this recipe in particular, the forms created will always be linked to the form template you published to the **TwoLibs1** SharePoint form library, even though forms are also stored in the **TwoLibs2** SharePoint form library.

39 Prevent form submission if a check box has not been selected

Problem

You have an InfoPath form with an "I have read and understood these terms and conditions" check box. You want to prevent users from submitting the form if they have not selected the terms and conditions check box.

Solution

In this solution, you want to prevent submission of a form. The action is to submit the form. This is an action that must go on a rule on a source, which in this case is the submit button on the toolbar or any other button or control you want to use to submit the form.

Then there is a check box that has a value that determines whether the form should be submitted or not, so this check should become a condition on the submit rule, that is, if the check box is selected submission is allowed to take place and if the check box is not selected submission is not allowed to take place.

And finally, to let the user know why the form cannot be submitted, you should display a message. In this solution, a message is shown to the user using text on a section control, which is hidden when the form opens, but appears as soon as the user tries to submit the form and the check box has not been selected.

Showing/hiding is a formatting action, so you must create a **Formatting** rule on a target. The section control is being hidden, so the section control is the target. The formatting of the target should be driven by the value of a field that is set when the form is submitted and the check box is not checked. The latter indicates that you should create a hidden field and a second **Action** rule on the submit button that sets the value of this hidden field based on a condition that the check box is selected or not selected.

Do you see the thought process? Don't worry if you don't; at the end of this recipe, we will go through it again. Just assume for now that you can configure an InfoPath form to be submitted using a rule and then add a condition on this rule to check whether the terms and conditions check box has been selected.

To allow a form to be submitted based on the selection of a check box:

1. In InfoPath, create a new **Blank Form** template.

2. Add a second view to the form template (see recipe *13 Add a second view to a form template*) and name it **Submit View**.

3. Switch back to **View 1** (the default view), and add a **Check Box** control and a **Section** control to the view. Name the check box control **termsConditionsCheck**.

4. Type the text "You must accept the terms and conditions before submitting the form" on the section control.

5. On the **Fields** task pane under the **myFields** group, add a hidden field as described in recipe *11 Add a hidden field* with the name **isSectionVisible**, the data type **Text (string)**, and a default value equal to **0**.

6. Click the section control to select it, and then click **Home ➤ Rules ➤ Manage Rules**.

7.   On the **Rules** task pane, click **New ➤ Formatting**.

8.   On the **Rules** task pane under **Formatting**, select the **Hide this control** check box.

9.   On the **Rules** task pane under **Condition**, click the text **None**.

10. On the **Condition** dialog box, select **isSectionVisible** from the first drop-down list box, select **is equal to** from the second drop-down list box, select **Type text** from the third drop-down list box, type **0** in the text box, and then click **OK**. The following condition should now appear on the **Rules** task pane under **Condition**:

```
isSectionVisible = "0"
```

This condition allows the rule to run to hide the section if the value of the **isSectionVisible** field is equal to **0**.

11. Click **Data ➤ Submit Form ➤ Submit Options**.

12. On the **Submit Options** dialog box, select the **Allow users to submit this form** check box, select the **Perform custom action using Rules** option, click **Advanced**, select **Leave the form open** in the **After submit** drop-down list box, and click **OK**. With this you have configured the form to be submitted using rules and to have the form remain open once it has been submitted. After you close the **Submit Options** dialog box, the **Rules** task pane for the **Form Submit** event should appear.

13. On the **Rules** task pane ensure that **Form Submit** is being shown below the title bar, and then click **New ➤ Action**.

14. On the **Rules** task pane under **Condition**, click the text **None – Rule runs when form is submitted**.

15. On the **Condition** dialog box, select **termsConditionsCheck** from the first drop-down list box, select **is equal to** from the second drop-down list box, select **TRUE** from the third drop-down list box, and click **OK**. The following condition should now appear on the **Rules** task pane under **Condition**:

```
termsConditionsCheck = TRUE
```

This condition allows the **Form Submit** rule to run if the **termsConditionsCheck** check box has been selected.

16. On the **Rules** task pane, click **Add** ➤ **Switch views**.

17. On the **Rule Details** dialog box, select **Submit View** from the **View** drop-down list box, and click **OK**. The following action should now appear on the **Rules** task pane under **Run these actions**:

```
Switch to view: Submit View
```

Note: This solution simulates submitting the form by switching to a different view for testing purposes. If you have a destination to submit to, you could configure a **Submit data** action (instead of a **Switch views** action) with a corresponding data connection that does a real submit.

18. On the **Rules** task pane, select the **Don't run remaining rules if the condition of this rule is met** check box, because after the form has been submitted, you do not want any more rules to run.

19. On the **Rules** task pane, click **New** ➤ **Action** to add a second **Action** rule.

20. On the **Rules** task pane under **Condition**, add a condition just like you did in step 15 that says:

```
termsConditionsCheck = FALSE
```

This condition allows the rule that sets the value of the **isSectionVisible** field to be equal to **1** to run if the **termsConditionsCheck** check box has not been selected, which means that if a user tries to submit the form and the check box has not been selected, the section will be made visible.

21. On the **Rules** task pane, click **Add** ➤ **Set a field's value**.

22. On the **Rule Details** dialog box, click the button behind the **Field** text box.

23. On the **Select a Field or Group** dialog box, select **isSectionVisible**, and click **OK**.

24. On the **Rule Details** dialog box, type **1** in the **Value** text box, and click **OK**. The following action should now appear on the **Rules** task pane under the **Run these actions** section:

```
Set a field's value: isSectionVisible = "1"
```

25. Preview the form.

When the form opens, click the **Submit** button on the Ribbon. The section should appear displaying the message that you must accept the terms and conditions before submitting the form. Select the check box and click the **Submit** button again. The **Submit View** should appear as an indication that the form has been submitted.

Discussion

The solution described above is a typical example of running a rule based on whether a certain condition has been met or not. In this case, if a user has not selected the check box, the form should not be submitted, but instead, a message should appear.

This solution contains both **Action** and **Formatting** rules. Let us try to identify them by dissecting the requirement.

The form is submitted. This is an action, a **Submit data** action on a rule for the **Form Submit** event to be more precise. Note: You used a **Switch views** action instead of a **Submit data** action in this recipe for testing purposes.

Form submission depends on whether the check box is selected or not. This is a condition for submitting the form, so a condition that should go on the rule for the **Form Submit** event. This results in a rule with the condition

```
termsConditionsCheck = TRUE
```

and the action

```
Switch to view: Submit View
```

when submitting the form. And because you do not want any more rules to run if the condition for this rule is met, you need to disable all other rules that would run after this rule by selecting the **Don't run remaining rules if the condition of this rule is met** check box.

A message should appear if the user tries to submit the form, but has not selected the check box. The appearing of a message on a section control can only be done through the use of a **Formatting** rule. And **Formatting** rules are set on targets instead of sources. You used a section control to show the message, so you have to add a **Formatting** rule on the section control (the target).

The showing/hiding of the section depends on whether the check box is selected and should only be shown when the form is being submitted. This means that you have to create a hidden field (**isSectionVisible**) that is set to a value that indicates that the section control should be shown. The value of the hidden field should be set by a rule on the **Submit Form** event to be equal to the value (any value unequal to 0; you used a value equal to 1) that makes the section control visible if the check box has not been selected. This is why you must set the condition

```
termsConditionCheck = FALSE
```

and the action

```
Set a field's value: isSectionVisible = "1"
```

on a second rule for submitting the form.

The entire logic for submitting the form based on conditions is visualized in the following flow chart.

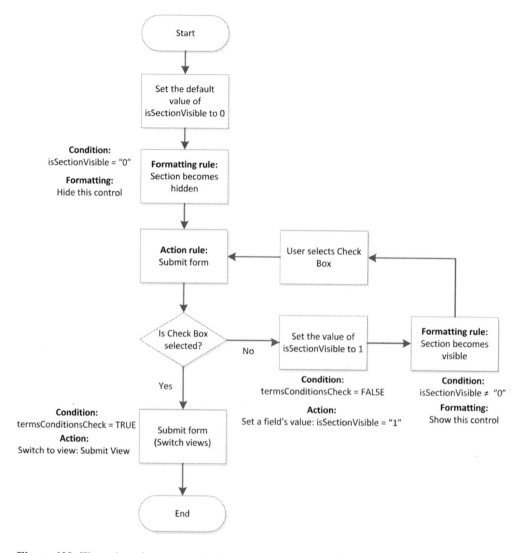

Figure 108. Flow chart for preventing form submission if a check box is not selected.

40 Submit form data to one Access database table

Problem

You want to use InfoPath to create, update, and delete records in an Access database table.

Solution

You can use the **Database** form template in InfoPath to design a form to maintain data that is stored in an Access database.

Suppose you have an Access database named **RunningShoes.accdb**, which has a table named **Brand** and another table named **Model** in it.

Brand has two columns:

1. BrandID (autonumber; primary key)
2. BrandName (text)

Model has three columns:

1. ModelID (autonumber; primary key)
2. ModelName (text)
3. BrandID (number; foreign key related to the BrandID column in **Brand**)

To submit data to the **Brand** Access database table:

1. In InfoPath, click **File ➤ New ➤ Database**, and then click **Design Form** to create a new **Database** form template. The **Data Connection Wizard** should appear.

2. On the **Data Connection Wizard**, click **Select Database**.

3. On the **Select Data Source** dialog box, browse to and select the **RunningShoes.accdb** Access database file, and then click **Open**. After you have selected the database, the **Select Table** dialog box should appear.

4. On the **Select Table** dialog box, select **Brand**, and click **OK**.

5. On the **Data Connection Wizard**, click **Next**.

6. On the **Data Connection Wizard**, you can read that InfoPath created a submit connection for the form template, and gave it the name **Main connection submit**. Ensure that the **Enable submit for this connection** check box is selected, and click **Finish**.

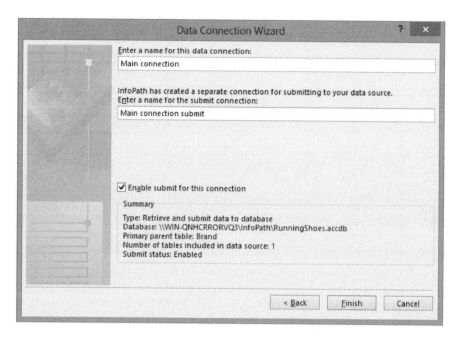

Figure 109. The last screen of the Data Connection Wizard in InfoPath 2013.

7. InfoPath automatically adds **New Record** and **Run Query** buttons to the view of the form template. The **New Record** button is used to clear form fields in preparation for entering data for a new record, and the **Run Query** button is used to retrieve data from the database. But before you can do all this, you must add a few fields to the view.

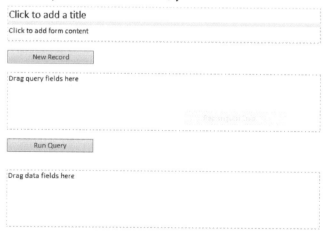

Figure 110. InfoPath design canvas after binding the form template to a database.

On the **Fields** task pane, you will see two groups in the Main data source: **queryFields** and **dataFields**. The **queryFields** group contains fields you can use for querying data in the database table, and the **dataFields** group contains fields and groups that can be used to enter data in or display data from the database table. On the **Fields** task pane, expand all of the groups, and examine the fields and groups under **queryFields** and **dataFields**.

Figure 111. Main data source of an InfoPath form bound to a database table.

8. On the **Fields** task pane under **dataFields**, click the **Brand** repeating group, drag it to the view of the form template, drop it on the text that says "Drag data fields here", and select **Repeating Section** from the context menu that appears.

9. On the **Fields** task pane under **dataFields**, expand the **Brand** repeating group, click **BrandName**, drag it to the view of the form template, and drop it inside of the repeating section you added in the previous step.

10. Preview the form. When the form opens, click the **Run Query** button to view all of the data in the table. You may see the following message appear when you click the **Run Query** button.

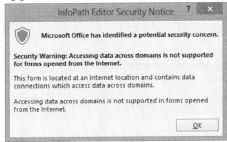

Figure 112. Security message when trying to connect to a local Access database.

To bypass security messages when previewing the form, give the form template **Full Trust** as follows:

a. In InfoPath Designer 2013, click **File ➤ Form Options**.

b. On the **Form Options** dialog box, select **Security and Trust** in the **Category** list, deselect the **Automatically determine security level (recommended)** check box, select the **Full Trust** option, and click **OK**.

c. Preview the form again.

11. To add a new record to the database table, click **New Record**, type in a brand name in the **BrandName** text box, and click **Submit**. After you click **Submit**, the form will close, because it is configured by default to close after submit, but you can configure it to remain open by going to **Data ➤ Submit Form ➤ Submit Options ➤ Advanced** and selecting **Leave the form open** in the **After submit** drop-down list box.

12. Now that you have seen how to retrieve all records and add a new one, it is time to add a query filter, to retrieve one specific record. On the **Fields** task pane, expand the **queryFields** group, expand the **Brand** group, drag **BrandName** to the view of the form template, and drop it on the text that says "Drag query fields here".

13. Preview the form.

When the form opens, type a brand name into the **BrandName** text box under the **New Record** button and then click **Run Query**. If a record is found in the database table for the brand name you typed in, then its details should appear in the text box below the **Run Query** button.

Discussion

As you saw in the solution described above, you can add a filter to query records from a database table. However, wildcard searches are not supported when you use the method described above. If you want to design a form template that can perform wildcard searches in a database table, you will have to write code to provide such functionality.

The security message "Accessing data across domains is not supported for forms opened from the Internet" is displayed when InfoPath identifies the form and data source as being located in two different domains. InfoPath checks cross-domain access if the security for the form is set to **Domain** or **Automatically determine security level (recommended)**, which it was set to before you set it to **Full Trust**. The solution is to put the InfoPath form template and Access database in the same domain.

InfoPath uses the security model of Internet Explorer to apply security to forms, so before you publish the InfoPath form template to the same domain as where the Access database is located, you must configure Internet Security on your computer.

Suppose the Access database is located somewhere on the network. It makes sense then to publish the form template to a network location in the same domain as where the Access database is located.

The recognition of network (UNC) paths is not enabled by default in the **Internet Options**, so you must enable this as follows:

1. In InfoPath, click **File ➤ Options**.

2. On the **InfoPath Options** dialog box, click **More Options**.

3. On the **Options** dialog box on the **General** tab, click **Internet Options**. Note: You can also open the **Internet Properties** dialog box via the menu in Internet Explorer.

4. On the **Internet Properties** dialog box, click the **Security** tab, select **Local Intranet**, and click **Sites**.

5. On the **Local intranet** dialog box, deselect the **Automatically detect intranet network** check box, select the **Include all network paths (UNCs)** check box, and click **Advanced**.

6. On the **Local intranet** dialog box, type in the UNC path to the network location, click **Add**, and then click **Close**.

7. On the **Local intranet** dialog box, click **OK**.

8. On the **Internet Properties** dialog box, click **OK**.

9. On the **Options** dialog box, click **OK**.

10. On the **InfoPath Options** dialog box, click **OK**.

11. Click **File ➤ Form Options**.

12. On the **Form Options** dialog box, select **Security and Trust** in the **Category** list, select the **Domain** option, and click **OK**. This will set the form template's security level back to **Domain** trust instead of **Full Trust**.

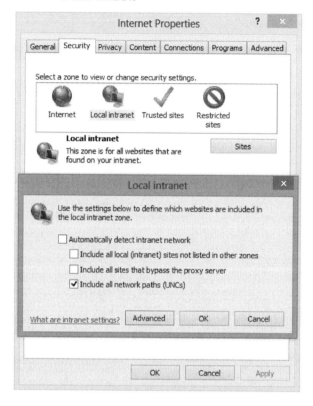

Figure 113. Local intranet dialog box including network paths as websites.

Now you must design a form template that uses the Access database that is located on the network, publish the form template to the network location (also see recipe *12 Publish an InfoPath form template*) in the same domain as where the Access database is located, and then you should be able to use that published form template to open an InfoPath form without getting the cross-domain access message. Be careful with using mapped network drives for the network location, since not all users may be using the same drive letter mappings for a certain network location.

It is always best to use the full network path when publishing a form template instead of a mapped network drive to a network location, because in the latter case, InfoPath may still see the form template and data source as being located in different domains.

To see where a form template is located or has been published, look at the bottom left corner in InfoPath Filler 2013 or the bottom right corner in InfoPath Designer 2013. That location should be the same location where the Access database is located.

FORM TEMPLATE'S LOCATION: \\WIN-QNHCRRORVQ3\INFOPATH\FORM1_PUB.XSN

Figure 114. Form template's location in InfoPath Filler 2013.

PUBLISH LOCATION: \\WIN-QNHCRRORVQ3\INFOPATH\FORM1_PUB.XSN

Figure 115. Publish location in InfoPath Designer 2013.

Tip:

Whenever you have included external data sources in an InfoPath form template and get data source access errors or warnings, check whether the security level of the form template has been set to **Domain** (and not **Restricted**), and then analyze where you have published the form template and whether the external data sources the form is trying to access are located in the same domain as the form template. If not, make sure that they are.

You may see the following warning message appear after you click the **Run Query** button to retrieve data when filling out a form in InfoPath Filler 2013:

You are working offline. InfoPath will use offline data instead of connecting to external data sources. If no offline data is available, some form elements, such as drop-down lists, may be blank.

If you get this message, in InfoPath Filler 2013, click **File ➤ Info ➤ Reconnect**, and then try again.

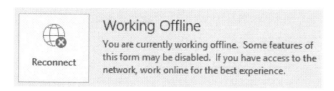

Figure 116. Reconnect button in InfoPath Filler 2013 for switching back to working online.

41 Submit form data to database tables with a one-to-many relationship

Problem

You want to use InfoPath to create, update, and delete records in two Access database tables that have a one-to-many relationship defined between them.

Solution

You can use the **Database** form template in InfoPath to design a form to manage data that is stored in two related Access database tables that have a one-to-many relationship between them.

Suppose you have an Access database named **RunningShoes.accdb**, which has a table named **Brand** and another table named **Model** in it.

Brand has two columns:

1. BrandID (autonumber; primary key)
2. BrandName (text)

Model has three columns:

1. ModelID (autonumber; primary key)
2. ModelName (text)
3. BrandID (number; foreign key related to the BrandID column in **Brand**)

To submit data to the **Brand** and **Model** Access database tables:

1. In InfoPath, create a new **Database** form template. When you click
    File ➤ New ➤ Database ➤ Design Form, the **Data Connection
    Wizard** should appear.

2. On the **Data Connection Wizard**, click **Select Database**, and then
    browse to and select the **RunningShoes.accdb** Access database file.
    After you have selected the database, the **Select Table** dialog box
    should appear.

3. On the **Select Table** dialog box, select **Brand** (which represents the
    "one" side of the relationship between the tables), and click **OK**.

4. On the **Data Connection Wizard**, click **Add Table**.

5. On the **Add Table or Query** dialog box, select **Model** (which
    represents the "many" side of the relationship between the tables), and
    click **Next**.

6. On the **Edit Relationship** dialog box, click **Finish**.

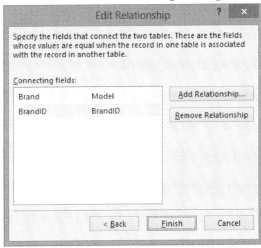

Figure 117. Edit Relationship dialog box in InfoPath 2013.

Note: If you gave the columns that bind the two tables together the
same name, InfoPath should automatically find the correct fields to
relate to each other. In this case, InfoPath found **BrandID** in the
Brand table and related it to **BrandID** in the **Model** table. If InfoPath

automatically created an incorrect relationship, you must select the relationship in the **Connecting fields** list, and then click **Remove Relationship**. Once you have deleted the incorrect relationship, click **Add Relationship** and choose the correct field from each table to relate to each other.

7. On the **Data Connection Wizard**, click **Next**.

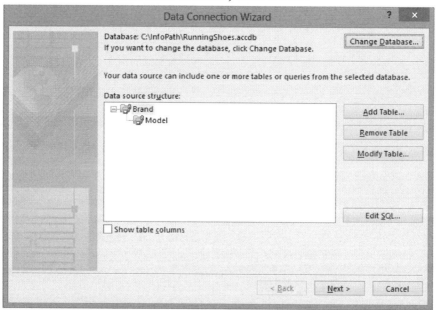

Figure 118. The data source for the database tables on the Data Connection Wizard.

8. On the **Data Connection Wizard**, you can read that InfoPath created a submit connection for the form template, and gave it the name **Main connection submit**. Ensure that the **Enable submit for this connection** check box is selected, and click **Finish**.

9. InfoPath automatically adds **New Record** and **Run Query** buttons to the view of the form template. The **New Record** button can be used to clear form fields in preparation for entering data for a new record, and the **Run Query** button can be used to retrieve data from the database. But before you can do all this, you must add a few fields to the form template.

On the **Fields** task pane, you will see two groups in the Main data source: **queryFields** and **dataFields**. The **queryFields** group contains fields you can use for querying data in the database tables, and the **dataFields** group contains fields and groups that can be used to enter data in or display data from the database tables. On the **Fields** task pane, expand all of the groups, and examine the fields and groups under **queryFields** and **dataFields**.

Figure 119. Main data source of an InfoPath form bound to two database tables.

10. On the **Fields** task pane under **dataFields**, click the **Brand** repeating group, drag it to the view of the form template, drop it on the text that says "Drag data fields here", and select **Repeating Section** from the context menu that appears.

11. On the **Fields** task pane under **dataFields**, expand the **Brand** repeating group, click **BrandName**, drag it to the view of the form template, and drop it inside of the repeating section you added in the previous step.

12. On the **Fields** task pane under **dataFields**, click the **Model** repeating group, drag it to the view of the form template, drop it below the **BrandName** text box, and select **Repeating Table** from the context menu that appears. Delete the **ModelID** and **BrandID** columns from the repeating table, because they are not required to be able to enter new records, since these fields have the **autonumber** data type assigned

to them in the database. To delete a column from a repeating table, right-click anywhere in the column you want to delete, and select **Delete** ➤ **Columns** from the context menu that appears or click anywhere in the column you want to delete and then select **Layout** ➤ **Rows & Columns** ➤ **Delete** ➤ **Columns** under **Table Tools** on the Ribbon.

13. Preview the form.

When the form opens, click the **Run Query** button to view all of the data in the table. If you get a security message, follow the instructions in step 10 of recipe *40 Submit form data to one Access database table*.

To add new records to the database tables, click **New Record**, type in a brand name, add a few model names to the repeating table, and then click **Submit**. Open the Access database and verify that the new records have been added to the database tables.

Discussion

Submitting to Access database tables that have a many-to-many relationship with each other is not supported in InfoPath. You will have to write custom code, if you want to submit data to tables that have a many-to-many relationship with each other.

And always remember to set primary keys on any tables you want to submit data to from within an InfoPath form, otherwise the submit action might fail.

Note that you must always have data that is new or that has changed on a form before submitting the form. If you click **Submit** without performing any changes to the data in the form, you will see a message appear saying:

The form cannot be submitted because of an error.

And if you look at the details for the message by clicking on the **Show Details** button on the message box, it will say:

InfoPath cannot submit the form.

The form does not contain any new data to submit to the data source.

Read-only views and controls after submit

Sometimes you may want to make one or more controls or an entire view with controls read-only immediately after an InfoPath form has been submitted, or after an InfoPath form has been submitted and is subsequently reopened.

The following three recipes discuss how you can make a control or an entire view read-only after a submit action has taken place.

42 Switch to a read-only view on submit

Problem

You added a read-only view to an InfoPath form template. Now you want to have the form switch to the read-only view when the form is submitted.

Solution

You can use rules to submit an InfoPath form and then switch to a read-only view after submit.

To switch to a read-only view on submit:

1. In InfoPath, create a new **Blank Form** template.

2. Add a read-only view to the form template as described in recipe *15 Add a read-only view* and remove the ability for users to switch views through the menu (deselect the **Show on the View menu when filling out this form** check box on the **View Properties** dialog box). When you are done, switch back to the default view via the **View** drop-down list box under the **Views** group on the **Page Design** tab.

3. Click **Data ➤ Submit Form ➤ Submit Options**.

4. On the **Submit Options** dialog box, select the **Allow users to submit this form** check box, select the **Perform custom action using Rules** option, click **Advanced**, select **Leave the form open** in the **After submit** drop-down list box, and click **OK**. This will cause the form to remain open once it has been submitted.

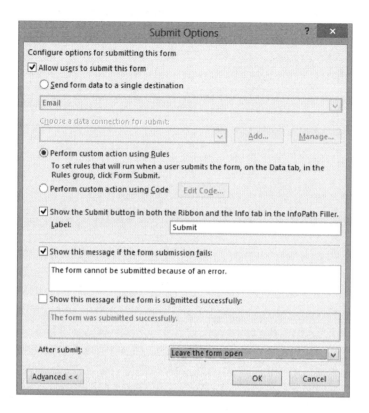

Figure 120. Submit Options dialog box in InfoPath 2013.

5. On the **Rules** task pane, ensure that **Form Submit** is listed under the title bar, and then click **New ➤ Action**.

6. On the **Rules** task pane, click **Add ➤ Submit data** to add an action to submit the form to a destination of your choice. This could be for example to a list of e-mail recipients (see recipe *37 Submit a form to a single destination using rules*) or to a SharePoint form library (see recipe *38 Submit a form to multiple destinations using rules*).

7. On the **Rules** task pane, click **Add ➤ Switch views** to add a second action to the rule.

8. On the **Rule Details** dialog box, select the read-only view from the **View** drop-down list box, and click **OK**.

9. Preview the form.

When the form opens, click the **Submit** button. The form should switch to and display the read-only view as well as remain open after it has been submitted.

Discussion

There are two things you must be aware of in the solution described above:

1. Because you want to switch to and display a read-only view when the form is submitted, you need to keep the form open after it has been submitted.

2. Because you want to switch views when the form is submitted, you must use rules for submitting the form and add a **Switch views** action rule as the last rule to run during the **Form Submit** event.

Question

1. Can you add **Validation** and **Formatting** rules to the **Form Submit** event?

43 Switch to a read-only view when a form is opened after submission

Problem

You added a read-only view to an InfoPath form template. Now you want to have the form switch to the read-only view as soon as a user opens the form after it has been submitted.

Solution

Switching to a specific view when a form is opened on subsequent times after it has been submitted, is a conditional action, which means that you must first set a flag to track whether the form has been submitted and then when the form is opened, check the value of the flag and if it has been set to a particular value that indicates that the form has been submitted, switch to the read-only view.

To switch to a read-only view when a form is opened after it has been submitted:

1. In InfoPath, create a new **Blank Form** template.

2. Add a read-only view to the form template as described in recipe *15 Add a read-only view* and remove the ability for users to switch views through the menu (deselect the **Show on the View menu when filling out this form** check box on the **View Properties** dialog box). When you are done, switch back to the default view via the **View** drop-down list box under the **Views** group on the **Page Design** tab.

3. Add a hidden field named **isFormSubmitted** (see recipe *11 Add a hidden field*) to the Main data source of the form.

4. Click **Data** ➤ **Submit Form** ➤ **Submit Options**.

5. On the **Submit Options** dialog box, select the **Allow users to submit this form** check box, select the **Perform custom action using Rules** option, and click **OK**.

6. On the **Rules** task pane, ensure that **Form Submit** is listed under the title bar, and then click **New** ➤ **Action**.

7. On the **Rules** task pane, click **Add** ➤ **Set a field's value**.

8. On the **Rule Details** dialog box, click the button behind the **Field** text box.

9. On the **Select a Field or Group** dialog box, select the **isFormSubmitted** field, and click **OK**.

10. On the **Rule Details** dialog box, type **submitted** in the **Value** text box, and click **OK**. With this you are setting the value of the **isFormSubmitted** field to be equal to the text **submitted** when the form is being submitted.

11. On the **Rules** task pane, click **Add** ➤ **Submit data** to add an action to submit the form to a destination of your choice. This could be to a list of e-mail recipients (select the **Send the form data as an attachment** option and the **Attach the form template to ensure that users can open the form** check box on the **Data Connection Wizard**, and send the e-mail to yourself for testing purposes) or to a SharePoint form

library for example. Click **OK** on the **Rule Details** dialog box when you are done.

12. Click **Data ➤ Rules ➤ Form Load** to open the **Rules** task pane for the **Form Load** event. The **Form Load** event runs whenever the form opens.

13. On the **Rules** task pane, ensure that **Form Load** is listed under the title bar, and then click **New ➤ Action**.

14. On the **Rules** task pane, click **Add ➤ Switch views**.

15. On the **Rule Details** dialog box, select the read-only view from the **View** drop-down list box, and click **OK**.

16. On the **Rules** task pane under **Condition**, click the text **None – Rule runs when form is opened**.

17. On the **Condition** dialog box, select **isFormSubmitted** from the first drop-down list box, leave **is equal to** selected in the second drop-down list box, select **Type text** from the third drop-down list box, type **submitted** in the text box, and click **OK**. The **Condition** on the **Rules** task pane should now say:

```
isFormSubmitted = "submitted"
```

With this you have created a rule that will run when the form opens, check whether the **isFormSubmitted** field contains the text **submitted**, and if it does, switch to the read-only view.

18. Preview the form.

When the form opens, click **Submit** to submit the form. When you reopen the form that was submitted, it should display the read-only view. For example, if you submitted the form to an e-mail recipient, that e-mail recipient must open the e-mail in Outlook and verify that the form displays the read-only view when viewed in Outlook.

44 Make a control read-only upon submit

Problem

You have a text box control on an InfoPath form which you want users to be able to edit the first time the form is opened, but then after the form is submitted and subsequently reopened, you do not want users to be able to edit the text that was entered into the text box anymore.

Solution

You can use conditional formatting and a hidden field to make a control read-only upon submit.

To make a text box control read-only upon submit:

1. In InfoPath, create a new **Blank Form** template.

2. Add a **Text Box** control to the view of the form template and name it **field1**.

3. On the **Fields** task pane under the **myFields** group, add a field with the name **isSubmitted** and the data type **True/False (boolean)**.

4. Click the text box to select it, and then click **Home ➤ Rules ➤ Manage Rules** to open the **Rules** task pane.

5. On the **Rules** task pane, click **New ➤ Formatting**.

6. On the **Rules** task pane, select the **Disable this control** check box.

7. On the **Rules** task pane under **Condition**, click the text **None**, and then add a condition that says:

```
isSubmitted = TRUE
```

With this you have added a rule that will disable the text box whenever the value of the **isSubmitted** field is equal to **TRUE**.

8. Click **Data ➤ Submit Form ➤ Submit Options**.

9. On the **Submit Options** dialog box, select the **Allow users to submit this form** check box, select the **Perform custom action using Rules** option, and click **OK**.

10. On the **Rules** task pane, ensure that **Form Submit** is listed under the title bar, and then add a new **Action** rule that sets the value of the **isSubmitted** field to **TRUE**. Note: You must type the text **true** in the **Value** text box on the **Rule Details** dialog box and not use the formula button behind the **Value** field. The action you added should say:

    ```
    Set a field's value: isSubmitted = "true"
    ```

11. On the **Rules** task pane, add a **Submit data** action rule to submit the form to a destination of your choice, for example to a SharePoint form library or to a list of e-mail recipients (select the **Send the form data as an attachment** option and the **Attach the form template to ensure that users can open the form** check box on the **Data Connection Wizard**, and send the e-mail to yourself for testing purposes).

12. Preview the form.

When the form opens, the text box should be editable. Type a piece of text in the text box and then submit the form. Once you submit the form and open the form that was submitted, the text box should be read-only.

Discussion

In the solution described above, you used a Boolean hidden field in the Main data source to keep track of whether the form had been submitted or not. You thereby set the value of the hidden field through an **Action** rule that ran just before the form was submitted.

Important:

> If you want the values that have been entered into fields to be stored in a form, you must always run any rules or actions that set the values of those fields before you run the rule or action that submits the form.

In step 10 of the solution described above, you did not use the **Insert Formula** dialog box when configuring the action that sets the value of the **isSubmitted** field, but rather entered a static piece of text directly in the

Value text box on the **Rule Details** dialog box. However, if you want to use the formula button behind the **Value** text box to enter the value of the **isSubmitted** field, you must enter the following formula on the **Insert Formula** dialog box:

```
true()
```

for the solution to work. The resulting action should then say:

```
Set a field's value: isSubmitted = true()
```

on the **Rules** task pane.

Important:

> If you enter **true()** as a static piece of text directly in the **Value** text box on the **Rule Details** dialog box, it will not be recognized as the **true** InfoPath function or the Boolean value **TRUE**.

Chapter 7: Input Controls

Input controls are controls that allow you to enter data and store it in the Main data source of an InfoPath form. Input controls, a few of which include text boxes, date pickers, and drop-down list boxes, are the most frequently used controls in InfoPath.

Text Boxes

A text box is the most basic control you can add to an InfoPath form. Text boxes allow users to enter textual data on a form.

While a text box is by default bound to a field that has the data type **Text (string)**, you can also bind it to fields that have other data types assigned to them. For example, you could create a text box that only accepts numbers as its input by binding it to a field that has a numeric data type such as **Whole Number (integer)** or **Decimal (double)**. Another example is creating a text box that displays the current time by binding the text box to a field that has the **Time (time)** data type.

09:55:24 AM

Figure 121. A text box displaying the current time.

45 Display the current time on a form when it opens

Problem

You want to display the current time (without the date) whenever you open an InfoPath form.

Solution

You can use the **now** and **substring** functions to extract the current time and then use a text box with the **Time (time)** data type to display the time.

InfoPath 2013 Cookbook

To display the current time when an InfoPath form opens:

1. In InfoPath, create a new **Blank Form** template.

2. Add a **Text Box** control to the view of the form template, name it **currentTime**, change its data type to **Time (time)**, and select its **Read-only** property.

3. Set the **Default Value** of the text box to be equal to the following formula:

```
substring(now(), 12)
```

This formula extracts all of the characters from the date and time string starting from the character at position 12 until the end of the string. Another formula you could use to extract the time portion from a date and time string is:

```
substring-after(now(), "T")
```

In the formula above, the **substring-after** function first looks for a **T** in the date and time string and then returns everything that comes after that **T**.

4. Right-click the text box and select **Text Box Properties** from the context menu that appears.

5. On the **Text Box Properties** dialog box on the **Data** tab, click the **Format** button behind the **Data type** drop-down list box. This should open the **Time Format** dialog box. Note that you can also open the **Time Format** dialog box via the **Properties ➤ Properties ➤ Data Format** command on the Ribbon.

6. On the **Time Format** dialog box, select the **Display the time like this** option, select the time format you want to use to display the time as, and then click **OK**.

7. On the **Text Box Properties** dialog box, click **OK**.

8. Preview the form.

When the form opens, the current time should appear in the text box, formatted using the format you specified on the **Time Format** dialog box.

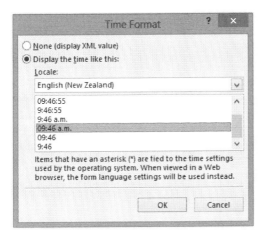

Figure 122. Time Format dialog box in InfoPath 2013.

Discussion

The **now** function returns the current date and time in the following format: **yyyy-MM-ddThh:mm:ss**. The part of this string that comes after the **T**, represents the time. So **yyyy** represents the year, **MM** represents the month, **dd** represents the day, **hh** represents the hours, **mm** represents the minutes, and **ss** represents the seconds. A concrete example of a date and time would be **2013-03-01T13:03:33**.

So to get the current time, you can pass the result of the **now** function to the **substring** function and extract the time by returning the part of the date and time string that starts at position number 12 (so after the **T**) and runs until the end of the string with counting starting at 1. By not specifying the third argument in the **substring** function, you are telling InfoPath that the function should grab all of the characters till the end of the string.

You could have also specified the amount of characters to extract from the date and time string returned by the **now** function by using the following formula:

```
substring(now(), 12, 8)
```

As you saw in the solution described above, you can also use the **substring-after** function to first look for the **T** in the date and time string returned by the **now** function, and then return the time portion that comes after the **T** as follows:

```
substring-after(now(), "T")
```

A second way to display the current time on an InfoPath form is by using a **Calculated Value** control instead of a **Text Box** control. A **Calculated Value** control is read-only by default, which is what you are after when you are displaying the current time.

You have the following two options when using a **Calculated Value** control:

1. Add a field to the Main data source and then bind it to a **Calculated Value** control.

2. Use a formula to display the result of a calculation in a **Calculated Value** control.

The first option works similar to using a text box control. This option would allow you to store the current time in the form when the form is saved or submitted.

With the second option, the time would not be stored in the InfoPath form once the form is saved or submitted, because there is no field in the Main data source to store it in (the control is not bound to any field). You can use the second option if you want to show the current time at startup, but not save it in the form itself.

After you have added a **Calculated Value** control to the form template, you would have to do the following to be able to display the current time:

1. Open the **Calculated Value Properties** dialog box.

2. On the **Calculated Value Properties** dialog box on the **General** tab, ensure that the **Data source** option is selected, and then click the formula button behind the **XPath** text box.

3. On the **Insert Formula** dialog box, enter the following formula

   ```
   substring(now(), 12, 8)
   ```

   or

   ```
   substring-after(now(), "T")
   ```

and click **OK**.

4. On the **Calculated Value Properties** dialog box on the **General** tab under **Result**, select **Time** from the **Format as** drop-down list box, and click **Format**.

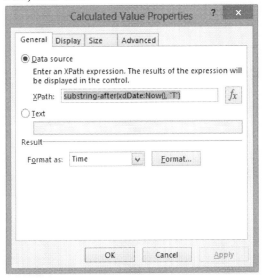

Figure 123. Calculated Value Properties dialog box with a formula.

5. On the **Time Format** dialog box, select the time format you want to use to display the time as, and then click **OK**.

6. On the **Calculated Value Properties** dialog box, click **OK**.

Note: When you click on a **Calculated Value** control to add it to the view of a form template, the **Insert Calculated Value** dialog box opens. You can add the formula via this dialog box, but will still have to open the **Calculated Value Properties** dialog box after the control has been added to the view of the form template to be able to format the result as a time.

Alternatively, you can just click **OK** on the **Insert Calculated Value** dialog box immediately after you click on the **Calculated Value** control to add it to the view of the form template without entering a formula, and then open the **Calculated Value Properties** dialog box to configure the properties of the control.

Tip:

> If you want to see the format of the date and time that InfoPath uses or exactly what the **now** function returns, you can add a text box control to a form template and then set the **Default Value** of the control to be equal to a formula that uses the **now** function. You can use this technique to see what any function in InfoPath returns.

46 Calculate the sum of text boxes

Problem

You have three text box controls on an InfoPath form and want to calculate the sum of the first two text boxes and place the result of the calculation in the third text box.

Solution

You can bind the text boxes to fields that have a numeric data type assigned to them and then use the plus operator (+) in a formula to calculate the sum of the values entered into the text boxes.

To calculate the sum of two text boxes:

1. In InfoPath, create a new **Blank Form** template.

2. Add three **Text Box** controls to the view of the form template, change their data type to **Decimal (double)**, and name them **number1**, **number2**, and **totalSum**, respectively.

3. Set the **Default Value** of the **totalSum** text box to be equal to the following formula:

    ```
    number1 + number2
    ```

    where **number1** is the field bound to the first text box and **number2** is the field bound to the second text box. Leave the **Refresh value when formula is recalculated** check box selected on the **Properties** dialog box. What this formula does is add the values of the **number1** and **number2** text boxes together to return the sum of the values.

4. Preview the form.

When the form opens, enter numbers in the first and in the second text box. The sum of the numbers you entered should appear in the third text box.

Discussion

In the solution described above, you saw how to use the plus operator (+) to calculate the sum of values stored within text boxes. Note that if you had two more text boxes (**number3** and **number4**), you would have had to use a formula such as

```
number1 + number2 + number3 + number4
```

to be able to calculate the sum of the values of the four text boxes. Note that instead of setting the **Default Value** of the **totalSum** text box as you have done in the solution described above, you could have also added a button control to the view of the form template and used the formula in an **Action** rule on the button to set the value of the **totalSum** text box.

A second way to calculate the sum of fields in InfoPath is to use the **sum** function. But because the **sum** function is best used with repeating fields (fields that are located for example in a repeating table, a repeating section, a numbered list, etc.), it would not have had much of an effect in this recipe, because the text boxes were bound to single fields, not repeating fields. For an example of using the **sum** function with a repeating table, see recipe *107 Add a sum field to a repeating table*.

Note that you changed the data type of the text boxes to **Decimal (double)** in the solution described above. While you can perform a summation on fields that have the **Text (string)** data type assigned to them, if users are going to be entering only numbers, it makes sense to choose a numeric data type (**Whole Number (integer)** or **Decimal (double)**) for the text boxes.

InfoPath 2013 Cookbook

In addition, by choosing a numeric data type, you do not have to add data validation to the text boxes to force users to enter a number (also see recipe *30 Check whether a number was entered*). Choosing a numeric data type also allows you to format numbers via the **Data Format** command under the **Properties** group on the **Properties** tab for the text box controls or by clicking the **Format** button behind the **Data type** drop-down list box on the **Text Box Properties** dialog box of the text box controls.

Figure 124. Data Format command on the Properties tab in InfoPath 2013.

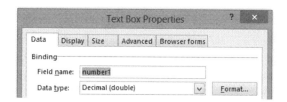

Figure 125. Format button on the Text Box Properties dialog box in InfoPath 2013.

Both commands allow you to access a numeric format dialog box (the **Decimal Format** dialog box in this case), so that you can configure how numbers that are entered into the corresponding text box should be displayed.

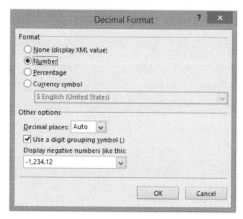

Figure 126. Decimal Format dialog box in InfoPath 2013.

188

Check Boxes and Option Buttons

Check boxes and option or radio buttons allow users to select one or more options that they are presented with on a form. So when do you use check boxes and when do you use option (radio) buttons?

Use check boxes when you want to present a user with multiple options that are not mutually exclusive. For example, a set of options such as Word/Access/Excel/InfoPath asking users to select all of the Microsoft Office applications they are familiar with would be a good candidate for check boxes, because in this case a user can select none, one, or several options.

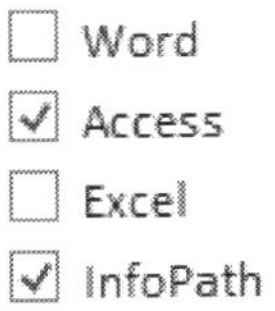

☐ Word
☑ Access
☐ Excel
☑ InfoPath

Figure 127. Check Box controls on an InfoPath form.

Use option buttons when you want to present a user with multiple options that are mutually exclusive, meaning that the user is allowed to select only one option. For example, yes/no questions are good candidates for option buttons, and so is a set of options such as male/female/unspecified, because in such cases only one option should be selected by the user.

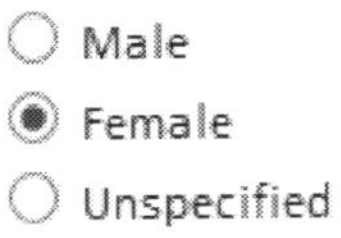

○ Male
◉ Female
○ Unspecified

Figure 128. Option Button control on an InfoPath form.

47 Validate a check box

Problem

You have a check box control on an InfoPath form and want to validate whether the check box has been selected or not.

Solution

You can use a **Validation** rule to validate whether a check box has been selected or not.

To validate a check box:

1. In InfoPath, create a new **Blank Form** template.

2. Add a **Check Box** control to the view of the form template and name it **isSelected**.

3. Add a **Text Box** control to the view of the form template, and name it **checkBoxMustBeSelected**.

4. Add a **Validation** rule to the check box control with a **Condition** that says:

```
isSelected = FALSE
and
checkBoxMustBeSelected is not blank
```

   and a **ScreenTip** that says: "You must select the check box". What this rule does is display the screen tip and a red dashed border around the check box if you type a piece of text in the text box without first selecting the check box.

5. Preview the form.

When the form opens, type a piece of text into the text box without first selecting the check box. A red dashed border should appear around the check box and when you hover with the mouse pointer over it, you should see the screen tip appear. Now select the check box and watch the red dashed border disappear.

Discussion

The key to understanding check box validation lies in paying close attention to what has been set for the **Value when cleared** and **Value when checked** properties of the check box.

The two aforementioned properties can be set to have one of 5 values when the **Data type** for the check box is set to **True/False (boolean)**:

1. (Blank)
2. TRUE
3. FALSE
4. 1
5. 0

When you first add a check box to a form template, the **Value when cleared** property is set to **FALSE** by default, and the **Value when checked** property is set to **TRUE** by default.

TRUE and **FALSE** is a good pair to use for the checked and unchecked states of a check box, but can easily result in validation errors on the check box itself if you do not know that you should set the value of the check box using the **true** or **false** function instead of just setting the value to the text **TRUE** or **FALSE** when using the **Set a field's value** action in a rule. However, setting the value to the text **true** or **false** would work.

When you use **1** and **0** as the pair of values for the checked and unchecked states of a check box, you can avoid the ambiguity of using **TRUE** and **FALSE** and are less likely to make the mistake of incorrectly setting the value of the check box or not knowing whether to use text, a number, or a function to set the value, because 1 is equal to "1" (text) in InfoPath.

As you may have noticed on the **Check Box Properties** dialog box, InfoPath does not restrict you to only use the **True/False (boolean)** data type for a check box control. For example, you could also select **Date (date)** as the data type for a check box and define two dates for the **Value when cleared** and **Value when checked** properties, so that if a user selects the check box, a certain date instead of **TRUE** or **1** is stored in the field bound to the check box. This also applies to option buttons (see recipe *51 Select an option and have a text box appear on a different view*).

Note that the data validation on a check box must match the data type of the field bound to the check box. For example, if you use a date as the data type for a check box, you must perform a date validation instead of a validation on whether the field is equal to **TRUE/FALSE** or **1/0**.

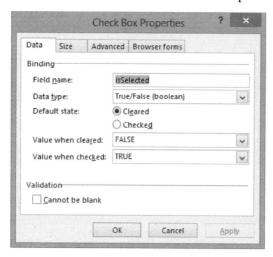

Figure 129. Checked and unchecked states of a check box set to TRUE and FALSE.

Question

1. In this recipe, you made the check box required based on whether the text box was empty or not. What is another way to make a check box required? And why did you not select that property?

48 Toggle a check box on and off when a button is clicked

Problem

You have a check box on an InfoPath form and want to be able to click a button and select the check box if it is deselected, or deselect the check box if it is selected.

Solution

You can use an **Action** rule on the button to change the value of the check box depending on the current value of the check box.

To toggle a check box on and off when a button is clicked:

1. In InfoPath, create a new **Blank Form** template.

2. Add a **Check Box** control and a **Button** control to the view of the form template. Name the check box control **isChecked**.

3. Add an **Action** rule to the button with a **Condition** that says:

    ```
    isChecked = FALSE
    ```

    and an action that says:

    ```
    Set a field's value: isChecked = "true"
    ```

    and select the **Don't run remaining rules if the condition of this rule is met** check box. The condition allows the rule to run if the **isChecked** check box has not been selected and then stops all remaining rules that have been defined on the button from running. If the condition is met, the rule sets the **isChecked** check box to be selected.

4. Add a second **Action** rule to the button with a **Condition** that says:

    ```
    isChecked = TRUE
    ```

    and an action that says:

    ```
    Set a field's value: isChecked = "false"
    ```

    and select the **Don't run remaining rules if the condition of this rule is met** check box. The condition allows the rule to run if the **isChecked** check box has been selected and then stops all remaining rules that have been defined on the button from running. If the condition is met, the rule sets the **isChecked** check box to be deselected.

5. Preview the form.

When the form opens, click the button. The check box should be selected. Click the button again. The check box should be deselected.

Discussion

In the solution described above, you made use of the **Don't run remaining rules if the condition of this rule is met** check box on a rule.

InfoPath generally runs **Action** rules on a control one after the other from top to bottom. And because you added two rules to the button and these two rules could inadvertently affect each other and cause unexpected behavior, because they are setting the value of the same field, i.e. the field bound to the check box, you must select the option to stop running any other rules as soon as the condition for one of these two rules has been met.

49 Make a field required based on the value of a check box

Problem

You have a date picker control on an InfoPath form and want to force users to enter a date in this date picker if a check box has been selected.

Solution

You can use a **Validation** rule with a condition that checks whether the check box has been selected and a date has been entered, and then display a message if the check box has been selected but a date has not been entered.

To make a field required based on the value of a check box:

1. In InfoPath, create a new **Blank Form** template.

2. Add a **Date Picker** control and a **Check Box** control to the view of the form template. Name the date picker control **dueDate** and the check box control **isUrgent**.

3. Because you want to check whether a date has been entered if the check box has been selected, you must add a **Validation** rule to the date picker control. Add a **Validation** rule to the date picker with a **Condition** that says:

```
isUrgent = TRUE
and
dueDate is blank
```

and a **ScreenTip** that says: "Please enter a due date". The condition allows the rule to run when the **isUrgent** check box has been selected and the **dueDate** date picker does not contain a date.

4. Preview the form.

When the form opens, you should see that the date picker control is not a required field, because there is no red asterisk being displayed in it. Once you select the check box, you should see a red asterisk appear in the date picker. And when you hover over the date picker, you should see the screen tip you specified earlier appear.

Discussion

In the solution described above, a field was made required based on a condition. If you have a field that must be required and does not depend on a condition being met for it to be required, it is best to select the **Cannot be blank** check box on the **Properties** dialog box of either the field or the control instead of adding a **Validation** rule to the field.

In summary:

- If you do not have any conditions that should be met for a field to be required, select the **Cannot be blank** property of the field.

- If you have a condition that should be met for a field to be required, use a **Validation** rule on the field.

50 Select a check box to move text from one field to another

Problem

You have two text boxes and one check box on an InfoPath form. When you select the check box, you want the text from the first text box to be moved to the second text box.

Solution

Moving is a combination of two actions: Copying and deleting. You can use an **Action** rule in InfoPath to first set the value of the second text box to be the same as that of the first text box, and then set the value of the first text box to be equal to an empty string. This will simulate the copy and delete actions that are required for moving text.

To select a check box to move text from one field to another:

1. In InfoPath, create a new **Blank Form** template.

2. Add two **Text Box** controls and one **Check Box** control to the view of the form template. Name the check box **moveText**, the first text box **textToMove**, and the second text box **copiedText**.

3. Add an **Action** rule to the check box that has a **Condition** that says:

    ```
    moveText = TRUE
    and
    textToMove is not blank
    ```

    and two actions that say:

    ```
    Set a field's value: copiedText = textToMove
    Set a field's value: textToMove = ""
    ```

    The first action copies the text from the first to the second text box, while the second action empties the first text box, thereby simulating moving text between the two text boxes. Note that to set the value of the **textToMove** text box to be equal to an empty string, you must leave the **Value** text box empty on the **Rule Details** dialog box.

4.   Preview the form.

When the form opens, type a piece of text in the first text box, and then select the check box. The text you entered in the first text box should appear in the second text box and disappear from the first text box.

Discussion

In the solution described above, you used a check box to move text from one text box to another. Note that you could have also used a button instead of a check box to perform the same action.

Exercise

Modify the solution in this recipe so that when the user clicks the check box for a second time (so the check box is deselected), the text is moved back to the first text box from the second text box. Hint: You must add a second **Action** rule to the check box.

51 Select an option and have a text box appear on a different view

Problem

You have an option button group on the default view of an InfoPath form template. Each option in the option button group has a corresponding text box on a second view of the form template. When you select one of the options on the first view, you want its corresponding text box to appear on the second view and you do not want the text boxes for the other non-selected options to appear on the second view.

InfoPath 2013 Cookbook

Solution

You can use a **Formatting** rule with a condition that shows/hides controls in InfoPath independent of the view on which they are located.

To select an option on one view and have a corresponding text box appear on a second view:

1. In InfoPath, create a new **Blank Form** template.

2. Add an **Option Button** control with 3 option buttons to **View 1** of the form template. Name the option button control **color**. Note that while there are three option buttons on the view of the form template, the Main data source of the form only contains one field for those three option buttons, so the value of only one option button – the selected option – will eventually be stored in the form.

3. Type the text **Red** behind the first option button, **Yellow** behind the second option button, and **Blue** behind the third option button.

4. Select the first option button, open its **Properties** dialog box, change the **Value when selected** property on the **Data** tab of the **Option Button Properties** dialog box to the text **red**, select the **This button is selected by default** check box, and then click **OK**.

5. Select the second option button, open its **Properties** dialog box, change the **Value when selected** property on the **Data** tab of the **Option Button Properties** dialog box to the text **yellow**, and click **OK**.

6. Select the third option button, open its **Properties** dialog box, change the **Value when selected** property on the **Data** tab of the **Option Button Properties** dialog box to the text **blue**, and click **OK**.

7. Add a second view named **View 2** to the form template as described in recipe *13 Add a second view to a form template*.

8. Add 3 **Text Box** controls to **View 2**. Name the text boxes **red**, **yellow**, and **blue**, respectively; and make the background color of each text box the same color as the name you gave the text box. You can do the latter by right-clicking a text box, selecting **Borders and Shading** from the drop-down menu that appears, and then on the **Shading** tab of the

Borders and Shading dialog box, select a color; or use the **Shading** command under the **Color** group on the **Properties** tab on the Ribbon for each control to set its background color.

9. Click the **red** text box to select it, and then add a **Formatting** rule to it with a **Condition** that says:

   color ≠ "red"

   and with a **Formatting** of **Hide this control**. You can compose the condition for this rule by selecting **is not equal to** from the second drop-down list box on the **Condition** dialog box and selecting **Type text** from the third drop-down list box, and then typing the text **red** in the text box. This rule will hide the **red** text box on **View 2** if the **red color** option button on **View 1** has not been selected.

10. Click the **yellow** text box to select it, and then add a **Formatting** rule to it with a **Condition** that says:

    color ≠ "yellow"

    and with a **Formatting** of **Hide this control**. This rule will hide the **yellow** text box on **View 2** if the **yellow color** option button on **View 1** has not been selected.

11. Click the **blue** text box to select it, and then add a **Formatting** rule to it with a **Condition** that says:

    color ≠ "blue"

    and with a **Formatting** of **Hide this control**. This rule will hide the **blue** text box on **View 2** if the **blue color** option button on **View 1** has not been selected.

12. Switch back to **View 1** (select **Page Design ➤ Views ➤ View ➤ View 1 (default)**) and add a **Button** control with an **Action** rule on it that switches to **View 2**.

13. Preview the form.

When the form opens, select the **Yellow** option button and then click the button to switch to the second view. The yellow text box should be visible and the other two text boxes should not be present on the view.

Discussion

The solution described above makes use of the principle that an InfoPath form has only one Main data source in which all of its data is stored, and that you can use views and controls to expose whatever data is stored within the Main data source.

In this example, controls exposing different fields in the Main data source are located on two different views, but you are still able to add rules (business logic) to the controls and have the controls depend on each other even if they are located on different views.

Remember:

> Controls are visual elements that you can add and place wherever you want to on a form template. Business rules do not depend on the placing or location of the controls themselves, but rather on the corresponding values of those controls stored in fields in the Main or Secondary data sources of the InfoPath form.

Exercise

Add a button control to **View 2** with an **Action** rule that switches to **View 1**. In addition, remove **View 2** from the **Current View** menu. Switch back to **View 1**. Preview the form. Can you select **View 2** from the **Current View** menu? Select the **Blue** option and then click the button on **View 1**. Click the button on **View 2**. Did you go back to **View 1**?

Drop-Down List Boxes

Drop-down list boxes allow you to display items to a user in a list that takes up the space of only one row, but can temporarily be expanded to display a list of multiple items.

Figure 130. A collapsed drop-down list box with Saucony as the selected item.

Figure 131. An expanded drop-down list box with Saucony as the currently selected item.

Drop-down list boxes are not difficult to work with once you understand how they function and understand the following two things:

1. You can fill a drop-down list box with items (also called "entries" in InfoPath). This can be one or multiple items, but is typically the latter. These items can be entered either manually, can come from a repeating field or group in the Main data source of the form, or can come from an external data source.

2. While a drop-down list box can display a list of multiple items, you can only select one item at a time from this list to be stored in the form. And it is the value of the selected item that is stored in the field that is bound to the drop-down list box.

In Figure 132, the drop-down list box is populated using a Secondary data source named **RunningShoes** where the **name** field under the **brand** repeating group in the Secondary data source is used to populate the display names (Mizuno, ASICS, Brooks, Saucony) of the items in the drop-down list box.

In addition, Saucony is the currently selected item in the drop-down list box, so this value is stored in the **selectedRunningShoe** field in the Main data source of the InfoPath form.

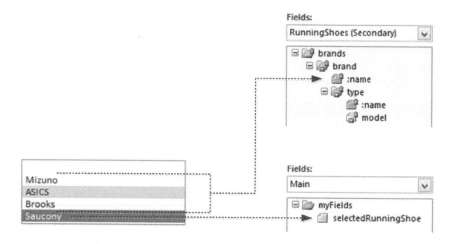

Figure 132. Relationship between a drop-down list box and data sources.

Remember:

> The field that is bound to a drop-down list box can contain only one value, i.e. the value of the selected item in the drop-down list box. This "rule" also applies to combo boxes and list boxes, but not to multiple-selection list boxes.

52 Populate a drop-down list box with static items

Problem

You have a drop-down list box on an InfoPath form and want to fill it with four static items.

Solution

You can manually configure the items that should be displayed in a drop-down list box.

To populate a drop-down list box with static items:

1. In InfoPath, create a new **Blank Form** template.

2. Add a **Drop-Down List Box** control to the view of the form template and name it **selectedRunningShoe**.

3. Right-click the **Drop-Down List Box** and select **Drop-Down List Box Properties** from the context menu that appears.

4. On the **Drop-Down List Box Properties** dialog box on the **Data** tab under **List box choices**, select the **Enter choices manually** option, and then click **Add**.

5. On the **Add Choice** dialog box, enter **Mizuno** in both the **Value** and the **Display name** text boxes, and click **OK**. Note that the values for the **Value** and the **Display name** properties need not be the same. You could for example also enter a **1** as the **Value** and **Mizuno** as the **Display name**. Just remember that whatever you put in the **Value** text box, will be what is later stored in the InfoPath form when a user selects an item from the drop-down list box.

6. Repeat the previous step to add entries for **ASICS**, **Brooks**, and **Saucony**.

7. If you look at the top of the entries list, you will see that an item with a **Display Name** of **Select** has been set as the **Default** item for the drop-down list box and that this item has a **Value** equal to an empty string. You can either keep this item as is or you can delete it and make another item the **Default** item as follows:

    a. Click the first item to select it, and then click **Remove**.

    b. Once the first item has been removed, the next item in line (**Mizuno**) should automatically become the **Default** item, so that when the form opens, **Mizuno** will appear immediately in the drop-down list box as the selected item. If you want to make another item the **Default** item, select that item (for example **ASICS**), and then click **Set Default**. You should see **Yes** appear in the **Default** column behind **ASICS**.

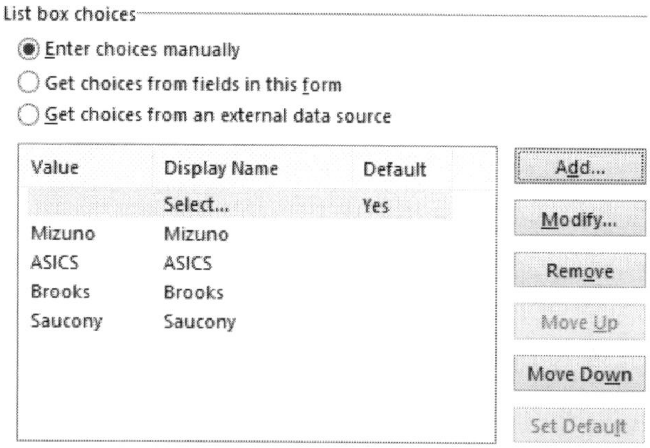

List box choices

⦿ Enter choices manually

◯ Get choices from fields in this form

◯ Get choices from an external data source

Value	Display Name	Default
	Select...	Yes
Mizuno	Mizuno	
ASICS	ASICS	
Brooks	Brooks	
Saucony	Saucony	

Add...

Modify...

Remove

Move Up

Move Down

Set Default

Figure 133. Default item set on the Drop-Down List Box Properties dialog box.

Value	Display Name	Default
Mizuno	Mizuno	
ASICS	ASICS	Yes
Brooks	Brooks	
Saucony	Saucony	

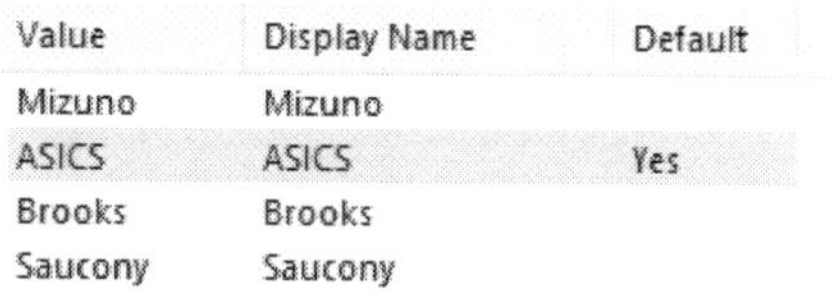

Figure 134. ASICS set as the Default item of the drop-down list box.

8. On the **Drop-Down List Box Properties** dialog box, click **OK**.

9. Preview the form.

When the form opens, **ASICS** should appear as the selected item in the drop-down list box if you followed the instructions in step 7. And when you click on the drop-down arrow of the drop-down list box to expand the list, you should see the static items you entered manually.

Discussion

In the solution described above, you added static items to a drop-down list box. Such items become part of the view the drop-down list box is located on and cannot be accessed through rules, which includes filtering or looking up data.

If you want to be able to access items that are used to fill a drop-down list box through rules, you must fill the drop-down list box with items from either a repeating field in the Main data source of the form as described in recipe *53 Populate a drop-down list box with data from a repeating table* or from an external data source as described in recipe *54 Populate a drop-down list box with data from an XML file.*

Exercise

Add a **List Box** control to the view of the form template and populate it the same way you populated the drop-down list box in this recipe.

53 Populate a drop-down list box with data from a repeating table

Problem

You have a drop-down list box on an InfoPath form and want to fill it with items that are contained in a repeating table on the same form.

Solution

You can configure the items displayed in a drop-down list box to come from fields in the same form as where the drop-down list box is located.

To populate a drop-down list box with data from a repeating table:

1. In InfoPath, create a new **Blank Form** template.

2. Add a **Repeating Table** control with one column to the view of the form template. Name the field within the repeating table **brandName**.

3. Add a **Drop-Down List Box** control to the view of the form template and name it **selectedRunningShoe**.

4. Right-click the **Drop-Down List Box** and select **Drop-Down List Box Properties** from the context menu that appears.

5. On the **Drop-Down List Box Properties** dialog box on the **Data** tab under **List box choices**, select the **Get choices from fields in this form** option, and then click the button behind the **Entries** text box.

6. On the **Select a Field or Group** dialog box, expand **group1**, select **group2**, and click **OK**.

7. On the **Drop-Down List Box Properties** dialog box, the **Value** and **Display name** text boxes should automatically be populated with the **brandName** field from the repeating table, which is what you want to use in this case, because you are going to display the names of running shoe brands in the drop-down list box. If you want to configure the value and display name yourself or if they were not automatically populated with the correct field, you can click the buttons behind the corresponding text boxes, and select a field of your choice via the **Select a Field or Group** dialog box.

8. On the **Drop-Down List Box Properties** dialog box, click **OK**.

9. Preview the form.

When the form opens, verify that the drop-down list box is empty. Add a couple of items to the repeating table, for example "Mizuno", "ASICS", "Brooks", and "Saucony". As you are adding items to the repeating table, expand the drop-down list box to see what it contains. The items you added to the repeating table should appear as items in the drop-down list box.

Discussion

In the solution described above, you saw how to use a field that is located in a repeating table to populate a drop-down list box. Note that this solution should work with any repeating field.

A repeating field is a single field that is located under a repeating group or a repeating field that is located under a single group.

For example, the repeating group bound to a repeating table control, a repeating section control, or a horizontal repeating table control, generally contains one or more fields. Such fields are repeating fields.

Figure 135. brandName is a repeating field due to group2, which is a repeating group.

Likewise, a bulleted list control, a numbered list control, a plain list control, and a multiple-selection list box control are generally bound to a repeating field that is located under a single group. Such a field is also a repeating field.

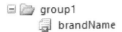

Figure 136. brandName is a repeating field under group1.

Exercise

Add a **Bulleted List** control to the view of the form template and use it to populate a drop-down list box the same way you populated the drop-down list box in this recipe. Hint: The **Entries** for the drop-down list box should come from a repeating field instead of a repeating group.

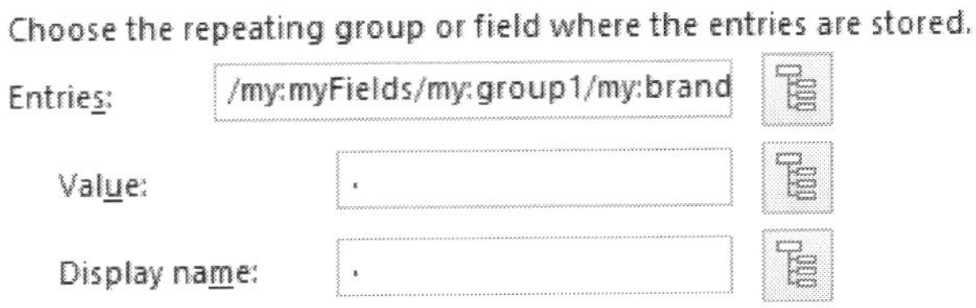

Choose the repeating group or field where the entries are stored.

Entries: /my:myFields/my:group1/my:brand

Value: .

Display name: .

The dots (.) in the **Value** and **Display name** text boxes refer to the value of the repeating field itself.

54 Populate a drop-down list box with data from an XML file

Problem

You have a drop-down list box on an InfoPath form and want to fill it with items that are contained in an XML file.

Solution

You can configure the items displayed in a drop-down list box to come from an external data source such as for example an XML file.

Suppose you have an XML file named **RunningShoes.xml** that has the following contents:

```xml
<?xml version="1.0" encoding="UTF-8"?>
<brands xmlns="uri:sym">
  <brand name="Mizuno">
    <type name="Control">
      <model>Wave Alchemy</model>
      <model>Wave Renegade</model>
    </type>
    <type name="Stability">
      <model>Wave Nirvana</model>
      <model>Wave Inspire</model>
      <model>Wave Nexus</model>
      <model>Wave Elixir</model>
    </type>
  </brand>
  <brand name="ASICS">
    <type name="Control">
      <model>GEL-Evolution</model>
      <model>GEL-Foundation</model>
    </type>
    <type name="Stability">
      <model>GEL-Kayano</model>
      <model>GEL-3020</model>
      <model>GEL-Turbulent</model>
      <model>GT-2150</model>
      <model>GEL-Phoenix 2</model>
      <model>GEL-1150</model>
    </type>
  </brand>
  <brand name="Brooks">
    <type name="Control">
      <model>Ariel</model>
      <model>Addiction</model>
    </type>
    <type name="Stability">
      <model>Trance</model>
      <model>Adrenaline</model>
    </type>
  </brand>
  <brand name="Saucony">
    <type name="Control">
```

```
      <model>ProGrid Stabil CS</model>
    </type>
    <type name="Stability">
      <model>ProGrid Omni</model>
      <model>ProGrid Hurricane</model>
      <model>Grid Tangent</model>
    </type>
  </brand>
</brands>
```

To populate a drop-down list box with data from an XML file:

1. In InfoPath, create a new **Blank Form** template.

2. Add a **Drop-Down List Box** control to the view of the form template and name it **selectedRunningShoe**.

3. Right-click the **Drop-Down List Box** and select **Drop-Down List Box Properties** from the context menu that appears.

4. On the **Drop-Down List Box Properties** dialog box on the **Data** tab under **List box choices**, select the **Get choices from an external data source** option, and then click **Add**. Note: If the form template already contains connections to external data sources, they should appear in the **Data source** drop-down list box, and you would not have to add any new ones unless the one you want to connect to is not listed. But because you just created a new form template, your form template should not contain any Secondary data sources, so you have to add one here.

5. On the **Data Connection Wizard**, leave the **Receive data** option selected and click **Next**.

6. On the **Data Connection Wizard**, select the **XML document** option, and click **Next**.

7. On the **Data Connection Wizard**, click **Browse**.

8. On the **Open** dialog box, browse to and select the **RunningShoes.xml** file, and then click **Open**.

9. On the **Data Connection Wizard**, click **Next**.

10. On the **Data Connection Wizard**, click **Next**.

11. On the **Data Connection Wizard**, name the data connection
    RunningShoes, leave the **Automatically retrieve data when form is
    opened** check box selected, and click **Finish**.

12. On the **Drop-Down List Box Properties** dialog box on the **Data** tab
    under **List box choices**, click the button behind the **Entries** text box.

13. On the **Select a Field or Group** dialog box, select a repeating group
    such as for example **brand**, and click **OK**. Selecting **brand** in this case
    will allow you to show the names of brands in the drop-down list box.

14. On the **Drop-Down List Box Properties** dialog box, the **Value** and
    Display name text boxes should automatically be populated with the
    @name field (attribute), which is what you want to use in this case,
    because you are going to display the names of running shoe brands in
    the drop-down list box. If you want to configure the value and display
    name yourself or if they were not automatically populated with the
    correct field, you can click the buttons behind the corresponding text
    boxes, and select a field of your choice via the **Select a Field or Group**
    dialog box.

15. On the **Drop-Down List Box Properties** dialog box, click **OK**.

16. Preview the form.

When the form opens the drop-down list box should contain the list of
running shoe brands from the XML file.

Discussion

Populating a drop-down list box with data from an external data source can
be done in one of two ways:

1. You can pre-add a data connection to the form template (see for
   example recipe *33 Get data from an XML file*), and then use the
   Secondary data source for this data connection to configure the
   choices for the drop-down list box.

2. You can add a new data connection when you are configuring the
   choices for the drop-down list box as you have done in the solution
   described above.

The field from the external data source you select for the **Display name** of a drop-down list box contains the values that users will be able to see in the drop-down list box. The field from the external data source you select for the **Value** of a drop-down list box remains invisible to users, but is the field that contains the value that will eventually be used for the selected item in the drop-down list box and the value that will eventually be stored in the form.

On the **Drop-Down List Box Properties** dialog box, you may have noticed a check box with the label **Show only entries with unique display names** at the bottom of the **Data** tab.

☐ Show only entries with unique display names

Figure 137. Show only entries with unique display names check box.

You may want to select this option if the external data source contains duplicate values for the field you are using as the **Display name**.

Important:

Always use a field from the external data source that contains unique values for the **Value** property of a drop-down list box. If you use a data source that contains duplicate values in a field and use this field to provide the values for the drop-down list box, you may experience unexpected behavior for the drop-down list box.

The values of the **Value** and **Display name** properties of the drop-down list box were set to be equal to the value of an attribute called **@name**. The *at* sign (**@**) indicates an attribute in XML. Attributes provide additional information about elements. For example, the XML structure of the **brand** repeating group was defined as follows:

```
<brands xmlns="uri:sym">
  <brand name="Mizuno">...</brand>
  <brand name="ASICS">...</brand>
  ...
</brands>
```

Here, **brands** and **brand** are XML elements, while **name** is an attribute of the **brand** element. The way you access attributes when using XPath is by prepending the *at* sign (@), so as in **@name**.

Had the XML structure for the **brand** repeating group been defined as follows:

```
<brands xmlns="uri:sym">
  <brand>
    <name>Mizuno</name>
    . . .
  </brand>
  <brand>
    <name>ASICS</name>
    . . .
  </brand>
  . . .
</brands>
```

then **name** would have been an element under the **brand** element. And the way you access an element when using XPath is by using the element's name, so as in **name**.

Exercise

If you have access to a SharePoint Server, try using data from a SharePoint list to populate the drop-down list box. See recipe *35 Get data from a SharePoint list* for how to add a data connection to a SharePoint list.

Exercise

You can populate multiple-selection list boxes and list boxes the same way you would populate a drop-down list box. Try using the technique described in this recipe to populate a multiple-selection list box or a list box control.

55 Filter a drop-down list box based on the first character

Problem

You have a drop-down list box and a text box on an InfoPath form and you want to type a character into the text box (for example, A, B, or C) and then have only those items that start with the character you specified appear as items in the drop-down list box.

Solution

You can apply a filter to the repeating group that you use to populate the drop-down list box when configuring the drop-down list box to get choices from either the form or an external data source.

To filter a drop-down list box based on the first character of items in the drop-down list box:

1. In InfoPath, create a new **Blank Form** template.

2. Add a **Text Box** control and a **Drop-Down List Box** control to the view of the form template. Name the text box **filterOnFirstLetter** and the drop-down list box **runningShoes**.

3. Add a **Receive data** connection as described in recipe *33 Get data from an XML file* to the same XML file you used in recipe *54 Populate a drop-down list box with data from an XML file*, and name the data connection **RunningShoes**.

4. Right-click the drop-down list box and select **Drop-Down List Box Properties** from the context menu that appears.

5. On the **Drop-Down List Box Properties** dialog box on the **Data** tab under the **List box choices** section, select the **Get choices from an external data source** option, select **RunningShoes** from the **Data source** drop-down list box, and then click the button behind the **Entries** text box.

6. On the **Select a Field or Group** dialog box, select the **brand** repeating group, and then click **Filter Data**.

7. On the **Filter Data** dialog box, click **Add**.

8. On the **Specify Filter Conditions** dialog box, select **name** from the first drop-down list box, select **begins with** from the second drop-down list box, and select **Use a formula** from the third drop-down list box.

9. On the **Insert Formula** dialog box, click **Insert Field or Group**.

10. On the **Select a Field or Group** dialog box, select **Main** from the drop-down list box, select **filterOnFirstLetter**, and then click **OK**.

11. On the **Insert Formula** dialog box, click **OK**.

12. On the **Specify Filter Conditions** dialog box, click **OK**.

13. On the **Filter Data** dialog box, the filter should now say:

```
name begins with filterOnFirstLetter
```

which means that you have added a filter to the **brand** repeating group in the XML file to only show those brands for which their names start with the character specified in the **filterOnFirstLetter** field which is located in the Main data source of the form and bound to the text box control. On the **Filter Data** dialog box, click **OK**.

14. On the **Select a Field or Group** dialog box, click **OK**.

15. On the **Drop-Down List Box Properties** dialog box, ensure that **@name** has been selected for the **Value** and **Display name** properties, and then click **OK**.

16. Preview the form.

When the form opens, type the first letter of any of the items in the drop-down list box into the text box. The items in the drop-down list box should be filtered to contain the matching items.

Discussion

In the solution described above, you used the **Filter Data** button on the **Select a Field or Group** dialog box to filter the entries within a Secondary data source based on the value of a field in the Main data source of the InfoPath form. You can use the **Filter Data** button whenever you want to select specific items within a Secondary data source through filtering.

Note that filtering can only be applied to items in a drop-down list box if that drop-down list box has been populated with values stored in either the Main data source or in a Secondary data source (see recipe *53 Populate a drop-down list box with data from a repeating table* and recipe *54 Populate a drop-down list box with data from an XML file*). You cannot filter items that have been manually added to a drop-down list box as described in recipe *52 Populate a drop-down list box with static items*.

To complete this recipe, you should restrict users to only be able to enter one character into the text box by setting a maximum length on the text box through a **Validation** rule (see recipe *31 Set a maximum length on text in a text box*).

If filtering on the first letter of items is too restrictive, you could also use **contains** in the filter condition instead of **begins with**. The filter would then look for an occurrence of the text that you type into the text box in any item of the drop-down list box.

56 Automatically select the first item in a drop-down list box

Problem

You have a drop-down list box on an InfoPath form and want to have it automatically display the first item as selected.

Solution

You can set the **Default Value** of the field bound to the drop-down list box to be equal to the value of the first item in the list of items in the drop-down list box.

To automatically select the first item in a drop-down list box:

1. In InfoPath, use the same form template you created in recipe *54 Populate a drop-down list box with data from an XML file.*

2. Click the drop-down list box to select it, and then click **Properties ➤ Properties ➤ Default Value**.

3. On the **Field or Group Properties** dialog box on the **Data** tab under **Default Value**, click the formula button behind the **Value** text box.

4. On the **Insert Formula** dialog box, click **Insert Field or Group**.

5. On the **Select a Field or Group** dialog box, select **RunningShoes (Secondary)** from the drop-down list box, expand the **brand** repeating group, select **name**, and click **OK**. The following should now be displayed in the **Formula** text box on the **Insert Formula** dialog box:

    ```
    @name
    ```

6. On the **Insert Formula** dialog box, select the **Edit XPath (advanced)** check box, and then modify the formula from:

    ```
    xdXDocument:GetDOM("RunningShoes")/ns1:brands/ns1:brand/@name
    ```

    to

    ```
    xdXDocument:GetDOM("RunningShoes")/ns1:brands/ns1:brand[1]/@name
    ```

    What this formula does is select the **@name** attribute of the first **brand** repeating group by using an index filter (**[1]**) on **brand**. Remember that **@name** was configured to provide the value for the **Value** property of the drop-down list box, so you must set the **Default Value** to be equal to the first **@name** attribute in the list of brand names in the drop-down list box.

7. On the **Insert Formula** dialog box, click **OK**. The formula for the default value on the **Field or Group Properties** dialog box should now say:

```
brand[1]/@name
```

8. On the **Field or Group Properties** dialog box, click **OK**.

9. Preview the form.

When the form opens, the first item (Mizuno) should appear as the selected item in the drop-down list box.

Discussion

In the solution described above, you set the value of the field bound to the drop-down list box to be equal to the value of the first item in a Secondary data source. Had you populated the drop-down list box with static items as described in recipe *52 Populate a drop-down list box with static items*, then you would have had to set the value of the field bound to the drop-down list box to be equal to the value of one of the static items from the drop-down list box.

For example, if **Mizuno** is the first static item in the drop-down list box, then **Mizuno** should also be the value of the **Default Value** property of the field bound to the drop-down list box for it to be shown as the selected item when the form opens. Alternatively, you can also set **Mizuno** as the **Default** item when adding the static items to the drop-down list box (also see recipe *52 Populate a drop-down list box with static items*).

You can use either rules or default values to set the value of a field:

- Use default values if you want a field to start up with a particular (default) value that does not depend on any conditions.

- Use rules when the setting of the value of a field is triggered by clicking or changing data on another field and/or if the setting of the value of the field depends on a condition. Because you cannot add conditions to default values, you must use rules to be able to set conditions that need to be met before setting the value of a field.

Filters in XPath expressions are specified between square brackets ([ ]). In the solution described above, you used **[1]** as a filter on the **brand** repeating group to find the first item in the Secondary data source for the XML file. Always remember that in XPath, counting starts at 1, and not at 0.

57 Clear the selected item in a drop-down list box

Problem

You have a drop-down list box on an InfoPath form and have selected an item in it. Now you want to click a button to clear the selected item in the drop-down list box.

Solution

You can use a rule to set the value of the field that is bound to the drop-down list box to be equal to an empty string. This will clear the drop-down list box selection.

To clear the selected item in a drop-down list box:

1. In InfoPath, create a new **Blank Form** template.

2. Add a **Drop-Down List Box** control and a **Button** control to the view of the form template.

3. Configure the drop-down list box to be filled with items from an external data source, with items from fields in the form, or with items that have been entered manually (also see recipe *52 Populate a drop-down list box with static items*, recipe *53 Populate a drop-down list box with data from a repeating table*, and recipe *54 Populate a drop-down list box with data from an XML file*).

4. Add an **Action** rule to the button that says:

    ```
    Set a field's value: field1 = ""
    ```

    where **field1** is the field that is bound to the drop-down list box.

5. Preview the form.

When the form opens, select an item from the drop-down list box and then click the button. The drop-down list box should be reset to display an empty item or its non-selected state.

58 Count the amount of items in a drop-down list box

Problem

You have filled a drop-down list box on an InfoPath form with data from a data source and want to know how many items are in the drop-down list box.

Solution

When you fill a drop-down list box with items from a data source, you typically bind the drop-down list box to a repeating field or group either in the Main or in a Secondary data source. So to find out how many items are in a drop-down list box, you must use the **count** function on the repeating field or group used to fill the drop-down list box.

To count the amount of items in a drop-down list box:

1. In InfoPath, create a new **Blank Form** template.

2. Add a **Drop-Down List Box** control to the view of the form template and populate it with items from a data source as described in recipe *54 Populate a drop-down list box with data from an XML file*.

3. Add a **Text Box** control to the view of the form template. You will use this text box to display the amount of items in the drop-down list box.

4. Right-click the text box and select **Text Box Properties** from the context menu that appears.

5. On the **Text Box Properties** dialog box, click the formula button behind the **Value** text box under **Default Value**.

6. On the **Insert Formula** dialog box, type

    ```
    count(
    ```

and then click **Insert Field or Group**.

7. On the **Select a Field or Group** dialog box, select the Secondary data source from the drop-down list box (this would be **RunningShoes (Secondary)** if you followed the steps in recipe *54 Populate a drop-down list box with data from an XML file*), click the repeating group (**brand** in this case), and click **OK**.

8. On the **Insert Formula** dialog box, type

)

   to close the **count** function. The formula should now resemble the following:

   count(brand)

   or

   count(xdXDocument:GetDOM("RunningShoes")/ns1:brands/ns1:brand)

   if you select the **Edit XPath (advanced)** check box. Click **Verify Formula** to check that the formula does not contain any errors, and then click **OK**.

9. On the **Text Box Properties** dialog box, leave the **Refresh value when formula is recalculated** check box selected, and then click **OK**.

10. Preview the form.

When the form opens, the text box should display the amount of items in the drop-down list box.

Discussion

The **count** function in InfoPath takes a field or group as its argument and counts the number of instances of that field or group.

In the solution described above, **brand** is the repeating group that is used to populate the drop-down list box, and represents items in the Secondary data source. If you want to count the amount of items in the Secondary data source, you must count the number of instances of the **brand** repeating group in the Secondary data source, which the solution does by using the formula:

```
count(brand)
```

You can also use the technique described in this recipe if you populate a drop-down list box with items from a repeating group or field in the Main data source of the form.

You cannot use this technique if you have manually populated a drop-down list box with items as described in recipe *52 Populate a drop-down list box with static items*. When you manually add items to a drop-down list box, those items become part of the view on which the drop-down list box is located and not part of a data source, and therefore you cannot access static items in a drop-down list box using rules in InfoPath.

Important:

> You can only use rules in InfoPath on fields that are located in either the Main or Secondary data sources of a form; not on views. Views are static elements of a form template. Their appearance is stored and defined in a **view.xsl** file that is part of the form template. The **view.xsl** file is constructed at design time and is not accessible via rules in InfoPath at runtime (when the form is being filled out).

You can verify that items that have been entered manually to populate a drop-down list box are indeed part of the view by exporting the source files of the InfoPath form template (via **File ➤ Publish ➤ Export Source Files**), opening the **view.xsl** file in Notepad, and searching for the items from the drop-down list box.

Exercise

Apply the technique described in this recipe on a drop-down list box that is populated with items from fields in the form as described in recipe *53 Populate a drop-down list box with data from a repeating table*.

Hint: the **count** function should work on the repeating group that is used to populate the drop-down list box.

---

59 Check if an item exists in a drop-down list box

Problem

You have a drop-down list box that is populated from an external data source. You want to know whether a particular item exists in the drop-down list box.

Solution

You can use the **count** function and a filter on a Secondary data source to check whether a particular item exists in a drop-down list box that is bound to that Secondary data source.

To check whether an item exists in a drop-down list box:

1. In InfoPath, create a new **Blank Form** template.

2. Add a **Drop-Down List Box** control, a **Text Box** control, and a **Section** control to the view of the form template. Name the drop-down list box **selectedItem** and the text box **itemToLookup**.

3. Type the text "Item exists" within the section control. The section control will be used to display a message as to whether the piece of text typed into the text box exists in the drop-down list box.

4. Configure the drop-down list box to be filled with items as described in recipe *54 Populate a drop-down list box with data from an XML file*. Select **@name** under the **brand** repeating group for both the **Value** and the **Display name** properties of the drop-down list box.

5. Click the section control to select it, and then click **Home ➤ Rules ➤ Manage Rules**.

6. On the **Rules** task pane, ensure that **group1** (the group bound to the section control) is displayed below the title bar of the **Rules** task pane

as the group you are adding the rule to, and then click **New ➤ Formatting**.

7. On the **Rules** task pane, select the **Hide this control** check box. This will hide the section control if the item does not exist in the drop-down list box, so does not exist in the Secondary data source that the drop-down list box is populated from.

8. To determine whether an item exists you can count the number of items in the drop-down list box that have a value that is equal to the value typed into the **itemToLookup** text box. If the count is zero, no item exists that has the value of the text string you typed in, so the section control must be hidden. You can now use this information to construct a condition for the **Formatting** rule on the section control. On the **Rules** task pane under **Condition**, click the text **None**.

9. On the **Condition** dialog box, select **Use a formula** from the third drop-down list box. You are going to misuse the **Insert Formula** dialog box to construct a formula that counts the items that have a value equal to the value of **itemToLookup**.

10. On the **Insert Formula** dialog box, type

    ```
    count(
    ```

    and then click **Insert Field or Group**.

11. On the **Select a Field or Group** dialog box, select **RunningShoes (Secondary)** from the drop-down list box, select the **brand** repeating group, and then click **Filter Data**.

12. On the **Filter Data** dialog box, click **Add**.

13. On the **Specify Filter Conditions** dialog box, leave **name** selected in the first drop-down list box, leave **is equal to** selected in the second drop-down list box, and then select **Select a field or group** from the third drop-down list box.

14. On the **Select a Field or Group** dialog box, select **Main** from the drop-down list box, select **itemToLookup**, and click **OK**. This filter condition compares the brand **name** from the Secondary data source to

the value of the **itemToLookup** field, which is bound to the text box and which is located in the Main data source of the form.

15. On the **Specify Filter Conditions** dialog box, click **OK**.

16. On the **Filter Data** dialog box, the expression should say:

```
name = itemToLookup
```

Click **OK**.

17. On the **Select a Field or Group** dialog box, click **OK**.

18. On the **Insert Formula** dialog box, type

```
) = 0
```

to complete the formula. The formula should now resemble the following:

```
count(brand[@name = itemToLookup]) = 0
```

This formula counts the **brand** repeating group nodes in the Secondary data source that are used to populate the drop-down list box where the **name** of a **brand** is equal to the value of the **itemToLookup** field in the Main data source of the InfoPath form and checks whether the result is **0**, so whether there are no **brand** repeating group nodes that have a **name** that is the same as the text typed into the **itemToLookup** text box. Note that the constructed XPath expression is using square brackets ([ ]) as an indication that the **brand** nodes are being filtered on their **name** being equal to **itemToLookup**.

19. On the **Insert Formula** dialog box, click **OK**.

20. On the **Condition** dialog box, select **The expression** from the first drop-down list box, and then delete the last round bracket and everything before **count** in the expression. You should then be left with the following expression:

```
count(xdXDocument:GetDOM("RunningShoes")/ns1:brands/ns1:brand[@
name = xdXDocument:get-DOM()/my:myFields/my:itemToLookup]) = 0
```

21. On the **Condition** dialog box, click **OK**.

22. Preview the form.

When the form opens, type the name of an item that exists in the drop-down list box into the text box and tab or click away from the text box. The section with the text "Item exists" should appear. Now type a text string that does not exist in the drop-down list box into the text box. The section should disappear.

Discussion

To check whether an item exists in a drop-down list box, you must populate the drop-down list box with items from either an external (Secondary) data source or from a repeating group or field in the Main data source of the form (see recipe *53 Populate a drop-down list box with data from a repeating table* and recipe *54 Populate a drop-down list box with data from an XML file*), because you cannot use rules to look up items in a drop-down list box that has been manually populated with items (see recipe *52 Populate a drop-down list box with static items*), since such items become part of the view and not part of the data source of a form (see the discussion section of recipe *58 Count the amount of items in a drop-down list box*).

Exercise

In the solution described above, users must type in a brand name exactly as it is displayed in the drop-down list box, otherwise the item will not be found. This means that the filter being applied is case-sensitive. For example, if a user types "mizuno" into the text box, "Mizuno" will not be found, since the two strings are different.

Try using the **translate** function (see for example recipe *18 Capitalize text in a text box*) to make the filter case-insensitive, so that when "mizuno" is typed into the text box, "Mizuno" is found.

Hint: The resulting expression for the condition to hide the section should resemble the following:

```
count(xdXDocument:GetDOM("RunningShoes")/ns1:brands/ns1:brand[
translate(@name, "abcdefghijklmnopqrstuvwxyz",
"ABCDEFGHIJKLMNOPQRSTUVWXYZ") = translate(xdXDocument:get-
DOM()/my:myFields/my:itemToLookup,
"abcdefghijklmnopqrstuvwxyz", "ABCDEFGHIJKLMNOPQRSTUVWXYZ")])
= 0
```

You can construct this formula after you have performed step 18 of the solution described above by selecting the **Edit XPath (advanced)** check box on the **Insert Formula** dialog box, and then manually modifying the formula by nesting the **@name** and the **itemToLookup** fields each in their own **translate** function. The purpose of the **translate** function is to capitalize both strings, so that the resulting comparison for "mizuno" in the text box and "Mizuno" in the drop-down list box would be

```
"MIZUNO" = "MIZUNO"
```

instead of

```
"mizuno" ≠ "Mizuno"
```

60 Populate a text box based on an item selected in a drop-down list box

Problem

You have a drop-down list box that is filled with items from an XML file. Not all of the data from the XML file can be displayed through the drop-down list box, so you want to be able to select an item from the drop-down list box, and then have a text box filled with additional information from the XML file that corresponds to the item you selected.

Solution

You can use a filter condition to perform a lookup in the Secondary data source for the XML file that is used to populate the drop-down list box, to find additional information that pertains to the selected item in the drop-down list box, and then populate the text box with this information.

In this recipe you will use an XML file named **MonthNames.xml** that has the following contents:

```
<?xml version="1.0" encoding="UTF-8" ?>
<months>
  <month>
    <number>01</number>
    <name>January</name>
  </month>
  <month>
    <number>02</number>
    <name>February</name>
  </month>
  <month>
    <number>03</number>
    <name>March</name>
  </month>
  <month>
    <number>04</number>
    <name>April</name>
  </month>
  <month>
    <number>05</number>
    <name>May</name>
  </month>
  <month>
    <number>06</number>
    <name>June</name>
  </month>
  <month>
    <number>07</number>
    <name>July</name>
  </month>
  <month>
    <number>08</number>
    <name>August</name>
  </month>
  <month>
    <number>09</number>
    <name>September</name>
  </month>
  <month>
    <number>10</number>
    <name>October</name>
```

```
  </month>
  <month>
    <number>11</number>
    <name>November</name>
  </month>
  <month>
    <number>12</number>
    <name>December</name>
  </month>
</months>
```

To populate a text box based on an item selected in a drop-down list box:

1. In InfoPath, create a new **Blank Form** template.

2. Add a **Drop-Down List Box** control to the view of the form template and populate it with data from an XML file (see recipe *54 Populate a drop-down list box with data from an XML file*). Use the **MonthNames.xml** file to populate the drop-down list box and select **number** as the **Value** and **name** as the **Display name** for the drop-down list box. Name the drop-down list box **selectedMonthNumber**.

3. Add a **Text Box** control to the view of the form template and name the text box **monthName**.

4. Add an **Action** rule to the drop-down list box that sets the value of the text box to be equal to the value of the drop-down list box. The action for the rule should say:

```
Set a field's value: monthName = .
```

where **monthName** is the field bound to the text box and the dot (**.**) represents the field bound to the drop-down list box the rule is running on.

When you preview the form and select a month from the drop-down list box, you should see a number appear in the text box instead of a month name. This is because while you see a month name (**Display name**) in the drop-down list box, in reality, the **Value** (the month number) of the drop-down list box is stored in the field (**selectedMonthNumber**) bound to the drop-down list box when you select an item. So you must perform a lookup in the Secondary data source that populates the drop-down list box to find the month name based on the month number that was selected and stored in the field bound to the drop-down list box. And doing a lookup basically means filtering the Secondary data source that is used to fill the drop-down list box on the selected month number. You will do that next.

5. Click on the action you added in step 4.

6. On the **Rule Details** dialog box, click the formula button behind the **Value** text box.

7. On the **Insert Formula** dialog box, clear the **Formula** text box by deleting the formula you constructed previously, and then click **Insert Field or Group**.

8. On the **Select a Field or Group** dialog box, select **MonthNames (Secondary)** from the drop-down list box, expand the **month** repeating group, click **name**, and then click **Filter Data**.

9. On the **Filter Data** dialog box, click **Add**. You want to add a filter where the number in the XML file is the same as the selected month number in the drop-down list box. The first number should come from the Secondary data source containing month names, and the second number should come from the **selectedMonthNumber** field in the Main data source that is bound to the drop-down list box.

10. On the **Specify Filter Conditions** dialog box, select **Select a field or group** from the first drop-down list box.

11. On the **Select a Field or Group** dialog box, ensure that **MonthNames (Secondary)** is selected in the drop-down list box, select **number**, and then click **OK**.

12. On the **Specify Filter Conditions** dialog box, leave **is equal to** selected in the second drop-down list box, and then select **Select a field or group** from the third drop-down list box.

13. On the **Select a Field or Group** dialog box, select **Main** from the drop-down list box, select **selectedMonthNumber** (which is the field that is bound to the drop-down list box), and then click **OK**.

14. On the **Specify Filter Conditions** dialog box, click **OK**.

15. On the **Filter Data** dialog box, click **OK**.

16. On the **Select a Field or Group** dialog box, click **OK**.

17. On the **Insert Formula** dialog box, select the **Edit XPath (advanced)** check box. The formula should now resemble the following:

```
xdXDocument:GetDOM("MonthNames")/months/month/name[../number =
xdXDocument:get-DOM()/my:myFields/my:selectedMonthNumber]
```

What the expression above does is retrieve all of the **name** fields in the **MonthNames** Secondary data source

```
xdXDocument:GetDOM("MonthNames")/months/month/name
```

and then filter those **name** fields

```
[ ... ]
```

on the value of the **number** field in the Secondary data source

```
../number
```

being equal to (=) the value of the **selectedMonthNumber** field in the Main data source

```
xdXDocument:get-DOM()/my:myFields/my:selectedMonthNumber
```

which contains the selected month number from the drop-down list box.

18. Click **OK** when closing all dialog boxes.

19. Preview the form.

When the form opens, select a month from the drop-down list box. The same month name as shown in the drop-down list box should appear in the text box.

Discussion

In the formula in step 17 of the solution described above, you can see that

```
xdXDocument:get-DOM()
```

gives you a reference to the Main data source when you are writing XPath expressions, while

```
xdXDocument:GetDOM("MonthNames")
```

gives you a reference to a Secondary data source named **MonthNames**.

You need not be concerned with these references when you are constructing XPath expressions through dialog boxes in InfoPath, but just be aware of them in case you want to manually start writing and/or modifying XPath expressions later down the track.

61 Cascading drop-down list boxes using an XML file

Problem

You have an XML file containing the names, types, and models of running shoes. You want to add three drop-down list boxes to an InfoPath form and have the first drop-down list box be populated with all of the running shoe brand names, the second drop-down list box with only the running shoe types belonging to the selected brand in the first drop-down list box, and the third drop-down list box with only the running shoe models belonging to the selected brand in the first drop-down list box and the selected type in the second drop-down list box.

Solution

Creating cascading or dependent drop-down list boxes entails filtering the data sources used to populate the drop-down list boxes on values that are selected elsewhere and which are often located in the Main data source of an InfoPath form.

To create cascading drop-down list boxes using data contained in one XML file:

1. In InfoPath, create a new **Blank Form** template.

2. Add a **Drop-Down List Box** control to the view of the form template, populate it with data from an XML file as described in recipe *54 Populate a drop-down list box with data from an XML file*, and name it **shoeBrand**. A user can select a running shoe brand from this drop-down list box.

3. Add a second **Drop-Down List Box** control to the view of the form template and name it **shoeType**. This drop-down list box should be populated with the types of running shoes that are available for a chosen running shoe brand.

4. Open the **Drop-Down List Box Properties** dialog box for the **shoeType** drop-down list box.

5. On the **Drop-Down List Box Properties** dialog box on the **Data** tab, select the **Get choices from an external data source** option, select **RunningShoes** from the **Data source** drop-down list box, and then click the button behind the **Entries** text box.

6. On the **Select a Field or Group** dialog box, expand the **brand** repeating group, select the **type** repeating group, and click **Filter Data**.

7. On the **Filter Data** dialog box, click **Add**.

8. You want to add a filter that will return only those **type** repeating groups that fall under the selected **brand** from the first drop-down list box. For this you must add a filter that compares the brand **name** from the XML file to the **shoeBrand** value selected in the first drop-down list box on the form. On the **Specify Filter Conditions** dialog box, select **Select a field or group** from the first drop-down list box.

9. On the **Select a Field or Group** dialog box, ensure that **RunningShoes (Secondary)** is selected in the drop-down list box, select the **name** field that is directly located under the **brand** repeating group, and click **OK**.

10. On the **Specify Filter Conditions** dialog box, leave **is equal to** selected in the second drop-down list box, and then select **Select a field or group** from the third drop-down list box.

11. On the **Select a Field or Group** dialog box, select **Main** from the drop-down list box, select **shoeBrand**, and click **OK**.

12. On the **Specify Filter Conditions** dialog box, click **OK**.

13. On the **Filter Data** dialog box, click **OK**.

14. On the **Select a Field or Group** dialog box, click **OK**.

15. On the **Drop-Down List Box Properties** dialog box, the **@name** attribute under the **type** repeating group should have been automatically selected for the **Value** and **Display name** properties. Leave this as is, and click **OK**.

16. Before you continue, preview the form to see whether the types for each brand are automatically being listed in the **shoeType** drop-down list box when you select a **shoeBrand**.

17. Add a third **Drop-Down List Box** control to the view of the form template and name it **shoeModel**.

18. Do the same thing as you did for the **shoeType** drop-down list box, but then instead of the **type** repeating group, select the **model** repeating field, and add a filter condition that compares the type's name in the XML file (**name** field under the **type** repeating group in the **RunningShoes** Secondary data source) to the type's name selected in the **shoeType** drop-down list box in the Main data source, and a second filter condition that compares the brand's name from the XML file (**name** field under the **brand** repeating group in the **RunningShoes** Secondary data source) to the brand's name selected in the **shoeBrand** drop-down list box in the Main data source. The resulting filter should resemble the following:

```
name = shoeType
and
name = shoeBrand
```

where the first **name** is the **name** field under the **type** repeating group, and the second **name** is the **name** field under the **brand** repeating group in the **RunningShoes** Secondary data source. Note: To join the two filter conditions together you must click the **And** button behind the first filter condition when you are on the **Specify Filter Conditions** dialog box (also see the discussion section of recipe *32 Show/hide sections based on a drop-down list box selection*).

19. Add an **Action** rule to the **shoeBrand** drop-down list box with two actions that say:

```
Set a field's value: shoeType = ""
Set a field's value: shoeModel = ""
```

These two actions ensure that any previously selected values in the **shoeType** and **shoeModel** drop-down list boxes are cleared when an item is selected from the **shoeBrand** drop-down list box. This is necessary to prevent items that do not exist in the list of filtered items from appearing in the drop-down list boxes.

20. Add an **Action** rule to the **shoeType** drop-down list box with an action that says:

```
Set a field's value: shoeModel = ""
```

This action ensures that any previously selected value in the **shoeModel** drop-down list box is cleared when an item is selected from the **shoeType** drop-down list box. This is necessary to prevent items that do not exist in the list of filtered items from appearing in the **shoeModel** drop-down list box.

21. Preview the form.

When the form opens, the second and third drop-down list boxes should be empty. Select a brand from the first drop-down list box. The second drop-down list box should now contain running shoe types. Select a type from the second drop-down list box. The third drop-down list box should now contain running shoe models for the shoe brand and shoe type you selected in the first and second drop-down list boxes.

Discussion

Figure 138 is a visual representation of how cascading drop-down list boxes are set up in InfoPath.

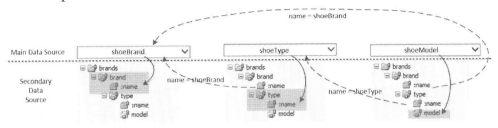

Figure 138. Relationship between data sources with filters to set up cascading lists.

In this figure, **shoeBrand**, **shoeType**, and **shoeModel** are all fields in the Main data source and are bound to drop-down list box controls. These fields store the selected value for each drop-down list box.

The **shoeBrand** drop-down list box is populated by the **name** field under the **brand** repeating group in the Secondary data source, the **shoeType** drop-down list box is populated by the **name** field under the **type** repeating group in the Secondary data source, and the **shoeModel** drop-down list box is populated by the **model** repeating field in the Secondary data source.

The **shoeType** drop-down list box has a filter set on it to only show those type names where the brand **name** in the Secondary data source is equal to the **shoeBrand** in the Main data source.

The **shoeModel** drop-down list box has a filter set on it to only show those models where the brand **name** in the Secondary data source is equal to the **shoeBrand** in the Main data source and the type **name** in the Secondary data source is equal to the **shoeType** in the Main data source.

Date Pickers and Date and Time Pickers

InfoPath 2013 comes with two date controls: **Date Picker** and **Date and Time Picker**. **Date Picker** controls allow you to select or enter dates, while **Date and Time Picker** controls allow you to select or enter dates in addition to entering times. A **Date and Time Picker** control is a control that is a combination of a **Date Picker** control for entering a date and a **Text Box** control for entering a time.

When selecting a date from a **Date Picker** or a **Date and Time Picker** control, you can make use of a calendar to select a date.

Figure 139. Date Picker calendar in InfoPath 2013.

A drawback of the date picker controls in InfoPath is that you cannot select a specific year from the calendar. For example, if you currently have the calendar open on the year 2013 and you want to select a date in 2012 or 1997, you would have to click on the forward or backward arrows on the calendar to navigate through each month until you arrive at the desired year. A workaround is to use a drop-down list box to select the starting year for the date picker (see recipe *64 Set the year of a date in a date picker using a drop-down list box*) or enter the date manually into the date picker control.

62 Display the current date in a date picker

Problem

You have a date picker on an InfoPath form and want this date picker to display the current date whenever the form opens.

Solution

You can set the **Default Value** of the date picker to be equal to a formula that uses the **today** function.

To display the current date in a date picker:

1. In InfoPath, create a new **Blank Form** template.

2. Add a **Date Picker** control to the view of the form template.

3. Right-click the date picker control and select **Date Picker Properties** from the context menu that appears.

4. On the **Date Picker Properties** dialog box on the **Data** tab, use the formula button to set the **Default Value** to be equal to the following formula:

    ```
    today()
    ```

5. On the **Date Picker Properties** dialog box, click **OK**.

6. Preview the form.

When the form opens, the current date should appear in the date picker control.

Discussion

You can also apply the technique described in the solution above if you are using a **Date and Time Picker** control instead of a **Date Picker** control.

The **now** function returns the current system date and time in the following format: **yyyy-MM-ddThh:mm:ss**, while the **today** function only returns the current system date in the following format: **yyyy-MM-dd**. Both functions return dates and times as strings.

The part of the string that comes after the **T**, represents the time. So **yyyy** represents the year, **MM** represents the month, **dd** represents the day, **hh** represents the hours, **mm** represents the minutes, and **ss** represents the seconds.

A concrete example of a date and time returned by the **now** function would be for example **2013-03-01T13:03:33** and a concrete example of a date returned by the **today** function would be for example **2013-03-01**.

Because a **Date and Time Picker** control consists of two controls (a date and a time) you must use the **now** function instead of the **today** function if you want to set its **Default Value**.

Exercise

Add a **Date and Time Picker** control to the form template and set its **Default Value** to be equal to the current date and time using the **now** function in a formula. As a test, also try setting the default value using the **today** function to see what happens.

63 Extract the year from a date picker

Problem

You have a date picker control on an InfoPath form and you want to extract the year number from the date that has been selected in the date picker and put this year number in a text box.

Solution

You can use the **substring** function to extract the year number from a date.

To extract the year from a date picker:

1. In InfoPath, create a new **Blank Form** template.

2. Add a **Date Picker** control and a **Text Box** control to the view of the form template. Name the date picker **selectedDate** and the text box **selectedYear**.

3. Add an **Action** rule to the date picker with an action that says:

   ```
   Set a field's value: selectedYear = substring(., 1, 4)
   ```

   where **selectedYear** is the field that is bound to the text box control. What this rule does is set the value of the **selectedYear** text box to be equal to the formula:

```
substring(., 1, 4)
```

This formula extracts the first 4 characters from the string representation of the date. InfoPath date fields have the format **yyyy-MM-dd** and InfoPath date/time fields have the format **yyyy-MM-ddThh:mm:ss**, where **yyyy** represents the year, **MM** represents the month, **dd** represents the day, **hh** represents the hours, **mm** represents the minutes, and **ss** represents the seconds. For example, September 15, 2013 at 3 p.m. would be represented by **2013-09-15** as the value of a date picker and by **2013-09-15T15:00:00** as the value of a date and time picker in InfoPath. So to extract the year, you must retrieve the part of the date string that starts at position 1 and is 4 characters long.

4.   Preview the form.

When the form opens, select or enter a date in the date picker. The year number for the date you selected or entered should appear in the text box.

Discussion

The **substring** function can be used to retrieve part of or an entire text string. The **substring** function takes 2 or 3 arguments:

1.   The text string from which to retrieve part of or the whole string.

2.   The position in the text string where the substring starts. The position number always starts at 1 (and not 0) for the first character. If the piece of text string you are looking for starts at position 3, enter a 3.

3.   Optionally, the amount of characters contained in the piece of text string you want to retrieve. If you do not specify an amount, all of the characters starting from the starting position you specified until the end of the string will be returned.

Here are a few examples of how the **substring** function works:

*   `substring("InfoPath is fun", 1, 8)` returns **InfoPath**.
*   `substring("InfoPath is fun", 13)` returns **fun**.

Having extracted the year from a date string, you now also know how to extract the day number, month number, hours, minutes, and seconds. The month starts at position 6 in the date string and has a length of 2 characters. The day starts at position 9 in the date string and has a length of 2 characters, etc.

Exercise

With what you have learned about the **substring** function, try to extract the month number and the day number from the date picker, and then try to extract the hours from a date and time picker control.

64 Set the year of a date in a date picker using a drop-down list box

Problem

You have a date picker control on an InfoPath form and want to be able to select a year from a drop-down list box and have the date picker automatically display the 1st of January of that year.

Solution

You can use the **concat** function to construct a date string based on the value of the year selected from the drop-down list box and then use a rule to set the value of the date picker to be equal to the constructed date string.

To set the year of the date in a date picker control using a drop-down list box:

1. In InfoPath, create a new **Blank Form** template.

2. Add a **Drop-Down List Box** control and a **Date Picker** control to the view of the form template. Name the drop-down list box **selectedYear** and the date picker **selectedDate**.

3. Right-click the drop-down list box and select **Drop-Down List Box Properties** from the context menu that appears.

4. On the **Drop-Down List Box Properties** dialog box on the **Data** tab under **List box choices**, leave the **Enter choices manually** option selected, and then click **Add**.

5. On the **Add Choice** dialog box, type a year, for example 2011, in the **Value** and **Display name** text boxes, and click **OK**.

6. Repeat steps 4 and 5 to add more years, for example, 2012, 2013, etc. On the **Drop-Down List Box Properties** dialog box, click **OK** when you are done adding the years.

7. Add an **Action** rule to the drop-down list box control with an action that says:

```
Set a field's value: selectedDate = concat(., "-01-01")
```

where **selectedDate** is the field that is bound to the date picker control. What this rule does is set the value of the **selectedDate** date picker to be equal to the concatenation of the value of the selected year from the drop-down list box and the static piece of text "-01-01". A sample result would be 2013-01-01, which has the correct format for a date that can be displayed in a date picker control in InfoPath.

8. Preview the form.

When the form opens, select a year from the drop-down list box. The 1st of January of the year you selected from the drop-down list box should appear in the date picker control. And when you click on the calendar icon on the right-hand side of the date picker control, the calendar should open and display the 1st of January of the year you selected from the drop-down list box.

Discussion

InfoPath date fields have the format **yyyy-MM-dd** and InfoPath date/time fields have the format **yyyy-MM-ddThh:mm:ss**, where **yyyy** represents the year, **MM** represents the month, **dd** represents the day, **hh** represents the hours, **mm** represents the minutes, and **ss** represents the seconds.

For example, September 15, 2013 at 3 p.m. would be represented by **2013-09-15** as the value of a date picker and by **2013-09-15T15:00:00** as the value of a date and time picker in InfoPath.

So had you used a date and time picker control instead of a date picker control in the solution described above, you would have had to change the formula to be the following:

```
concat(., "-01-01T00:00:00")
```

instead of

```
concat(., "-01-01")
```

or set the time part of the date and time picker to be whatever you wanted it to be, but in any case equal to a valid time, otherwise InfoPath would reject the constructed date and time value as a valid value for a date and time picker control.

65 Display the month name for a selected date

Problem

You have a date picker control on an InfoPath form and want to extract the month number from the date and display the month name elsewhere on the form.

Solution

Because InfoPath does not offer a function to retrieve the month name from a date, you must use a workaround that uses the **substring** function to extract the month number from a date, and then look up the month name in either an external data source (e.g. an XML file) or a repeating field in the form. In this recipe you will use the **MonthNames.xml** file that you also used in recipe *60 Populate a text box based on an item selected in a drop-down list box*.

To display the month name for a selected date:

1. In InfoPath, create a new **Blank Form** template.

2. Add a **Date Picker** control to the view of the form template and name it **completionDate**.

3. Add a **Receive data** connection to the **MonthNames.xml** file you used in recipe *60 Populate a text box based on an item selected in a drop-down list box* (also see recipe *33 Get data from an XML file*).

4. Add a **Calculated Value** control to the view of the form template.

5. On the **Insert Calculated Value** dialog box, click the formula button behind the **XPath** text box.

6. On the **Insert Formula** dialog box, click **Insert Field or Group**.

7. On the **Select a Field or Group** dialog box, select **MonthNames (Secondary)** from the drop-down list box, expand the **month** repeating group, select the **name** field, and click **Filter Data**.

8. On the **Filter Data** dialog box, click **Add**.

9. You are going to construct a formula that retrieves all of the names of the months, but with a filter that will look for the month name that has the same number as the month number of the date that was selected in the date picker. On the **Specify Filter Conditions** dialog box, select **number** from the first drop-down list box, leave **is equal to** selected in the second drop-down list box, and select **Use a formula** from the third drop-down list box.

10. On the **Insert Formula** dialog box, type

```
substring(
```

and then click **Insert Field or Group**.

11. On the **Select a Field or Group** dialog box, select **Main** from the drop-down list box, select **completionDate**, and click **OK**.

12. On the **Insert Formula** dialog box, type

```
, 6, 2)
```

to complete the formula. The final formula should resemble the following:

```
substring(completionDate, 6, 2)
```

or the following if you have the **Edit XPath (advanced)** check box selected:

```
substring(xdXDocument:get-DOM()/my:myFields/my:completionDate,
6, 2)
```

What this formula does is extract the month number from the **completionDate** date picker. Remember that dates have the format **yyyy-MM-dd** in InfoPath, so the **substring** function extracts 2 characters starting from the 6th position in the date string. This results in **MM** being returned, so the number for the month.

13. On the **Insert Formula** dialog box click **OK**.

14. On the **Specify Filter Conditions** dialog box, click **OK**.

15. On the **Filter Data** dialog box, the filter should say:

```
number = substring(completionDate, 6, 2)
```

This filter says that the month number in the Secondary data source for the XML file should be the same as the month number extracted from the **completionDate** field in the Main data source. Click **OK**.

16. On the **Select a Field or Group** dialog box, click **OK**. The final formula should now say:

```
name[number = substring(completionDate, 6, 2)]
```

or the following if you have the **Edit XPath (advanced)** check box selected:

```
xdXDocument:GetDOM("MonthNames")/months/month/name[../number =
substring(xdXDocument:get-DOM()/my:myFields/my:completionDate,
6, 2)]
```

With this you have added a filter on the month names to perform a lookup in the Secondary data source to find the one month name for which the month number in the Secondary data source for the XML file is the same as the month number extracted from the date that is selected in the **completionDate** date picker, which is bound to a field that is located in the Main data source of the form.

17. On the **Insert Formula** dialog box, click **OK**.

18. On the **Insert Calculated Value** dialog box, click **OK**.

19. Preview the form.

When the form opens, select a date from the date picker. The month name should have been retrieved from the XML file and displayed in the calculated value control.

Question

1. How would you have to modify the formula that sets the value of the calculated value control so that it displays the date that is selected or entered via the date picker in the following format: **dd MMMM yyyy**. So for example, if you enter **2013-01-13** into the date picker, the calculated value control should display the date as **13 January 2013**. Hint: You must use the **concat** and **substring** functions.

66 Set a date picker to display the previous month in its calendar

Problem

You have a date picker on an InfoPath form and want it to display the 1st of the previous month instead of the current month.

Solution

You can use rules, functions, and formulas to set the date of the date picker to be equal to the first of the previous month.

To set a date picker to display the previous month in its calendar:

1. In InfoPath, create a new **Blank Form** template.

2. Add a **Date Picker** control to the view of the form template and name it **datePreviousMonth**.

3. The logic to calculate the date for the previous month is as follows:

   a. If it is currently January, you want the date in the date picker to be the 1st of December of the previous year.

   b. If it is currently not January, you want the date in the date picker to be the 1st of the previous month in the same year.

   What this logic means is that you must set conditions on rules, and the conditions must determine whether it is currently January or not. And because you have to set conditions on rules, you cannot set the **Default Value** of the date picker, but must rather use an **Action** rule on another control or on the form itself to trigger setting the date of the date picker. Here you will set the date when the form opens. So click **Data ➤ Rules ➤ Form Load**. This should open the **Rules** task pane.

4. On the **Rules** task pane, add an **Action** rule to the **Form Load** event with an action that says:

   ```
   Set a field's value: datePreviousMonth = today()
   ```

   where **datePreviousMonth** is the field bound to the date picker control and `today()` is the **today** function that returns the current date. This rule initializes the date picker to contain the current date. This rule does not have conditions and should always be the first rule in the list of rules.

5. On the **Rules** task pane, add a second **Action** rule to the **Form Load** event with a **Condition** that says:

   ```
   number(substring(my:datePreviousMonth, 6, 2)) > 1
   and
   number(substring(my:datePreviousMonth, 6, 2)) < 11
   ```

   and an action that says:

   ```
   Set a field's value: datePreviousMonth =
   concat(substring(datePreviousMonth, 1, 4), "-0",
   ```

```
string(number(substring(datePreviousMonth, 6, 2)) - 1), "-01")
```

and select the **Don't run remaining rules if the condition of this rule is met** check box. This rule sets the value of the **datePreviousMonth** field when the current month falls between February and October (inclusive). This rule is added to make the concatenation easier as a zero should be added in front of any month number less than 10. Remember that dates in InfoPath have the format **yyyy-MM-dd**, so any month number is expected to consist of 2 characters, and not 1. Note: You must use the **The expression** option to define the expressions for the condition on the rule.

6. On the **Rules** task pane, add a third **Action** rule to the **Form Load** event with a **Condition** that says:

```
number(substring(my:datePreviousMonth, 6, 2)) >= 11
```

and an action that says:

```
Set a field's value: datePreviousMonth =
concat(substring(datePreviousMonth, 1, 4), "-",
string(number(substring(datePreviousMonth, 6, 2)) - 1), "-01")
```

and select the **Don't run remaining rules if the condition of this rule is met** check box. This rule sets the value of the **datePreviousMonth** field when the current month falls in or after November. This rule is added to make the concatenation easier as a zero should not be added in front of a month number greater than 9. Note: You must use the **The expression** option to define the expression for the condition on the rule.

7. On the **Rules** task pane, add a fourth **Action** rule to the **Form Load** event with a **Condition** that says:

```
number(substring(my:datePreviousMonth, 6, 2)) = 1
```

and an action that says:

```
Set a field's value: datePreviousMonth =
concat(string(number(substring(datePreviousMonth, 1, 4)) - 1),
"-12-01")
```

and select the **Don't run remaining rules if the condition of this rule is met** check box. This rule sets the value of the **datePreviousMonth** field to December of the previous year when the current month is January. Note: You must use the **The expression** option to define the expression for the condition on the rule.

8. Preview the form.

When the form opens, the first of the previous month should appear in the date picker, depending on the date that is currently set on your system. To test other months, you could change your system date and then reopen the form to see whether it displays the correct previous month.

Tip:

When you use the **The expression** option on the **Condition** dialog box, there is no facility to construct an expression. It is best to select the **Use a formula** option in the third drop-down list box as soon as you open the **Condition** dialog box. This will open the **Insert Formula** dialog box where you can select fields and insert functions. Once you are happy with your constructed formula, you can click **OK**, and then on the **Condition** dialog box, select **The expression** from the first drop-down list box. InfoPath will add a field (whichever field was selected in the first drop-down list box before you selected **The expression** from the first drop-down list box) and an equal sign in front of your constructed formula, so you must correct the expression in the text box by removing these additions. See for example recipe *31 Set a maximum length on text in a text box.*

Discussion

In the solution described above, you used the following InfoPath functions to construct the date for the previous month:

- **number**, which converts a string to a number so that you can perform mathematical calculations.

- **string**, which converts a number to a string, so that you can use the result in the **concat** function.

- **concat**, which combines two or more fields or strings into one string.

- **substring**, which returns a specific part of a string.

67 Display the name of the day for a selected date

Problem

You have a date picker control on an InfoPath form and want to select a date from the date picker and have the name of the day corresponding to the date be displayed on the form.

Solution

You can use the **substring** function and a formula that is based on using the year, month, and day to calculate a day number where Sunday is 0 and Saturday is 6.

To display the name of the day for a selected date:

1. In InfoPath, create a new **Blank Form** template.

2. Add a **Date Picker** control to the view of the form template, name the date picker control **myDate**, and set its **Default Value** to be equal to the following formula:

```
today()
```

3. On the **Fields** task pane, add a text field named **dayName** under the **myFields** group, right-click it, drag it to the view of the form template, and when you drop it, select **Calculated Value** from the context menu that appears.

4. On the **Fields** task pane under the **dayName** field, add a field of type **Field (attribute)** with the name **day** and the data type **Whole Number (integer)**.

5. Once added, double-click the **day** field, and then on the **Field or Group Properties** dialog box, set its **Default Value** to be equal to the following formula:

    ```
    number(substring(myDate, 9, 2))
    ```

    and ensure that the **Refresh value when formula is recalculated** check box is selected on the **Field or Group Properties** dialog box. This formula extracts the day number from the **myDate** date picker.

6. On the **Fields** task pane under the **dayName** field, add a field of type **Field (attribute)** with the name **month** and the data type **Whole Number (integer)**.

7. Once added, double-click the **month** field, and then on the **Field or Group Properties** dialog box, set its **Default Value** to be equal to the following formula:

    ```
    number(substring(myDate, 6, 2))
    ```

    and ensure that the **Refresh value when formula is recalculated** check box is selected on the **Field or Group Properties** dialog box. This formula extracts the month number from the **myDate** date picker.

8. On the **Fields** task pane under the **dayName** field, add a field of type **Field (attribute)** with the name **year** and the data type **Whole Number (integer)**.

9. Once added, double-click the **year** field, and then on the **Field or Group Properties** dialog box, set its **Default Value** to be equal to the following formula:

    ```
    number(substring(myDate, 1, 4))
    ```

    and ensure that the **Refresh value when formula is recalculated** check box is selected on the **Field or Group Properties** dialog box. This formula extracts the year number from the **myDate** date picker.

10. Set the **Default Value** of the **dayName** field to be equal to the following formula:

```
(@my:day + number(@my:year - (floor((14 - @my:month) div 12)))
+ floor(number(@my:year - (floor((14 - @my:month) div 12))) div
4) - floor(number(@my:year - (floor((14 - @my:month) div 12)))
div 100) + floor(number(@my:year - (floor((14 - @my:month) div
12))) div 400) + floor((31 * number(@my:month + 12 * (floor((14
- @my:month) div 12)) - 2)) div 12)) mod 7
```

and ensure that the **Refresh value when formula is recalculated** check box is selected. This is a formula used to calculate a number for a day of the week. It uses the value of the **myDate** date picker to calculate a number between 0 and 6, with 0 representing Sunday and 6 representing Saturday.

11. Add 7 **Action** rules to the **dayName** field with the following conditions and actions:

   a. Condition:

   ```
   dayName = "0"
   ```

   Action:

   ```
   Set a field's value: . = "Sunday"
   ```

   b. Condition:

   ```
   dayName = "1"
   ```

   Action:

   ```
   Set a field's value: . = "Monday"
   ```

   c. Condition:

   ```
   dayName = "2"
   ```

   Action:

   ```
   Set a field's value: . = "Tuesday"
   ```

   d. Condition:

```
dayName = "3"
```

Action:

```
Set a field's value: . = "Wednesday"
```

e. Condition:

```
dayName = "4"
```

Action:

```
Set a field's value: . = "Thursday"
```

f. Condition:

```
dayName = "5"
```

Action:

```
Set a field's value: . = "Friday"
```

g. Condition:

```
dayName = "6"
```

Action:

```
Set a field's value: . = "Saturday"
```

where the dot (.) represents the context node, which in this case is the **dayName** field. Ensure that the **Don't run remaining rules if the condition of this rule is met** check box is selected for each one of the rules above.

12. Preview the form.

When the form opens, the current date should appear in the date picker and the name of the week day should appear in the calculated value control. Select a different date from the date picker and see how the week day name changes.

Discussion

In the solution described above, you used attributes on a field to help make a formula shorter and more legible. However, you could have also just referenced the **myDate** field in each **substring** function and arrive at the following formula for the **Default Value** for the **dayName** field:

```
(number(substring(../my:myDate, 9, 2)) +
number(number(substring(../my:myDate, 1, 4)) - (floor((14 -
number(substring(../my:myDate, 6, 2))) div 12))) +
floor(number(number(substring(../my:myDate, 1, 4)) - (floor((14 -
number(substring(../my:myDate, 6, 2))) div 12))) div 4) -
floor(number(number(substring(../my:myDate, 1, 4)) - (floor((14 -
number(substring(../my:myDate, 6, 2))) div 12))) div 100) +
floor(number(number(substring(../my:myDate, 1, 4)) - (floor((14 -
number(substring(../my:myDate, 6, 2))) div 12))) div 400) +
floor((31 * number(number(substring(../my:myDate, 6, 2)) + 12 *
(floor((14 - number(substring(../my:myDate, 6, 2))) div 12)) - 2))
div 12)) mod 7
```

There are two types of fields you can create in InfoPath:

1. Elements
2. Attributes

An attribute can be seen as a property of an element, and can be used to provide additional information for an element.

You can add an attribute to either a **group** or an element **field** in InfoPath.

Figure 140. Day, month, and year attributes under the dayName field (element).

While creating fields as elements instead of attributes will suit most of your scenarios, there may be times when you want to define properties on an element. In such cases, you can add fields as attributes on an element as shown in the solution described above.

68 Force Sundays to be selected from a date picker

Problem

You have a date picker control on an InfoPath form and want to force users to always select a date that falls on a Sunday.

Solution

You can use a **Validation** rule to check whether the date that is selected or entered in a date picker falls on a Sunday.

To force Sundays to be selected from a date picker control:

1. In InfoPath, create a new **Blank Form** template.

2. Add a **Date Picker** control to the view of the form template, name the date picker control **myDate**, and set its **Default Value** to be equal to the following formula:

    ```
    today()
    ```

3. On the **Fields** task pane, add a hidden text field (see recipe *11 Add a hidden field*) named **dateParts** under the **myFields** group.

4. On the **Fields** task pane under the **dateParts** field, add a field of type **Field (attribute)** with the name **day** and the data type **Whole Number (integer)**.

5. Once added, double-click the **day** field, and then on the **Field or Group Properties** dialog box, set its **Default Value** to be equal to the following formula:

    ```
    number(substring(myDate, 9, 2))
    ```

    and ensure that the **Refresh value when formula is recalculated** check box is selected on the **Field or Group Properties** dialog box. This formula extracts the day number from the **myDate** date picker.

6. On the **Fields** task pane under the **dateParts** field, add a field of type **Field (attribute)** with the name **month** and the data type **Whole Number (integer)**.

7. Once added, double-click the **month** field, and then on the **Field or Group Properties** dialog box, set its **Default Value** to be equal to the following formula:

    ```
    number(substring(myDate, 6, 2))
    ```

    and ensure that the **Refresh value when formula is recalculated** check box is selected on the **Field or Group Properties** dialog box. This formula extracts the month number from the **myDate** date picker.

8. On the **Fields** task pane under the **dateParts** field, add a field of type **Field (attribute)** with the name **year** and the data type **Whole Number (integer)**.

9. Once added, double-click the **year** field, and then on the **Field or Group Properties** dialog box, set its **Default Value** to be equal to the following formula:

    ```
    number(substring(myDate, 1, 4))
    ```

    and ensure that the **Refresh value when formula is recalculated** check box is selected on the **Field or Group Properties** dialog box. This formula extracts the year number from the **myDate** date picker.

10. Set the **Default Value** of the **dateParts** field to be equal to the following formula:

    ```
    (@my:day + number(@my:year - (floor((14 - @my:month) div 12)))
    + floor(number(@my:year - (floor((14 - @my:month) div 12))) div
    4) - floor(number(@my:year - (floor((14 - @my:month) div 12)))
    div 100) + floor(number(@my:year - (floor((14 - @my:month) div
    12))) div 400) + floor((31 * number(@my:month + 12 * (floor((14
    - @my:month) div 12)) - 2)) div 12)) mod 7
    ```

    and ensure that the **Refresh value when formula is recalculated** check box is selected. This is a formula used to calculate a number for a day of the week. It uses the value of the **myDate** date picker to calculate a number between 0 and 6, with 0 representing Sunday and 6 representing Saturday.

11. Add a **Validation** rule to the **myDate** date picker with a **Condition** that says:

```
dateParts ≠ "0"
```

(**dateParts** is not equal to 0) and a **ScreenTip** that says: "You must select a Sunday". This rule checks whether the selected date is not a Sunday and then displays a message.

12. Preview the form.

When the form opens, select a date that does not fall on a Sunday. A red dashed border should appear around the date picker and when you hover over the date picker you should see the screen tip message appear. Then select a date that falls on a Sunday. The red dashed border should disappear.

Discussion

See the discussion section of recipe *67 Display the name of the day for a selected date* for an explanation of the difference between elements and attributes in InfoPath.

69 Display the time of a date and time picker in a drop-down list box

Problem

You have a date and time picker control on an InfoPath form and want to change the text box of the time part of the date and time picker control into a drop-down list box control for easy selection of a certain time of a day.

Solution

You can use a Secondary data source that contains times and bind this to a drop-down list box control to provide the hours for a date and time picker control.

256

To change the time text box of a date and time picker control into a drop-down list box:

1. In InfoPath, create a new **Blank Form** template.

2. Add a **Date and Time Picker** control to the view of the form template and name it **theDateAndTime**.

3. Select the text box control (time part) of the date and time picker control and press **Delete** on your keyboard to delete it.

4. Add a **Receive data** connection to an XML file (see recipe *33 Get data from an XML file*) that has the following contents:

```xml
<?xml version="1.0" encoding="UTF-8"?>
<datetimetimes xmlns="urn:sym">
  <selectedTime/>
  <times><date/><time>01:00</time><datetime/></times>
  <times><date/><time>02:00</time><datetime/></times>
  <times><date/><time>03:00</time><datetime/></times>
  <times><date/><time>04:00</time><datetime/></times>
  <times><date/><time>05:00</time><datetime/></times>
  <times><date/><time>06:00</time><datetime/></times>
  <times><date/><time>07:00</time><datetime/></times>
  <times><date/><time>08:00</time><datetime/></times>
  <times><date/><time>09:00</time><datetime/></times>
  <times><date/><time>10:00</time><datetime/></times>
  <times><date/><time>11:00</time><datetime/></times>
  <times><date/><time>12:00</time><datetime/></times>
  <times><date/><time>13:00</time><datetime/></times>
  <times><date/><time>14:00</time><datetime/></times>
  <times><date/><time>15:00</time><datetime/></times>
  <times><date/><time>16:00</time><datetime/></times>
  <times><date/><time>17:00</time><datetime/></times>
  <times><date/><time>18:00</time><datetime/></times>
  <times><date/><time>19:00</time><datetime/></times>
  <times><date/><time>20:00</time><datetime/></times>
  <times><date/><time>21:00</time><datetime/></times>
  <times><date/><time>22:00</time><datetime/></times>
  <times><date/><time>23:00</time><datetime/></times>
  <times><date/><time>00:00</time><datetime/></times>
</datetimetimes>
```

and name the data connection **DateTimeTimes**.

5. Click the date picker to select it, and then click **Home ➤ Rules ➤ Manage Rules**.

6. On the **Rules** task pane, click **New ➤ Action**, add a **Condition** that says:

```
theDateAndTime is not blank
```

and then click **Add ➤ Set a field's value**.

7. On the **Rule Details** dialog box, click the button behind the **Field** text box.

8. On the **Select a Field or Group** dialog box, select **DateTimeTimes (Secondary)** from the drop-down list box, expand the **times** repeating group, select the **date** field under the **times** repeating group, and click **OK**. With this you are setting all of the **date** fields in the Secondary data source.

9. On the **Rule Details** dialog box, click the button behind the **Value** text box.

10. On the **Insert Formula** dialog box, construct a formula that says:

```
substring-before(., "T")
```

and then click **OK**. This formula extracts the string that comes before the **T** in the date and time string, which is the same as extracting only the date part from the date and time string.

11. On the **Rule Details** dialog box, click **OK**. The action on the **Rules** task pane should now say:

```
Set a field's value: date = substring-before(., "T")
```

where **date** is the **date** field under the **times** repeating group in the **DateTimeTimes** Secondary data source. This rule sets all of the **date** fields in the Secondary data source to be equal to the date part of the date and time picker control. The date part has the format **yyyy-MM-dd**. If you look at the XML file, you will see that all of the **date** nodes start out as empty fields.

12. On the **Fields** task pane, select **DateTimeTimes (Secondary)** from the drop-down list box, right-click the **selectedTime** field, and then drag-and-drop it onto the view of the form template. When you drop it, select **Drop-Down List Box** from the context menu that appears.

13. Open the **Drop-Down List Box Properties** dialog box, and then set the list box choices to come from the **DateTimeTimes** Secondary data source and to have the **times** repeating group as the **Entries**, the **datetime** field as the **Value** and the **time** field as the **Display name** for the drop-down list box (also see recipe *54 Populate a drop-down list box with data from an XML file*). Click **OK** when you are done.

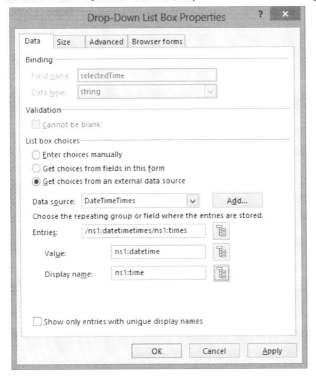

Figure 141. Drop-down list box bound to the Secondary data source containing times.

14. Add a **Formatting** rule to the **selectedTime** drop-down list box with a **Condition** that says:

```
theDateAndTime is blank
```

and a **Formatting** of **Disable this control**. This rule disables the drop-down list box if no date has been selected or entered in the date part of the date and time picker control. Note: Remember that **theDateAndTime** field is located in the Main data source of the form, so you must select **Main** from the drop-down list box on the **Select a Field or Group** dialog box when constructing the condition for the rule.

15. On the **Fields** task pane, select **DateTimeTimes (Secondary)** from the drop-down list box, and then click **date** under the **times** repeating group to select it. Then on the **Rules** task pane, add an **Action** rule to the **date** field that says:

```
Set a field's value: datetime = concat(., "T", time, ":00")
```

where **datetime** and **time** are fields that are located in the **DateTimeTimes** Secondary data source. This rule sets the values of all of the **datetime** fields in the Secondary data source by concatenating the **date** and **time** values from the Secondary data source with a resulting format of **yyyy-MM-ddThh:mm:ss**, which is suitable to be used as the format for the value of a date and time picker control.

16. Add a second **Action** rule to the **date** field under the **times** repeating group in the Secondary data source with a **Condition** that says:

```
selectedTime is not blank
and
theDateAndTime is not blank
```

and that has an action that says:

```
Set a field's value: selectedTime =
concat(substring(theDateAndTime, 1, 10),
substring(selectedTime, 11, 9))
```

This rule ensures that if a time has previously been selected, and you select a different date, the selected time in the drop-down list box is refreshed to reflect the new date and the previously selected time, because the formula concatenates the date part from the date picker and the time part from the drop-down list box. While you may only see a date in the date picker and a time in the drop-down list box, both controls store a date and time as their value. So

```
substring(theDateAndTime, 1, 10)
```

results in the date part of the date picker being extracted, and

```
substring(selectedTime, 11, 9)
```

results in the time part of the value of the selected item in the drop-down list box being extracted (excluding any time zone information).

17. Add a third **Action** rule to the **date** field under the **times** repeating group in the Secondary data source with a **Condition** that says:

```
selectedTime is blank
and
theDateAndTime is not blank
```

and that has an action that says:

```
Set a field's value: selectedTime = theDateAndTime
```

This rule ensures that the first time a date is selected from the date picker, the time in the drop-down list box is automatically set to 12 a.m. if no time has been selected.

18. Click the drop-down list box to select it, and then add an **Action** rule to it with an action that says:

```
Set a field's value: theDateAndTime = .
```

This rule sets the value of the field bound to the date and time picker control to be equal to the date and time value of the item selected in the drop-down list box. This is necessary, because the date and time picker control will have a time of 00:00 when you select a date from the date picker, because its time part will not have been set yet. Its time part should be set when you select a time from the drop-down list box.

19. Click **Data ➤ Rules ➤ Form Load**.

20. On the **Rules** task pane, ensure that **Form Load** is listed under the title bar, and then click **New ➤ Action**, and add two actions that say:

```
Set a field's value: date = substring-before(theDateAndTime,
"T")
Set a field's value: selectedTime = theDateAndTime
```

This rule ensures that when a previously saved form is opened with a previously selected date and time, the correct time is displayed in the drop-down list box.

21. Preview the form.

When the form opens, the drop-down list box should be disabled and you should see 00:00 in it as the time. When you select a date from the date picker control, the drop-down list box should be enabled. Select a time from the drop-down list box, and then save the form somewhere locally on disk. Open the form (XML file) you just saved in Notepad. You should see the date and time picker field with a value that contains your selected date from the date picker and your selected time from the drop-down list box. Double-click the form you saved to open it again in InfoPath Filler 2013. The date and time should be correctly displayed both in the date picker and in the drop-down list box.

Discussion

The trick to understanding the solution described above is to realize that while you are seeing a date in the date picker and a time in the drop-down list box control, the fields that these controls are bound to store a date and time as their value. So any rule you add to set the value of these controls should have a date and time format (**yyyy-MM-ddThh:mm:ss**).

Data from Secondary data sources is never persisted (stored) in the InfoPath form (XML file) itself. In the solution described above, you used a Secondary data source to be able to display a drop-down list box with times and then select a time from this drop-down list box without having all of the date and time values stored in the form once the form was saved. This is a best practice that will keep your forms uncluttered, light, and containing only relevant data.

Tip:

> If you need to use a field purely as a way to perform a calculation or any other processing, and do not need to store the final value of this field in the Main data source of the form, you can use a Secondary data source that contains "helper fields". This will keep data in your forms uncluttered and relevant.

In the solution described above, there are several rules being applied to fields. Whenever you have so many rules that can affect each other, you need to be careful and aware of which field change triggers which rule. You can click **Data ➤ Rules ➤ Rule Inspector** to open the **Rule Inspector** dialog box to view these rules. And if you click on any of the fields (for example **date**) on the left-hand side of the **Rule Inspector** dialog box, the right-hand side should show all of the rules that depend on the field you selected, rules that are triggered by a change in the field, and rules that may change the field. You can always use this information to try to troubleshoot a form that has many rules and is exhibiting unexpected behavior.

The date picker has one action rule that can be triggered:

1. If **theDateAndTime** is not blank (so a date has been entered into the date picker), an action will set the **date** field in the Secondary data source to be equal to the date part of the date picker.

The **date** field in the Secondary data source has 3 action rules that can be triggered:

1. If a change takes place on the **date** field, the **datetime** fields in the Secondary data source are set. This rule always runs.

2. If the **selectedTime** field in the Secondary data source is not blank (so a time has been selected once before from the drop-down list box) and the **theDateAndTime** field in the Main data source is not blank (so a date has been entered into the date picker), then the **selectedTime** field will be set to be equal to a concatenation of the date part of the date picker and the time part of itself, separated by a "T".

3. If the **selectedTime** field in the Secondary data source is blank (so a time has yet to be selected from the drop-down list box for the first time) and the **theDateAndTime** field in the Main data source is not blank (a date has been entered into the date picker), then the **selectedTime** field will be set to be equal to the value of the date picker.

The **selectedTime** field in the Secondary data source has one action rule that can be triggered:

1. If a change takes place on the **selectedTime** field, the date picker (**theDateAndTime** field) is set to be equal to the value of the **selectedTime** field. This rule always runs.

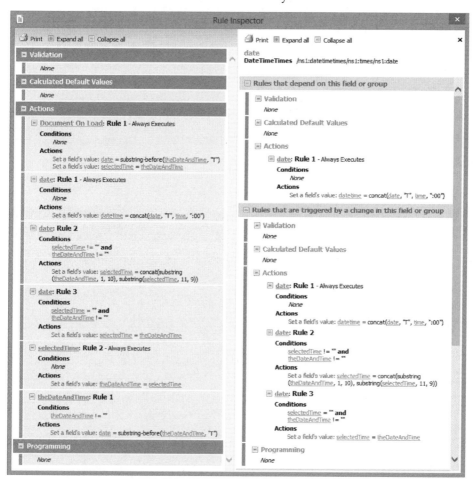

Figure 142. Rule Inspector dialog box showing dependencies on the right-hand side.

Now let us take a look at a few scenarios to see how these rules are triggered and work.

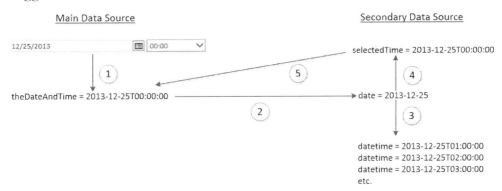

In the figure above, a user enters a date of December 25, 2013 in the date picker. This action causes the following chain of events:

1. The value of the **theDateAndTime** field is set to 2013-12-25T00:00:00. The time is set to 00:00:00, because no time has been selected.

2. Because the value of the **theDateAndTime** field changed from blank to 2013-12-25T00:00:00, it triggers the rule that sets the value of the **date** field in the Secondary data source.

3. Because the value of the **date** field in the Secondary data source changed from an empty string to 2013-12-25, it triggers the rule that sets the **datetime** fields in the Secondary data source.

4. Because the value of the **date** field in the Secondary data source changed from an empty string to 2013-12-25 and **selectedTime** is blank and **theDateAndTime** is not blank, it triggers rule number 3 on the **date** field that sets the value of the **selectedTime** field.

5. Because the value of the **selectedTime** field changed from blank to 2013-12-25T00:00:00, it triggers the rule on the **selectedTime** field that sets the value of the **theDateAndTime** field. And because the **theDateAndTime** field was already set to 2013-12-25T00:00:00, no change takes place, so the rule on the **theDateAndTime** field does not run again, and all actions stop.

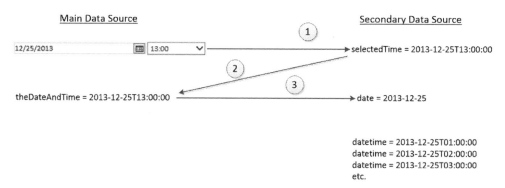

In the figure above, a user selects a time of 13:00 from the drop-down list box. This action causes the following chain of events:

1. The value of the **selectedTime** field is set to 2013-12-25T13:00:00.

2. Because the value of the **selectedTime** field changed from 2013-12-25T00:00:00 to 2013-12-25T13:00:00, it triggers the rule on the **selectedTime** field that sets the value of the **theDateAndTime** field to 2013-12-25T13:00:00.

3. Because the value of the **theDateAndTime** field changed from 2013-12-25T00:00:00 to 2013-12-25T13:00:00, it triggers the rule that sets the value of the **date** field in the Secondary data source. But because the date part of the **theDateAndTime** field is equal to 2013-12-25 and the **date** field in the Secondary data source was already set to this value, no change takes place, so none of the rules on the **date** field are triggered, and all actions stop.

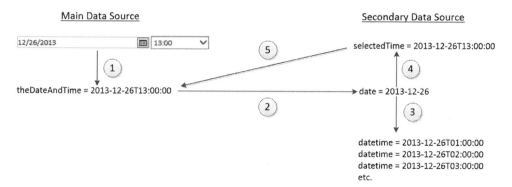

In the figure above, a user changes the date to December 26, 2013 in the date picker. This action causes the following chain of events:

1. The value of the **theDateAndTime** field is set to 2013-12-26T13:00:00.

2. Because the value of the **theDateAndTime** field changed from 2013-12-25T13:00:00 to 2013-12-26T13:00:00, it triggers the rule that sets the value of the **date** field in the Secondary data source.

3. Because the value of the **date** field in the Secondary data source changed from 2013-12-25 to 2013-12-26, it triggers the rule that sets the **datetime** fields in the Secondary data source.

4. Because the value of the **date** field in the Secondary data source changed from 2013-12-25 to 2013-12-26 and **selectedTime** is not blank and **theDateAndTime** is not blank, it triggers rule number 2 on the **date** field that sets the value of the **selectedTime** field.

5. Because the value of the **selectedTime** field changed from 2013-12-25T13:00:00 to 2013-12-26T13:00:00, it triggers the rule on the **selectedTime** field that sets the value of the **theDateAndTime** field. But because the **theDateAndTime** field was already set to this value, no change takes place, and all actions stop.

In the figure above, a user clears the date picker. This action causes the following event:

1. The value of the **theDateAndTime** field is set to NIL (blank). Because the value of the **theDateAndTime** field changed from 2013-12-26T13:00:00 to blank, it does not trigger the rule that sets the value of the **date** field in the Secondary data source, which only runs when the **theDateAndTime** field is not blank, so all actions stop.

Hopefully the scenarios explained above have increased your understanding of how rules are triggered and how changes on one field can have a cascading effect on the values of other fields.

70 Add 7 days to a date in a date picker

Problem

You have two date picker controls on an InfoPath form. You want users to be able to select a date in one date picker and have the other date picker automatically populate itself with a date that lies 7 days in the future.

Solution

You can use the **addDays** function to add an amount of days to a date.

To add 7 days to the date displayed in a date picker:

1. In InfoPath, create a new **Blank Form** template.

2. Add two **Date Picker** controls to the view of the form template. Name the first date picker **selectedDate**, and the second date picker **calculatedDate**.

3. Open the **Date Picker Properties** dialog box of the **calculatedDate** date picker, and then set the **Default Value** to be equal to the following formula:

    ```
    addDays(selectedDate, 7)
    ```

    This formula adds 7 days to **selectedDate** and returns the result as a date.

4. Preview the form.

When the form opens, select a date from the first date picker. The date in the second date picker should automatically get calculated and set to be equal to a date that lies 7 days in the future.

Discussion

The **addDays** function adds days to a date or date and time value. The **addDays** function accepts two arguments: The first argument is the date you want to add a number of days to, and the second argument is the amount of days you want to add to the date.

If you want to add an amount of days to the date of a **Date and Time Picker** control instead of a **Date Picker** control, you can use the **addSeconds** function instead of the **addDays** function.

The **addSeconds** function adds seconds to a time or date and time, and takes two arguments: A time and the amount of seconds to add.

There are 60 seconds in a minute, 60 minutes in an hour, and 24 hours in a day. Suppose you want to add 3 days and 5 hours to the date and time specified in a **Date and Time Picker** control, you would have to specify a total amount of 277200 seconds (3 days x 24 hours x 60 minutes x 60 seconds + 5 hours x 60 minutes x 60 seconds) as the second argument of the **addSeconds** function.

Exercise

The same way you can add days to a date, you can subtract days from a date by placing a minus sign before the amount of days, so for example:

```
addDays(selectedDate, -7)
```

Try it out!

Exercise

Add a **Date and Time Picker** control to the form template and set its **Default Value** to be equal to 9 days and 3 hours in the future starting from today. Hint: You must use the **now** function as the first argument of the **addSeconds** function.

71 Check whether a start date falls before an end date

Problem

You have start and end date picker controls on an InfoPath form and want to ensure that the start date always falls before the end date.

Solution

You can use a **Validation** rule and the fact that dates in InfoPath are represented by strings that can easily be compared with each other to check whether the start date falls before the end date.

To check whether a start date falls before an end date:

1. In InfoPath, create a new **Blank Form** template.

2. Add two **Date Picker** controls to the view of the form template. Name the first date picker **startDate** and the second date picker **endDate**.

3. Click the **startDate** date picker to select it, and then select **Home ➤ Rules ➤ Add Rule ➤ Is After ➤ Show Validation Error**.

4. On the **Rule Details** dialog box, click the formula button behind the text box.

5. On the **Insert Formula** dialog box, click **Insert Field or Group**.

6. On the **Select a Field or Group** dialog box, select **endDate**, and click **OK**.

7. On the **Insert Formula** dialog box, click **OK**.

8. On the **Rule Details** dialog box, click **OK**. The **Rules** task pane should automatically open if it was not already being displayed. On the **Rules** task pane, InfoPath should have created a **Validation** rule that has a **Condition** that says:

```
startDate > endDate
and
startDate is not blank
```

and the **ScreenTip** "Enter a date on or before endDate". You can change the screen tip if you wish.

9.   Preview the form.

When the form opens, select an end date and then enter a start date that falls after the end date. A red dashed border should appear around the start date and when you hover with the mouse pointer over it, you should see the screen tip appear. Enter a start date that falls before the end date. The red dashed border should disappear.

Discussion

In a similar way as described in the solution above, you can also add a **Validation** rule to the **endDate** date picker to check whether the end date falls before the start date. The only difference is that you must use the **Is Before** menu item instead of the **Is After** menu item when adding the rule to the **endDate** date picker.

Remember, the **Add Rule** command on the **Home** tab under the **Rules** group provides shortcuts to adding rules in InfoPath. You can also use the **Manage Rules** command to construct and add similar rules yourself.

If you click on the condition for the **Validation** rule on the **Rules** task pane, and then select **The expression** from the first drop-down list box for each expression in the condition, you should see the following two expressions appear:

```
msxsl:string-compare(., ../my:endDate) > 0

. != ""
```

As you can see from the first expression, InfoPath uses a function that compares strings when doing a date comparison. The **msxsl:string-compare** function is not accessible via the **Insert Function** dialog box, but you can still type it in manually and use it on the **Insert Formula** dialog box. The **msxsl:string-compare** function takes two strings as its arguments, compares them alphabetically, and returns:

- 0 if both strings are the same.

- -1 if the first string is less than the second string, so the first string falls before the second string.

- 1 if the first string is greater than the second string, so the first string falls after the second string.

Question

1. Knowing what you now know about the **msxsl:string-compare** function, what would the following expression return?

```
msxsl:string-compare("01", "1")
```

72 Keep two date pickers within a 7-day date range from each other

Problem

You have two date picker controls on an InfoPath form and want to check whether the dates are within 7 days of each other.

Solution

You can use a **Validation** rule to prevent two dates from being more than 7 days apart from each other.

To keep two date pickers within a 7-day date range from each other:

1. In InfoPath, create a new **Blank Form** template.

2. Add two **Date Picker** controls to the view of the form template and name them **startDate** and **endDate**, respectively.

3. Add a **Validation** rule to the **endDate** date picker that has a **Condition** that says:

```
startDate is not blank
and
endDate is not blank
and
endDate > addDays(startDate, 7)
```

and the **ScreenTip** "Enter a date that falls within 7 days from the start date". Note: To construct the third expression for the condition, on the **Condition** dialog box, you must select **endDate** from the first drop-down list box, select **is greater than** from the second drop-down list box, select **Use a formula** from the third drop-down list box, and then construct the formula using the **addDays** function.

4. Preview the form.

When the form opens, select a start date, and then select an end date that is more than 7 days in the future. A red dashed border should appear around the end date, and when you hover over the end date, the screen tip message you specified earlier should appear. Now select an end date that is within 7 days from the start date. The red dashed border should disappear.

Discussion

The following condition on the **Validation** rule in the solution described above prevents the rule from running if either a start date or an end date has not been entered (so is blank):

```
startDate is not blank
and
endDate is not blank
```

You can use the technique described in the solution above to also check dates in the past by subtracting days using the **addDays** function. For example, if you want to check whether the start date falls in the past but stays within 7 days of the end date, then you can use the formula

```
addDays(endDate, -7)
```

when constructing the condition for a **Validation** rule on the **startDate** date picker.

73 Calculate a person's age based on a date of birth in a date picker

Problem

You have a date picker control on an InfoPath form that is used to enter a date of birth. You want to be able to calculate a person's age from the selected date of birth.

Solution

You can use **Action** rules with conditions to calculate an age based on a date of birth selected in a date picker control.

To calculate a person's age based on a date of birth entered in a date picker:

1. In InfoPath, create a new **Blank Form** template.

2. Add a **Date Picker** control to the view of the form template and name it **dob**.

3. Add a **Text Box** control to the view of the form template, name it **age**, change its data type to **Whole Number (integer)**, and set it to be **Read-only**.

4. Add an **Action** rule to the date picker control without a condition and with the following action:

    ```
    Set a field's value: age = number(substring(today(), 1, 4)) -
    number(substring(., 1, 4))
    ```

    This rule calculates the amount of years between the current year and the birth year.

5. Add a second **Action** rule to the date picker control that has a **Condition** that says:

    ```
    number(substring(xdDate:Today(), 9, 2)) <
    number(substring(../my:dob, 9, 2))
    and
    number(substring(xdDate:Today(), 6, 2)) =
    number(substring(../my:dob, 6, 2))
    or
    ```

```
number(substring(xdDate:Today(), 6, 2)) <
number(substring(../my:dob, 6, 2))
```

and that has the following action:

```
Set a field's value: age = number(substring(today(), 1, 4)) -
number(substring(., 1, 4)) - 1
```

This rule subtracts 1 year from the age if the current date falls within the same month but before the day of birth or if the current month falls before the month of the date of birth. Note: To construct each expression for the condition listed above, select **The expression** from the first dropdown list box on the **Condition** dialog box and then enter the expression.

6.   Add a third **Action** rule to the date picker control that has a **Condition** that says:

```
age < 0
```

and that has the following action:

```
Set a field's value: age = 0
```

This rule sets the age to be equal to 0 if the calculated age is less than 0.

7.   Preview the form.

When the form opens, enter any date of birth and see whether the age is calculated correctly. Note: You can type the date directly into the date picker control instead of using the calendar of the date picker control to select a date. For example, you can type **1985-03-21** directly into the date picker. The date should then be correctly reformatted by InfoPath and the calculated age should appear in the text box.

Discussion

The solution described above makes use of the fact that **Action** rules run in order from top to bottom (see the section about *Action rules* in Chapter 4). This means that when the first rule has run, the age is set to a certain amount of years. This value is overwritten by rule 2 (the one that subtracts 1 year from the age) if the person's day of birth has yet to take place in the current year. And finally, rule 3 overwrites the age with a zero, if the calculated age from any of the two previous rules resulted in a number less than zero.

If the expressions for the condition in the solution above look like magic to you, review the tip given in recipe *66 Set a date picker to display the previous month in its calendar* that explains making use of a technique when constructing formulas to be used as expressions in conditions for rules.

74 Calculate the difference in days between a date picker and today

Problem

You have a date picker control on an InfoPath form and want to know how many days there are between the current date (today) and the selected date in the date picker.

Solution

You can use the Julian Day formula as described on Wikipedia (see `http://en.wikipedia.org/wiki/Julian_day`) to calculate the difference between today and a date picker using **Action** rules.

To calculate the difference in days between the selected date in a date picker and today:

1. In InfoPath, create a new **Blank Form** template.

2. Add a **Date Picker** control to the view of the form template and name it **selectedDate**.

3. On the **Fields** task pane under the **selectedDate** field, add a **Field (attribute)** named **jdn_selectedDate** of data type **Text (string)**.

4. On the **Fields** task pane under the **myFields** group, add a **Field (element)** with the name **currentDate**, the data type **Date (date)**, and a **Default Value** equal to the following formula:

```
today()
```

Note that to set the **Default Value**, you must open the **Field or Group Properties** dialog box after adding the field to the Main data source.

5.   On the **Fields** task pane under the **currentDate** field, add a **Field (attribute)** named **jdn_currentDate** of data type **Text (string)**.

6.   Add a **Text Box** control named **difference** to the view of the form template, and select the **Read-only** property of the text box.

7.   On the **Fields** task pane under the **myFields** group, add a group named **JulianDayCalculator**.

8.   On the **Fields** task pane under the **JulianDayCalculator** group, add 7 fields of type **Field (element)** with the data type **Whole Number (integer)** and the following names: **day, month, year, a, y, m, JDN**.

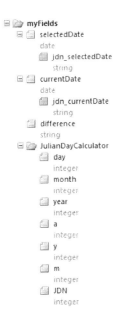

Figure 143. Main data source of the InfoPath form.

9.   Set the **Default Value** of field **a** to be equal to the following formula:

```
(14 - ../my:month) div 12
```

Note: You must click the formula button behind the **Value** text box on the **Field or Group Properties** dialog box to open the **Insert Formula** dialog box and enter the formula.

10. Set the **Default Value** of field **y** to be equal to the following formula:

```
../my:year + 4800 - ../my:a
```

11. Set the **Default Value** of field **m** to be equal to the following formula:

```
../my:month + 12 * ../my:a - 3
```

12. Set the **Default Value** of field **JDN** to be equal to the following formula:

```
../my:day + ((153 * ../my:m + 2) div 5) + 365 * ../my:y +
(../my:y div 4) - (../my:y div 100) + (../my:y div 400) - 32045
```

13. Add an **Action** rule to the **selectedDate** field with the following actions:

```
Set a field's value: day = number(substring(., 9, 2))
Set a field's value: month = number(substring(., 6, 2))
Set a field's value: year = number(substring(., 1, 4))
Set a field's value: @jdn_selectedDate = JDN
```

This rule sets the day, month, and year for the Julian Day calculator based on the values from the selected date and then calculates the Julian Day Number (JDN) for the selected date.

14. Add a second **Action** rule to the **selectedDate** field with the following actions:

```
Set a field's value: day = number(substring(currentDate, 9, 2))
Set a field's value: month = number(substring(currentDate, 6,
2))
Set a field's value: year = number(substring(currentDate, 1,
4))
Set a field's value: @jdn_currentDate = JDN
Set a field's value: difference =
ceiling(number(@jdn_selectedDate) - number(@jdn_currentDate))
```

This rule sets the day, month, and year for the Julian Day calculator based on the values from the current date, calculates the Julian Day Number (JDN) for the current date, and then calculates the difference between the selected date and the current date.

15. Preview the form.

When the form opens, select a date that lies in the future. A positive amount of days should appear in the **difference** text box. And then select a date that lies in the past. A negative amount of days should appear in the **difference** text box.

Discussion

The Julian Day formula calculates a number for a certain date in time. The solution described above calculates the Julian Day Number for the selected date and the Julian Day Number for the current date and then subtracts them from each other to find the difference.

The first **Action** rule calculates the Julian Day Number for the selected date. By setting the values of the **day**, **month**, and **year** fields under the **JulianDayCalculator** group, the values of the **a**, **y**, **m**, and **JDN** fields are recalculated. And then the last action in this rule is to temporarily store the result of the calculation in the **@jdn_selectedDate** attribute under the **selectedDate** field.

The second **Action** rule calculates the Julian Day Number for the current date. By setting the values of the **day**, **month**, and **year** fields under the **JulianDayCalculator** group, the values of the **a**, **y**, **m**, and **JDN** fields are recalculated. The result of the calculation is then temporarily stored in the **@jdn_currentDate** attribute under the **currentDate** field.

And finally, the difference between **@jdn_selectedDate** and **@jdn_currentDate** is calculated to give you the date difference. The **ceiling** function is used in the final date difference calculation to round the difference up to the nearest integer and prevent decimals from appearing in the result.

Note: Because actions in a rule are also executed from top to bottom just like rules are executed from top to bottom, you could have combined the two **Action** rules into one big **Action** rule containing 9 actions. The solution described above splits them up into two **Action** rules for clarity.

Caveat: Date difference calculations using the Julian Day formula may produce incorrect amounts of days when calculating negative differences for dates in different months.

75 Calculate the difference in days between two date pickers

Problem

You have two date picker controls on an InfoPath form and want to know how many days there are between the two dates.

Solution

You can use the Julian Day formula as described on Wikipedia (see `http://en.wikipedia.org/wiki/Julian_day`) to calculate the difference between two date picker controls using **Action** rules.

To calculate the difference in days between two date picker controls:

1. In InfoPath, create a new **Blank Form** template.

2. Add a **Date Picker** control to the view of the form template and name it **startDate**.

3. On the **Fields** task pane under the **startDate** field, add a **Field (attribute)** named **jdn_startDate** of data type **Text (string)**.

4. Add a **Date Picker** control to the view of the form template and name it **endDate**.

5. On the **Fields** task pane under the **endDate** field, add a **Field (attribute)** named **jdn_endDate** of data type **Text (string)**.

6. Add a **Text Box** control named **difference** to the view of the form template and make the text box **Read-only**.

7. On the **Fields** task pane under the **myFields** group, add a group named **JulianDayCalculator**.

8. On the **Fields** task pane under the **JulianDayCalculator** group, add 7 fields of type **Field (element)** with the data type **Whole Number (integer)** and the following names: **day, month, year, a, y, m, JDN**.

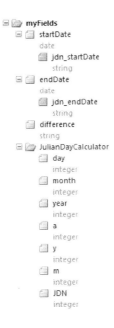

Figure 144. Main data source of the InfoPath form.

9. Set the **Default Value** of field **a** to be equal to the following formula:

```
(14 - ../my:month) div 12
```

Note: You must click the formula button behind the **Value** text box on the **Field or Group Properties** dialog box to open the **Insert Formula** dialog box and enter the formula.

10. Set the **Default Value** of field **y** to be equal to the following formula:

```
../my:year + 4800 - ../my:a
```

11. Set the **Default Value** of field **m** to be equal to the following formula:

```
../my:month + 12 * ../my:a - 3
```

12. Set the **Default Value** of field **JDN** to be equal to the following formula:

```
../my:day + ((153 * ../my:m + 2) div 5) + 365 * ../my:y +
(../my:y div 4) - (../my:y div 100) + (../my:y div 400) - 32045
```

13. Add an **Action** rule to the **startDate** field with the following 8 actions:

```
Set a field's value: day = number(substring(., 9, 2))
Set a field's value: month = number(substring(., 6, 2))
Set a field's value: year = number(substring(., 1, 4))
Set a field's value: @jdn_startDate = JDN
Set a field's value: day = number(substring(endDate, 9, 2))
Set a field's value: month = number(substring(endDate, 6, 2))
Set a field's value: year = number(substring(endDate, 1, 4))
Set a field's value: @jdn_endDate = JDN
```

This rule calculates the Julian Day Number (JDN) first for the start date and then for the end date when a start date is entered.

14. Add a second **Action** rule to the **startDate** field with a **Condition** that says:

```
startDate is not blank
and
endDate is not blank
```

and that has the following action:

```
Set a field's value: difference = ceiling(number(@jdn_endDate)
- number(@jdn_startDate))
```

This rule calculates the date difference if both the start date and the end date have been entered.

15. Add an **Action** rule to the **endDate** field with the following 8 actions:

```
Set a field's value: day = number(substring(., 9, 2))
Set a field's value: month = number(substring(., 6, 2))
Set a field's value: year = number(substring(., 1, 4))
Set a field's value: @jdn_endDate = JDN
Set a field's value: day = number(substring(startDate, 9, 2))
Set a field's value: month = number(substring(startDate, 6, 2))
```

```
Set a field's value: year = number(substring(startDate, 1, 4))
Set a field's value: @jdn_startDate = JDN
```

This rule calculates the Julian Day Number (JDN) first for the end date and then for the start date when an end date is entered.

16. Add a second **Action** rule to the **endDate** field with a **Condition** that says:

```
startDate is not blank
and
endDate is not blank
```

and that has the following action:

```
Set a field's value: difference = ceiling(number(@jdn_endDate)
- number(@jdn_startDate))
```

This rule calculates the date difference if both the start date and the end date have been entered.

17. Preview the form.

When the form opens, select a date for the start date and then a date that lies in the future for the end date. The date difference should appear in the **difference** text box and should be a positive amount of days. Select an end date that lies in the past. A negative amount of days should appear in the **difference** text box.

Discussion

The Julian Day formula calculates a number for a certain date in time. The solution described above follows the same logic as that described in the discussion section of recipe *74 Calculate the difference in days between a date picker and today* where the selected date can be seen as the end date and the current date can be seen as the start date.

76 Calculate the difference between two dates in a repeating table

Problem

You have two date picker controls that are located within a repeating table control on an InfoPath form and want to calculate the difference between two dates that are entered on any row of the repeating table.

Solution

You can use the Julian Day formula as described on Wikipedia (see `http://en.wikipedia.org/wiki/Julian_day`) to calculate the difference between two date picker controls that are located in a repeating table control on an InfoPath form.

To calculate the difference in days between two date picker controls in a repeating table control:

1. In InfoPath, create a new **Blank Form** template.

2. Add a **Repeating Table** control with 3 columns to the view of the form template. Name the fields in the repeating table **startDate**, **endDate**, and **difference**, respectively.

3. Change the **startDate** and **endDate** text boxes into date picker controls as described in recipe *6 Change a text box into a date picker*.

4. Make the **difference** text box **Read-Only**.

5. Add an **Action** rule to the **startDate** field with a **Condition** that says:

```
startDate is not blank
and
endDate is not blank
```

and that has the following action:

```
Set a field's value: difference = ((number(substring(endDate,
9, 2))) + ((153 * ((number(substring(endDate, 6, 2))) + 12 *
((14 - (number(substring(endDate, 6, 2)))) / 12) - 3) + 2) / 5)
+ 365 * ((number(substring(endDate, 1, 4))) + 4800 - ((14 -
```

```
(number(substring(endDate, 6, 2)))) / 12)) +
(((number(substring(endDate, 1, 4))) + 4800 - ((14 -
(number(substring(endDate, 6, 2)))) / 12)) / 4) -
(((number(substring(endDate, 1, 4))) + 4800 - ((14 -
(number(substring(endDate, 6, 2)))) / 12)) / 100) +
(((number(substring(endDate, 1, 4))) + 4800 - ((14 -
(number(substring(endDate, 6, 2)))) / 12)) / 400) - 32045) -
((number(substring(., 9, 2))) + ((153 * ((number(substring(.,
6, 2))) + 12 * ((14 - (number(substring(., 6, 2)))) / 12) - 3)
+ 2) / 5) + 365 * ((number(substring(., 1, 4))) + 4800 - ((14 -
(number(substring(., 6, 2)))) / 12)) + (((number(substring(.,
1, 4))) + 4800 - ((14 - (number(substring(., 6, 2)))) / 12)) /
4) - (((number(substring(., 1, 4))) + 4800 - ((14 -
(number(substring(., 6, 2)))) / 12)) / 100) +
(((number(substring(., 1, 4))) + 4800 - ((14 -
(number(substring(., 6, 2)))) / 12)) / 400) - 32045)
```

This rule calculates the date difference if both the start date and the end date have been entered. See the discussion section for how you can construct the formula.

6. Add an **Action** rule to the **endDate** field with a **Condition** that says:

```
startDate is not blank
and
endDate is not blank
```

and that has the following action:

```
Set a field's value: difference = ((number(substring(., 9, 2)))
+ ((153 * ((number(substring(., 6, 2))) + 12 * ((14 -
(number(substring(., 6, 2)))) / 12) - 3) + 2) / 5) + 365 *
((number(substring(., 1, 4))) + 4800 - ((14 -
(number(substring(., 6, 2)))) / 12)) + (((number(substring(.,
1, 4))) + 4800 - ((14 - (number(substring(., 6, 2)))) / 12)) /
4) - (((number(substring(., 1, 4))) + 4800 - ((14 -
(number(substring(., 6, 2)))) / 12)) / 100) +
(((number(substring(., 1, 4))) + 4800 - ((14 -
(number(substring(., 6, 2)))) / 12)) / 400) - 32045) -
((number(substring(startDate, 9, 2))) + ((153 *
((number(substring(startDate, 6, 2))) + 12 * ((14 -
(number(substring(startDate, 6, 2)))) / 12) - 3) + 2) / 5) +
365 * ((number(substring(startDate, 1, 4))) + 4800 - ((14 -
(number(substring(startDate, 6, 2)))) / 12)) +
(((number(substring(startDate, 1, 4))) + 4800 - ((14 -
(number(substring(startDate, 6, 2)))) / 12)) / 4) -
```

```
(((number(substring(startDate, 1, 4))) + 4800 - ((14 -
(number(substring(startDate, 6, 2)))) / 12)) / 100) +
(((number(substring(startDate, 1, 4))) + 4800 - ((14 -
(number(substring(startDate, 6, 2)))) / 12)) / 400) - 32045)
```

This rule calculates the date difference if both the start date and the end date have been entered. See the discussion section for how you can construct the formula.

7. Preview the form.

When the form opens, select a date for the start date and then a date that lies in the future for the end date. The date difference should appear in the **difference** text box and should be a positive amount of days. Select an end date that lies in the past. A negative amount of days should appear in the **difference** text box. Add a second row to the repeating table and select dates again. The difference for the second row should appear.

Discussion

The solution described above makes use of the same technique described in recipe *75 Calculate the difference in days between two date pickers* with the difference that all of the separate parts of the formula have been joined together to form one big formula.

The base formula to calculate the Julian Day Number (JDN) is as follows:

```
../my:day + ((153 * ../my:m + 2) div 5) + 365 * ../my:y + (../my:y
div 4) - (../my:y div 100) + (../my:y div 400) - 32045
```

To get one big formula that contains all of the separate calculations, you must replace the individual fields with their corresponding formulas as listed in the following table.

Field	Replace with Formula
`../my:a`	`((14 - ../my:month) div 12)`

Field	Replace with Formula
../my:y	(../my:year + 4800 - ../my:a)
../my:m	(../my:month + 12 * ../my:a - 3)
../my:day	(number(substring(., 9, 2)))
../my:month	(number(substring(., 6, 2)))
../my:year	(number(substring(., 1, 4)))

Once you have replaced all of the fields, you should wind up with a formula such as the following:

```
(number(substring(., 9, 2))) + ((153 * ((number(substring(., 6,
2))) + 12 * ((14 - (number(substring(., 6, 2)))) div 12) - 3) + 2)
div 5) + 365 * ((number(substring(., 1, 4))) + 4800 - ((14 -
(number(substring(., 6, 2)))) div 12)) + (((number(substring(., 1,
4))) + 4800 - ((14 - (number(substring(., 6, 2)))) div 12)) div 4)
- (((number(substring(., 1, 4))) + 4800 - ((14 -
(number(substring(., 6, 2)))) div 12)) div 100) +
(((number(substring(., 1, 4))) + 4800 - ((14 - (number(substring(.,
6, 2)))) div 12)) div 400) - 32045
```

The formula above runs on the context node (the dot in the formula) and calculates the Julian Day Number for either the **startDate** or the **endDate** field. To calculate the Julian Day Number for the value of the **endDate** field when the context node is the **startDate** field, you must replace all of the dots in the formula above with

```
../my:endDate
```

which should then result in the following formula:

```
(number(substring(../my:endDate, 9, 2))) + ((153 *
((number(substring(../my:endDate, 6, 2))) + 12 * ((14 -
(number(substring(../my:endDate, 6, 2)))) div 12) - 3) + 2) div 5)
+ 365 * ((number(substring(../my:endDate, 1, 4))) + 4800 - ((14 -
(number(substring(../my:endDate, 6, 2)))) div 12)) +
(((number(substring(../my:endDate, 1, 4))) + 4800 - ((14 -
(number(substring(../my:endDate, 6, 2)))) div 12)) div 4) -
(((number(substring(../my:endDate, 1, 4))) + 4800 - ((14 -
(number(substring(../my:endDate, 6, 2)))) div 12)) div 100) +
(((number(substring(../my:endDate, 1, 4))) + 4800 - ((14 -
(number(substring(../my:endDate, 6, 2)))) div 12)) div 400) - 32045
```

So the formula above calculates the Julian Day Number for the **endDate** field when the calculation is being performed from within the **startDate** field (the context node).

To get the final difference between the two Julian Day Numbers (JDN), you must subtract the first formula from the second formula as in

```
(JDN formula for endDate) - (JDN formula for startDate)
```

which should result in the following big formula:

```
((number(substring(../my:endDate, 9, 2))) + ((153 *
((number(substring(../my:endDate, 6, 2))) + 12 * ((14 -
(number(substring(../my:endDate, 6, 2)))) div 12) - 3) + 2) div 5)
+ 365 * ((number(substring(../my:endDate, 1, 4))) + 4800 - ((14 -
(number(substring(../my:endDate, 6, 2)))) div 12)) +
(((number(substring(../my:endDate, 1, 4))) + 4800 - ((14 -
(number(substring(../my:endDate, 6, 2)))) div 12)) div 4) -
(((number(substring(../my:endDate, 1, 4))) + 4800 - ((14 -
(number(substring(../my:endDate, 6, 2)))) div 12)) div 100) +
(((number(substring(../my:endDate, 1, 4))) + 4800 - ((14 -
(number(substring(../my:endDate, 6, 2)))) div 12)) div 400) -
32045)
 -
((number(substring(., 9, 2))) + ((153 * ((number(substring(., 6,
2))) + 12 * ((14 - (number(substring(., 6, 2)))) div 12) - 3) + 2)
div 5) + 365 * ((number(substring(., 1, 4))) + 4800 - ((14 -
(number(substring(., 6, 2)))) div 12)) + (((number(substring(., 1,
4))) + 4800 - ((14 - (number(substring(., 6, 2)))) div 12)) div 4)
- (((number(substring(., 1, 4))) + 4800 - ((14 -
(number(substring(., 6, 2)))) div 12)) div 100) +
(((number(substring(., 1, 4))) + 4800 - ((14 - (number(substring(.,
6, 2)))) div 12)) div 400) - 32045)
```

288

You can then use the formula above in an **Action** rule on the **startDate** field to set the value of the **difference** field.

You must then go through the same process to construct a big formula that calculates the difference between the **startDate** and the **endDate** fields when the calculation is being performed from within the **endDate** field (the context node). That formula should resemble the following:

```
((number(substring(., 9, 2))) + ((153 * ((number(substring(., 6,
2))) + 12 * ((14 - (number(substring(., 6, 2)))) div 12) - 3) + 2)
div 5) + 365 * ((number(substring(., 1, 4))) + 4800 - ((14 -
(number(substring(., 6, 2)))) div 12)) + (((number(substring(., 1,
4))) + 4800 - ((14 - (number(substring(., 6, 2)))) div 12)) div 4)
- (((number(substring(., 1, 4))) + 4800 - ((14 -
(number(substring(., 6, 2)))) div 12)) div 100) +
(((number(substring(., 1, 4))) + 4800 - ((14 - (number(substring(.,
6, 2)))) div 12)) div 400) - 32045)
     -
((number(substring(../my:startDate, 9, 2))) + ((153 *
((number(substring(../my:startDate, 6, 2))) + 12 * ((14 -
(number(substring(../my:startDate, 6, 2)))) div 12) - 3) + 2) div
5) + 365 * ((number(substring(../my:startDate, 1, 4))) + 4800 -
((14 - (number(substring(../my:startDate, 6, 2)))) div 12)) +
(((number(substring(../my:startDate, 1, 4))) + 4800 - ((14 -
(number(substring(../my:startDate, 6, 2)))) div 12)) div 4) -
(((number(substring(../my:startDate, 1, 4))) + 4800 - ((14 -
(number(substring(../my:startDate, 6, 2)))) div 12)) div 100) +
(((number(substring(../my:startDate, 1, 4))) + 4800 - ((14 -
(number(substring(../my:startDate, 6, 2)))) div 12)) div 400) -
32045)
```

Note:

You may have noticed that the Julian Day Number formula does not always return a whole number, for example when the start date and the end date are in different months. To correct this issue, you can nest the formulas from steps 5 and 6 in the **ceiling** function to convert the result of the date difference calculation into a whole number if the end date is greater than the start date (a positive date difference). For example:

```
ceiling( [date difference formula goes here] )
```

77 Count the amount of holidays between two date pickers

Problem

You have two date picker controls on an InfoPath form and a list of dates for holidays and weekends in an XML file. You want users to be able to enter two dates and then display the amount of holidays between those two dates on the InfoPath form.

Solution

You can use a filter and the **count** function in InfoPath to determine how many of the dates listed in the XML file fall between dates specified in two date picker controls.

To count the amount of holidays between two date pickers:

1. In Notepad, create an XML file that has the following contents representing dates for holidays and weekends:

    ```
    <holidays>
      <holiday><date>2013-06-30</date></holiday>
      <holiday><date>2013-07-04</date></holiday>
      <holiday><date>2013-07-06</date></holiday>
      <holiday><date>2013-07-07</date></holiday>
    </holidays>
    ```

    and name the file **holidays.xml**. Note: You must fill this XML file with all of the dates for holidays and weekends you would like to account for.

2. In InfoPath, create a new **Blank Form** template.

3. Add a **Receive data** connection that gets data from the **holidays.xml** file (see recipe *33 Get data from an XML file*) and name the data connection **holidays**.

4. Add two **Date Picker** controls to the view of the form template and name them **startDate** and **endDate**, respectively.

5. Add a **Button** control to the view of the form template and label it **Calculate**.

6. Add a **Text Box** control to the view of the form template and name it **nonBusinessDays**.

7. Click the **Calculate** button to select it, and then click **Home ➤ Rules ➤ Manage Rules**.

8. On the **Rules** task pane, click **New ➤ Action**.

9. On the **Rules** task pane, click **Add ➤ Set a field's value**.

10. On the **Rule Details** dialog box, click the button behind the **Field** text box.

11. On the **Select a Field or Group** dialog box, leave **Main** selected in the drop-down list box, select the **nonBusinessDays** field, and click **OK**.

12. On the **Rule Details** dialog box, click the formula button behind the **Value** text box.

13. On the **Insert Formula** dialog box, click **Insert Field or Group**.

14. On the **Select a Field or Group** dialog box, select **holidays (Secondary)** from the drop-down list box, expand the **holiday** repeating group, select **date**, and then click **Filter Data**.

15. On the **Filter Data** dialog box, click **Add**.

16. On the **Specify Filter Conditions** dialog box, leave **date** selected in the first drop-down list box, select **is greater than or equal to** from the second drop-down list box, and then select **Select a field or group** from the third drop-down list box.

17. On the **Select a Field or Group** dialog box, select **Main** from the drop-down list box, select **startDate**, and click **OK**. With this you have specified that a **date** in the **holidays** Secondary data source should be greater than or equal to the **startDate** field which is bound to the first date picker control.

18. On the **Specify Filter Conditions** dialog box, click **And** to add a second condition.

19. Repeat steps 16 and 17, but then select **is less than or equal to** from the second drop-down list box, and select **endDate** in the **Main** data source for the third drop-down list box.

20. On the **Specify Filter Conditions** dialog box, click **OK**.

21. On the **Filter Data** dialog box, the filter condition should now say:

```
date ≥ startDate
and
date ≤ endDate
```

What this filter condition does is allow a **date** to be returned from the **holidays** Secondary data source if that **date** falls on or between the **startDate** and the **endDate** specified in the Main data source of the form. Click **OK**.

22. On the **Select a Field or Group** dialog box, click **OK**. The formula on the **Insert Formula** dialog box should now say:

```
date[msxsl:string-compare(., startDate) >= 0 and msxsl:string-
compare(., endDate) <= 0]
```

The entire formula now returns a node-set that contains all of the **date** fields in the **holidays** Secondary data source that fall on or between the **startDate** and **endDate** specified in the Main data source.

23. The last step is to count the amount of **date** fields returned by the formula, so that you can display how many dates that fall on or between the date picker dates are holidays. On the **Insert Formula** dialog box, manually modify the formula by placing a **count** function around it as follows:

```
count( formula goes here )
```

So the final formula should resemble the following:

```
count(date[msxsl:string-compare(., startDate) >= 0 and
msxsl:string-compare(., endDate) <= 0])
```

or

```
count(xdXDocument:GetDOM("holidays")/holidays/holiday/date[msxs
l:string-compare(., xdXDocument:get-
DOM()/my:myFields/my:startDate) >= 0 and msxsl:string-
compare(., xdXDocument:get-DOM()/my:myFields/my:endDate) <= 0])
```

if you have the **Edit XPath (advanced)** check box selected on the
Insert Formula dialog box.

24. On the **Insert Formula** dialog box, click **Verify Formula** to ensure
that the formula does not contain any errors, and then click **OK**.

25. On the **Rule Details** dialog box, click **OK**. The action on the **Rules**
task pane should now say:

```
Set a field 's value: nonBusinessDays =
count(date[msxsl:string-compare(., startDate) >= 0 and
msxsl:string-compare(., endDate) <= 0])
```

26. Preview the form.

When the form opens, select a start date and an end date from the date
picker controls, thereby keeping in mind which dates are currently present
in the **holidays.xml** file. Click the **Calculate** button and verify that the
amount returned is indeed the amount of holidays between the two dates
you specified through the date pickers.

Discussion

In the solution described above, you used the **Filter Data** button on the
Select a Field or Group dialog box to construct a filter expression that
could filter the entries in the Secondary data source based on the values of
fields in the Main data source of the InfoPath form. This filter expression
was used to be able to return a node-set containing **date** fields in the
holidays Secondary data source that satisfied a condition.

You then used the result of the filtering within the **count** function. The
count function counts the number of instances of a field or group. You can
use it on a repeating field or a repeating group. In this case, you used the
count function to be able to count the amount of **date** fields in the

holidays Secondary data source that fell on or between the specified start date and end date.

While you used an XML file containing dates for holidays in this recipe, you could have also used for example a SharePoint list or a database table containing dates for holidays, which should make the process of having to manually maintain the list of holidays easier, since you would not have to update the form template every time you update the list of holidays.

Note that if you do not want to use a Secondary data source that is manually populated with dates for holidays and weekends, so that you can perform a calculation in InfoPath, you must either write code or find another solution that does not involve having to manually maintain a list of holidays and weekends.

Exercise

Try to combine this recipe with recipe *75 Calculate the difference in days between two date pickers* to come up with a solution that calculates the difference between two date pickers, and excludes holidays and weekends that are listed in an XML file.

Multiple-Section List Boxes

A **Multiple-Selection List Box** is a close cousin of the **Drop-Down List Box** and the normal **List Box** with the difference that you have the ability to select and store multiple items in it instead of just one.

Figure 145. Multiple-Selection List Box in InfoPath 2013.

And because a multiple-selection list box is a close cousin of the other types of list boxes in InfoPath, you can populate it by using the same technique you used to populate a drop-down list box (see recipe *52 Populate a drop-down list box with static items*, recipe *53 Populate a drop-down list box with data from a repeating table*, and recipe *54 Populate a drop-down list box with data from an XML file*).

The big difference between a multiple-selection list box and the other types of list boxes in InfoPath is the data source structure. A multiple-selection list box must be bound to a repeating field instead of a non-repeating field as is the case with other types of list boxes.

When you look at the data source structure for a field bound to a multiple-selection list box, you will see a similar structure on the **Fields** task pane as the one shown in the following figure.

Figure 146. Data source structure for a field bound to a Multiple-Selection List Box.

In the figure shown above, **field1** is the field that is bound to a multiple-selection list box. As you can see from the small blue icon with an arrow on the field, the field is a repeating field, which means that **group1**, which serves as the container for **field1**, will contain multiple **field1** nodes in it once you select multiple items from the multiple-selection list box. To fully understand how this works, add a multiple-selection list box to a form template, populate it with a few items, preview the form, select a few items, save the form locally on disk, and then open the form (XML file) in Notepad.

78 Select one or more items by default in a multi-select list box

Problem

You have a multiple-selection list box on an InfoPath form. When a user opens a new form, you want a couple of items in the multiple-selection list box to be selected by default.

Solution

You must configure the multiple-selection list box to have default values if you want one or more items to be selected at startup.

To display one or more items as selected in a multiple-selection list box:

1. In InfoPath, create a new **Blank Form** template.

2. Add a **Multiple-Selection List Box** control to the view of the form template.

3. You can populate a multiple-selection list box with items using the same methods you used when populating a drop-down list box. The method for configuring a multiple-selection list box to display one or more items as selected at startup depends on the method you have chosen to populate the multiple-selection list box.

    If you have populated the multiple-selection list box with static items as described in recipe *52 Populate a drop-down list box with static items* and want one of those items to be selected at startup:

    a. Open the **Multiple-Selection List Box Properties** dialog box.

    b. On the **Multiple-Selection List Box Properties** dialog box on the **Data** tab, select the item you want to display as selected at startup, and then click **Set default**. A **Yes** should appear in the **Default** column behind the item you selected.

    c. On the **Multiple-Selection List Box Properties** dialog box, click **OK**.

Note that once you have set an item to be the default item, you can only remove that default setting by selecting a different item and setting that item to be the default item. To return to having no items selected in the multiple-selection list box:

a. Click **Data ➤ Form Data ➤ Default Values**.

b. On the **Edit Default Values** dialog box, expand the group node that contains the repeating field for the multiple-selection list box, click the repeating field to select it, and then empty the **Default value** text box.

c. On the **Edit Default Values** dialog box, click **OK**.

If you have populated the multiple-selection list box with items as described in recipe *52 Populate a drop-down list box with static items*, recipe *53 Populate a drop-down list box with data from a repeating table*, or recipe *54 Populate a drop-down list box with data from an XML file*, and want one or multiple items to be selected at startup:

a. Click **Data ➤ Form Data ➤ Default Values**.

b. On the **Edit Default Values** dialog box, expand the group node that contains the repeating field for the multiple-selection list box.

c. On the **Edit Default Values** dialog box, right-click the repeating field and select **Add another <field name> below** from the context menu that appears.

d. Repeat the previous step until you have an amount of repeating fields that is the same as the amount of items you want to display as selected in the multiple-selection list box.

e. On the **Edit Default Values** dialog box, select the first repeating field, and then in the **Default value** text box, enter a piece of text that corresponds to the value of the item you want to have displayed as selected.

f. Repeat the previous step for the other items you want to display as selected.

g. On the **Edit Default Values** dialog box, click **OK**.

4. Preview the form.

Discussion

In the solution described above, you learned two main techniques you can use to display items as selected in a multiple-selection list box:

1. By using the **Set default** command on the **Multiple-Selection List Box Properties** dialog box. This method can only be used if you have populated a multiple-selection list box with static items.

2. By adding repeating fields with default values via the **Edit Default Values** dialog box.

Because you cannot remove a default item once you have set it using the first technique, it is recommended that you always use the second technique to configure items in a multiple-selection list box to be selected at startup. Also note that the second method will automatically configure one item to be the default item on the **Multiple-Selection List Box Properties** dialog box if a multiple-selection list box has been populated with static items.

79 Limit a multi-select list box to a maximum of 3 selected items

Problem

You have a multiple-selection list box on an InfoPath form and want users to be able to select a maximum of 3 items in the multiple-selection list box.

Solution

You can add a section control and a hidden field that simulate performing data validation on a multiple-selection list box.

To limit a multiple-selection list box to a maximum of 3 selected items:

1. In InfoPath, create a new **Blank Form** template.

2. Add a **Multiple-Selection List Box** control to the view of the form template and name it **selectedItems**.

3. Populate the multiple-selection list box with either static or dynamic items. Keep it simple and just add 5 static items: **Item 1**, **Item 2**, **Item 3**, **Item 4**, and **Item 5**. Note: You can populate a multiple-selection list box the same way you populate a drop-down list box (see recipe *52 Populate a drop-down list box with static items*, recipe *53 Populate a drop-down list box with data from a repeating table*, and recipe *54 Populate a drop-down list box with data from an XML file*).

4. Add a **Section** control to the view of the form template and then type the text "Maximum 3 items allowed" inside of the section control. You can change the color of the text to red if you wish.

5. Click the section control to select it, and then click **Home** ➤ **Rules** ➤ **Manage Rules**.

6. On the **Rules** task pane, ensure that **group2** is displayed under the title bar, and then click **New** ➤ **Formatting** to add a **Formatting** rule to the **group2** section control.

7. On the **Rules** task pane, select the **Hide this control** check box. This should hide the section control when the condition on the rule has been met.

8. On the **Rules** task pane under **Condition**, click the text **None**.

9. On the **Condition** dialog box, select **Use a formula** from the third drop-down list box. You are going to misuse the **Insert Formula** dialog box to construct a formula that you can use as an expression on the **Condition** dialog box.

10. On the **Insert Formula** dialog box, type

    ```
    count(
    ```

    and then click **Insert Field or Group**.

11. On the **Select a Field or Group** dialog box, expand the **group1** group, select the **selectedItems** repeating field under the **group1** group, and then click **Filter Data**.

12. On the **Filter Data** dialog box, click **Add**.

13. On the **Specify Filter Conditions** dialog box, leave **selectedItems** selected in the first drop-down list box, select **is not blank** from the second drop-down list box, and then click **OK**.

14. On the **Filter Data** dialog box, click **OK**.

15. On the **Select a Field or Group** dialog box, click **OK**.

16. The resulting formula on the **Insert Formula** dialog box should now resemble the following:

```
count(selectedItems[. != ""]
```

Type

```
) <= 3
```

to close the **count** function and require the amount of items to be less than or equal to 3. The final formula should now resemble the following:

```
count(selectedItems[. != ""]) <= 3
```

17. On the **Insert Formula** dialog box, select the **Edit XPath (advanced)** check box, select the entire formula, and then copy it by pressing **Ctrl+C**.

18. On the **Insert Formula** dialog box, click **Cancel**.

19. On the **Condition** dialog box, select **The expression** from the first drop-down list box, delete the entire expression from the text box, and then press **Ctrl+V** to paste the formula you copied earlier into the text box. The expression for the condition should say:

```
count(../my:group1/my:selectedItems[. != ""]) <= 3
```

This condition allows the rule to run to hide the section when there are 3 or less non-blank items selected in the multiple-selection list box, so shows the section when more than 3 non-blank items have been selected.

20. On the **Condition** dialog box, click **OK**.

21. Click anywhere behind the text on the section control to place the cursor, and then add a **Text Box** control within the section control. Name the text box **itemCount**, change its data type to **Whole Number (integer)**, and select its **Cannot be blank** property. You are going to use this text box to keep track of the amount of selected items in the multiple-selection list box and perform data validation for the multiple-selection list box.

22. Add a **Formatting** rule to the **itemCount** text box control with a **Condition** that says:

```
true()
```

and with a **Formatting** of **Hide this control**. Because you want the **itemCount** text box to be present on the view of the form template, but always remain invisible to users, this rule makes use of the **true** function to always run and hide the text box control (also see recipe *27 Disable a button on a read-only view*).

23. Add an **Action** rule to the **selectedItems** multiple-selection list box with an action that says:

```
Set a field's value: itemCount = count(selectedItems[. != ""])
```

where **itemCount** is the field bound to the text box. Note that you must manually enter the following formula on the **Insert Formula** dialog box to get the correct expression:

```
count(../my:selectedItems[. != ""])
```

What this expression does is navigate from the context node (an item that has been selected in the multiple-selection list box) up to the parent **group1** group node of the multiple-selection list box, retrieve all of the **selectedItems** fields under the **group1** group node of which their values are not empty strings, and then the formula returns the amount of non-blank items in the multiple-selection list box by using the **count** function.

24. Open the **Text Box Properties** dialog box and set the **Default Value**
of the **itemCount** text box to be equal to the following formula:

```
count(selectedItems[. != ""])
```

or

```
count(../../my:group1/my:selectedItems[. != ""])
```

if you have the **Edit XPath (advanced)** check box selected on the
Insert Formula dialog box. This formula returns the amount of non-
blank items that have been selected in the multiple-selection list box
and uses that amount to set the **Default Value** of the **itemCount** text
box. Ensure that you leave the **Refresh value when formula is
recalculated** check box selected on the **Text Box Properties** dialog
box, so that whenever an item is deselected in the multiple-selection list
box, the value of the **itemCount** text box is updated.

25. Add a **Validation** rule to the **itemCount** text box with a **Condition**
that says:

```
itemCount > 3
```

and a **ScreenTip** that says: "Maximum 3 items allowed". Because the
itemCount text box has been hidden (so users cannot enter any data
into it), if more than 3 items are selected in the multiple-selection list
box and a user tries to save the form despite the section control telling
her about the error, InfoPath will display the following error to the
user: *This form contains validation errors. Errors are marked with either a red
asterisk (required fields) or a red, dashed border (invalid values).*

Figure 147. Message shown when a user tries to save a form with validation errors.

If the user clicks **Yes**, she can still save the form with validation errors. However, if the form has been enabled to be submitted and the user tries to submit the form with validation errors, she will see the following message appear and will not be able to submit the form: *InfoPath cannot submit the form because it contains validation errors. Errors are marked with either a red asterisk (required fields) or a red, dashed border (invalid values).*

Figure 148. Message shown when a user tries to submit a form with validation errors.

26. Preview the form.

When the form opens, select more than 3 items in the multiple-selection list box. You should see the section containing the error message appear. Try to save the form. Read the message on the message box that appears and then click **No**. Deselect items in the multiple-selection list box until you have less than 4 items selected. The section containing the error message should disappear.

Discussion

Because the option to add custom **Validation** rules to a multiple-selection list box is disabled in InfoPath, the solution described above used a hidden text box to add data validation, which would have otherwise been applied to the multiple-selection list box, and a section control to be able to display an error message to the user.

Whenever an item is selected in the multiple-selection list box, the value of the hidden text box is updated. You may have noticed that whenever an item is deselected in the multiple-selection list box, the value of the hidden text box is not updated. To correct this problem, you set the default value of the hidden text box to be equal to a formula that counts the amount of non-blank selected items in the multiple-selection list box.

80 Show or hide sections using a multiple-selection list box

Problem

You have data in an XML file and you want to use a multiple-selection list box to show data from that XML file based on the items that are selected in the multiple-selection list box.

Solution

You can use conditional formatting on a repeating section to filter and display data based on selections from a multiple-selection list box.

In this recipe, you will use the **RunningShoes** XML file you used in recipe *54 Populate a drop-down list box with data from an XML file.*

To show or hide sections using a multiple-selection list box:

1. In InfoPath, create a new **Blank Form** template.

2. Add a **Multiple-Selection List Box** control to the view of the form template and name the multiple-selection list box **shoeBrand**.

3. Add a **Receive data** connection to the XML file you used in recipe *54 Populate a drop-down list box with data from an XML file* and follow the same steps to populate the multiple-selection list box with items from the Secondary data source. Select the **brand** repeating group for the **Entries** property, and the **name** field (under the **brand** repeating group) for both the **Value** and the **Display name** properties of the multiple-selection list box.

4. On the **Fields** task pane, select **RunningShoes (Secondary)** from the drop-down list box, right-click the **brand** repeating group, and then drag-and-drop it onto the view of the form template. Select **Repeating Section with Controls** from the context menu that appears when you drop it.

5. Click the repeating section to select it, and then click **Home ➤ Rules ➤ Manage Rules**.

6. On the **Rules** task pane, ensure that **brand** is displayed under the title bar, and then click **New ➤ Formatting** to add a **Formatting** rule to the **brand** repeating group.

7. On the **Rules** task pane, select the **Hide this control** check box. This should hide any repeating section for which the condition on the rule has been met.

8. Because you want to hide all repeating sections for which the brand name has not been selected in the multiple-selection list box, you must add a condition that counts the amount of repeating sections (items in the Secondary data source) for which the brand name has been selected in the multiple-selection list box (**shoeBrand** repeating fields in the Main data source), and if the count is zero, hide the repeating section. On the **Rules** task pane under **Condition**, click the text **None**.

9. On the **Condition** dialog box, select **Use a formula** from the third drop-down list box. You are going to misuse the **Insert Formula** dialog box to construct a formula that you can use as an expression on the **Condition** dialog box.

10. On the **Insert Formula** dialog box, type

    ```
    count(
    ```

    and then click **Insert Field or Group**.

11. On the **Select a Field or Group** dialog box, ensure that **RunningShoes (Secondary)** is selected in the drop-down list box, expand the **brand** repeating group, select the **name** field under the **brand** repeating group, and then click **Filter Data**.

12. On the **Filter Data** dialog box, click **Add**.

13. On the **Specify Filter Conditions** dialog box, leave **name** selected in the first drop-down list box, leave **is equal to** selected in the second drop-down list box, and select **Select a field or group** from the third drop-down list box.

14. On the **Select a Field or Group** dialog box, select **Main** from the drop-down list box, expand the **group1** group, select the **shoeBrand** repeating field, and then click **OK**.

15. On the **Specify Filter Conditions** dialog box, click **OK**.

16. On the **Filter Data** dialog box, click **OK**.

17. On the **Select a Field or Group** dialog box, click **OK**.

18. The resulting formula on the **Insert Formula** dialog box should now resemble the following:

```
count(@name[. = shoeBrand]
```

Type

```
)
```

to close the **count** function. The final formula should now resemble the following:

```
count(@name[. = shoeBrand])
```

19. On the **Insert Formula** dialog box, select the **Edit XPath (advanced)** check box, select the entire formula, and then copy it by pressing **Ctrl+C**.

20. On the **Insert Formula** dialog box, click **Cancel**.

21. On the **Condition** dialog box, select **The expression** from the first drop-down list box, delete the entire expression from the text box, and then press **Ctrl+V** to paste the formula you copied earlier into the text box. Type the following after the formula you just pasted:

```
= 0
```

This checks whether the result of the **count** function is equal to **0**. The resulting expression should look like the following:

```
count(@name[. = xdXDocument:get-
DOM()/my:myFields/my:group1/my:shoeBrand]) = 0
```

What this expression does is return the amount of names of shoe brands in the Secondary data source for which the name of the shoe brand in the Secondary data source is the same as the name of the shoe brand that has been selected in the multiple-selection list box, which is located in the Main data source. If a shoe brand is found in the Secondary data source for a selected shoe brand in the multiple-selection list box, the count will be unequal to 0, so the repeating section for that shoe brand should be displayed. If a shoe brand has not been selected in the multiple-selection list box, the count will be equal to 0, so the repeating section for that shoe brand should be hidden.

22. On the **Condition** dialog box, click **OK**.

23. Preview the form.

When the form opens, no repeating sections should be visible. As you select shoe brands from the multiple-selection list box, their corresponding repeating sections should appear. And if you deselect a shoe brand, its corresponding repeating section should disappear.

Discussion

In the solution described above, you filtered data in a Secondary data source based on items selected in a multiple-selection list box.

A good way to understand how multiple-selection list boxes work is to add one with a couple of static items to the view of an InfoPath form template, preview the form, select a couple of items, save the form locally on disk, and then open the XML file for the form in Notepad.

If you do this, you will notice that the value stored in the field bound to the control is not one single value as is the case with drop-down list boxes, combo boxes, and list boxes, but that it consists of several values including one that is empty. Note that you can prevent the empty item from being saved by deselecting the check box for the repeating field that is bound to the multiple-selection list box on the **Edit Default Values** dialog box, which you can access via **Data ➤ Form Data ➤ Default Values**.

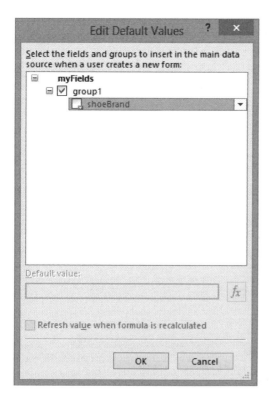

Figure 149. Deselected repeating field to remove the empty item from a multi-select list.

If you look at the **Fields** task pane after you have added a multiple-selection list box to the view of an InfoPath form template, you will also see that it is constructed using a repeating field under a group.

Figure 150. Group and repeating field representing a multiple-selection list box.

Armed with the knowledge that a multiple-selection list box consists of a repeating field, you now also know that you can come up with creative solutions that make use of functions that take a repeating group or field as their arguments, such as the **count**, **sum**, **avg**, and **eval** functions do.

You can also use the technique of filtering and counting to determine whether a particular item has been selected in a multiple-selection list box. For example, suppose you have a multiple-selection list box named **field1** that contains 5 items with corresponding values of 1 through 5. If a user selects the item that has a value equal to 3, you want a text box named **field2** to be emptied.

The way you could go about creating such a solution is to add an **Action** rule to the multiple-selection list box with a **Condition** that says:

```
count(../my:field1[. = "3"]) > 0
```

and an action that says:

```
Set a field's value: field2 = ""
```

where **field2** is the field that is bound to the text box. Note that you must select the **The expression** option on the **Condition** dialog box to enter the expression for the condition.

Because the **Action** rule is running on the multiple-selection list box, which is bound to the repeating field **field1**, the expression first navigates to the parent **group1** group before retrieving all of the **field1** fields under the **group1** group

```
../my:field1
```

and then filtering those **field1** fields on the value of the item you want to find (the item that has a value equal to 3 in this case)

```
../my:field1[. = "3"]
```

and then finally using the **count** function to count the amount of filtered items returned

```
count(../my:field1[. = "3"])
```

If this amount is greater than 0, it means that the item was found. Now whenever a user selects the item that has a value equal to 3 in the multiple-selection list box, the text box will be emptied.

81 Display items from a multiple-selection list box as multi-line text

Problem

You have a multiple-selection list box on an InfoPath form and want to be able to select a few items from it, click on a button, and have the selected items be transferred to a multi-line text box and displayed as text with one item on each line.

Solution

You can use the **eval** function to evaluate a list of items in either a repeating field or repeating group and concatenate all of the items in one string. And to add line breaks between the items, you can use the XML character for a line break in a Secondary data source and add it to the items when concatenating them through the **eval** function.

To display items from a multiple-selection list box as multi-line text:

1. In InfoPath, create a new **Blank Form** template.

2. Add a **Multiple-Selection List Box** control, a **Text Box** control, and a **Button** control to the view of the form template. Name the multiple-selection list box **allItems** and name the text box **selectedItems**.

3. Populate the multiple-selection list box with either static or dynamic items. Keep it simple and just add 3 static items: **Item 1**, **Item 2**, and **Item 3**. Note: You can populate a multiple-selection list box the same way you populate a drop-down list box (see recipe *52 Populate a drop-down list box with static items*, recipe *53 Populate a drop-down list box with data from a repeating table*, and recipe *54 Populate a drop-down list box with data from an XML file*).

4. Open the **Properties** dialog box for the text box, and then on the **Display** tab, select the **Multi-line** check box to make the text box accept and display multiple lines of text. Click **OK** when you are done.

5. Add a **Receive data** connection to an XML file (see recipe *33 Get data from an XML file*) that has the following contents:

```
<break>
  <value>&#xD;</value>
</break>
```

The **value** field in this XML file will be used to add line breaks to text added to the multi-line text box. Name the data connection **break**.

6. On the **Fields** task pane under the **myFields** group, add a hidden text field named **break** (see recipe *11 Add a hidden field*).

7. On the **Fields** task pane, double-click the **break** field you just added to open its **Properties** dialog box.

8. On the **Field or Group Properties** dialog box on the **Data** tab under **Default Value**, click the formula button behind the **Value** text box.

9. On the **Insert Formula** dialog box, click **Insert Field or Group**.

10. On the **Select a Field or Group** dialog box, select **break (Secondary)** from the drop-down list box, select the **value** field, and click **OK**.

11. On the **Insert Formula** dialog box, click **OK**.

12. On the **Field or Group Properties** dialog box, ensure that the **Refresh value when formula is recalculated** check box is selected, and click **OK**. With this you have set the **Default Value** of the **break** hidden field to be equal to the value of the **value** field under the **break** group in the Secondary data source for the XML file.

13. Add an **Action** rule to the button that sets the value of the **selectedItems** text box to be equal to the following formula:

```
eval(eval(allItems[. != ""], "concat(., ../../my:break)"),
"..")
```

where **allItems** is the repeating field bound to the multiple-selection list box.

14. Preview the form.

When the form opens, select a few items in the multiple-selection list box and then click the button. The items you selected should have been copied over to the text box and each item should have been displayed on a separate line.

Discussion

The **eval** function returns the values of a field or group, and takes two arguments. The first argument defines the field or group the **eval** function should operate on, and the second argument defines the expression to calculate for the field or group. Usually, the **eval** function is nested within a function that operates on a field or group, such as **sum** or **avg**.

In the solution described above, you used the **eval** function twice. The first **eval** function (the inner one) was used as follows:

```
eval(allItems[. != ""], "concat(., ../../my:break)")
```

The preceding formula takes a selected item in the multiple-selection list box that is not an empty string, and returns the concatenation of that item with a line break.

The **allItems** field in the formula represents the repeating field the **eval** function should work on, and the second argument represents the expression the **eval** function should perform on that repeating field, so the result of the evaluation.

Let us first dissect the expression for the first argument in the **eval** function above.

```
allItems[. != ""]
```

The filter expression

```
[. != ""]
```

prevents the **eval** function from evaluating any **allItems** repeating field that has an empty string as its value. Remember that a multiple-selection list box has at least one empty item by default unless you have configured it not to have one. So to prevent empty items from appearing in the final multi-line text, you need to filter them out as the expression above does.

Let us now dissect the expression for the second argument in the **eval** function.

```
concat(., ../../my:break)
```

The dot (.) represents the context node (**allItems** repeating field) the **eval** function is working on, while

```
../../my:break
```

represents the field for the line break. The field for the line break is located under the **myFields** group in the Main data source, and if you have an **allItems** repeating field as the context (starting) node, you must first navigate upwards to the **group1** parent node of the **allItems** node using the double-dot notation (..), and then upwards again to the **myFields** group node (which in turn is the parent node of the **group1** node) using the double-dot notation again, before you can navigate back down to the **break** node, which then results in the

```
../../my:break
```

XPath expression used in the **concat** function.

So finally, the **eval** function works on each non-blank **allItems** node in the multiple-selection list box to return the value of the concatenation of that **allItems** node with a line break (**break** node).

```
eval(allItems[. != ""], "concat(., ../../my:break)")
```

The second **eval** function (the outer one) is used to retrieve the contents of all of the **allItems** nodes in the multiple-selection list box as a string. The most basic formula to do this is the following:

```
eval(allItems, "..")
```

The preceding formula returns the value of the anonymous parent

```
".."
```

which is a concatenated string of the contents of all of the parent's children (**allItems** nodes). The latter is a W3C standard.

In the final formula, you want to get the contents of all of the **allItems** nodes, but you also want to apply the concatenation you constructed earlier for each **allItems** node, so that the line break is included between the concatenated contents of all of the **allItems** nodes.

So you must replace

```
allItems
```

in the previous formula with the **eval** formula you constructed earlier, because you want the **eval** function to work on the formula you constructed earlier, and the result of the evaluation to be the contents of the anonymous parent.

The final formula would then be the following when you combine the two **eval** functions:

```
eval(eval(allItems[. != ""], "concat(., ../../my:break)"), ".."))
```

Chapter 8: Objects

Objects are controls in InfoPath that do not store any data in the Main data source of an InfoPath form, that store a special type of data, or that store data that can be converted into binary data such as images and files.

Calculated Values

A **Calculated Value** control can be used to display the result of a formula, the value of a field in a data source, or static text. Because a **Calculated Value** control displays text as read-only, users are unable to interact with this control, so it is mostly used for displaying and not for entering data. In addition, a **Calculated Value** control is ideal to use if you want to display the result of a formula without having to bind the control to a field in the Main or a Secondary data source of a form.

When you click to add a **Calculated Value** control to the view of a form template from either the **Controls** group on the Ribbon or the **Controls** task pane, the **Insert Calculated Value** dialog box will appear.

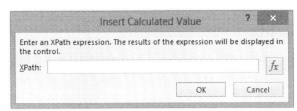

Figure 151. The Insert Calculated Value dialog box in InfoPath 2013.

From here, you can do one of three things:

1. Click **OK** to just add the control to the view without configuring it.

2. Enter a static piece of text such as for example "This is just a label" into the **XPath** text box and then click **OK**. Note that you must enter the text with double quotes around it for it to be accepted as a string by InfoPath.

3. Click the formula button behind the **XPath** text box to open the **Insert Formula** dialog box to select a field or construct a formula.

While you can use the **Properties ➤ Color ➤ Borders** command to add borders to the control, the control itself does not have any borders when you first add it to the view of a form template.

Figure 152. A Calculated Value control as it appears on the view of a form template.

Once you have added a **Calculated Value** control to the view of a form template, you can open its **Properties** dialog box to configure it.

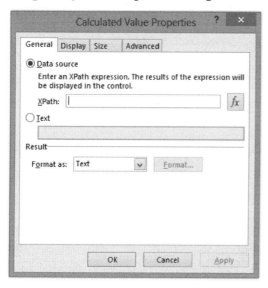

Figure 153. The Calculated Value Properties dialog box in InfoPath 2013.

The **Calculated Value Properties** dialog box allows you to use a formula to set the value of the control, select a field or enter an XPath expression to bind the control to a field in the Main or a Secondary data source, set the value of the control to be equal to a static piece of text, or format the result displayed in the control as **Text**, **Decimal**, **Whole Number**, **Date**, **Time**, or **Date and Time**.

Note that unlike on the **Insert Calculated Value** dialog box, if you want to enter a static piece of text for the control via the **Calculated Value Properties** dialog box, you can select the **Text** option and then enter the text wihout double quotes around it.

82 Dynamically change the label of a text box when an option is selected

Problem

You have an option button control on an InfoPath form with three options and want the label of a text box to dynamically change whenever one of those options is selected.

Solution

You can use an **Action** rule on the option button control to change the value of a field that is used as the source for the label of the text box.

To dynamically change the label of a text box when an option is selected:

1. In InfoPath, create a new **Blank Form** template.

2. Add an **Option Button** control with 3 options to the view of the form template, name the field bound to the option button control **title**, and label the options **Male**, **Female**, and **Unknown**, respectively.

3. Open the **Option Button Properties** dialog box for the first option, change its **Value when selected** property to **Mr**, and then click **OK**.

4. Repeat the previous step for the other two options, but then change their **Value when selected** properties to **Mrs** and **Sir/Madam**, respectively.

5. Add a **Receive data** connection to an XML file (see recipe *33 Get data from an XML file*) that has the following contents:

    ```
    <control>
      <label>Sir/Madam</label>
    </control>
    ```

    and name the data connection **DynamicLabel**.

6. On the **Fields** task pane, select **DynamicLabel (Secondary)** from the drop-down list box, right-click **label**, drag it to the view of the form

template, drop it, and select **Calculated Value** from the context menu that appears when you drop it.

7. Add a **Text Box** control to the view of the form template just behind the calculated value control (resize the calculated value control if necessary). If InfoPath automatically added a static label in front of the text box, delete that label, since you will be using the calculated value control to display the label for the text box.

8. Add an **Action** rule to the option button control with an action that says:

```
Set a field's value: label = .
```

where **label** is the **label** field that is located in the **DynamicLabel** Secondary data source, and the dot (**.**) represents the context node, which in this case is the **title** field bound to the option button control. Note that you could also use a formula with the **concat** function to dynamically construct or append text to the label.

9. Preview the form.

When the form opens, the text "Sir/Madam" should appear in front of the text box as its label. Select an option, for example **Female**. The text "Mrs" should now appear in front of the text box.

Discussion

A **Calculated Value** control displays text as read-only and is the perfect control to use when you want to display labels on an InfoPath form.

In the solution described above, you saw how to use a field that is located in a Secondary data source, bind it to a **Calculated Value** control, and dynamically set the value of that field to be equal to the value of an option button, so that the label that is displayed in front of a text box changes as different options are selected.

While you could have also used a field in the Main data source of the form to achieve the same result, using a field in a Secondary data source keeps the Main data source free from irrelevant information, which what a label contains is.

The default value for the field in the Secondary data source was set in the XML file itself, since you cannot set the **Default Value** of a field that is located in a Secondary data source directly at design time. However, had you not set the default value of the field in the XML file itself, then you could have also used the **Form Load** event to set its value as follows:

1. Click **Data ➤ Rules ➤ Form Load**.

2. On the **Rules** task pane, add an **Action** rule to the **Form Load** event with an action that says:

```
Set a field's value: label = "Sir/Madam"
```

where **label** is the **label** field that is located in the **DynamicLabel** Secondary data source, and "Sir Madam" is a static piece of text.

3. Preview the form.

When the form opens, the text "Sir/Madam" should appear by default as the label for the text box.

Buttons and Picture Buttons

Button controls in InfoPath do not store any data and are not linked to any fields in the Main data source of a form. The only purpose of buttons is to perform actions when the user clicks on them.

There are two types of button controls in InfoPath 2013:

1. A normal **Button** control that has a textual caption.

   Figure 154. Normal button control in InfoPath 2013.

2. A **Picture Button** control that allows you to use images for a button.

   Figure 155. Picture Button control in InfoPath 2013.

These two types of button controls do not differ in functionality; only in the way they look, because one displays images and the other displays text.

A **Picture Button** control must be configured to use images that define the way the button looks. Therefore, it has two properties you can set to point to images:

1. Picture
2. Hover Picture

The **Picture** property can be set to point to an image that defines the normal state of the button and the **Hover Picture** property can be set to point to an image that defines the way the button looks when the user hovers with a mouse pointer over the button. Note that setting the **Hover Picture** property of a picture button is optional. If you do not set it, the image for the normal state of the button will also be used for the hover state of the button.

Figure 156. A Picture Button control with its Picture property set to an image.

To set the image for a **Picture Button** control, you can either click **Properties ➤ Picture Button ➤ Picture** or on the **Picture Button Properties** dialog box, click **Browse** under the **Picture** section on the **General** tab.

If you want to use one and the same image for several picture buttons, so reuse an image, it is best to first add that image as a resource file to the form template, and then on the **General** tab of the **Picture Button Properties** dialog box, select the image you added as a resource file to the form template from the **Picture** drop-down list box.

A resource file is a file that is used to display additional information in a form template. When you save or publish an InfoPath form template, resource files are included in the form template (the XSN file).

To add an image as a resource file to a form template:

1. Click **Data ➤ Form Data ➤ Resource Files**.

2. On the **Resource Files** dialog box, click **Add**.

3. On the **Add File** dialog box, browse to and select the image file you want to add, and then click **OK**.

4. Repeat steps 2 and 3 to add as many images as you like, and then on the **Resource Files** dialog box, click **OK**.

All of the images you add as resources files to the form template should then appear in the **Picture** and **Hover picture** drop-down list boxes on the **General** tab of the **Picture Button Properties** dialog box of the **Picture Button** control. You can then select an image from either drop-down list box to be used as a picture or a hover picture for the **Picture Button** control.

By adding images as resource files to a form template and then assigning them to picture button controls, you reduce the amount of files that are stored in a form template. For example, if you were to add two picture buttons to the view of a form template and then use the **Picture** command on the **Properties** tab on the Ribbon to add the same image to each picture button, you would wind up with two instances of the same image stored in the form template. However, if you first add the image you want to use on both picture buttons to the form template as a resource file and then use the **Picture Button Properties** dialog box to select that image from the **Picture** drop-down list box for each picture button, you would wind up with only one image stored in the form template. So whenever possible, use resource files instead of directly assigning images to picture buttons, since this should help keep the size of the form template down, which in turn should help forms load faster.

Tip:

A best practice is to use resource files whenever you have external files your InfoPath forms need to access. By adding such files as resource files to a form template, you remove the dependency of requiring access to external locations, which may become unavailable from time to time.

83 Change the label of a button when the button is clicked

Problem

You have a button on an InfoPath form and you want the label of this button to display a certain piece of text when the button is clicked.

Solution

You can use a rule on the button to change the value of a field that is used as the source for the label of the button.

To change the label of a button when the button is clicked:

1. In InfoPath, create a new **Blank Form** template.

2. Add a **Button** control to the view of the form template.

3. Add a hidden field of data type **Text (string)**, with the name **buttonLabel**, and that has a **Default Value** equal to the text **Not Clicked** to the Main data source of the form (also see recipe *11 Add a hidden field*).

4. Right-click the button and select **Button Properties** from the context menu that appears.

5. On the **Button Properties** dialog box on the **General** tab, click the formula button behind the **Label** text box.

6. On the **Insert Formula** dialog box, click **Insert Field or Group**.

7. On the **Select a Field or Group** dialog box, select **buttonLabel**, and click **OK**.

8. Click **OK** when closing all dialog boxes.

9. Add an **Action** rule to the button with an action that says:

    ```
    Set a field's value: buttonLabel = "Clicked"
    ```

    This rule sets the value of the **buttonLabel** hidden field to be equal to the static piece of text "Clicked".

10. Preview the form.

When the form opens for the first time, the label of the button should display the text **Not Clicked**. When you click the button, the label should change into the text **Clicked**.

Discussion

The **Label** property of a button can be set to be equal to a static piece of text, to the result of a calculation, or to the value of a field as the solution described above demonstrates. So to create a dynamic label, you must use the formula button behind the **Label** property on the **Button Properties** dialog box to construct a formula that returns a piece of text.

In the solution described above, you used a hidden field in the Main data source to set the label of the button. Because all fields that are part of the Main data source are eventually stored in the XML of the InfoPath form and because the label of a button is not data that you would call relevant to whatever data is typically stored in an InfoPath form (a label is just descriptive data), you may want to use a field in a Secondary data source instead to set the label of a button as follows:

1. In Notepad, create an XML file that has the following contents:

    ```
    <label>
      <value>Not Clicked</value>
    </label>
    ```

    and name the XML file **label.xml**.

2. In InfoPath, add an XML data connection to the **label.xml** file to the form template (see recipe *33 Get data from an XML file*) and name the data connection **label**.

3. Right-click the button and select **Button Properties** from the context menu that appears.

4. On the **Button Properties** dialog box on the **General** tab, click the formula button behind the **Label** text box.

5. On the **Insert Formula** dialog box, click **Insert Field or Group**.

6. On the **Select a Field or Group** dialog box, select **label (Secondary)** from the drop-down list box, select the **value** field, and click **OK**.

7. Click **OK** when closing all dialog boxes.

8. Click the button to select it, and then select **Home ➤ Rules ➤ Add Rule ➤ When This Button Is Clicked ➤ Set a Field's Value**.

9. On the **Rule Details** dialog box, click the button behind the **Field** text box.

10. On the **Select a Field or Group** dialog box, select **label (Secondary)** from the drop-down list box, select the **value** field, and click **OK**.

11. On the **Rule Details** dialog box, type **Clicked** in the **Value** text box, and then click **OK**. With this you have set the **value** field in the **label** Secondary data source to be equal to the text **Clicked** when the button is clicked. The final **Action** rule should say:

```
Set a field's value: value = "Clicked"
```

where **value** is the field that is located under the **label** group in the **label** Secondary data source. This rule sets the value of the **value** field in the **label** Secondary data source to be equal to the static piece of text "Clicked".

12. Preview the form.

When the form opens, the label of the button should display the text **Not Clicked**. When you click the button, the label should change into the text **Clicked**.

84 Add line breaks to the label of a button

Problem

You have a button on an InfoPath form with a very long label, for example "First Line Second Line Third Line". You want to break the label into 3 lines of text with "First Line", "Second Line", and "Third Line" each being displayed on a separate line.

Solution

You can use a formula for the label of a button to break the label into multiple lines of text.

To add line breaks to the label of a button:

1. In Notepad, create an XML file that has the following contents:

    ```
    <break>
      <value>&#xD;</value>
    </break>
    ```

    and name the XML file **LineBreak.xml**.

2. In InfoPath, create a new **Blank Form** template.

3. Add a **Button** control to the view of the form template.

4. Add a **Receive data** connection that gets data from the **LineBreak.xml** file to the form template (see recipe *33 Get data from an XML file*) and name the data connection **LineBreak**.

5. Right-click the button and select **Button Properties** from the context menu that appears.

6. On the **Button Properties** dialog box on the **General** tab, click the formula button behind the **Label** text box.

7. On the **Insert Formula** dialog box, construct a formula that uses the **concat** function and says:

    ```
    concat("First Line", value, "Second Line", value, "Third Line")
    ```

    where **value** is the field that is located under the **break** group node in the **LineBreak** Secondary data source for the XML file.

8. Click **OK** when closing all dialog boxes.

9. Preview the form.

When the form opens, the text for the label of the button should appear on three separate lines.

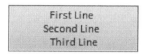

Figure 157. Button with label displayed on three separate lines.

Discussion

In the solution described above, you assigned a value equal to

```
&#xD;
```

which represents a carriage-return in XML, to an element in an XML file and thus also to a field in a Secondary data source, and then used it in a formula to add line breaks to text. Likewise, you could also use

```
&#x9;
```

in an XML file to add tab stops to a piece of text.

85 Enable a button by clicking on another button

Problem

You have two button controls on an InfoPath form, one of which is disabled. You want to be able to click on the button that is enabled to enable the button that is disabled.

Solution

You can add a **Formatting** rule to the button that is disabled to enable that button when the value of a field is set to a particular value, and you can add an **Action** rule to the button that is enabled to set the value of the field that enables the disabled button.

To enable a button by clicking on another button:

1. In Notepad, create an XML file that has the following contents:

    ```
    <button>
      <isEnabled>No</isEnabled>
    </button>
    ```

    and name the XML file **ButtonState.xml**.

2. In InfoPath, create a new **Blank Form** template.

3. Add two **Button** controls to the view of the form template.

4. Add a **Receive data** connection that gets data from the **ButtonState.xml** file to the form template (see recipe *33 Get data from an XML file*) and name the data connection **ButtonState**.

5. Add a **Formatting** rule to the second button with a **Condition** that says:

    ```
    isEnabled = "No"
    ```

    and a **Formatting** of **Disable this control**. Note that you must select **Select a field or group** from the first drop-down list box on the **Condition** dialog box, and then select **ButtonState (Secondary)** from the drop-down list box on the **Select a Field or Group** dialog box to be able to select the **isEnabled** field for the condition. This rule disables the second button when the value of the **isEnabled** field in the **ButtonState** Secondary data source is equal to the text **No**.

6. Add an **Action** rule to the first button that says:

    ```
    Set a field's value: isEnabled = "Yes"
    ```

    where the **isEnabled** field is located in the **ButtonState** Secondary data source. This rule sets the value of the **isEnabled** field to be equal to a piece of text that is not equal to **No** (the text **Yes** in this case), so that the **Formatting** rule on the second button is triggered to enable the second button when the first button is clicked.

7. Preview the form.

When the form opens, the second button should be disabled and non-clickable. Click the first button. The second button should now be enabled and clickable.

Discussion

In the solution described above, you saw how to use a field in a Secondary data source as an intermediary for disabling a button and enabling that same button when another button is clicked. Note that you could have also used a field in the Main data source of the form to achieve the same result. A field in a Secondary data source was used in this case to keep the InfoPath form free from irrelevant data, which is what a helper field such as the **isEnabled** field contains.

86 Create a tabbed interface using buttons

Problem

You want to design an InfoPath form where users can click on buttons that represent tabs to switch between tab pages.

Solution

You can use views to represent tab pages and buttons to represent tabs along with **Action** rules on the buttons to switch between the views.

To create a tabbed interface using buttons:

1. In InfoPath, create a new **Blank Form** template.

2. On the **Fields** task pane, add a hidden field named **lastClicked** to the Main data source of the form as described in recipe *11 Add a hidden field*.

3. Add two views named **View 2** and **View 3** to the form template (also see recipe *13 Add a second view to a form template*).

4. Switch back to **View 1** and delete the page layout that InfoPath added by default to the view.

5. Add a custom table with two rows and one column to **View 1**.

6. Add 3 **Button** controls behind each other in the first row of the custom table. Ensure that the custom table is wide enough to accommodate all of the buttons on one row. Label the button controls **Tab 1**, **Tab2**, and **Tab 3**, respectively.

7. Type the static piece of text "Tab 1" in the second row of the custom table. This text will just be used to see which view is currently being displayed.

Figure 158. The three buttons representing tabs on View 1 in InfoPath 2013.

8. Add an **Action** rule to the first button with an action that says:

```
Switch to view: View 1
```

This action switches to **View 1** when the first button is clicked.

9. Add a second action to the rule on the first button that says:

```
Set a field's value: lastClicked = "1"
```

This action sets the value of the **lastClicked** hidden field in the Main data source to be equal to **1** as an indication that the first button was the last button that the user clicked.

10. Add a **Formatting** rule to the first button with a **Condition** that says:

```
lastClicked = "1"
```

and a **Formatting** that sets the background color of the button to a light blue color.

11. Add an **Action** rule to the second button with an action that says:

```
Switch to view: View 2
```

This action switches to **View 2** when the second button is clicked.

12. Add a second action to the rule on the second button that says:

```
Set a field's value: lastClicked = "2"
```

This action sets the value of the **lastClicked** hidden field in the Main data source to be equal to **2** as an indication that the second button was the last button that the user clicked.

13. Add a **Formatting** rule to the second button with a **Condition** that says:

```
lastClicked = "2"
```

and a **Formatting** that sets the background color of the button to a light blue color.

14. Add an **Action** rule to the third button with an action that says:

```
Switch to view: View 3
```

This action switches to **View 3** when the third button is clicked.

15. Add a second action to the rule on the third button that says:

```
Set a field's value: lastClicked = "3"
```

This action sets the value of the **lastClicked** hidden field in the Main data source to be equal to **3** as an indication that the third button was the last button that the user clicked.

16. Add a **Formatting** rule to the third button with a **Condition** that says:

```
lastClicked = "3"
```

and a **Formatting** that sets the background color of the button to a light blue color.

17. Click the square in the upper left-hand corner of the custom table to select the entire table including the controls and text in it (or press **Ctrl+A** to select everything on the view), and then press **Ctrl+C** to copy the custom table with controls.

18. Switch to **View 2**, delete the default page layout, and then press **Ctrl+V** to paste the custom table and controls you copied from **View 1**.

19. Repeat the previous step for **View 3**. Copying and pasting the table and controls like this should make all 3 views look identical. In addition, you should notice that the **Action** and **Formatting** rules you defined on the buttons have also been copied along with the controls.

20. Switch to **View 2**, change the "Tab 1" text into "Tab 2".

21. Switch to **View 3**, change the "Tab 1" text into "Tab 3".

22. Click **Data ➤ Rules ➤ Form Load** to open the **Rules** task pane for the **Form Load** event.

23. Add an **Action** rule to the **Form Load** event with two actions that say:

    ```
    Switch to view: View 1
    Set a field's value: lastClicked = "1"
    ```

    This rule switches to **View 1** when the form opens and displays the first button as the selected button.

24. Preview the form.

When the form opens, **Tab 1** (**View 1**) should appear and the background color of the first button should be light blue. Click on any of the other two buttons to bring forward those tabs (views) and see the background color of the corresponding buttons change to light blue.

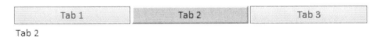

Tab 2

Figure 159. The tabbed interface in InfoPath 2013.

Discussion

In the solution described above, you saw how to create a basic tabbed interface using buttons and views. Such a solution is handy to use for example when you want to break controls up into separate groups or if you want to place controls on separate views and give the user a way to easily access those views by clicking on buttons.

Note that you could also use picture buttons instead of normal buttons to provide similar functionality and perhaps a slicker looking interface using images for the buttons (tabs).

In the solution described above, you also saw how to copy tables, controls, and rules from one view to another. Always be careful when copying rules, since references to fields may wind up being incorrect. So always double-check any rules you may have copied using either the method described in this recipe, or the **Copy Rule** or **Copy All Rules** command.

You may notice that for example when you click on the third button, the first button may get a black border around it as an indication that it has the focus. This is technically incorrect, since the third button should have the focus. You can change this behavior by specifying tab indexes for the buttons.

To specify the tab index for a button:

1. Open the **Button Properties** dialog box.

2. On the **Button Properties** dialog box, click the **Advanced** tab.

3. On the **Button Properties** dialog box on the **Advanced** tab, enter a number in the **Tab index** counter text box. The control that should receive the focus first on a view should get a tab index equal to **1** assigned to it. The control that should receive the focus next after the user presses **Tab** on the keyboard, should get a tab index equal to **2** assigned to it, etc.

For the buttons in the solution described above, the tab indexes should be assigned as listed in the following table:

View	Button	Tab Index
1	Tab 1	1
1	Tab 2	2
1	Tab 3	3
2	Tab 1	3

2	Tab 2	1
2	Tab 3	2
3	Tab 1	2
3	Tab 2	3
3	Tab 3	1

Note that because buttons are used to switch between the views, you could choose to remove the view names from the **Current View** menu by deselecting the **Show on the View menu when filling out this form** check box on the **General** tab on the **View Properties** dialog box for each view.

File Attachments

File Attachment controls allow you to attach files to InfoPath forms.

Figure 160. File Attachment control in InfoPath 2013.

To add a file to a file attachment control, you must first open the InfoPath form and then do one of two things to attach a file to the control:

1. Click on the text that says "Click here to attach a file".

2. Hover with the mouse pointer over the control until a paperclip icon appears in the upper left-hand corner, click on the icon to open the context menu, and then select **Attach** from the context menu.

Figure 161. Attach menu item on the context menu of a File Attachment control.

Once you attach a file to a file attachment control, the context menu will be expanded to contain more menu items of which you can use the **Cut** or **Remove** menu items to delete the file contained within the file attachment control.

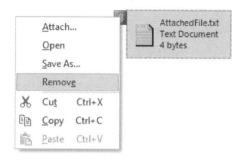

Figure 162. Remove menu item to delete the file contained within the control.

Any file you attach to an InfoPath form is stored within the InfoPath form itself as what is called a Base64 encoded string. To see what the contents of a file attachment control looks like: Save the InfoPath form locally on disk and then open it in Notepad. The contents of the file attachment control should look something like the following:

```
x01GQRQAAAABAAAAAAAAABEAAAARAAAASQBuAGYAbwBQAGEAdABoADIAMAAxADAALgB
0AHgAdAAAAEluZm9QYXRoIGlzIGNvb2wh
```

Such a piece of text string, while illegible to you, can be converted back to a binary file by InfoPath or by using code.

A file attachment control has several properties you can configure. If you look at the **Data** tab on the **File Attachment Properties** dialog box, you will find the following properties you can configure:

1. **Show file placeholder**
   This option allows the file attachment control to be empty at startup and displays the text "Click here to attach a file" in it.

2. **Specify default file**
   This option allows you to select a file to be included in the file attachment control by default. You are still able to replace the file when filling out the form.

3. **Allow the user to browse, delete, and replace files**
   When deselected, this option disables the **Attach**, **Remove**, **Cut**, and **Paste** menu items on the context menu of the file attachment control. When selected, all menu items are enabled.

4. **Cannot be blank**
   When selected, this option will make the file attachment control a mandatory field.

5. **Allow the user to attach only the following file types**
   This option is enabled for InfoPath Filler Forms and is disabled for Web Browser Forms. When enabled, it allows you to specify the file extensions of files that are allowed to be placed in the file attachment control.

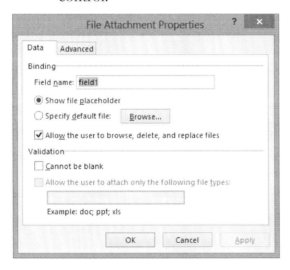

Figure 163. File Attachment Properties dialog box in InfoPath 2013.

You may have noticed that the **Paste** menu item on the context menu of the file attachment control is not always enabled. This menu item only becomes enabled when you have previously used the **Copy** menu item on the same or on another file attachment control on the form, and want to paste the file you copied to the same or to another file attachment control on the form. The **Copy** and **Paste** menu items effectively allow you to copy and paste files between file attachment controls on an InfoPath form.

87 Check if a file has been attached to a file attachment control

Problem

You have a file attachment control on an InfoPath form and want to check whether the user has attached a file to it.

Solution

To check whether a file is present within a file attachment control, you must check whether the field bound to the file attachment control has a value.

To check if a file has been attached to a file attachment control:

1. In InfoPath, create a new **Blank Form** template.

2. Add a **File Attachment** control, a **Button** control, and a **Text Box** control to the view of the form template. Name the file attachment control **myAttachment** and the text box **message**.

3. Add an **Action** rule to the button with a **Condition** that says:

   ```
   myAttachment is blank
   ```

   and an action that says:

   ```
   Set a field's value: message = "Attachment is not present"
   ```

   where **message** is a field that is located in the Main data source of the form and that is bound to the text box control, and where "Attachment is not present" is a static piece of text. This rule displays the message "Attachment is not present" in the text box when you click the button and no file has been attached to the file attachment control.

4. Add a second **Action** rule to the button with a **Condition** that says:

   ```
   myAttachment is not blank
   ```

   and an action that says:

```
Set a field's value: message = "Attachment is present"
```

This rule displays the message "Attachment is present" in the text box when you click the button and a file has been attached to the file attachment control.

5.   Preview the form

When the form opens, click the button before attaching a file to the file attachment control. The message "Attachment is not present" should appear in the text box. Attach a file to the file attachment control and then click the button again. The message "Attachment is present" should appear in the text box.

88 Clear a file attachment control

Problem

You have a file attachment control on an InfoPath form and want to be able to delete any file that has been attached to the file attachment control.

Solution

You can use an **Action** rule to set the value of the field that is bound to a file attachment control to be equal to an empty string to be able to clear the file attachment control and delete any file that has been attached to the file attachment control.

To clear a file attachment control:

1.   In InfoPath, create a new **Blank Form** template.

2.   Add a **File Attachment** control and a **Button** control to the view of the form template. Name the file attachment control **myAttachment**.

3.   Click the button to select it, and then select **Home ➤ Rules ➤ Add Rule ➤ When This Button Is Clicked ➤ Set a Field's Value**.

4.   On the **Rule Details** dialog box, click the button behind the **Field** text box.

5. On the **Select a Field or Group** dialog box, select **myAttachment**, and click **OK**.

6. On the **Rule Details** dialog box, leave the **Value** text box empty, and click **OK**. Note that leaving the **Value** text box empty results in the value being set to an empty string.

7. Preview the form.

When the form opens, attach a file to the file attachment control. Once you have attached a file, click the button. The file that you attached to the file attachment control should disappear.

89 Make an attachment read-only – method 1

Problem

You have a file attachment control and a check box control on an InfoPath form. You want users to be able to add a file to the file attachment control, but when the check box is selected, you want users to be able to only view the file that is stored within the file attachment control, but not change or delete it.

Solution

You can use conditional formatting on section controls containing file attachment controls to hide a modifiable file attachment control and show a read-only file attachment control containing the same file.

To make a file attachment control read-only:

1. In InfoPath, create a new **Blank Form** template.

2. Add two **Section** controls, one **File Attachment** control, and one **Check Box** control to the view of the form template. Name the file attachment control **myAttachment** and the check box control **isAttachmentReadOnly**.

3. Move the **File Attachment** control that is located on the view of the form template from its current location outside of both **Section** controls to a location inside of the first **Section** control. Note: To

move a control, click it, hold the left mouse button pressed down, and then drag it to a new location on the view of the form template.

4. On the **Fields** task pane, drag the **myAttachment** field to the view of the form template and drop it inside of the second section control. Select **File Attachment** from the context menu that appears when you drop the field inside of the second section control. Now you have two **File Attachment** controls on the view of the form template pointing to the same field in the Main data source of the form. You can also see that the two file attachment controls are pointing to the same field by hovering over the small blue info icon on either control. The tooltip text "myAttachment (Control stores duplicate data)" should appear.

5. Delete all empty lines within and between the **Section** controls, so that when one section control is hidden the other will move up or down to seamlessly take its place.

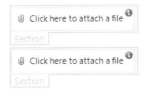

Figure 164. Two section controls without blank lines in or between them.

6. Right-click the second **File Attachment** control and select **File Attachment Properties** from the context menu that appears.

7. On the **File Attachment Properties** dialog box on the **Data** tab, deselect the **Allow the user to browse, delete, and replace files** check box, and click **OK**. The file attachment control in the second section is the read-only file attachment control, so users should not be able to alter its contents.

8. Click the first **Section** control to select it, and then add a **Formatting** rule to it with a **Condition** that says:

```
isAttachmentReadOnly = TRUE
```

and a **Formatting** of **Hide this control**. This rule will hide the first **Section** control that contains the modifiable file attachment control if the value of the **isAttachmentReadOnly** field is equal to **TRUE**, and show the **Section** control if the value of the **isAttachmentReadOnly** field is equal to **FALSE**. Note: Make sure you click on the text on the control that says "Section" and then on the **Rules** task pane double-check that **group1** is displayed below the title bar of the **Rules** task pane before you add the **Formatting** rule.

9. Click the second **Section** control to select it, and then add a **Formatting** rule to it with a **Condition** that says:

```
isAttachmentReadOnly = FALSE
```

and a **Formatting** of **Hide this control**. This rule will hide the second **Section** control that contains the read-only file attachment control if the value of the **isAttachmentReadOnly** field is equal to **FALSE**, and show the **Section** control if the value of the **isAttachmentReadOnly** field is equal to **TRUE**. Note: Make sure you click on the text on the control that says "Section" and then on the **Rules** task pane double-check that **group2** is displayed below the title bar of the **Rules** task pane before you add the **Formatting** rule.

10. Preview the form.

When the form opens, the modifiable file attachment control should appear. Attach a file to it. Then select the **isAttachmentReadOnly** check box. This action should hide the modifiable file attachment control and show the read-only file attachment control. You should not see anything move on the form, because the second section control should seamlessly take the place of the first section control. When you hover over the file attachment control and then click on the paperclip icon in its upper left-hand corner, you should only see options to **Open, Save As**, or **Copy** the file stored in the file attachment control, but not to **Attach, Remove, Cut**, or **Paste** the file.

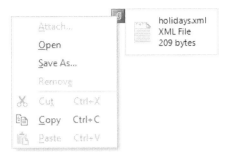

Figure 165. Menu of the file attachment control containing a file that cannot be modified.

Discussion

A file attachment control does not have a read-only property you can set to make it read-only, neither does it support conditional formatting when it is placed on a Web Browser Form, but you can still make a file attachment control read-only in one of two ways:

1. Use conditional formatting on a section control containing the file attachment control.

2. Place the file attachment control on a read-only view (see recipe *15 Add a read-only view*).

The first method was used in the solution described above. The second method is explained in recipe *90 Make an attachment read-only – method 2*.

Note that a file attachment control has a property called **Allow the user to browse, delete, and replace files** that you can turn on or off at design time to make the file stored in a file attachment control readable but not modifiable. You can use this property to make a file attachment control read-only if the state of the control does not depend on any conditions.

In the solution described above, the first file attachment control is used as a modifiable file attachment control so should be hidden if the check box, which indicates that the file attachment control is read-only, is selected.

The second file attachment control is used as a read-only file attachment control so should be hidden if the check box, which indicates that the file attachment control is read-only, is not selected.

You could delete the check box from the view of the form template to make the field it is bound to a hidden field (see recipe *11 Add a hidden field*). You could then set the value of this hidden field to **TRUE**, for example as soon as the form has been submitted (see recipe *44 Make a control read-only upon submit*), so that the next time the form opens, the file attachment control will be read-only. This is how you would go about making a file attachment control read-only when a form is submitted.

When section controls are hidden, they give up the space they normally take up on a form when they are visible. To make two section controls look like one and the same (without any visual displacements when one is shown and the other is hidden, and vice versa), you must ensure that there are no lines or spaces between the two section controls and that they have the same size. This trick was used in the solution described above to make two file attachment controls look like one and the same.

90 Make an attachment read-only – method 2

Problem

You have a file attachment control on an InfoPath form and want users to be able to add a file to it, but once the form has been submitted, you want to allow users to only view the file that is stored within the file attachment control, but not change or delete it.

Solution

You can use a read-only view with a modifiable file attachment control and a non-read-only view with a read-only file attachment control to make a file attachment control read-only.

To make a file attachment control read-only:

1. In InfoPath, create a new **Blank Form** template.

2. Add a **File Attachment** control to the default view of the form template and name it **myAttachment**.

3. Add a view named **Read-Only View** to the form template and make it read-only (see recipe *15 Add a read-only view*).

4. On the **Fields** task pane, drag the **myAttachment** field to the **Read-Only View** view, drop it, and select **File Attachment** from the context menu that appears when you drop it. Note: Placing the file attachment control on the read-only view will make the file attachment control inaccessible and users will only be able to see that it contains a file, but not open or view the file it contains.

5. Add a **Button** control to the **Read-Only View** view, and label it **View Attachment**. The read-only view will not affect the functioning of the button control, because buttons are not disabled or made read-only when placed on read-only views.

6. Add a third view named **Attachment View** to the form template. This view will be used as a view to limit access to the file attachment control and allow users to view any file the file attachment control contains, but not modify the file stored within the file attachment control.

7. On the **Fields** task pane, drag the **myAttachment** field to the **Attachment View** view, drop it, and select **File Attachment** from the context menu that appears when you drop it.

8. Because the **Attachment View** view is not read-only, you must disable the option for users to change the file in the file attachment control. So right-click the file attachment control and select **File Attachment Properties** from the context menu that appears.

9. On the **File Attachment Properties** dialog box on the **Data** tab, deselect the **Allow the user to browse, delete, and replace files** check box, and click **OK**.

10. Add a **Button** control to the **Attachment View** view, and label it **Back**.

11. Add an **Action** rule to the **Back** button on the **Attachment View** view with an action that says:

```
Switch to view: Read-Only View
```

This rule allows the user to navigate back to the **Read-Only View** view when the **Back** button is clicked.

12. Switch to the **Read-Only View** view, and then add an **Action** rule to the **View Attachment** button on the **Read-Only View** view with an action that says:

```
Switch to view: Attachment View
```

This rule allows the user to navigate to the **Attachment View** view when the **View Attachment** button is clicked.

13. Configure the form to be submitted and then to switch to the **Read-Only View** view on submit (see recipe *42 Switch to a read-only view on submit* and recipe *43 Switch to a read-only view when a form is opened after submission*).

14. Remove the **View menu** option on each one of the three views by deselecting the **Show on the View menu when filling out this form** check box on the **General** tab on the **View Properties** dialog box for each view.

15. Ensure that you have made **View 1 (default)** the startup view in the **View** drop-down list box on the **Page Design** tab.

16. Preview the form.

When the form opens, the default view should appear. Attach a file to the file attachment control and then click **Submit**. The form should then display the read-only view.

If you click the paperclip icon on the file attachment control, you should see that all of the menu items are disabled. And if you double-click the file in the file attachment control, the file should not open, so the user cannot read it.

Figure 166. Inaccessible file attachment control on a read-only view in InfoPath 2013.

Click the **View Attachment** button. The form should switch to and display the **Attachment View** view. If you now click the paperclip icon on the file attachment control, you should see the **Open**, **Save As**, and **Copy** menu items enabled, and when you double-click the file in the file attachment control, you should be able to open and view the file.

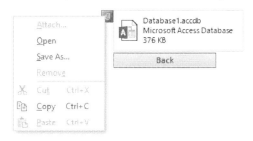

Figure 167. Readable but not modifiable file attachment control in InfoPath 2013.

Discussion

A file attachment control does not have a read-only property you can set to make it read-only, neither does it support conditional formatting when it is placed on a Web Browser Form, but you can still make a file attachment control read-only in one of two ways:

1. Use conditional formatting on a section control containing the file attachment control.

2. Place the file attachment control on a read-only view (see recipe *15 Add a read-only view*).

The first method was explained in recipe *89 Make an attachment read-only – method 1*. The second method was used in the solution described above.

The drawback of placing a file attachment control on a read-only view is that you are then unable to open or view the file stored within the file attachment control. To overcome this drawback, you can add a second non-read-only view to the form template, place a file attachment control on it, and bind the same field that is bound to the file attachment control on the read-only view to the file attachment control on the non-read-only view. This should allow you to open the file stored within the file attachment control. And then to prevent users from modifying the contents of the file attachment control, you can disallow browsing, deleting, and replacing of files through a property of the file attachment control. The last step would be to add buttons to the views to allow users to switch from the read-only view to the non-read-only view and vice versa.

91 Add multiple files to a file attachment control

Problem

You have a file attachment control on an InfoPath form and want to attach more than one file to the form by using this file attachment control.

Solution

A file attachment control can only contain one file at a time. To be able to store multiple files under the same field name in InfoPath, you must add a file attachment field to a repeating group, which you can then bind to either a **Repeating Table** or a **Repeating Section** control.

To add multiple files to a file attachment control:

1. In InfoPath, create a new **Blank Form** template.

2. Add a **Repeating Table** control with one column to the view of the form template.

3. Delete the text box control that InfoPath automatically added to the repeating table when you added the control to the view. Remember to also delete the field that the text box is bound to on the **Fields** task pane.

4. Place the cursor in the empty repeating table cell, and then click **Home ➤ Controls ➤ File Attachment** to add a file attachment control to the repeating table. Name the file attachment control **myAttachment**.

5. Preview the form.

When the form opens, attach a file using the file attachment control in the repeating table. If you want to attach more files to the form, you can click **Insert item** on the repeating table to add a new row to the repeating table, and then attach a second file. Continue adding as many rows to the repeating table as necessary to attach files to the form.

Chapter 9: Container Controls

Container controls include sections, repeating tables, repeating sections, and regions. Container controls as the name suggests are controls that can serve as a container for other controls.

Repeating tables and repeating sections are among the most often used container controls in InfoPath, so in this chapter you will learn how to use these controls.

Sections

Section controls are controls that can contain other controls or on which you can write text. Section controls are often used to group related controls and can be bound to group nodes in a data source (Main or Secondary).

Section controls are ideal candidates to use for displaying error messages, because they give up their visible space when they are hidden. In addition, because the use of pop-up error message boxes is discouraged when using InfoPath browser forms, you can use section controls instead to provide error display functionality in the browser when creating InfoPath Web Browser Forms.

And as you have already seen in recipe *89 Make an attachment read-only – method 1*, section controls can also be used to perform swapping tricks in InfoPath, again because of the space that they give up when they are hidden.

InfoPath comes with different types of section controls:

- **Section** – This control represents a single section that is static and always present on a form. It cannot be added or removed when the form is being filled out.

- **Optional Section** – This control represents a single section, which you can add or remove while filling out a form. It does not appear on the form by default; users have to add it to the form.

- **Choice Section** – This control represents a single section that can be replaced by a different section while filling out a form.

- **Repeating Section** – This control represents a section that repeats. You can insert additional sections while filling out a form.

- **Repeating Recursive Section** – This control represents a section that repeats and that can be inserted within itself.

Of all of the section controls mentioned above, only the first type of section control is non-dynamic, i.e. it cannot be added or removed while filling out a form. In addition, the first three types of section controls are single section controls, which means that only one section is displayed on the form at any given point in time.

92 Use sections to display error messages

Problem

You have an InfoPath form on which you want to use section controls to display error messages or other types of messages to the user, but you do not want these messages to be stored in the InfoPath form itself.

Solution

To avoid storing error messages in the Main data source of an InfoPath form, you can use an XML file as a Secondary data source that can temporarily hold error messages you want to display on the InfoPath form.

You must construct the XML file that will be used to display error messages in such a way that you can add section controls to the form template when you drag groups from the Secondary data source and place them on the view.

An XML file that has the following structure and contents should allow you to add section controls when you drag-and-drop one of its groups onto the view of the form template:

```
<messages>
  <message1><placeholder/></message1>
```

```
    <message2><placeholder/></message2>
    <message3><placeholder/></message3>
    <message4><placeholder/></message4>
</messages>
```

To use section controls to display error messages:

1.   In InfoPath, create a new **Blank Form** template.

2.   Add a data connection to the **messages** XML file above (see recipe *33 Get data from an XML file*) and name the data connection **Messages**.

3.   Add a **Text Box** control to the view of the form template and name it **myTextBox**.

4.   On the **Fields** task pane, select **Messages (Secondary)** from the drop-down list box.

5.   On the **Fields** task pane, drag-and-drop the **message1** group onto the view of the form template and place it below the text box. Delete any empty lines within the section control. Also delete the **placeholder** text box control that is located within the section control and replace it with the message you want to display, for example "You must enter a piece of text".

6.   Add a second **Text Box** control to the view of the form template and place it below the section control.

7.   Add a **Formatting** rule to the section control with a **Condition** that says:

```
myTextBox is not blank
```

and a **Formatting** of **Hide this control**, where **myTextBox** is a field that is located in the Main data source of the form and that is bound to the first text box control on the view. This rule ensures that when the first text box is empty, the section will become visible, and soon after you type something into the first text box and move off the text box by clicking or tabbing away from the text box, the section will become hidden.

8.   Preview the form.

When the form opens, the section with the message should be visible. Type something in the first text box and move to the second text box. The section should disappear. Empty the first text box. The section should appear. Save the form to disk, open it in Notepad, and then verify that the message has not been stored in the InfoPath form (XML file).

Discussion

If you need to use fields or groups in InfoPath as a way to help you do something else or as in the solution described above to display error messages, it is best to use a Secondary data source (for example an XML file) instead of creating a field or group in the Main data source of the form.

When you use a Secondary data source, the data from the data source will not be stored in the form itself, so will also not unnecessarily make forms large, bulky, and/or contain data that is unrelated or irrelevant to other data contained in the form itself.

Important:

All data that is part of the Main data source of a form will be permanently stored in the form itself (XML file that represents the InfoPath form). Any data that is stored in Secondary data sources you have added to a form template will not be stored in the form, so will be lost when you save or submit and then close the form. The data of Secondary data sources is never persisted in an InfoPath form.

In the solution described above, the **placeholder** field within the **message1** group was replaced by a static message saying "You must enter a piece of text". If you want to make the error message dynamic (so set it at runtime using a rule), you can use the **placeholder** field within the **message1** group, and change the **placeholder** text box into a **Calculated Value** control so that it displays as a label without any borders around it and becomes read-only within the section control. And then you can use an **Action** rule to dynamically set the value of the **placeholder** field to be equal to the message you want to display (also see recipe *82 Dynamically change the label of a text box when an option is selected*).

93 Make a field mandatory when a specific choice section is selected

Problem

You have a choice section control on an InfoPath form and want to make a text box control mandatory whenever one specific choice section is added to the form.

Solution

You can use a **Validation** rule with an **is present** condition to check whether the choice section has been selected by a user, and then if it has been, make the text box mandatory.

To make a field mandatory when a specific choice section is selected:

1. In InfoPath, create a new **Blank Form** template.

2. Add a **Choice Group** control to the view of the form template. The choice group control should contain two choice section controls named **group2** and **group3**. Rename **group2** to **travelRequest** and rename **group3** to **travelExpense**.

3. Click to place the cursor within the choice group control, but outside of and below the second choice section control, and then click **Home ➤ Controls ➤ Choice Section** to add a third choice section to the choice group control. Rename the third choice section you added to **travelReimbursement**.

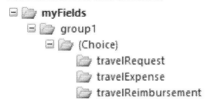

Figure 168. A choice group with 3 choice sections.

4. Type the static pieces of text "Travel Request", "Travel Expense", and "Travel Reimbursement" inside of their corresponding choice sections,

so that you know which choice section is being displayed when the form is being filled out. In a real-world scenario, you would add other controls within the choice section controls. We are just keeping things simple here by adding static pieces of text to the choice sections.

5. Add a **Text Box** control to the view of the form template and name it **mandatoryTravelExpense**. You will be making this text box a required field if the user adds the **travelExpense** choice section to the form.

6. Select the text box, and then click **Home ➤ Rules ➤ Manage Rules**.

7. On the **Rules** task pane, click **New ➤ Validation**.

8. On the **Rules** task pane, type "This field is mandatory" in the **ScreenTip** text box, and then under **Condition**, click the text **None**.

9. On the **Condition** dialog box, select **Select a field or group** from the first drop-down list box.

10. On the **Select a Field or Group** dialog box, expand **group1** (which is the group node that is bound to the choice group control), expand **(Choice)**, select the **travelExpense** group, and click **OK**.

11. On the **Condition** dialog box, select **is present** from the second drop-down list box, and click **And**.

12. On the **Condition** dialog box, select **mandatoryTravelExpense** from the first drop-down list box for the second expression, select **is blank** from the second drop-down list box for the second expression, and click **OK**. The condition on the **Rules** task pane should now say:

```
travelExpense is present
and
mandatoryTravelExpense is blank
```

This rule checks whether the group node that is bound to the **travelExpense** choice section is present in the Main data source of the form, so whether it was selected by a user, and if it is present and the **mandatoryTravelExpense** text box is blank, the validation error is displayed.

13. Preview the form.

When the form opens, you should see the **travelRequest** choice section appear. Hover over it until you see a control appear in its top left-hand corner. Click the control and select **Replace with travelExpense** from the context menu that appears. You should now see the **travelExpense** choice section appear in addition to a red asterisk in the text box. And when you hover over the text box, you should see the validation error message appear. Enter a piece of text in the text box. The red asterisk should disappear.

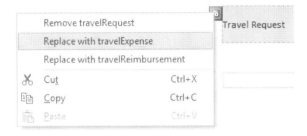

Figure 169. Replacing the travelRequest with the travelExpense choice section.

Discussion

In the solution described above, you used an **is present** condition to check whether a choice section was selected by a user.

When you replace a choice section with a different choice section, the choice section that was replaced is removed from the Main data source of the form. This means that if you want to check whether a particular choice section was selected by a user, you must check whether the group node that is bound to that choice section is present in the Main data source of the form. And this is why you must use **is present** in the condition for a rule.

You might be wondering: Why use **is present** instead of **is not blank** in the condition for the rule? The simple reason for this is that **is not blank** is typically used to check the value of a field; not the presence of a group. A section control is a container control, so technically speaking it should not have a value. Therefore, you should not use **is blank** or **is not blank** with section controls that can be removed from a form while it is being filled out (for example **Optional Section** and **Choice Section**), but instead you should use **is present** or **is not present** to check whether the group nodes that are bound to such section controls are present in the Main data source of the form or not. Note that InfoPath does allow you to use **is blank** and **is not blank** checks on removable sections that contain other controls that are bound to fields or groups under the group nodes bound to the removable sections.

Choice group controls start up with one choice section selected by default. In the solution described above, this was the **travelRequest** choice section. You can change the choice section a choice group starts up with by default through the **Edit Default Values** dialog box, which you can open via **Data ➤ Form Data ➤ Default Values**.

Figure 170. travelReimbursement selected as the default choice section.

When testing the InfoPath form created in the solution described above, you saw that you could replace a choice section with another choice section through a context menu on the choice section control. You can change the text that is displayed for the menu items that are listed in this context menu through the **Section Commands** dialog box of each choice section control, which you can access by clicking on the **Customize Commands** button on the **Data** tab of the **Choice Section Properties** dialog box of a choice section control.

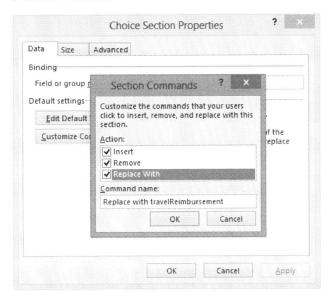

Figure 171. The Section Commands dialog box for a choice section control.

Repeating Tables and Repeating Sections

A repeating control in InfoPath is a control to which you can add rows or sections, or from which you can remove rows or sections. A section is a control that can contain other controls and is often used to group related controls.

There are 5 types of repeating controls in InfoPath:

1. Repeating Table
2. Repeating Section
3. Horizontal Repeating Table (only available in InfoPath Filler Forms)
4. Repeating Recursive Section (only available in InfoPath Filler Forms)
5. Repeating Choice Group (only available in InfoPath Filler Forms)

Repeating Table and **Repeating Section** controls are the most commonly used repeating controls in InfoPath. Structurally, there is no difference between a **Repeating Table** and a **Repeating Section** control. While they look different on an InfoPath form, their data source structure is similar. You can verify this by adding a **Repeating Table** control to the view of an InfoPath form template and then looking at how the Main data source changed on the **Fields** task pane. Then add a **Repeating Section** control to the view of the form template, add 3 **Text Box** controls within the repeating section, and then look at the Main data source on the **Fields** task pane again. You should see a similar structure for both the repeating table and the repeating section.

Figure 172. Data source of a repeating table or repeating section on the Fields task pane.

As you can see from the figure shown above, the data structure of a repeating table or a repeating section consists of:

1. A non-repeating group (**group1**)
2. A repeating group (**group2**)
3. One or more fields (**field1**, **field2**, **field3**)

If we now take the repeating table shown in Figure 173, **group1** would represent the table itself (so the container for all of the rows and columns), **group2** would represent a row in the table, and **field1**, **field2**, and **field3**, would represent the columns.

A table can have one or more rows, so one or more **group2** nodes, which is why **group2** is called a repeating group. **field1**, **field2**, and **field3** are repeated along with the **group2** nodes to form table cells that contain data.

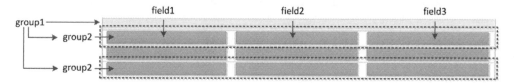

Figure 173. Relationship between a repeating table and nodes in the data source.

The name **Repeating Table** is a little bit misleading, because the table itself is not repeated, but its rows are.

Repeating table rows and repeating sections can be filtered using either conditional formatting (see for example recipe *111 Hide a row of a repeating table when a check box is selected*) or the **Filter Data** command, which is available on repeating tables and repeating sections that are bound to repeating groups in the Main data source of a form (see the discussion section of recipe *121 Master/detail functionality with one master and two detail lists*).

94 4 Ways to add a control to a repeating table

Problem

You have a repeating table on an InfoPath form template or a repeating group in the Main data source of the form and want to add a rich text box control to one of its columns.

Solution

There are four ways you can add a rich text box control (or any other type of control) to a repeating table.

Method 1 for adding a control (a rich text box in this case) to a repeating table:

1. In InfoPath, create a new **Blank Form** template.

2. Add a **Repeating Table** control with one column to the view of the form template.

3. InfoPath automatically adds a text box in the newly added column (if you have the **Automatically create data source** check box selected on the **Controls** task pane). Because you want to place your own control in the column, you must delete the text box that InfoPath added. So select the text box control and press **Delete** on your keyboard. And because the field that the text box was bound to still exists in the Main data source, you must click on the drop-down arrow on the right-hand side

of that field on the **Fields** task pane, and select **Delete** from the drop-down menu that appears to delete the field from the Main data source.

4. Click within the empty column to place the cursor inside of the cell of the repeating table, and then click **Home ➤ Controls ➤ Rich Text Box** or if you have the **Controls** task pane open, click **Rich Text Box** to add a rich text box control to the column of the repeating table. You can use this method to select any other control you want to add to a repeating table.

Method 2 for adding a control (a rich text box in this case) to a repeating table:

1. In InfoPath, create a new **Blank Form** template.

2. Add a **Repeating Table** control with one column to the view of the form template.

3. Click on the text box in the column of the repeating table to select it, and then click **Properties ➤ Properties ➤ Field Properties**.

4. On the **Field or Group Properties** dialog box on the **Data** tab, select **Rich Text (XHTML)** from the **Data type** drop-down list box, and click **OK**. The text box control in the repeating table now displays the message "Control cannot store this data type" when you hover over it.

Figure 174. "Control cannot store this data type" error message in InfoPath 2013.

5. Right-click the text box and select **Change Control ➤ Rich Text Box** from the context menu that appears. The message should disappear.

Method 3 for adding a control (a rich text box in this case) to a repeating table:

1. In InfoPath, create a new **Blank Form** template.

2. Add a **Repeating Table** control to the view of the form template.

3. On the **Fields** task pane, click the drop-down arrow behind **group2** (the repeating group bound to the repeating table), and select **Add** from

the drop-down menu that appears.

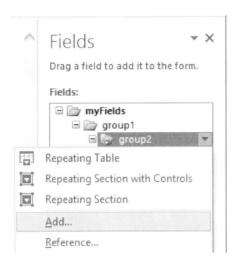

Figure 175. Add menu item on drop-down menu of the repeating group.

4. On the **Add Field or Group** dialog box, enter a name for the field (for example **myRichTextBox**), select **Rich Text (XHTML)** from the **Data type** drop-down list box, and click **OK**.

5. Right-click any column in the repeating table, and select **Insert ➤ Columns to the Right** from the context menu that appears.

6. InfoPath automatically adds a text box in the newly added column (if you have the **Automatically create data source** check box selected on the **Controls** task pane). Because you want to place your own control in the column, you must delete the text box that InfoPath added. So select the text box control and press **Delete** on your keyboard. And because the field that the text box was bound to still exists in the Main data source, you must click on the drop-down arrow on the right-hand side of that field on the **Fields** task pane, and select **Delete** from the drop-down menu that appears to delete the field from the Main data source.

7. On the **Fields** task pane, drag the **myRichTextBox** field to the view of the form template and drop it inside of the cell of the column you just added. It should automatically get bound to a **Rich Text Box** control.

Method 4 for adding a control (a rich text box in this case) to a repeating table:

1. In InfoPath, create a new **Blank Form** template.

2. Add a **Repeating Table** control to the view of the form template.

3. Add a **Rich Text Box** control to the view of the form template on a location anywhere outside of the repeating table.

4. On the **Fields** task pane, select the field that is bound to the rich text box (this field is named **field4** if you started with a new form template and accepted the default of 3 columns in the repeating table), click on the drop-down arrow on the right-hand side of the field, and select **Move** from the drop-down menu that appears.

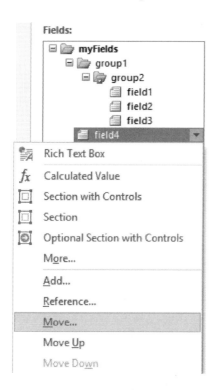

Figure 176. Moving field4 to another location in the Main data source.

5. On the **Move Field or Group** dialog box, expand **group1**, select **group2** (which is bound to the repeating table), and then click **OK**.

Figure 177. Moving myField to a location under group2.

field4 should now be located under **group2** on the **Fields** task pane.

Figure 178. Field4 moved to a location under group2.

If you hover over the rich text box on the view of the form template, you should see a message saying "Control cannot store data correctly" appear. This is because the rich text box should now be moved to a column inside of the repeating table, since the field that it is bound to is located under the repeating group node that is bound to the repeating table.

6. Delete one of the text boxes that InfoPath automatically added to the repeating table, and then drag-and-drop the rich text box into the empty cell within the repeating table. The message should disappear.

Discussion

All of the methods described in this recipe make use of the same principle, i.e. that you must first have a field of type **Rich Text (XHTML)** under the repeating group node that is bound to the repeating table, and then you can bind this field to a **Rich Text Box** control that is located inside of the repeating table control on the view of the form template.

The four methods described in this recipe can be used to add any type of control to a repeating table. The only thing you must be aware of is that you must select the right data type and/or create the right structure for a field to be able to bind it to the control you desire. The easiest method from the four methods to add any type of control to a repeating table would probably be the first method.

Beginners often make the mistake of first adding a control to the view of a form template and then dragging-and-dropping that control into a repeating table control. If you do this, you may see a message saying

Control cannot repeat here

appear on the control you dragged-and-dropped into the repeating table.

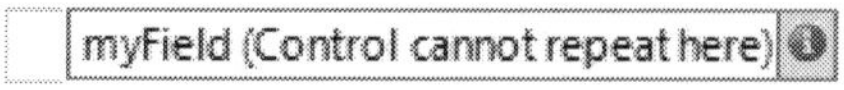

myField (Control cannot repeat here)

Figure 179. "Control cannot repeat here" message on a control in a repeating table.

This is because that control is not bound to a field that is part of the repeating group that the repeating table is bound to. If you look on the **Fields** task pane at the location of the field that is bound to the control, you should see that it is not located below the repeating group that the repeating table is bound to.

So to correct this message, you must move the field to a location under the repeating group that the repeating table is bound to by using the **Move** menu item in the drop-down menu of the field on the **Fields** task pane, and then on the **Move Field or Group** dialog box, select the repeating group that the repeating table is bound to as you did in method 4 in the solution described above.

Note that once you have used the **Move** menu item to move a field to a location under a repeating group, you can use the **Move Up** or **Move Down** menu item in the drop-down menu for that field to move the field up or down in the list of fields under the repeating group.

Exercise

In this recipe you learned four ways to add a control to a repeating table. Use the first method to add a repeating table within a cell of another repeating table to create nested repeating tables. What does the Main data source look like after you have done this?

Exercise

Try using one of the four methods to add a **Multiple-Selection List Box** control to a column of the repeating table.

---

95 Remove the first empty row of a repeating table

Problem

You have a repeating table control on an InfoPath form. When the form opens, the repeating table displays an empty row by default. You want the repeating table to start up with no rows.

Solution

You can remove the default row that a repeating table starts up with through the **Edit Default Values** dialog box.

To remove the first empty row of a repeating table:

1. In InfoPath, create a new **Blank Form** template.

2. Add a **Repeating Table** control to the view of the form template.

3. Click **Data** ➤ **Form Data** ➤ **Default Values**.

4. On the **Edit Default Values** dialog box, expand **group1**, deselect the check box in front of **group2** or right-click **group2** and select **Exclude this group from the initial form** menu item in the drop-down menu that appears, and then click **OK**.

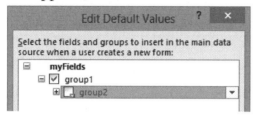

Figure 180. Removing the first empty row from a repeating table.

5. Preview the form.

When the form opens, the repeating table should not contain any rows.

Discussion

In the solution described above, you saw how to use the **Edit Default Values** dialog box to prevent a repeating table from having any rows when a new InfoPath form opens.

You could have also used a **Formatting** rule to hide the first empty row of a repeating table instead of removing it (see recipe *110 Hide the first row of a repeating table*). Whether you hide or remove the first empty row is up to you. But typically, if you want to store data in the first row of the repeating table, but not display this data to the user, you may want to choose to hide the first row. In all other cases, you may want to choose to remove the row.

Note:

> The option to exclude the repeating group bound to a repeating table is only available if you have one repeating group node (**group2** in this recipe) for a repeating table on the **Edit Default Values** dialog box. If you have multiple repeating group nodes defined for a repeating table (also see recipe *96 Display a fixed amount of rows in a repeating table*), you must first remove all of them and leave only one for the option to exclude the repeating group to become available again.

96 Display a fixed amount of rows in a repeating table

Problem

You have a repeating table on an InfoPath form and want to always display 3 rows in it in addition to not allowing users to add or delete any rows.

Solution

You can add a default amount of rows to a repeating table and configure properties of the repeating table to disallow the addition and deletion of rows.

Note: If you want to allow users to add or delete rows, but not go over a certain amount of rows in the repeating table, see recipe *114 Limit the amount of rows added to a repeating table to a maximum*.

To display a fixed amount of rows in a repeating table:

1. In InfoPath, create a new **Blank Form** template.

2. Add a **Repeating Table** control to the view of the form template.

3. Click **Data** ➤ **Form Data** ➤ **Default Values**.

4. On the **Edit Default Values** dialog box, expand **group1**, right-click **group2**, and select **Add another group2 above** or **Add another**

group2 below from the drop-down menu that appears.

Figure 181. Selecting to add another group2 as a default row to a repeating table.

5. Repeat the previous step so that you wind up having a total of 3 **group2** nodes.

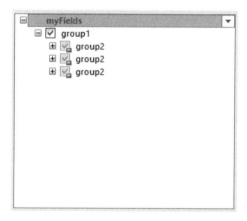

Figure 182. Default group2 nodes representing 3 default rows in a repeating table.

These 3 **group2** nodes will appear as 3 empty default rows when the form opens. Note that you can also add default values to the fields in the 3 default rows by expanding any of the **group2** nodes, selecting one of the fields (for example **field1**) under the selected **group2** node, and then entering a value or constructing a formula for the **Default value** text box on the **Edit Default Values** dialog box.

6. On the **Edit Default Values** dialog box, click **OK**.

7. Right-click the repeating table and select **Repeating Table Properties** from the context menu that appears.

8. On the **Repeating Table Properties** dialog box on the **Data** tab, deselect the **Allow users to insert and delete rows** check box, and click **OK**. This should prevent the **Insert item** command and the drop-down menu for adding and removing rows from appearing on the repeating table.

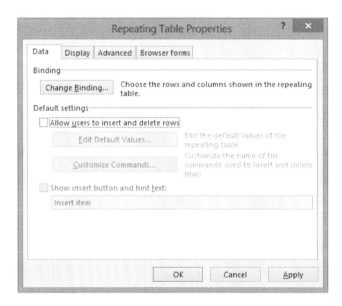

Figure 183. Disallowing users to insert and delete rows.

9. Preview the form.

When the form opens, you should see 3 rows appear in the repeating table. And when you hover over any row, you should not see controls for adding or removing rows appear on the left-hand side of the repeating table, so the amount of rows is effectively fixed at 3.

Discussion

In the solution described above, you saw how to configure a repeating table in such a way to make it display a fixed amount of rows. You thereby removed all of the commands with which a user can add or delete rows.

If you open the **Repeating Table Properties** dialog box again, and select the **Allow users to insert and delete rows** check box, you will see a button named **Customize Commands** become enabled. Click on this button to open the **Table Commands** dialog box where you can select which commands to enable or disable on the repeating table.

Figure 184. The Table Commands dialog box with only the Remove command enabled.

Any commands you select on the **Table Commands** dialog box, will appear as a menu item on the control that appears on the left-hand side of a repeating table row whenever you hover over a row.

Note that you can also customize the piece of text that is displayed for a menu item representing a command on the table. For example, in Figure 184 and Figure 185, the text "Remove this row" was used for the **Remove** command on a repeating table. In addition, only the **Remove** command was enabled on the **Table Commands** dialog box, so only a menu item to remove a row will appear in the drop-down menu for a row of the repeating table.

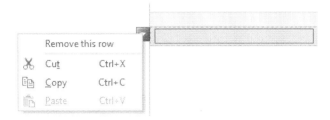

Figure 185. Drop-down menu containing commands for a row of a repeating table.

A repeating table also comes by default with a command named **Insert item**, which is displayed immediately below the last row of the repeating table and which users can use to insert a row.

Figure 186. The "Insert item" command of a repeating table.

You can select or deselect the **Show insert button and hint text** check box on the **Data** tab of the **Repeating Table Properties** dialog box to show or hide the **Insert item** command. And if you choose to show it, you can also change the piece of text that is displayed for the command. For example, if a repeating table contains a list of products, you can change the text to say "Insert product" instead of "Insert item".

Figure 187. The text of the "Insert item" command changed to "Insert product".

97 Make an entire repeating table read-only

Problem

You have a repeating table on an InfoPath form which you want to make read-only in its entirety.

Solution

You can make a repeating table read-only by making each field in the repeating table read-only by disabling the control.

To make a repeating table read-only:

1. In InfoPath, create a new **Blank Form** template.

2. Add a **Repeating Table** control to the view of the form template.

3. Click **Home ➤ Rules ➤ Manage Rules**.

4. Click one of the fields in the repeating table to select it, and then on the **Rules** task pane, click **New ➤ Formatting**.

5. On the **Rules** task pane under **Formatting**, select the **Disable this control** check box.

6. On the **Rules** task pane under **Condition**, click the text **None**.

7. On the **Condition** dialog box, select **The expression** from the first drop-down list box, replace the text in the text box with

    ```
    true()
    ```

    and click **OK**.

8. On the **Rules** task pane, right-click the rule you just added, and select **Copy Rule** from the drop-down menu that appears.

9. Click another field in the repeating table that you want to make read-only to select it, and then on the **Rules** task pane, click the **Paste Rule** command below the title bar to paste the rule. Repeat this step for all of the other fields you want to make read-only.

10. Preview the form.

When the form opens, you should not be able to change any of the read-only fields in the repeating table.

Discussion

By setting the expression for a condition on a rule to be equal to the **true** function, that rule will always run and run as soon as the form opens.

Text box controls have a **Read-only** property you can set to make the controls read-only, but many controls in InfoPath do not have such a property. If a control does not have a read-only property, then you must use conditional formatting to disable the control and make it read-only. Note that in the solution described above, you could have selected the **Read-only** property of the text boxes instead of using conditional formatting to make the controls in the repeating table read-only.

But you cannot apply conditional formatting to all controls in InfoPath either, because not all controls support it. For example, a file attachment control on a Web Browser Form does not support conditional formatting. In such cases, you would have to configure the control to disallow the user to browse, delete, and replace files (in the case of the file attachment control) or put the control on a read-only view (see recipe *15 Add a read-only view*).

In the solution described above, you made the controls in the rows of the repeating table read-only, but users were still able to add and delete rows. If you do not want to allow users to add or delete rows, you must deselect the **Allow users to insert and delete rows** check box on the **Repeating Table Properties** dialog box (see the discussion section of recipe *96 Display a fixed amount of rows in a repeating table*). This will make the repeating table completely read-only. And if you want the repeating table to be read-only based on a condition, you can apply the same trick as explained in recipe *114 Limit the amount of rows added to a repeating table to a maximum* to switch between a readable and a read-only version of the repeating table based on a condition.

98   Make rows of a repeating table read-only by using check boxes

Problem

You have a repeating table on an InfoPath form and want to disable a row so that fields in it cannot be modified when you select a check box within that row.

Solution

You can use conditional formatting on a field in a row of a repeating table to disable it whenever a check box in the same row as that field is selected.

To make rows of a repeating table read-only by using check boxes:

1. In InfoPath, create a new **Blank Form** template.

2. Add a **Repeating Table** control with 3 columns to the view of the form template.

3. Replace the third text box in the repeating table with a **Check Box** control.

4. Right-click the check box control and select **Check Box Properties** from the context menu that appears.

5. On the **Check Box Properties** dialog box, change the name to **isLocked**, change the data type to **True/False (boolean)**, select the **Cleared** option as the default state, select **FALSE** for the **Value when cleared** property, select **TRUE** for the **Value when checked** property, and then click **OK**.

6. For each field in the repeating table that you want to lock or make read-only, add a **Formatting** rule to the field with a **Condition** that says:

   ```
   isLocked = TRUE
   ```

   and that has a **Formatting** of **Disable this control**.

7. Preview the form.

When the form opens, enter text in any of the fields for which you set up a **Formatting** rule, and then select the check box in the same row as that field. The field should become read-only and you should not be able to modify the text in that field. Add more rows to the repeating table and try locking fields in other rows.

Discussion

While the solution described above locks fields on an individual basis, there might be instances when you want to lock all of the fields in a row collectively. Because a repeating table does not support disabling a row through conditional formatting, you could choose to hide the row instead.

99 Count the number of rows in a repeating table – method 1

Problem

You have a repeating table on an InfoPath form and want to know how many rows the repeating table contains.

Solution

You can use the **count** function in a formula to determine how many rows a repeating table contains.

To count the number of rows in a repeating table from a field that is located outside of the repeating table:

1. In InfoPath, create a new **Blank Form** template.

2. Add a **Repeating Table** control to the view of the form template.

3. Add a **Text Box** control to the view of the form template and name it **totalCount**. This text box should be located somewhere outside of the repeating table.

4. Click the **totalCount** text box to select it, and then click **Properties ➤ Properties ➤ Default Value**.

5. On the **Field or Group Properties** dialog box, set the **Default Value** of the **totalCount** text box to be equal to the following formula:

```
count(group2)
```

where **group2** is the repeating group that is bound to the repeating table and that represents rows in the repeating table.

6. On the **Field or Group Properties** dialog box, leave the **Refresh value when formula is recalculated** check box selected, and click **OK**.

7. Preview the form.

When the form opens, a 1 should appear in the text box, because the repeating table starts up displaying 1 row. Insert another row. The value of the text box should increase to 2. Remove a row. The number in the text box should decrease by 1.

Discussion

The **count** function in InfoPath is a function that takes a field or group as its argument and counts the number of instances of that field or group. You generally use the **count** function on repeating groups or repeating fields.

In the solution described above, **group2** is the repeating group that is bound to the repeating table, so represents a row in the repeating table. If you want to count the amount of rows in the repeating table, you must count the number of instances of **group2** in the repeating table, which the solution does by using the formula:

```
count(group2)
```

The solution described above makes use of a field that is located outside of the repeating table and not inside of the repeating table to count the amount or rows. If you want to count rows from inside of the repeating table, you must use a technique that navigates to either the parent repeating **group2** node of the current context node or the grandparent **group1** node of the current context node, and then count the amount of **group2** nodes (see recipe *100 Count the number of rows in a repeating table – method 2*).

100 Count the number of rows in a repeating table – method 2

Problem

You have a repeating table on an InfoPath form and want to know how many rows the repeating table contains.

Solution

You can use the **count** function together with the **preceding-sibling** and **following-sibling** XPath axes in a formula to determine how many rows a repeating table contains. Or you can use the **count** function together with an XPath expression that navigates to the container **group1** node of the repeating table before counting the amount of **group2** nodes of the repeating table.

To count the number of rows in a repeating table from a field that is located inside of the repeating table:

1. In InfoPath, create a new **Blank Form** template.

2. Add a **Repeating Table** control with 2 columns to the view of the form template.

3. Click the **field2** text box in the repeating table to select it, and then click **Properties** ➤ **Properties** ➤ **Default Value**.

4. On the **Field or Group Properties** dialog box, set the **Default Value** of **field2** to be equal to the following formula:

```
count(../preceding-sibling::*) + count(../following-sibling::*)
+ 1
```

What this formula does is:

a. Start at the context node, which is **field2**. This is the node on which you are currently setting the default value.

b. Move to its parent

```
..
```

which is a **group2** node.

c. Get all of the sibling nodes preceding the **group2** node

```
../preceding-sibling::*
```

so get all of the **group2** nodes that are located before the **group2** node of the context node.

d. Count all of the **group2** nodes that are located before the **group2** node of the context node

```
count(../preceding-sibling::*)
```

e. Get all of the sibling nodes following the **group2** node

```
../following-sibling::*
```

so get all of the **group2** nodes that are located after the **group2** node of the context node.

f. Count all of the **group2** nodes that are located after the **group2** node of the context node

```
count(../following-sibling::*)
```

g. Add a **1** to the total, because the **group2** node of the context node is omitted by both the **preceding-sibling** and **following-sibling** XPath axes, so you must include it to complete the total count. This gives the final formula:

```
count(../preceding-sibling::*) + count(../following-
sibling::*) + 1
```

You could also use the following formula to set the **Default Value** of **field2** and achieve the same results:

```
count(../../my:group2)
```

This formula navigates to the parent node (**group1**) of the parent node (**group2**) of the context node (**field2**), before navigating down to retrieve and count all of the **group2** nodes in the repeating table.

5. On the **Field or Group Properties** dialog box, leave the **Refresh value when formula is recalculated** check box selected, and click **OK**.

6. Preview the form.

When the form opens, a 1 should appear in the text box bound to **field2**. Click **Insert item** to insert a new row. The number in the **field2** text box should now be a 2. Insert and remove rows to see how the count changes.

Discussion

An XPath axis defines a node-set (set of nodes) relative to the current node. The **preceding-sibling** XPath axis selects all of the sibling nodes that are located before the current node, while the **following-sibling** XPath axis selects all of the sibling nodes that are located after the current node. In the solution described above,

```
count(../preceding-sibling::*)
```

counts all of the **group2** nodes that are located before the **group2** node above the current field (**field2**), while

```
count(../following-sibling::*)
```

counts all of the **group2** nodes that are located after the **group2** node above the current field (**field2**). And because the **group2** node of the current field (**field2**) is excluded by both XPath axes, you must add a 1 to the total sum, which gives you the final formula:

```
count(../preceding-sibling::*) + count(../following-sibling::*) + 1
```

which counts the amount of rows in a repeating table from a field located within the repeating table.

Figure 188 visually explains how the XPath navigation in this recipe works:

1. The navigation starts at the context node, which is a **field2** node in a row of the repeating table.

2. The parent of the context node is retrieved. This is the **group2** node above the **field2** node.

3. Starting from the **group2** node of the **field2** node, all of the **group2** nodes preceding the current **group2** node are retrieved.

4. Starting from the **group2** node of the **field2** node, all of the **group2** nodes following the current **group2** node are retrieved.

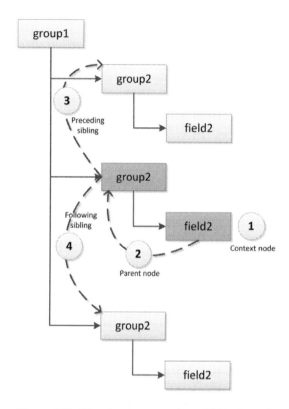

Figure 188. Visual representation of XPath navigation using axes.

Other useful XPath axes you could use in InfoPath formulas include:

- Ancestor – selects all of the ancestors (parent, grandparent, etc.) of the current node.

- Ancestor-or-self – selects all of the ancestors (parent, grandparent, etc.) of the current node and the current node itself.

- Child – selects all of the children of the current node.

- Descendant – selects all of the descendants (children, grandchildren, etc.) of the current node.

- Descendant-or-self – selects all of the descendants (children, grandchildren, etc.) of the current node and the current node itself.

- Parent – selects the parent of the current node.

- Preceding – Selects all of the nodes that appear before the current node, except for ancestors, attribute nodes, and namespace nodes.

- Self – selects the current node.

Note that just like in recipe *99 Count the number of rows in a repeating table – method 1* , in this recipe you had to leave the **Refresh value when formula is recalculated** check box on the **Field or Group Properties** dialog box selected, so that the total amount of rows is updated both when a row is added as well as removed from the repeating table. This also means that the same total amount of rows will be displayed in all of the **field2** text boxes in the rows of the repeating table. If you want to display sequential numbers in a field in a repeating table, you can use the technique described in recipe *103 Automatically number repeating table rows*.

101 Count the number of rows changed in a repeating table

Problem

You have a repeating table on an InfoPath form and want to know in how many rows values were changed.

Solution

You can use the **count** function and a filter condition to count the amount of rows that have been changed in a repeating table.

To count the number of rows that have been changed in a repeating table:

1. In InfoPath, create a new **Blank Form** template.

2. Add a **Repeating Table** control with 4 columns to the view of the form template. Name the text boxes in the repeating table **firstName**, **lastName**, **hasChanged**, and **oldValue**, respectively.

3. Change the third text box in the repeating table into a **Check Box** control.

4. Right-click the check box control and select **Check Box Properties** from the context menu that appears.

5. On the **Check Box Properties** dialog box, change the data type to **True/False (boolean)**, select the **Cleared** option as the default state, select **FALSE** for the **Value when cleared** property, select **TRUE** for the **Value when checked** property, and then click **OK**.

6. Add an **Action** rule to the **firstName** text box in the repeating table that has a **Condition** that says:

```
oldValue ≠ normalize-space(concat(., " ", lastName))
```

and an action that says:

```
Set a field's value: hasChanged = true()
```

where **oldValue** is the field that is bound to the last text box control in the repeating table, the dot (.) represents the **firstName** text box in the repeating table, **lastName** is the field that is bound to the second text box control in the repeating table, **hasChanged** is the field that is bound to the check box control in the repeating table and `true()` is the **true** function, which you must set by using the **Insert Formula** dialog box. This rule sets the value of the field that is bound to check box in the repeating table to be equal to **TRUE** whenever the value of the **firstName** text box changes and the concatenation of the values of the **firstName** and **lastName** fields is not the same as the value of the **oldValue** field. Note that the **normalize-space** function is used to remove unwanted spaces from around the concatenated string (also see recipe *20 Join two text strings and remove spaces if either text string is empty*).

7. Add a second **Action** rule to the **firstName** text box in the repeating table that has a **Condition** that says:

```
oldValue = normalize-space(concat(., " ", lastName))
```

and an action that says:

```
Set a field's value: hasChanged = false()
```

where `false()` is the **false** function, which you must set by using the
Insert Formula dialog box. This rule sets the value of the field that is
bound to check box in the repeating table to be equal to **FALSE**
whenever the value of the **firstName** text box changes and the
concatenation of the values of the **firstName** and **lastName** fields is
the same as the value of the **oldValue** field.

8. Copy both **Action** rules from the **firstName** text box and paste them
   onto the **lastName** text box in the repeating table, and ensure that you
   correct the conditions to be equal to

```
oldValue ≠ normalize-space(concat(firstName, " ", .))
```

for the first **Action** rule, and

```
oldValue = normalize-space(concat(firstName, " ", .))
```

for the second **Action** rule, where the dot (.) represents the **lastName**
text box in the repeating table. Note that you can copy both rules by
first right-clicking the **firstName** field on the **Fields** task pane and
selecting **Copy All Rules** from the drop-down menu that appears, and
then right-clicking the **lastName** field on the **Fields** task pane and
selecting **Paste All Rules** from the drop-down menu that appears.

9. Add a **Calculated Value** control to the view of the form template that
   has its **XPath** property set to a formula that says:

```
count(group2[hasChanged = string(true())])
```

or

```
count(my:group1/my:group2[my:hasChanged = string(true())])
```

if you have the **Edit XPath (advanced)** check box selected on the
Insert Formula dialog box. This rule returns the amount of **group2**

groups for which their **hasChanged** fields have a value equal to
TRUE. Note that you must use the **Filter Data** button on the **Select a
Field or Group** dialog box to set up a filter condition when you select
group2 to add it to the formula.

10. On the **Fields** task pane, add a hidden text field (see recipe *11 Add a
    hidden field*) named **isLoading** under the **myFields** group. You will use
    this hidden field to keep track of when the **Form Load** event is
    executing.

11. Click **Data ➤ Rules ➤ Form Load**.

12. On the **Rules** task pane, add an **Action** rule to the **Form Load** event
    with 4 actions that say:

    ```
    Set a field's value: isLoading = "1"
    Set a field's value: hasChanged = true()
    Set a field's value: hasChanged = false()
    Set a field's value: isLoading = "0"
    ```

    where **isLoading** is the hidden field in the Main data source,
    hasChanged is the field that is bound to the check box control in the
    repeating table, `true()` is the **true** function, and `false()` is the **false**
    function, which you must set by using the **Insert Formula** dialog box.
    The purpose of this rule is to:

    a. Indicate when the **Form Load** event has started running (`isLoading`
       `= "1"`) and has ended (`isLoading = "0"`).

    b. Trigger any rules that have been defined on the **hasChanged** field in
       the repeating table by changing the value of all of the **hasChanged**
       fields in the repeating table first to **TRUE** and then to **FALSE**.

    c. Set the values of all of the **hasChanged** fields that are bound to the
       check boxes in the repeating table to be equal to **FALSE** whenever
       the form opens. This is to ensure that the values of the fields that are
       bound to the check boxes are reset for forms that have been
       previously saved and reopened.

13. Add an **Action** rule to the **hasChanged** check box in the repeating
    table that has a **Condition** that says:

```
isLoading = "1"
```

and an action that says:

```
Set a field's value: oldValue = normalize-
space(concat(firstName, " ", lastName))
```

where **isLoading** is the hidden field in the Main data source, **oldValue** is the field that is bound to the last text box control in the repeating table, and the **concat** function is used to concatenate the values of the **firstName** and **lastName** text boxes in the repeating table. This rule only runs when a new or an existing form is loading (so being opened) to record the original values of the **firstName** and **lastName** fields in the **oldValue** field in each row of the repeating table.

14. Preview the form.

When the form opens, a 0 should appear in the calculated value control. Add a second row to the repeating table. You should still see a 0 in the calculated value control. Change the value of the second text box in the second row to something that is not an empty string and click away. The check box in the second row should be selected and a 1 should appear in the calculated value control. Continue changing the values of the text boxes to see how those changes affect the count. Also restore text boxes to their original values to see how that affects the count.

Discussion

The **count** function takes a field or group as its argument and counts the number of instances of that field or group. You generally use the **count** function on repeating groups or repeating fields.

In the solution described above, you used the **count** function together with a filtered node-set to count the amount of rows that were changed in a repeating table. The filtered node-set contained only those **group2** group nodes for which their corresponding **hasChanged** fields had a value equal to **TRUE**.

Note that while you left the check box and the last text box present in the repeating table, once you have the functionality working as you would like it to work, you should remove both controls from the repeating table on the view of the form template and leave the corresponding **hasChanged** and **oldValue** fields present in the Main data source, so that users cannot manually change their values. The purpose of both fields is to keep track of which rows have been updated, so they should not be accessible to users.

Caveat: If a row is deleted, it is not counted as a change. And if a row is added, it is not counted as a change unless values in the newly added row are changed.

102 Count the number of occurrences of a word in a repeating table

Problem

You have a repeating table on an InfoPath form and want to know in how many rows the word "Apple" appears in the first column of the repeating table.

Solution

You can use the **count** and **contains** functions to search for and count the number of a particular text string in a field in a repeating table.

To count the number of occurrences of the word "Apple" in a field in a repeating table:

1. In InfoPath, create a new **Blank Form** template.

2. Add a **Repeating Table** control and a **Text Box** control to the view of the form template.

3. Add 5 default rows to the repeating table (see recipe *96 Display a fixed amount of rows in a repeating table*) and fill the first field (**field1**) in each row with random words, of which 2 of them should contain the word "Apple".

4. Set the **Default Value** of the text box to be equal to the following formula:

```
count(../my:group1/my:group2/my:field1[contains(., "Apple")])
```

You can construct this formula as follows:

a. Open the **Properties** dialog box for the text box and click the formula button behind the **Default Value** text box.

b. On the **Insert Formula** dialog box, click **Insert Function**.

c. On the **Insert Function** dialog box, select **Field** in the **Categories** list, select **count** in the **Functions** list, and click **OK**.

d. On the **Insert Formula** dialog box, double-click the text that says "double click to insert field".

e. On the **Select a Field or Group** dialog box, expand the **group1** group, expand the **group2** repeating group, select **field1**, and click **Filter Data**. **field1** contains the text strings you want to search in, but because you only want to return **field1** instances that contain the word "Apple", you must add a filter that makes use of the **contains** function.

f. On the **Filter Data** dialog box, click **Add**.

g. On the **Specify Filter Conditions** dialog box, select **field1** from the first drop-down list box, select **contains** from the second drop-down list box, select **Type text** from the third drop-down list box, type **Apple** in the text box, and click **OK**. Note: You could have also used the **Use a formula** drop-down menu item in the third drop-down list box to select a field or construct a formula that has a value you want to use as the word to search for.

h. Click **OK** when closing all dialog boxes.

5. Preview the form.

When the form opens, the text box should display a 2 as an indication that the word "Apple" appears in two rows in the first column of the repeating table.

Discussion

The **contains** function in InfoPath takes two arguments: A field or text string to search within, and a field or text string to search for. The **contains** function returns **TRUE** if the first field or text string contains the second field or text string. Otherwise, it returns **FALSE**.

As you may already know, filter expressions are put between square brackets in the XPath expression for fields. The filter expression is

```
[contains(., "Apple")]
```

in the formula

```
count(../my:group1/my:group2/my:field1[contains(., "Apple")])
```

What the formula above says when you read it from right to left is: Return all of the **field1** fields that contain the word "Apple" under the **group2** repeating groups under the **group1** group, and then count how many of those **field1** fields were returned. In essence, you are counting the number of **field1** fields that contain the word "Apple".

You may have noticed that if **field1** contains an instance of the word "apple", so a word that has all lowercase characters, the **contains** function does not find such instances. This is because the **contains** function is looking for an exact match of the word.

To make the **contains** function look for any match, you must first convert the word you are searching for to either uppercase or lowercase, and then perform a search for either "APPLE" or "apple".

You can use the **translate** function (also see recipe *18 Capitalize text in a text box*) to convert a word to uppercase by using

```
translate("My Word", "abcdefghijklmnopqrstuvwxyz",
"ABCDEFGHIJKLMNOPQRSTUVWXYZ")
```

or to lowercase by using

```
translate("My Word", "ABCDEFGHIJKLMNOPQRSTUVWXYZ",
"abcdefghijklmnopqrstuvwxyz")
```

In the solution described above, you can replace the formula with the following formula to be able to perform a non-case-sensitive search.

```
count(../my:group1/my:group2/my:field1[contains(translate(.,
"ABCDEFGHIJKLMNOPQRSTUVWXYZ", "abcdefghijklmnopqrstuvwxyz"),
"apple")])
```

This formula uses the **translate** function within the **contains** function to convert **field1** instances to lowercase before comparing them to the word "apple".

103 Automatically number repeating table rows

Problem

You have a repeating table on an InfoPath form and want the first column of the repeating table to contain a number that is automatically calculated whenever you add a row to or remove a row from the repeating table.

Solution

You can use the **preceding-sibling** XPath axis to automatically number rows in a repeating table.

To automatically number repeating table rows:

1. In InfoPath, create a new **Blank Form** template.

2. Add a **Repeating Table** control to the view of the form template.

3. Right-click the text box in the first column of the repeating table and select **Change Control > Calculated Value** from the context menu that appears.

4. With the first field (**field1**) still selected, click **Properties > Properties > Default Value**.

5. On the **Field or Group Properties** dialog box on the **Data** tab under the **Default Value** section, click the formula button behind the **Value** text box.

6. On the **Insert Formula** dialog box, select the **Edit XPath (advanced)** check box.

7. On the **Insert Formula** dialog box, type the following formula in the **Formula** text box:

```
count(../preceding-sibling::*) + 1
```

What this formula does is:

a. Start at the context node, which is **field1**. This is the node on which you are currently setting the default value.

b. Move to its parent

```
..
```

which is a **group2** node.

c. Get all of the sibling nodes preceding the **group2** node

```
../preceding-sibling::*
```

so get all of the **group2** nodes that are located before the **group2** node of the context node.

d. Count all of the **group2** nodes that are located before the **group2** node of the context node

```
count(../preceding-sibling::*)
```

and add a **1** to it

```
count(../preceding-sibling::*) + 1
```

because if the context node's parent is the first **group2** node in the repeating table, the amount will be zero (0), while you want the amount to be 1.

8. On the **Insert Formula** dialog box, click **Verify Formula** to ensure that the formula does not contain any errors. Click **OK** to close the message box that says whether the formula contains or does not contain errors. Correct any errors if necessary.

9. On the **Insert Formula** dialog box, click **OK**.

10. On the **Field or Group Properties** dialog box, ensure that the **Refresh value when formula is recalculated** check box is selected, and then click **OK**. This will ensure that whenever you add a row to or delete a row from the repeating table, all of the **field1** field values in the repeating table will be recalculated and updated.

11. Preview the form.

When the form opens, add a couple of rows to the repeating table and see how the rows are sequentially numbered. Then remove rows to see how the numbers are recalculated.

Discussion

In the solution described above, you used the **preceding-sibling** XPath axis and the **count** function to count the amount of **group2** repeating groups that preceded a particular **group2** repeating group (the parent of the context node) and added a 1 to the result to be able to sequentially number rows in a repeating table.

The **preceding-sibling** XPath axis was first introduced in recipe *100 Count the number of rows in a repeating table – method 2*, so you can refer to the discussion section of that recipe to get more information about the XPath axis and how it works.

104 Copy data from the previous row to a new row in a repeating table

Problem

You have a repeating table on an InfoPath form and whenever you enter values into a row and then click the **Insert item** command to insert a new row, you want the values from the previous row to be copied over to the new row.

Solution

You can use the **preceding-sibling** XPath axis to retrieve all of the previous rows starting from the context row and then apply a filter to return only the first row preceding the context row.

To copy data from the previous row to a new row in a repeating table:

1. In InfoPath, create a new **Blank Form** template.

2. Add a **Repeating Table** control to the view of the form template.

3. Set the **Default Value** of each field in the repeating table to be equal to the following formula:

```
../preceding-sibling::my:group2[1]/my:field1
```

The formula above has been set on the first field (**field1**) in the repeating table. You will have to change the last part of this formula for each field you add the formula to. For example, for **field2**, the formula would become:

```
../preceding-sibling::my:group2[1]/my:field2
```

Deselect the **Refresh value when formula is recalculated** check box on the **Properties** dialog box after you have set the default value. This is to prevent all fields from being updated (recalculated) if you go back and edit data in an existing row.

4. Preview the form.

When the form opens, enter data in the first row of the repeating table, and then click **Insert item** to add a new row. The text string(s) from the first row should have been copied over to the second row. Now change some text in the second row and click **Insert item** to add a third row. The text from the second row should now appear in the third row.

Go back to the first row and change some text. If you deselected the **Refresh value when formula is recalculated** check box (as specified in step 3 of the solution) for the default value, the data in the subsequent rows (2 and 3) should not change when you click away from the row. Go back to an existing row, click on the control on the left-hand side of the row, and select **Insert group2 after** from the drop-down menu that appears. A new row should be inserted after the row you are currently on and the values from the current row should appear in the new row.

Discussion

The formula used in this recipe can be constructed as follows (also see Figure 189):

1. The context node is the node you are setting the default value on (**field1** in this case).

2. You want to set the value of **field1** to be equal to the value of the **field1** in the preceding row, so you must navigate to the preceding row. And to do this, you must find the **group2** node that is the preceding sibling of the **group2** node that is the parent of the **field1** context node. So first you must use

   `..`

   to navigate to the parent of **field1**. This gives you

   `..`

   as the formula.

3. Then you must find all of the **group2** sibling nodes preceding the **group2** node of the **field1** context node, so you must use

   ```
   preceding-sibling::my:group2
   ```

   This results in

   ```
   ../preceding-sibling::my:group2
   ```

   as the formula.

4. Once you have all of the preceding **group2** nodes, you only want the first **group2** node preceding the **group2** node of the **field1** context node, so must add a filter (**[1]**) that returns only the first preceding **group2** node. This results in

   ```
   ../preceding-sibling::my:group2[1]
   ```

   as the formula.

5. And once you have the first preceding **group2** node, you can navigate down to find the **field1** node under that **group2** node. This results in the final formula:

```
../preceding-sibling::my:group2[1]/my:field1
```

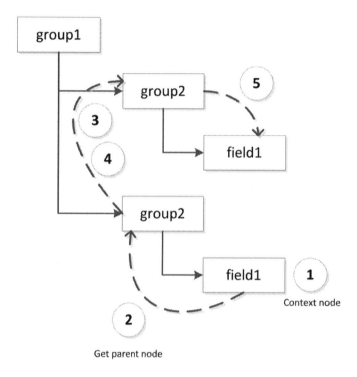

Figure 189. Flow chart for getting the value of a field in the previous row.

105 Auto-populate a repeating table with week periods

Problem

You have a repeating table on an InfoPath form and want to automatically populate two date picker controls in the first and second columns with week periods, where you fill in the first date in the repeating table and then have all of the other date picker controls automatically populate themselves.

Solution

You can expand on the technique described in recipe *104 Copy data from the previous row to a new row* to automatically calculate dates and date periods in a repeating table.

To automatically populate a repeating table with week periods:

1. In InfoPath, create a new **Blank Form** template.

2. Add a **Repeating Table** control with 3 columns to the view of the form template.

3. Change the first two text boxes in the repeating table into **Date Picker** controls (see recipe *6 Change a text box into a date picker*). Name the first date picker control **startDate** and the second date picker control **endDate**. Leave the third text box a text box, but change its name to **previousDate** and delete the column for the text box and the text box itself from the repeating table, but not from the Main data source (by doing this you will be making it a hidden field; see recipe *11 Add a hidden field*). You will be using **previousDate** as a field to help perform calculations in the repeating table.

4. To create a week period, you must first add 6 days to the value of **startDate**. This means that the value of **endDate** should be set to be equal to a formula that adds 6 days to the value of **startDate**. So set the **Default Value** of **endDate** to be equal to the following formula:

    ```
    addDays(startDate, 6)
    ```

    and ensure that the **Refresh value when formula is recalculated** check box is selected.

5. Once you have calculated the value of **endDate** for a week period, you want the next **startDate** to start one day after the last **endDate**. So here you have to apply the technique from recipe *104 Copy data from the previous row to a new row* to look up the **endDate** in the previous row of the repeating table, and then use the **addDays** function in a formula to add 1 day to it. But because the **addDays** function accepts a date as its first argument (and not an XPath axis), you must use a workaround

by first retrieving **endDate** in the previous row through an XPath expression using the **preceding-sibling** XPath axis, set **previousDate** to be equal to the result, and then use the **addDays** function to add 1 day to the value of **previousDate** and set the value of **startDate** to be equal to the result.

First set the **Default Value** of **previousDate** to be equal to the following formula:

```
../preceding-sibling::my:group2[1]/my:endDate
```

and then set the **Default Value** of **startDate** to be equal to the following formula:

```
addDays(previousDate, 1)
```

Ensure that the **Refresh value when formula is recalculated** check box is selected for both default values. Note: To set the default value of a hidden field (**previousDate**), you must open the **Field or Group Properties** dialog box for that field by double-clicking on the field on the **Fields** task pane, and then set its **Default Value** property.

6. Preview the form.

When the form opens, enter a date in the first date picker (start date). The end date should automatically appear in the second date picker. Click the **Insert item** command to add a new row to the repeating table. Both date pickers should now contain dates for the following week period. Continue adding rows to the repeating table and see how each row is populated with a week period.

106 Auto-populate a drop-down list box with past and future dates

Problem

You have a drop-down list box control on an InfoPath form, which you want to automatically populate with dates starting from the currently selected date and then going 7 days in the past and 7 days in the future.

Solution

You can use repeating fields in a Secondary data source of an InfoPath form to perform date calculations and then populate a drop-down list box with a fixed amount of dates that fall 7 days in the past and 7 days in the future starting from the currently selected date.

To auto-populate a drop-down list box with dates that fall 7 days in the past and 7 days in the future:

1. In InfoPath, create a new **Blank Form** template.

2. Add a data connection to an XML file (see recipe *33 Get data from an XML file*) that has the following contents:

```
<dateData>
  <dateRow><dateValue/><dateDisplay/><currentDate/></dateRow>
  <dateRow><dateValue/><dateDisplay/><currentDate/></dateRow>
  <dateRow><dateValue/><dateDisplay/><currentDate/></dateRow>
  <dateRow><dateValue/><dateDisplay/><currentDate/></dateRow>
  <dateRow><dateValue/><dateDisplay/><currentDate/></dateRow>
  <dateRow><dateValue/><dateDisplay/><currentDate/></dateRow>
  <dateRow><dateValue/><dateDisplay/><currentDate/></dateRow>
  <dateRow><dateValue/><dateDisplay/><currentDate/></dateRow>
  <dateRow><dateValue/><dateDisplay/><currentDate/></dateRow>
  <dateRow><dateValue/><dateDisplay/><currentDate/></dateRow>
  <dateRow><dateValue/><dateDisplay/><currentDate/></dateRow>
  <dateRow><dateValue/><dateDisplay/><currentDate/></dateRow>
  <dateRow><dateValue/><dateDisplay/><currentDate/></dateRow>
  <dateRow><dateValue/><dateDisplay/><currentDate/></dateRow>
  <dateRow><dateValue/><dateDisplay/><currentDate/></dateRow>
</dateData>
```

and name the data connection **DateData**.

3. Add a **Drop-Down List Box** control to the view of the form template, name it **selectedDate**, and change its data type to **Date (date)**.

4. With the drop-down list box still selected, click **Properties ➤ Properties ➤ Default Value**, and then set the **Default Value** of the field bound to the drop-down list box to be equal to the following formula:

```
today()
```

This formula ensures that the current date is displayed in the drop-down list box whenever a new form opens.

5. Add an **Action** rule to the **selectedDate** drop-down list box that has a **Condition** that says:

```
selectedDate is blank
```

and an action that says:

```
Set a field's value: . = today()
```

where the dot (**.**) represents the **selectedDate** field that is bound to the drop-down list box and today() is the **today** function. This rule ensures that whenever a user selects the blank item from the drop-down list box, the current date is automatically displayed.

6. Add a second **Action** rule without a condition to the **selectedDate** drop-down list box that has an action that says:

```
Set a field's value: currentDate = .
```

where **currentDate** is a field that is located under the **dateRow** repeating group under the **dateData** group in the **DateData** Secondary data source and where the dot (**.**) represents the **selectedDate** field that is bound to the drop-down list box. This rule ensures that whenever a user selects a date from the drop-down list box, the values of all of the **currentDate** fields in the Secondary data source are initialized and the rules on those fields executed.

7.   On the **Fields** task pane, select **DateData (Secondary)** from the drop-down list box, expand the **dateRow** repeating group, select the **currentDate** field, and then on the **Rules** task pane, add an **Action** rule without a condition to the **currentDate** field in the Secondary data source that has two actions that say:

```
Set a field's value: dateValue = addDays(., count(preceding-
sibling::dateRow) - 7)

Set a field's value: dateDisplay = concat(substring(dateValue,
9, 2), "/", substring(dateValue, 6, 2), "/",
substring(dateValue, 1, 4))
```

For the first action, you must enter the following formula on the **Insert Formula** dialog box:

```
addDays(., count(preceding-sibling::dateRow) - 7)
```

or

```
xdDate:AddDays(., count(../preceding-sibling::dateRow) - 7)
```

if you have the **Edit XPath (advanced)** check box selected on the **Insert Formula** dialog box. What this formula does is add an amount of days to the value of the **currentDate** field. Because the result of the **preceding-sibling** XPath axis expression starts at 0, the result of the **addDays** function will start at a date that falls 7 days in the past.

For the second action, you must enter the following formula on the **Insert Formula** dialog box:

```
concat(substring(dateValue, 9, 2), "/", substring(dateValue, 6,
2), "/", substring(dateValue, 1, 4))
```

This formula formats the resulting date from the **dateValue** field as **dd/MM/yyyy**. However, you can format this date in any other format you wish by using the **concat** and **substring** functions (also see for example Question 1 in recipe *65 Display the month name for a selected date*).

Note that the two actions in the rule on the **currentDate** field will run for each **currentDate** field in each **dateRow** repeating group in the Secondary data source, thereby setting the values of the corresponding **dateValue** and **dateDisplay** fields in each **dateRow** repeating group.

8. Click **Data ➤ Rules ➤ Form Load**.

9. On the **Rules** task pane, add an **Action** rule without a condition to the **Form Load** event that has an action that says:

```
Set a field's value: currentDate = selectedDate
```

where **currentDate** is a field that is located under the **dateRow** repeating group under the **dateData** group in the **DateData** Secondary data source and where **selectedDate** is the field that is bound to the drop-down list box. This rule ensures that whenever you open a form in which a date has been previously saved in the **selectedDate** field, the values of the **currentDate** fields in the **DateData** Secondary data source are set, so that the rule on the **currentDate** field can run to populate all of the **dateValue** and **dateDisplay** fields in the **DateData** Secondary data source.

10. Right-click the drop-down list box and select **Drop-Down List Box Properties** from the context menu that appears.

11. On the **Drop-Down List Box Properties** dialog box on the **Data** tab, select the **Get choices from an external data source** option, ensure that **DateData** is selected in the **Data source** drop-down list box, and then click the button behind the **Entries** text box.

12. On the **Select a Field or Group** dialog box, select the **dateRow** repeating group, and click **OK**.

13. On the **Drop-Down List Box Properties** dialog box, ensure that the **Value** property has been set to the **dateValue** field and that the **Display name** property has been set to the **dateDisplay** field.

14. On the **Drop-Down List Box Properties** dialog box, click **OK**.

15. Preview the form.

When the form opens, the current date should appear in the drop-down list box. And when you expand the drop-down list box, you should see 15 dates listed, 7 of which should fall in the past and another 7 should fall in the future starting from the currently selected date.

Figure 190. Expanded drop-down list box displaying 15 dates.

Discussion

In the solution described above, you used repeating fields in a Secondary data source to perform date calculations and display dates in a drop-down list box. Note that you could have also used repeating fields in the Main data source (so for example fields bound to a repeating table control on the form) to provide the same functionality. A Secondary data source was used in this case to keep the form free from irrelevant information. Had you used repeating fields in the Main data source, then all of the data pertaining to the date calculations would have wound up being stored along with the selected date itself in the InfoPath form when you saved or submitted the form.

107 Add a sum field to a repeating table

Problem

You have a repeating table on an InfoPath form that contains a field with a number, for example, an amount for lunch bought this week. You want to add a field to the repeating table that sums up all of the money you spent on lunch this week.

Solution

You can use the **sum** function to create a grand total field in a repeating table.

To add a sum field to a repeating table:

1. In InfoPath, create a new **Blank Form** template.

2. Add a **Repeating Table** control with one column to the view of the form template.

3. Open the **Text Box Properties** dialog box for the text box bound to **field1** in the repeating table, change the **Field name** to **lunchMoney**, change the **Data type** from **Text (string)** to **Decimal (double)**, and click **Format**.

4. On the **Decimal Format** dialog box under the **Format** section, select the **Number** option, and then under the **Other options** section, select **2** from the **Decimal places** drop-down list box, and click **OK**. This will display numbers with 2 digits after the decimal point. Note: You can also set the data type on the field itself, but you will not be able to apply a format to it. Remember that controls are visual elements that expose data stored in fields. Formatting a number to have 2 digits after the decimal point is a visual thing. Fields themselves cannot be seen without controls, so any visual display must be set on the control, not on the field.

5. On the **Text Box Properties** dialog box, click **OK**.

6. Open the **Repeating Table Properties** dialog box.

7. On the **Repeating Table Properties** dialog box, click the **Display** tab, select the **Include footer** check box, and click **OK**. An extra row should appear at the bottom of the repeating table.

8. Click in the bottom row of the repeating table to place the cursor in it, and then add a **Text Box** control to it. Change the data type for this

text box to **Decimal (double)**, and format the number to have 2
decimal places.

9. Set the **Default Value** of the text box in the footer of the repeating
    table to be equal to the following formula:

```
sum(lunchMoney)
```

or

```
sum(../my:group1/my:group2/my:lunchMoney)
```

if you have the **Edit XPath (advanced)** check box selected on the
Insert Formula dialog box. Ensure that the **Refresh value when
formula is recalculated** check box is selected when you set the default
value, so that every time when you add a row to the repeating table or
change the value of a **lunchMoney** field in the repeating table, the sum
is recalculated and updated.

10. Preview the form

When the form opens, add a few rows with amounts to the repeating table.
Every time you add a row with an amount, the sum should get updated.

Discussion

The **sum** function returns the sum of all fields in a group. Each field is first
converted to a number. In the solution described above, **lunchMoney**
repeats in the repeating table, so **sum** will return the sum of all
lunchMoney fields in the repeating table.

If you have two repeating tables on an InfoPath form with both repeating
tables having a total sum field that uses the **sum** function to calculate the
sum of a repeating field in the corresponding repeating table, you can use
the plus operator (+) as discussed in recipe *46 Calculate the sum of text boxes*
to calculate the sum of the two total sum fields in the repeating tables, or
you can use the plus operator together with the **sum** function to calculate
the total sum over both repeating tables as follows:

```
sum(field1) + sum(field2)
```

where **field1** is a (repeating) field in the first repeating table and **field2** is a (repeating) field in the second repeating table. This formula gives you the total sum over both repeating tables.

Exercise

The same way you added a sum field, try replacing it with a field that calculates the average of a list of numbers. Hint: You can use the **avg** function for this.

Tip:

> There are two ways to calculate the sum of fields in InfoPath: 1. Use the plus operator (+) and 2. Use the **sum** function. If you have single fields, i.e. fields that do not repeat, use the plus operator to calculate the sum. If you have a repeating field, e.g. a field in a repeating section, a repeating table, or a multiple-selection list box, use the **sum** function on that field to calculate the sum of a list of fields.

108 Add a running total sum to a repeating table

Problem

You have a repeating table on an InfoPath form and want that while a user is entering numbers into the first column of the repeating table, a running total is calculated and displayed in the second column of the repeating table.

Solution

You can use the **preceding** XPath axis and the **sum** function to create a running total field in a repeating table.

To add a running total sum to a repeating table:

1. In InfoPath, create a new **Blank Form** template.

2. Add a **Repeating Table** control with 2 columns to the view of the form template. Name the text box controls in the repeating table **number** and **runningTotal**, respectively.

3. Add an **Action** rule to the **number** text box in the repeating table with an action that says:

```
Set a field's value: runningTotal = . +
sum(preceding::my:number)
```

This formula calculates the sum of all of the **number** fields preceding the current **number** context node and adds the value of the current **number** context node to that sum.

4. Because the formula in the previous step does not recalculate correctly whenever you delete a row from the repeating table, you must apply a correction. And for that you must set the **Default Value** of the **runningTotal** text box to be equal to the following formula:

```
sum(preceding::my:number)
```

This formula calculates the sum of all of the **number** fields preceding the current **runningTotal** context node, which also includes the **number** field in the same row of the repeating table as the **runningTotal** context node. Leave the **Refresh value when formula is recalculated** check box selected on the **Properties** dialog box.

5. Preview the form.

When the form opens, a zero (0) should appear in the **runningTotal** text box. Enter a number in the **number** text box and click away from the field. The number you entered should appear in the **runningTotal** text box. Add a new row to the repeating table and enter another number in the **number** text box. Continue adding rows and entering numbers, while checking whether the running total in the **runningTotal** text box is correctly updated. Also remove rows and see whether the running total in the **runningTotal** text box is correctly updated.

InfoPath 2013 Cookbook

Discussion

In the solution described above, you saw how to use the **preceding** XPath axis together with the **sum** function to calculate a running total in a repeating table.

The **preceding** XPath axis is similar to the **preceding-sibling** XPath axis with the difference that the **preceding** XPath axis retrieves all of the nodes preceding the current context node (except for ancestors, attribute nodes, and namespace nodes), while the **preceding-sibling** XPath axis only retrieves sibling nodes preceding the current context node.

For example, to set the default value of the **runningTotal** field, you used the following formula:

```
sum(preceding::my:number)
```

Figure 191 explains the relationship between the different fields and groups that make up the repeating table.

Because you are setting the default value of the **runningTotal** field, the **runningTotal** field is the context node (the node where you start at; node number 1 in the figure). If you navigate upwards in the hierarchy, the context node has 4 nodes (fields and groups) preceding it, which includes a **number** node (2) under the same **group2** node (3) as the context node (1), but excludes nodes number 3 and 7, because they are ancestors of node number 1.

This means that if you want to calculate the sum of all of the **number** fields that precede the **runningTotal** field in a particular row of the repeating table, including the **number** field in the same row in which the **runningTotal** field is located,

```
preceding::my:number
```

would return all of the **number** fields you are looking for (nodes number 2 and 5 in the figure).

404

Likewise, when adding the **Action** rule to the **number** field (step 3 in the solution described above), the **number** field becomes the context node (for example node number 2 in the figure).

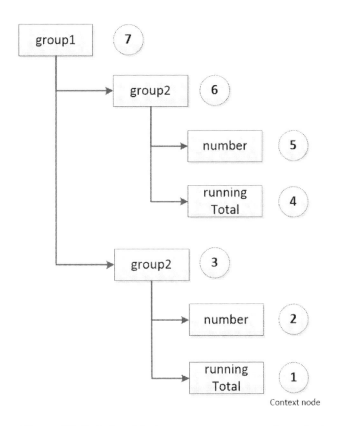

Figure 191. Relationship between a context node and other nodes in a hierarchy of nodes.

And because

```
preceding::my:number
```

would only return all of the **number** fields in rows preceding the row in which the context node is located (node number 5 in the figure) and exclude the current context node, you must add the value of the context node to the sum of the values of all of the preceding **number** fields to get the correct total, which results in the following formula:

```
. + sum(preceding::my:number)
```

109 Calculate the average of all fields in 3 repeating tables

Problem

You have three separate repeating table controls on an InfoPath form. Each repeating table contains a field in its footer displaying the average for that repeating table, but you would like to add an extra field to the form that displays the average of the values in all of the repeating tables.

Solution

You can use the **sum** and **count** functions in InfoPath to calculate the average of all fields that are located in three separate repeating tables on an InfoPath form.

To calculate the average of all fields in 3 repeating tables:

1. In InfoPath, create a new **Blank Form** template.

2. Add 3 **Repeating Table** controls with one column each to the view of the form template, and change the data type for the field in each repeating table to **Decimal (double)** to force users to enter only numbers in the fields. Note that you could also use the data type **Whole Number (integer)** to force users to enter only whole numbers in the fields.

3. Configure all of the repeating tables to start up with no rows as described in recipe *95 Remove the first empty row of a repeating table*.

4. Right-click the first repeating table control and select **Repeating Table Properties** from the context menu that appears.

5. On the **Repeating Table Properties** dialog box, click the **Display** tab, select the **Include footer** check box, and click **OK**.

6. Repeat the previous 2 steps for the other two repeating tables.

7. Add a **Text Box** control to the footer of the first repeating table control, change its data type to **Decimal (double)**, and name it **averageOfFields1**.

8. Repeat the previous step for the other two repeating tables, but name the text boxes **averageOfFields2** and **averageOfFields3**, respectively.

9. Set the **Default Value** of the **averageOfFields1** text box to be equal to the following formula:

   ```
   avg(field1)
   ```

   where **field1** is located in the first repeating table control. Leave the **Refresh value when formula is recalculated** check box selected. This formula calculates the average of all of the **field1** fields in the first repeating table.

10. Set the **Default Value** of the **averageOfFields2** text box to be equal to the following formula:

    ```
    avg(field2)
    ```

    where **field2** is located in the second repeating table control. Leave the **Refresh value when formula is recalculated** check box selected. This formula calculates the average of all of the **field2** fields in the second repeating table.

11. Set the **Default Value** of the **averageOfFields3** text box to be equal to the following formula:

    ```
    avg(field3)
    ```

    where **field3** is located in the third repeating table control. Leave the **Refresh value when formula is recalculated** check box selected. This formula calculates the average of all of the **field3** fields in the third repeating table.

12. Add a **Text Box** control to the view of the form template, leave its data type as **Text (string)**, and name it **averageOfAllFields**.

13. Set the **Default Value** of the **averageOfAllFields** text box to be equal to the following formula:

    ```
    (sum(field1) + sum(field2) + sum(field3)) / (count(field1) +
    count(field2) + count(field3))
    ```

where **field1**, **field2**, and **field3** are located in the three repeating tables. This formula calculates the average of all of the fields in all of the repeating tables. Leave the **Refresh value when formula is recalculated** check box selected.

14. Preview the form.

When the form opens, add rows to the repeating tables with a couple of numbers. While you are adding rows and entering numbers, the average of all of the fields should appear in the **averageOfAllFields** text box.

Discussion

In the solution described above, you saw how to use the **sum** and **count** functions to calculate the average of fields that are located in different repeating tables. While you were able to use the **avg** function on the repeating field in each repeating table to display an average of the fields in each repeating table in the footer, the **avg** function cannot be used with more than one repeating field when each repeating field belongs to a different repeating group. This is why you had to use a combination of the **sum** and **count** functions to calculate the average of all of the fields within the three repeating tables.

When the form first opens, you may see **NaN** displayed in the **averageOfAllFields** text box. **NaN** stands for **Not a Number**. Because all of the repeating tables contain no rows at startup, the division in the calculation of the average cannot be performed since there are no fields to perform a calculation on, which results in **NaN** being displayed in the text box.

If you do not want InfoPath to display **NaN** when the calculation fails, you could replace it with an empty string by adding an **Action** rule to the **averageOfAllFields** text box that sets its own value to an empty string whenever its value is equal to **NaN**. So the rule on the **averageOfAllFields** text box should say:

```
Set a field's value: . = ""
```

and the **Condition** on the rule should say:

```
averageOfAllFields = "NaN"
```

Note: If you are filling out forms via the browser, select the **Always** option on the **Browser forms** tab of the **Text Box Properties** dialog box for the **averageOfAllFields** text box to make sure that the rule also runs when rows are deleted from the repeating tables.

110 Hide the first row of a repeating table

Problem

You have a repeating table on an InfoPath form and want to hide the first row in that repeating table.

Solution

You can use the **preceding-sibling** XPath axis to find and then hide the first row of a repeating table.

To hide the first row of a repeating table:

1. In InfoPath, create a new **Blank Form** template.

2. Add a **Repeating Table** control to the view of the form template.

3. Select the repeating table and then click **Home ➤ Rules ➤ Manage Rules**.

4. On the **Rules** task pane, ensure that **group2** is listed below the title bar (if it is not, click the text "Repeating Table" on the repeating table to select it or click on **group2** in the Main data source). You want to add conditional formatting to the **group2** repeating group (so to rows in the table); not to an individual field within the repeating group.

5. On the **Rules** task pane, click **New ➤ Formatting**.

6. On the **Rules** task pane under **Formatting**, select the **Hide this control** check box.

7. On the **Rules** task pane under **Condition**, click the text **None**.

8. On the **Condition** dialog box, select **The expression** from the first drop-down list box, and then type the following expression into the text box:

```
count(preceding-sibling::*) = 0
```

9. On the **Condition** dialog box, click **OK**.

10. Preview the form.

When the form opens, the first row of the repeating table should not be visible.

Discussion

In the solution described above, you used the **preceding-sibling** XPath axis and the **count** function to count the amount of **group2** repeating groups that preceded a particular **group2** repeating group (the context node). The **preceding-sibling** XPath axis was first introduced in recipe *100 Count the number of rows in a repeating table – method 2*, so you can refer to the discussion section of that recipe to get more information about the XPath axis and how it works. What the

```
count(preceding-sibling::*) = 0
```

expression does is count the amount of rows (**group2** repeating groups) that are located before any row (**group2** group node) while going through all of the rows of the repeating table. Remember that you added the **Formatting** rule to a row (and all rows) of the repeating table, so the condition will be applied to all rows of the repeating table. And because only the first row has no rows preceding it, the expression for the condition will evaluate to **TRUE** for that row, so that row will be hidden.

Note that instead of hiding the first row you could also remove it from the initial form as described in recipe *95 Remove the first empty row of a repeating table*.

111 Hide a row of a repeating table when a check box is selected

Problem

You have a repeating table on an InfoPath form that represents a task list. You want to be able to select a check box in any row of the repeating table and then have that row become invisible.

Solution

You can use conditional formatting to hide rows of a repeating table.

To hide a row of a repeating table when a check box is selected:

1. In InfoPath, create a new **Blank Form** template.

2. Add a **Repeating Table** control with 2 columns to the view of the form template.

3. Delete the field from the second column both on the view of the form template and on the **Fields** task pane, and then place the cursor in the second empty cell and click **Home ➤ Controls ➤ Check Box** to add a **Check Box** control to it. Name the check box control **isHidden**.

4. Select the repeating table and then click **Home ➤ Rules ➤ Manage Rules**.

5. On the **Rules** task pane, ensure that **group2** is listed below the title bar (if it is not, click the text "Repeating Table" on the repeating table to select it or click on **group2** in the Main data source). You want to add conditional formatting to the repeating group (so to rows in the table); not to an individual field within the repeating group.

6. On the **Rules** task pane, click **New ➤ Formatting**.

7. On the **Rules** task pane under **Formatting**, select the **Hide this control** check box.

8. On the **Rules** task pane under **Condition**, click the text **None**.

411

9. On the **Condition** dialog box, select **isHidden** from the first drop-down list box, leave **is equal to** selected in the second drop-down list box, select **TRUE** from the third drop-down list box, and click **OK**. The following expression should now appear on the **Rules** task pane under **Condition**:

```
isHidden = TRUE
```

This rule hides any row in the repeating table if the **isHidden** check box in that row is selected.

10. Preview the form.

When the form opens, add a few rows to the repeating table and type some unique text in each row so that they are distinguishable. Select a check box in any row. That row should then disappear from view.

Discussion

If you hide a few rows in a repeating table and then save or submit the form, those rows will remain hidden from view but will also remain present in the Main data source of the form. You can see this if you save the InfoPath form and then open the XML file for the InfoPath form in Notepad.

Important:

> Using conditional formatting to hide rows does not delete the rows, but just hides them from view.

Exercise

Instead of hiding a row, try adding a **Formatting** rule to **field1** in the repeating table to display the text in **field1** as strikethrough when the check box is selected.

112 Highlight the last row of a repeating table

Problem

You have a repeating table on an InfoPath form and you want the last row of the repeating table to be continuously shown as highlighted with a distinguishable background color.

Solution

You can use conditional formatting on rows of a repeating table to highlight the last row of the repeating table.

To highlight the last row of a repeating table:

1. In InfoPath, create a new **Blank Form** template.

2. Add a **Repeating Table** control to the view of the form template.

3. Select the repeating table and then click **Home ➤ Rules ➤ Manage Rules**.

4. On the **Rules** task pane, ensure that **group2** is listed below the title bar (if it is not, click the text "Repeating Table" on the repeating table to select it or click on **group2** in the Main data source). You want to add conditional formatting to the repeating group (so to rows in the table); not to an individual field within the repeating group.

5. On the **Rules** task pane, click **New ➤ Formatting**.

6. On the **Rules** task pane, change the background color to a color of your choice.

7. On the **Rules** task pane under **Condition**, click the text **None**.

8. On the **Condition** dialog box, select **The expression** from the first drop-down list box, and then type the following expression into the text box:

```
count(following-sibling::*) = 0
```

9. On the **Condition** dialog box, click **OK**.

10. Preview the form.

When the form opens, the last row of the repeating table should appear as highlighted and should remain highlighted as you add rows to and remove rows from the repeating table.

Discussion

In the solution described above, you used the **following-sibling** XPath axis and the **count** function to count the amount of **group2** repeating groups that followed or came after a particular **group2** repeating group (the context node).

The **following-sibling** XPath axis works similar to the **preceding-sibling** XPath axis, which was first introduced in recipe *100 Count the number of rows in a repeating table – method 2*, with the difference that the **preceding-sibling** XPath axis looks behind and the **following-sibling** XPath axis looks ahead. What the

```
count(following-sibling::*) = 0
```

expression does is count the amount of rows (**group2** repeating group nodes) that follow any row while going through all of the rows of the repeating table. Remember that you added the **Formatting** rule to a row (and all rows) of the repeating table, so the condition will be applied to all rows of the repeating table. And because there are no rows that follow the last row, the expression for the condition will evaluate to **TRUE** for that row, so that row will be highlighted.

You may have noticed that the fields within the last row of the repeating table were not highlighted. This is because you applied formatting to the rows of the repeating table and not to the individual fields.

If you also want the fields to be highlighted, you can copy the rule you created earlier and apply it to each field within the repeating table as follows:

1. Click the repeating table to select it, and then click **Home ➤ Rules ➤ Manage Rules** to open the **Rules** task pane.
2. On the **Rules** task pane, click on the drop-down arrow on the right-hand side of the rule you created earlier, and select **Copy Rule** from

the drop-down menu that appears. Note: You can also use the **Copy Rule** command at the top of the task pane under the title bar.

3. Click on a field inside of the repeating table to select it, and then on the **Rules** task pane, click on the **Paste Rule** command at the top of the task pane under the title bar.

Figure 192. Paste Rule command enabled on the Rules task pane.

4. Repeat the previous step for each field that you want to highlight within the repeating table.

The same way you can highlight the last row of a repeating table, you can highlight the first row of a repeating table by using the following expression for the condition:

```
count(preceding-sibling::*) = 0
```

113 Highlight alternating rows in a repeating table

Problem

You have a repeating table on an InfoPath form and you want every second row of the repeating table to have a different background color compared to the other rows.

Solution

You can use conditional formatting on rows of a repeating table to highlight alternating rows in the repeating table.

To highlight alternating rows in a repeating table:

1. In InfoPath, create a new **Blank Form** template.

2. Add a **Repeating Table** control to the view of the form template.

3. Select the repeating table and then click **Home ➤ Rules ➤ Manage Rules**.

4. On the **Rules** task pane, ensure that **group2** is listed below the title bar (if it is not, click the text "Repeating Table" on the repeating table to select it or click on **group2** in the Main data source). You want to add conditional formatting to the repeating group (so to rows in the table); not to an individual field within the repeating group.

5. On the **Rules** task pane, click **New ➤ Formatting**.

6. On the **Rules** task pane under **Formatting**, change the background color to a color of your choice.

7. On the **Rules** task pane under **Condition**, click the text **None**.

8. On the **Condition** dialog box, select **The expression** from the first drop-down list box, and then type the following expression into the text box:

```
(count(preceding-sibling::*) + 1) mod 2 = 0
```

9. On the **Condition** dialog box, click **OK**.

10. Preview the form.

When the form opens, add a few rows to the repeating table. The second row and every second row thereafter should have the background color you specified as the formatting.

If you want to highlight the first row and then every second row thereafter, change the expression to be the following:

```
count(preceding-sibling::*) mod 2 = 0
```

And if you want to highlight every third row, you can use

```
(count(preceding-sibling::*) + 1) mod 3 = 0
```

Discussion

In the solution described above, you saw how to use the **preceding-sibling** XPath axis in a condition on a **Formatting** rule to highlight alternating rows in a repeating table.

The **preceding-sibling** XPath axis was first introduced in recipe *100 Count the number of rows in a repeating table – method 2*, so you can refer to the discussion section of that recipe to get more information about the XPath axis and how it works.

mod is an operator you can use to retrieve the remainder of the division of one number by another. For example, 19 mod 4 = 3 because 19 divided by 4 equals 4 with a remainder of 3 (4 x 4 = 16 and 19 – 16 = 3 so the remainder is 3). Likewise, 16 mod 4 = 0 because 16 divided by 4 equals 4 with a remainder of 0 (4 x 4 = 16 and 16 – 16 = 0 so the remainder is 0).

In the solution described above, every time the expression of the condition results in a zero, formatting is applied to a row. To be able to highlight every other row, you must first count how many rows are located before the context row (while going through all of the rows of the repeating table) and then if the count mod 2 equals 0, that row should be highlighted.

114 Limit the amount of rows added to a repeating table to a maximum

Problem

You have a repeating table on an InfoPath form and you want users to be able to add a maximum of 10 rows to the repeating table.

Solution

You can use conditional formatting on section controls that contain repeating tables that are bound to the same repeating group, to swap a normal repeating table with a repeating table to which no rows can be added as soon as the normal repeating table has reached a maximum amount of rows.

To limit the amount of rows added to a repeating table to a maximum:

1. In InfoPath, create a new **Blank Form** template.

2. Add a **Repeating Table** control to the view of the form template.

3. Delete the repeating table control from the view, but do not delete the repeating group it was bound to from the Main data source.

4. The repeating group (**group2**) of a repeating table generally lies under a container group (**group1**), so you can bind the container group to a section control. On the **Fields** task pane, click **group1**, drag it to the view of the form template, and drop it. It should automatically get bound to a **Section** control containing a **Repeating Table** control. Delete the empty lines below the repeating table control in the section control.

5. Repeat the previous step to bind **group1** to a second **Section** control on the view of the form template. Place the second section control below the first section control and ensure that there are no empty lines between the two section controls. InfoPath should now show information icons on all of the fields in both repeating tables saying that "Control stores duplicate data" (see Figure 193). Do not worry about this, because you will be showing only one repeating table at a time depending on how many **group2** rows are present.

6. Right-click the repeating table in the second section control, and select **Repeating Table Properties** from the context menu that appears.

7. On the **Repeating Table Properties** dialog box on the **Data** tab, deselect the **Show insert button and hint text** check box, and then click **Customize Commands**.

8. On the **Table Commands** dialog box, deselect all of the check boxes in the **Action** list except for the check box in front of the **Remove** action, select **Remove** in the **Action** list, change the **Command name** from **Remove group2** to **Remove row**, and then click **OK**.

9. On the **Repeating Table Properties** dialog box, click **OK**. With this you have configured the repeating table in the second section control to allow rows to be removed but not inserted.

10. Click the first section control (**group1**) to select it, and then click **Home ➤ Rules ➤ Manage Rules** to open the **Rules** task pane.

11. On the **Rules** task pane, ensure that **group1** is listed as the selected group below the title bar, and then click **New ➤ Formatting** to add a **Formatting** rule.

12. On the **Rules** task pane under **Formatting**, select the **Hide this control** check box, and then under **Condition** click the text **None**.

13. You want to hide the first section, which contains the repeating table to which users can add rows, if there are 10 or more rows in the repeating table. So on the **Condition** dialog box, select **The expression** from the first drop-down list box, type the following expression into the text box:

```
count(my:group2) >= 10
```

    and then click **OK**. Remember that you can use the **Use a formula** option in the third drop-down list box to construct the expression (also see recipe *31 Set a maximum length on text in a text box* where this technique was explained for the first time).

14. On the **Rules** task pane, right-click the rule you just added, and select **Copy Rule** from the drop-down menu that appears.

15. Click the second section control to select it. Note that while the second section control is bound to the same group node (**group1**) as the first section control, it is an entirely different control on the view of the form template. So on the **Rules** task pane, you should not see any rules listed for the second section control.

16. On the **Rules** task pane, click the **Paste Rule** command to paste the rule you just copied from the first section control onto the second section control.

17. On the **Rules** task pane under **Condition**, click the text **Number of occurrences of group2 ≥ 10**.

18. You want to hide the second section, which contains the repeating table from which rows can only be removed, if there are less than 10 rows in

the repeating table. So on the **Condition** dialog box, select **is less than** from the second drop-down list box, and then select **The expression** from the first drop-down list box. The following expression should now appear in the text box:

```
count(my:group2) < 10
```

Click **OK**.

19. Preview the form.

When the form opens, the repeating table should display one row. Add 8 rows to the repeating table and enter a couple of values in fields of the repeating table. When you click **Insert item** to add a 10th row, the **Insert item** command should disappear, and you should only be able to remove rows via the control on the left-hand side of each row of the repeating table. Remove a row. The **Insert item** command should appear again.

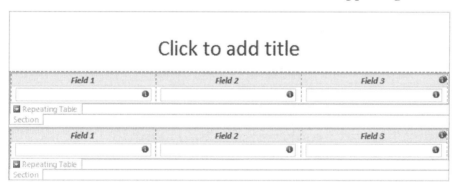

Figure 193. Two section controls containing a reference to the same repeating group.

Discussion

In the solution described above, you used the **count** function in the condition for a **Formatting** rule to be able to count the amount of rows in a repeating table (also see recipe *99 Count the number of rows in a repeating table – method 1*) and use this amount to show or hide sections containing repeating tables that were bound to the same repeating group in the Main data source.

Section controls give up their space when they are hidden and in this recipe you are making use of this fact. The trick behind this recipe is having one section replace another section by placing them in such a way on the view of the form template that there are no spaces between them, so that when one section replaces the other, there are no visual displacements taking place.

In this case, the section containing a repeating table to which users can add rows and from which users can delete rows was replaced by another section containing a repeating table from which users can only remove rows. Both repeating tables were bound to the same repeating group in the Main data source of the form, which means that both repeating tables displayed the same data stored in fields under the repeating group. So while the second repeating table replaced the first repeating table when a 10th row was added to the first repeating table, the user kept seeing the same data from the first repeating table displayed in the second repeating table without any visual displacements.

Note that while you could have added two extra section controls to place the repeating tables in, you reused and bound the container group (**group1**) of the repeating table twice to a section control on the view of the form template, which enabled you to then apply conditional formatting to two separate section controls bound to the same group node in the data source. This way you avoided having to add extra group nodes to the data source just for the purpose of showing/hiding repeating tables on the form.

115 Change a green repeating table to red if it contains more than 3 rows

Problem

You have a repeating table on an InfoPath form that has a green background color. As soon as you add more than 3 rows to the repeating table, you want the background color to change from green to red.

Solution

You can use conditional formatting on section controls that contain repeating tables that are bound to the same repeating group, to change the color of a repeating table based on the amount of rows in the repeating table.

To change a green repeating table to red if it contains more than 3 rows:

1. Follow steps 1 through 5 of recipe *114 Limit the amount of rows added to a repeating table to a maximum*.

2. Select the entire repeating table in the first section control, and then click **Properties ➤ Color ➤ Shading** and select a green color from the drop-down color picker that appears.

3. Select the entire repeating table in the second section control, and then click **Properties ➤ Color ➤ Shading** and select a red color from the drop-down color picker that appears.

4. Click the first section control (**group1**) to select it, and then click **Home ➤ Rules ➤ Manage Rules** to open the **Rules** task pane.

5. On the **Rules** task pane, ensure that **group1** is listed as the selected group below the title bar, and then click **New ➤ Formatting** to add a **Formatting** rule.

6. On the **Rules** task pane under **Formatting**, select the **Hide this control** check box, and then under **Condition** click the text **None**.

7. You want to hide the first section, which contains the green repeating table, if there are more than 3 rows in the repeating table, so on the **Condition** dialog box, select **The expression** from the first drop-down list box, type the following expression into the text box:

```
count(my:group2) > 3
```

and then click **OK**. Remember that you can use the **Use a formula** option in the third drop-down list box to construct the expression (also see recipe *31 Set a maximum length on text in a text box* where this technique was explained for the first time).

8. On the **Rules** task pane, right-click the rule you just added, and select **Copy Rule** from the drop-down menu that appears.

9. Click the second section control to select it. Note that while the second section control is bound to the same group node (**group1**) as the first section control, it is an entirely different control on the view of the form template. So on the **Rules** task pane, you should not see any rules listed for the second section control.

10. On the **Rules** task pane, click the **Paste Rule** command to paste the rule you just copied from the first section control onto the second section control.

11. On the **Rules** task pane under **Condition**, click the text **Number of occurrences of group2 > 3**.

12. You want to hide the second section, which contains the red repeating table, if there are 3 rows or less in the repeating table, so on the **Condition** dialog box, select **is less than or equal to** from the second-drop-down list box, and then select **The expression** from the first drop-down list box. The following expression should now appear in the text box:

```
count(my:group2) <= 3
```

Click **OK**.

13. Preview the form.

When the form opens, the repeating table should be green. Add a couple of rows to the repeating table. As soon as you go over 3 rows, the repeating table should turn red. Delete rows (by hovering over a row, clicking on the drop-down arrow icon that appears on the left-hand side of a row, and selecting **Remove group2** from the drop-down menu that appears) until you have 3 rows or less, at which point the repeating table should turn green again.

Discussion

The solution described above makes use of the same technique described in recipe *114 Limit the amount of rows added to a repeating table to a maximum*, so for more information you can refer to the discussion section of that recipe. The only difference is that in this recipe, the color of the repeating table was changed by swapping repeating tables and the amount of rows was not restricted. Note that the background colors you set on the repeating table controls cannot be accessed through rules, which is why you used section controls as containers to be able to switch colors on two controls that were bound to the same repeating group in the data source, so which displayed the same data in the same way, but with a different look and feel.

116 Shrinking drop-down list in a repeating table

Problem

You have a drop-down list box that is located in a repeating table. Whenever a user selects an item from the drop-down list box and adds a new row to the repeating table, the selected item should disappear from the drop-down list box that is located in the newly added row.

Solution

You can use a filter on the data source that is used to populate the drop-down list box to filter out all of the items that have already been selected in any other row of the repeating table.

To create a shrinking drop-down list in a repeating table:

1. In InfoPath, create a new **Blank Form** template.

2. Add a **Receive data** connection to the XML file you used in recipe *54 Populate a drop-down list box with data from an XML file* and name the data connection **RunningShoes**.

3. Add a **Repeating Table** control with one column to the view of the form template. Name the field within the repeating table **selectedRunningShoe**.

4. Right-click the text box within the repeating table and then select **Change Control ▶ Drop-Down List Box** from the context menu that appears.

5. Right-click the drop-down list box and select **Drop-Down List Box Properties** from the context menu that appears.

6. On the **Drop-Down List Box Properties** dialog box on the **Data** tab under **List box choices**, select the **Get choices from an external data source** option, select **RunningShoes** from the **Data source** drop-down list box, and then click the button behind the **Entries** text box.

7. On the **Select a Field or Group** dialog box, select the **brand** repeating group, and click **Filter Data**.

8. On the **Filter Data** dialog box, click **Add**.

9. On the **Specify Filter Conditions** dialog box, leave **name** selected in the first drop-down list box, leave **is equal to** selected in the second drop-down list box, and then select **Use a formula** from the third drop-down list box.

10. On the **Insert Formula** dialog box, click **Insert Field or Group**.

11. On the **Select a Field or Group** dialog box, select **Main** from the drop-down list box, expand the **group1** group node, expand the **group2** repeating group node, select **selectedRunningShoe**, and click **OK**.

12. On the **Insert Formula** dialog box, click **OK**.

13. On the **Specify Filter Conditions** dialog box, select **The expression** from the first drop-down list box. The expression in the text box should say:

```
@name = xdXDocument:get-
DOM()/my:myFields/my:group1/my:group2/my:selectedRunningShoe
```

What this filter condition does is return all of the **brand** repeating groups in the **RunningShoes** Secondary data source where the **name** field is equal to the value of any **selectedRunningShoe** field in the repeating table. But because you want the opposite, you must nest the filter condition in the **not** function and change it to say the following:

```
not(@name = xdXDocument:get-
DOM()/my:myFields/my:group1/my:group2/my:selectedRunningShoe)
```

This filter condition removes (filters out) all of the **brand** repeating groups from the **RunningShoes** Secondary data source where the **name** field is equal to any **selectedRunningShoe** field in the repeating table.

14. On the **Specify Filter Conditions** dialog box, click **OK**.

15. On the **Filter Data** dialog box, click **OK**.

16. On the **Select a Field or Group** dialog box, click **OK**.

17. On the **Drop-Down List Box Properties** dialog box, the **Value** and **Display name** text boxes should have automatically been populated with the **name** field (**@name** attribute). If you want to configure the value and display name yourself or if they were not automatically populated with the correct field, you can click the buttons behind the corresponding text boxes, and select a field of your choice via the **Select a Field or Group** dialog box.

18. On the **Drop-Down List Box Properties** dialog box, click **OK**.

19. Preview the form.

When the form opens, all of the items from the **RunningShoes** Secondary data source should be present in the drop-down list box in the first row of the repeating table. Select an item from the drop-down list box, and then click **Insert item** to add a second row to the repeating table. The item you selected in the first drop-down list box should not be present in the second drop-down list box. Continue adding rows until there are no items left in the drop-down list box. Also try removing rows from the repeating table to see items reappear in the drop-down list box.

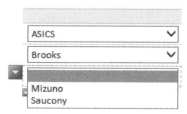

Figure 194. Drop-down list box containing less and less items as they are selected.

Discussion

In the solution described above, you saw that once you had selected all of the items from the drop-down list box, you were able to continue adding rows to the repeating table, but those rows would contain empty drop-down list boxes. If you want users not to be able to add rows to the repeating table once all of the items have been selected, you can perform a similar trick as the one described in recipe *114 Limit the amount of rows added to a repeating table to a maximum* by swapping the repeating table with a repeating table to which users cannot add rows as soon as all of the drop-down list box items have been selected. You can achieve such functionality as follows:

1. On the **Fields** task pane, right-click **group1** (the container group for the repeating group of the repeating table), drag it to the view of the form template, drop it, and select **Section** from the context menu that appears.

2. Repeat the previous step to add a second section control that is bound to the same **group1** group node to the view of the form template. Ensure that the section controls are placed directly under each other with no lines between them.

3. Select the repeating table that was already present on the view of the form template, press **Ctrl+X** on your keyboard to cut it, click anywhere inside of the first section control, and then press **Ctrl+V** on your keyboard to paste the repeating table in the first section control. Ensure that there are no extra lines above or below the repeating table inside of the section control.

4. Select the repeating table that is located in the first section control, press **Ctrl+C** on your keyboard to copy it, click anywhere inside of the second section control, and then press **Ctrl+V** on your keyboard to paste the repeating table in the second section control. And again, ensure that there are no extra lines above or below the repeating table inside of the second section control. You should see the message "Control stores duplicate data" appear on both repeating tables. Just ignore this message for now.

Figure 195. Repeating tables in two section controls.

5. Open the **Repeating Table Properties** dialog box for the second repeating table.

6. On the **Repeating Table Properties** dialog box on the **Data** tab, deselect the **Show insert button and hint text** check box, and then click **Customize Commands**.

7. On the **Table Commands** dialog box, deselect all of the check boxes except for the **Remove** check box. This should allow users to remove rows from the second repeating table, but not add any new rows. Note that you must leave the first repeating table configured as is, since users should be able to add rows to or remove rows from the first repeating table.

8. Click **OK** when closing all dialog boxes.

9. Add a **Formatting** rule to the first section control with a **Condition** that says:

```
count(my:group2) =
count(xdXDocument:GetDOM("RunningShoes")/ns1:brands/ns1:brand
)
```

and that has a **Formatting** of **Hide this control**. What this rule does is hide the first section control that contains the first repeating table (which is the repeating table users can use to add rows) as soon as the amount of rows that have been added to the repeating table is the same as the amount of brands in the **RunningShoes** Secondary data source, so as soon as all of the brands have been selected from the drop-down list box. Note that you can use the technique explained in recipe *31 Set a maximum length on text in a text box* to first construct the expression for the condition using the **Insert Formula** dialog box and then afterwards correct the expression on the **Condition** dialog box.

10. Add a **Formatting** rule to the second section control with a **Condition** that says:

```
count(my:group2) <
count(xdXDocument:GetDOM("RunningShoes")/ns1:brands/ns1:brand
)
```

and that has a **Formatting** of **Hide this control**. What this rule does is hide the second section control that contains the second repeating table (which is the repeating table users can use to remove, but not add rows) whenever the amount of rows that have been added to the repeating table is less than the amount of brands in the **RunningShoes** Secondary data source, so it shows the section control whenever the amount of rows in the repeating table is equal to or has exceeded the amount of selectable brands in the Secondary data source. Note that you can use the technique explained in recipe *31 Set a maximum length on text in a text box* to first construct the expression for the condition using the **Insert Formula** dialog box and then afterwards correct the expression on the **Condition** dialog box.

117 Cascading drop-down list boxes in a repeating table

Problem

You have a repeating table with two drop-down list boxes in it and want to be able to select an item from the first drop-down list box and then have the second drop-down list box populated with items related to the selected item in the first drop-down list box.

Solution

In this recipe, you will use the **RunningShoes** XML file that you also used in recipe *54 Populate a drop-down list box with data from an XML file*, but this time you will populate the first drop-down list box with brand names and the second drop-down list box should contain the running shoe models for the selected brand.

To create cascading drop-down list boxes in a repeating table:

1. In InfoPath, create a new **Blank Form** template.

2. Add a **Repeating Table** control with 2 columns to the view of the form template.

3. Add a **Drop-Down List Box** control to the first column of the repeating table (see recipe *94 4 Ways to add a control to a repeating table* for how to add controls other than text boxes to a repeating table) and a second drop-down list box to the second column of the repeating table. Name the first drop-down list box **brand** and the second drop-down list box **model**.

4. Populate the first drop-down list box with data from the **RunningShoes** XML file (see recipe *54 Populate a drop-down list box with data from an XML file*) by adding the XML file as a Secondary data source to the form template and then specifying it to be used as the data source for the drop-down list box. Use the **name** field under the **brand** repeating group for the **Value** and the **Display name** properties of the first drop-down list box.

5. Open the **Drop-Down List Box Properties** dialog box for the second drop-down list box, select the **RunningShoes** data source as the external data source the drop-down list box should get data from, and click the button behind the **Entries** text box.

6. On the **Select a Field or Group** dialog box, expand all of the nodes, select the **model** repeating field, and click **Filter Data**. Because the items in the second drop-down list box should depend on the brand that is selected from the first drop-down list box, you must add a filter that filters models on brands but that also only looks at the brand that is selected in the current row of the repeating table.

7. On the **Filter Data** dialog box, click **Add**.

8. On the **Specify Filter Conditions** dialog box, select **Select a field or group** from the first drop-down list box.

9. On the **Select a Field or Group** dialog box, ensure that **RunningShoes (Secondary)** is selected in the drop-down list box, select the **name** field under the **brand** repeating group, and click **OK**.

10. You want the brand name in the **RunningShoes** Secondary data source to be the same as the brand name selected in the first drop-down list box that is bound to a field that is located under the repeating group bound to the repeating table in the Main data source of the form. So on the **Specify Filter Conditions** dialog box, select **Select a field or group** from the third drop-down list box.

11. On the **Select a Field or Group** dialog box, select **Main** from the drop-down list box, expand the **group1** group node, expand the **group2** repeating group node, select the **brand** field, and click **OK**.

12. Click **OK** when closing all dialog boxes.

13. To prevent any previously selected item from appearing in the **model** drop-down list box whenever you reselect an item from the **brand** drop-down list box, you must add an **Action** rule to the **brand** drop-down list box to clear the **model** drop-down list box. So click the **brand** drop-down list box to select it, click **Home ➤ Rules ➤ Manage Rules**, and then on the **Rules** task pane add an **Action** rule with an action that says:

```
Set a field's value: model = ""
```

14. Preview the form.

When the form opens, verify that the second drop-down list box is empty, and then select a brand from the first drop-down list box. The second drop-down list box should now contain shoe models for the selected brand in the first drop-down list box. Add several rows to the repeating table, and then select a brand from the first drop-down list box in any row. When you look in the second drop-down list box in the same row as the drop-down list box from which you selected a brand, the second drop-down list box should contain the running shoe models for the brand you selected.

Discussion

In the solution described above, you saw how to use a filter on a data source to be able to create cascading drop-down list boxes in a repeating table.

If you reopen the **Drop-Down List Box Properties** dialog box for the **model** drop-down list box and navigate back to the **Specify Filter Conditions** dialog box by clicking on the button behind the **Entries** text box, **Filter Data** on the **Select a Field or Group** dialog box, and finally **Modify** on the **Filter Data** dialog box, and then select **The expression** from the first drop-down list box on the **Specify Filter Conditions** dialog box, you should see the following expression appear in the text box:

```
../../@name = current()/my:brand
```

While you could have entered such an expression manually or construct it by selecting **Use a formula** from the third drop-down list box on the **Specify Filter Conditions** dialog box together with the **Insert Formula** dialog box, you used dialog boxes in the solution described above to let InfoPath construct the expression for you, which hides much of the complexity behind such an expression.

If you do not know the XPath expression for a field, you can use the **Copy XPath** functionality in InfoPath to look it up. For example, to retrieve the full XPath expression for the **brand** field, you must click on **brand** on the **Fields** task pane, click on the drop-down arrow on the right-hand side of **brand**, and select **Copy XPath** from the drop-down menu that appears. This will copy the following XPath expression to the Windows clipboard:

```
/my:myFields/my:group1/my:group2/my:brand
```

Because **current()** gives you a reference to the current node, which in this case is the current row in a repeating table, and **my:group2** represents a row in the repeating table, you can delete everything in the XPath expression starting from **my:group2** going backwards and replace it with

```
current()
```

which will result in the following XPath expression:

```
current()/my:brand
```

The expression above returns the value of **brand** selected in the first column of the repeating table and located in the same row of the repeating table where the second drop-down list box is currently being populated.

If you look at the **Entries** text box on the **Drop-Down List Box Properties** dialog box of the **model** drop-down list box, you should see the following XPath expression:

```
/ns1:brands/ns1:brand/ns1:type/ns1:model[../../@name =
current()/my:brand]
```

The figure below shows how the **group2** group relates to a repeating table and where **current()** fits into the entire picture.

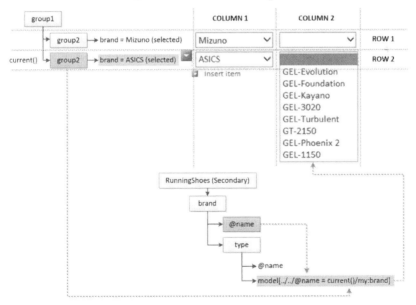

Figure 196. Relationship between repeating table, data sources, and current().

How to interpret Figure 196:

- The **RunningShoes** Secondary data source is used to populate the drop-down list boxes in both columns of the repeating table.

- The drop-down list box in the first column is populated with brand names (**RunningShoes ➤ brand ➤ @name**).

- Mizuno is selected as the brand in the drop-down list box in the first column and first row of the repeating table, and ASICS is selected as the brand in the drop-down list box in the first column and second row of the repeating table.

- The drop-down list box in the second column is populated with models (**RunningShoes ➤ model**), but is filtered on the brand name in the Secondary data source being equal to the selected brand name in the Main data source in the first column in the same row (**RunningShoes ➤ model** where **brand/@name = current()/my:brand**).

- The items in the drop-down list box in the second column and second row of the repeating table are being displayed, and because ASICS was selected in the drop-down list box in the first column and second row of the repeating table, the drop-down list box in the second column and second row of the repeating table displays ASICS running shoe models.

This recipe does not have to be restricted to looking up data in the same Secondary data source that is used to populate two drop-down list boxes. You could populate each drop-down list box with data from two different Secondary data sources and still use the technique described above to create dependent or cascading drop-down list boxes in a repeating table.

118 Export a repeating table's contents as a string

Problem

You have a repeating table that has one column containing a text box and you want all of the text entered in rows of the repeating table to be concatenated to form one long string.

Solution

You can use the **eval** function to export the contents of all of the rows of a repeating table.

To export a repeating table's contents as a string to a text box:

1. In InfoPath, create a new **Blank Form** template.

2. Add a **Repeating Table** control with one column and a **Text Box** control to the view of the form template.

3. Set the **Default Value** of the text box outside of the repeating table to be equal to the following formula:

    ```
    eval(group2, "..")
    ```

    and ensure that the **Refresh value when formula is recalculated** check box has been selected. In the formula above, **group2** represents the repeating group bound to the repeating table.

4. Preview the form.

When the form opens, type a piece of text in the text box within the repeating table. Move away from the text box by clicking elsewhere on the form. The second text box below the repeating table should display the value from the text box within the repeating table. Add a couple of rows to the repeating table with more text to see how the text in the text box below the repeating table is updated.

Discussion

The **eval** function returns the values of a field or group, and takes two arguments. The first argument defines the field or group the **eval** function should operate on, and the second argument defines the expression to calculate for the field or group. Usually, the **eval** function is nested within a function that operates on a field or group, such as **sum** or **avg**.

The formula in the solution described above returns the value of the anonymous parent

```
".."
```

which is a concatenated string of all of the parent's children (**group2** nodes). The latter is a W3C standard. If you have three rows in the repeating table with the text "a", "b", and "c", respectively, the resulting value of the formula would be "a b c".

119 Export a repeating table's contents to a text box with line breaks

Problem

You have a first name and a last name column in a repeating table to capture a list of contact names. You want to be able to loop through all of the names in the rows of the repeating table and construct a list of names (first name plus last name) that can be displayed as one piece of text in a multi-line text box with line breaks.

Solution

You can use the **eval** function to export the contents of all of the rows of a repeating table and add line breaks between the contents of the rows.

To export a repeating table's contents to a text box with line breaks:

1.   In InfoPath, create a new **Blank Form** template.

2.   Add a **Repeating Table** control with 3 columns to the view of the form template. Name the first text box in the repeating table **firstName**, the second text box **lastName**, and the third text box **lineBreak**. Make the **lineBreak** field hidden by deleting the repeating table column it is located in.

3.   Add a **Text Box** control to the view of the form template.

4.   Open the **Text Box Properties** dialog box, and then on the **Display** tab, select the **Multi-line** check box to make the text box accept line breaks and multiple lines of text. Click **OK** when you are done.

5.   Add a data connection to an XML file (see recipe *33 Get data from an XML file*) that has the following contents:

```
<break>
  <value>&#xD;</value>
</break>
```

and name the data connection **LineBreak**.

6. Set the **Default Value** of the **lineBreak** field in the repeating table to be equal to the value of the **value** field under the **break** group in the **LineBreak (Secondary)** data source. Note: To set the default value of a hidden field, you can double-click the hidden field on the **Fields** task pane to open its **Field or Group Properties** dialog box and then set its default value from there.

7. Set the **Default Value** of the multi-line text box to be equal to the following formula:

```
eval(eval(group2, 'concat(normalize-space(concat(my:firstName,
" ", my:lastName)), my:lineBreak)'), "..")
```

and ensure that the **Refresh value when formula is recalculated** check box is selected on the **Properties** dialog box.

8. Preview the form.

When the form opens, type a first name and a last name into the text boxes in the repeating table. As you type and leave the text boxes, the multi-line text box should get updated. Continue adding rows to the repeating table and typing names. The multi-line text box should eventually be populated with the names from the repeating table as a list of names displayed on separate lines.

Discussion

The **eval** function returns the values of a field or group, and takes two arguments. The first argument defines the field or group the **eval** function should operate on, and the second argument defines the expression to calculate for the field or group. Usually, the **eval** function is nested within a function that operates on a field or group, such as **sum** or **avg**.

In the solution described above, you used the **eval** function twice. The first **eval** function (the inner one) was used as follows:

```
eval(group2, 'concat(normalize-space(concat(my:firstName, " ",
my:lastName)), my:lineBreak)')
```

The preceding formula takes a **group2** node of the repeating table, and returns the concatenation of the **firstName**, **lastName**, and **lineBreak** fields under that **group2** node.

The **group2** in the formula is the group the **eval** function should work on (the context node), and the second argument is the expression the **eval** function should perform on that group, so the result of the evaluation.

Let us first dissect the expression for the second argument in the **eval** function above. First **firstName** and **lastName** under a **group2** node (the context node) are concatenated using the **concat** function. And a space is added between these two fields.

```
concat(my:firstName, " ", my:lastName)
```

Then the **normalize-space** function is used to remove unwanted empty spaces from around the concatenation of the first name and the last name (see recipe *20 Join two text strings and remove spaces if either text string is empty*)

```
normalize-space(concat(my:firstName, " ", my:lastName))
```

and a line break is appended to the result by using the **concat** function for a second time.

```
concat(normalize-space(concat(my:firstName, " ", my:lastName)),
my:lineBreak)
```

And finally, the **eval** function is used on a **group2** node in the repeating table to return the value of the concatenations of its fields (the expression between single quotes).

```
eval(group2, 'concat(normalize-space(concat(my:firstName, " ",
my:lastName)), my:lineBreak)')
```

The second **eval** function (the outer one) is used to retrieve the contents of all of the **group2** nodes as a string. The most basic formula to get this done is the following:

```
eval(group2, "..")
```

The preceding formula returns the value of the anonymous parent

```
".."
```

which is a concatenated string of the contents of all of the parent's children (**group2** nodes). The latter is a W3C standard. In the final formula, you want to get the contents of all of the **group2** nodes, but you also want to apply the concatenation you constructed earlier for each **group2** node, so that the line break is included between the concatenated contents of all of the **group2** nodes. So you must replace

```
group2
```

in the formula using the outer **eval** function with the **eval** formula you constructed earlier. This results in the following final formula when you combine the two **eval** formulas:

```
eval(eval(group2, 'concat(normalize-space(concat(my:firstName, " ",
my:lastName)), my:lineBreak)'), "..")
```

120 Copy data from a Secondary data source to the Main data source

Problem

You have a repeating table and a drop-down list box on an InfoPath form. The drop-down list box is being populated with data from an external data source. Whenever you select an item from this drop-down list box and add a new row to the repeating table, you want the data pertaining to the item you selected in the drop-down list box to be copied over to the new row of the repeating table.

Solution

You can use filters on a Secondary data source and default values on fields in a repeating table to copy data from a Secondary data source to a row of the repeating table.

To copy data from a Secondary data source to a repeating group in the Main data source:

1. In InfoPath, create a new **Blank Form** template.

2. Add a **Drop-Down List Box** control to the view of the form template and name it **selectedItem**.

3. Populate the drop-down list box with data from the **MonthNames.xml** file that you also used in recipe *60 Populate a text box based on an item selected in a drop-down list box* by adding the XML file as a Secondary data source to the form template and then specifying it to be used as the data source for the drop-down list box. Use the **month** repeating group as the **Entries**, the **number** field under the **month** repeating group as the **Value**, and the **name** field under the **month** repeating group as the **Display name** for the drop-down list box.

4. Add a **Repeating Table** control with 2 columns to the view of the form template. Name the text box controls in the repeating table **monthNumber** and **monthName**, respectively. In addition, configure the repeating table to not display a first empty row as described in recipe *95 Remove the first empty row of a repeating table*.

5. Set the **Default Value** of the **monthNumber** field in the repeating table to be equal to the following formula:

```
selectedItem
```

where **selectedItem** is a field in the Main data source and that is bound to the drop-down list box. Deselect the **Refresh value when formula is recalculated** check box on the **Properties** dialog box. Because you do not want any values in previously added rows of the repeating table to be overwritten when you add or remove a row, you must deselect the check box that refreshes the value of the **monthNumber** field in the repeating table.

6. Select the **monthName** field in the repeating table, and then click **Properties ➤ Properties ➤ Default Value**.

7. On the **Field or Group Properties** dialog box, click the formula button behind the **Value** text box.

8. On the **Insert Formula** dialog box, click **Insert Field or Group**.

9. On the **Select a Field or Group** dialog box, select **MonthNames (Secondary)** from the drop-down list box, expand the **month** repeating group, select the **name** field, and click **Filter Data**. Because you want to retrieve the name of the month that pertains to the selected item in the drop-down list box, you must add a filter to extract that information from the Secondary data source.

10. On the **Filter Data** dialog box, click **Add**.

11. On the **Specify Filter Conditions** dialog box, select **number** from the first drop-down list box, leave **is equal to** selected in the second drop-down list box, and then select **Select a field or group** from the third drop-down list box.

12. On the **Select a Field or Group** dialog box, select **Main** from the drop-down list box, select the **selectedItem** field, and click **OK**.

13. On the **Specify Filter Conditions** dialog box, click **OK**.

14. On the **Filter Data** dialog box, click **OK**.

15. On the **Select a Field or Group** dialog box, click **OK**. The formula on the **Insert Formula** dialog box should now say:

```
name[number = selectedItem]
```

What this formula does is return only those **name** fields from the Secondary data source where the value of their corresponding **number** field is equal to the value of the **selectedItem** field in the Main data source.

16. On the **Insert Formula** dialog box, click **OK**.

17. On the **Field or Group Properties** dialog box, deselect the **Refresh value when formula is recalculated** check box, and then click **OK**.

18. Preview the form.

When the form opens, select an item from the drop-down list box and then click the **Insert item** command on the repeating table. The number and name of the month you selected from the drop-down list box should appear in the newly inserted row. Select another item from the drop-down list box and add another row to the repeating table. The newly selected item should appear in the newly added row of the repeating table.

Discussion

In the solution described above, you saw how to use the default values of fields to pull data in from a Secondary data source to be able to copy data over to rows of a repeating table.

Because InfoPath does not provide an action with which you can set the values of fields in a particular row of a repeating table, you used the technique described in this recipe to be able to set the values of fields in newly added rows.

121 Master/detail functionality with one master and two detail lists

Problem

You have a list of running shoe brands with each brand having motion control running shoe models and stability running shoe models. You want to create an InfoPath form to display the brands in a repeating table and then when you select a brand, the corresponding motion control and stability running shoes are displayed in two detail lists.

Solution

You can use repeating tables and repeating sections to manually set up master/detail functionality in an InfoPath Filler Form.

To create master/detail functionality that has one master and two detail lists:

1. In InfoPath, create a new **Blank Form (InfoPath Filler)** template.

2. Add a **Repeating Table** with one column to the view of the form template and name the text box within the repeating table **brand**. You are going to use this repeating table as the master for master/detail functionality.

3. Right-click the repeating table and select **Repeating Table Properties** from the context menu that appears.

4. On the **Repeating Table Properties** dialog box, click the **Master/Detail** tab, select the **Set as master** option, enter a **Master ID** (for example, **RunningShoesMaster**), and then click **OK**. With this you have set the repeating table to be the master.

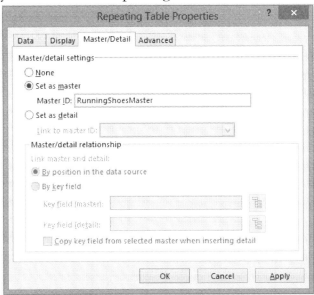

Figure 197. Setting a repeating table to be the master.

5. On the **Fields** task pane, right-click the **group2** repeating group, and select **Add** from the drop-down menu that appears.

6. On the **Add Field or Group** dialog box, type **motionControlRunningShoe** in the **Name** text box, leave **Field (element)** selected in the **Type** drop-down list box, leave **Text (string)** selected in the **Data type** drop-down list box, select the **Repeating** check box, and click **OK**.

7. Repeat the previous two steps, but name the repeating field **stabilityRunningShoe** instead of **motionControlRunningShoe**. The Main data source should now resemble the following figure:

Figure 198. Main data source of the InfoPath form.

8. The two repeating fields under the **group2** repeating group will serve as detail lists of the master. On the **Fields** task pane, right-click the **group2** repeating group, drag it to the view of the form template, drop it, and select **Repeating Section with Controls** from the context menu that appears. InfoPath should have added two **Bulleted List** controls for the **motionControlRunningShoe** and the **stabilityRunningShoe** repeating fields to the repeating section. InfoPath should have also added a text box control for the **brand** field to the repeating section. Delete this text box in addition to its label from the repeating section, but do not delete the **brand** field from the Main data source.

9. Right-click the repeating section and select **Repeating Section Properties** from the context menu that appears.

10. On the **Repeating Section Properties** dialog box on the **Data** tab, deselect the **Allow users to insert and delete sections** check box.

11. On the **Repeating Section Properties** dialog box, click the
Master/Detail tab, select the **Set as detail** option, select
RunningShoesMaster from the **Link to master ID** drop-down list
box, leave the **By position in the data source** option selected, and
click **OK**.

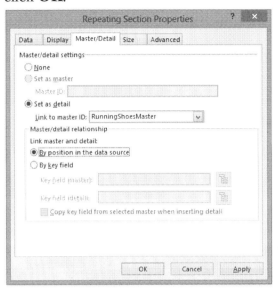

Figure 199. Setting a repeating section to display details.

12. Preview the form.

When the form opens, enter a running shoe brand (for example "Mizuno")
in the **brand** text box, and then enter a couple of motion control running
shoe models (for example "Wave Alchemy" and "Wave Renegade") in the
motion control running shoes list and a couple of stability running shoe
models (for example "Wave Nirvana", "Wave Elixir", "Wave Inspire", and
"Wave Nexus") in the stability running shoes list. Click the **Insert item**
command on the repeating table to add a new row. The lists should be
empty. Enter another running shoe brand (for example "Brooks") in the
brand text box, and then enter a couple of motion control running shoe
models (for example "Ariel" and "Addiction") in the motion control
running shoes list and a couple of stability running shoe models (for
example "Trance" and "Adrenaline") in the stability running shoes list. Now
when you click on the first row in the repeating table, you should see the

running shoe models for the first running shoe brand ("Mizuno") appear in the two bulleted lists.

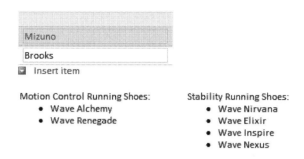

Figure 200. Running shoes (details) for the first running shoe brand in the master.

And when you click on the second row, the running shoe models for the second running shoe brand ("Brooks") should appear in the two bulleted lists.

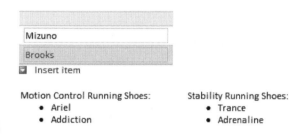

Figure 201. Running shoes (details) for the second running shoe brand in the master.

Discussion

In the solution described above, you saw how to manually set up master/detail functionality in an InfoPath form. Note that you cannot set up master/detail functionality in Web Browser Forms, which is why you created an InfoPath Filler Form in the solution above.

You can also add master/detail functionality to an InfoPath Filler Form by making use of a **Master/Detail** control. A **Master/Detail** control always consists of two parts:

1. A master control

2. A detail control

The master control is always a repeating table, while the detail control can be either a repeating table or a repeating section. In the solution described above you used a repeating section as the detail control.

If you wanted to recreate the solution described above using a **Master/Detail** control instead of performing manual steps to set up master/detail functionality, you would have to do the following:

1. Click **Home ➤ Controls ➤ Master /Detail**.

2. On the **Insert Master/Detail** dialog box, enter **1** for the **Number of columns in master** and **1** for the **Number of fields in detail**, and click **OK**.

3. Delete the text box in the repeating section for the detail.

4. Click inside of the repeating section for the detail to place the cursor, and then click **Home ➤ Controls ➤ Bulleted List** to add a bulleted list control to the repeating section for the detail.

5. Repeat the previous step to add a second bulleted list control to the repeating section for the detail.

While the Main data source may not look the same as in the solution described above (InfoPath places repeating fields under group nodes), the linking between the master and the two details is the same as described in the solution above.

The master is always linked to the detail through what is called a **Master ID**, which you assigned to the repeating table through its **Properties** dialog box. The detail must be linked to a master by selecting the **Master ID** of the master you want to link the detail to on the **Properties** dialog box of the repeating table or repeating section that represents the detail.

The detail can be linked to the master either by its position in the data source or by a key field. In the solution described above you linked it by its position in the data source. In this case, you bound the same repeating group (**group2**) that was bound to the master, to the detail and removed the field (**brand**) from the detail, because it was already being filled out through the master.

Note that had you tried to bind the **motionControlRunningShoe** and **stabilityRunningShoe** repeating fields to repeating tables and then tried to link those repeating tables to the **RunningShoesMaster** repeating table, InfoPath would have displayed the following message.

Figure 202. Incorrect context warning message in InfoPath 2013.

That is because the **motionControlRunningShoe** and **stabilityRunningShoe** repeating fields are located under the **group2** repeating group bound to the master.

If a repeating group or a repeating field you want to use as a detail is located under a repeating group bound to a master, you must also bind the repeating group that you bound to the master, to the detail to avoid the

The master that you just picked is in an incorrect context.

message from appearing. Another option to avoid this message from appearing would be not to have the repeating group or the repeating field you want to use for the detail, located under the repeating group bound to the master as shown in the following figure.

Figure 203. Main data source of a form with 3 independent repeating groups.

In the figure above, repeating groups **group4** and **group6** are not located under repeating group **group2**, but rather under **group3** and **group5**, which in turn are located under the **myFields** group. If you have such a scenario, you can bind **group2** to a repeating table and make that repeating table the master with a **Master ID** equal to **RunningShoesMaster** (step 4 in the solution described above), and then you must bind **group4** to a second repeating table and make that repeating table a detail by configuring it as shown in the following figure.

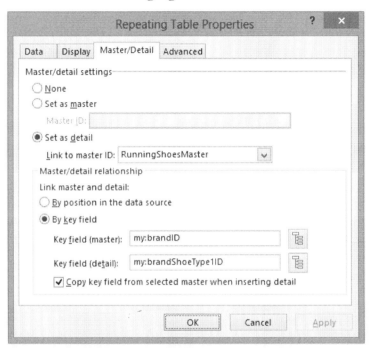

Figure 204. Using a key field to link a detail to a master.

And finally, you must bind **group6** to a third repeating table and make that repeating table the second detail for the same master as the first detail by configuring it as shown in the following figure.

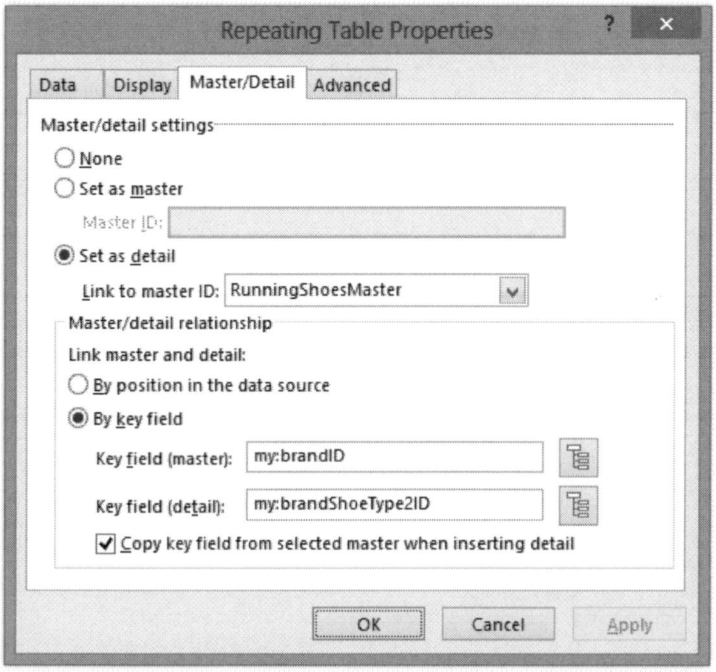

Figure 205. Using a key field to link a second detail to the same master.

Now whenever you insert a new brand in the master repeating table and assign a number to the **brandID** column, that number will automatically be copied over to the other two repeating tables when you add detail items to them.

Figure 206. One master repeating table linked to two detail repeating tables.

The data for a master/detail control must be located in the Main data source of a form for you to be able to use the control. This means that you cannot bind data from a Secondary data source to a master/detail control. So for example, if you add a data connection to an XML file, you cannot use a master/detail control to display this data.

However, if you create an InfoPath form template that is based on an XML file (via **File ➤ New ➤ XML or Schema**) or based on a database (via **File ➤ New ➤ Database**), the XML file or database will be used to create the Main data source of the form, so you will then also be able to use a master/detail control to display and/or enter data.

In recipe *41 Submit form data to database tables with a one-to-many relationship* you created a form template that was based on a database. Follow the instructions in steps 1 through 8 from that recipe, delete everything from the view of the form template except for the **Run Query** button, and then use what you learned in this recipe to bind the **Brand** repeating group under the **dataFields** group to a master repeating table and then bind the **Brand** repeating group for a second time to a repeating table to set up a detail repeating table. The second repeating table should contain a repeating table bound to the **Model** repeating group, which is what you want to display in the detail. Note that for the detail, you must configure the outer repeating table that contains the **Model** repeating table to set up the master/detail connection.

Note that you can bind a master/detail control to the data in the Main data source by dragging-and-dropping the **Brand** repeating group under the **dataFields** group from the **Fields** task pane onto the view of the form template, binding it to two repeating tables, and then linking the repeating tables to each other manually as described in the solution in this recipe; or you can add a **Master/Detail** control to the view of the form template as follows:

1. Click **Home ➤ Controls ➤ Master/Detail**.

2. On the **Master/Detail Binding** dialog box, expand the **dataFields** group, select the **Brand** repeating group, and click **OK**. This should add a master repeating table and a detail repeating section containing a repeating table bound to the **Model** repeating group to the view of

the form template.

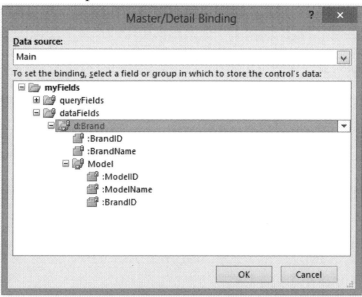

Figure 207. Master/Detail Binding dialog box in InfoPath 2013.

If you did everything correctly, when you open a new form and click the **Run Query** button, data should appear in the master repeating table, and when you click to select a row, the corresponding detail data should appear in the **Model** repeating table that is nested in the detail repeating table or section.

You may notice that the master repeating table contains a lot of rows and that therefore the detail appears lower down on the view after you retrieve data from the database. Repeating tables and repeating sections that are bound to repeating groups in the Main data source of an InfoPath form come with a **Filter Data** command you can use to reduce the amount of data being displayed in the control by filtering the data. For example, if you wanted to display only the brand names that contained the letters "broo" in the master repeating table, then you would have to modify the solution as follows:

1. On the **Fields** task pane, add a new **Field (element)** with the data type **Text (string)** and the name **filterOn** under the **myFields** group. Note that there is a padlock icon on all of the fields and

groups under the **queryFields** and **dataFields** groups, so you cannot modify them, which includes adding new fields to them. However, because the **myFields** group is not locked, you can add fields to it.

2. On the **Fields** task pane, drag the **filterOn** field to the view of the form template, and drop it. It should automatically get bound to a text box.

3. Open the **Repeating Table Properties** dialog box of the master repeating table, click the **Display** tab, and then under the **Filter** section, click **Filter Data**.

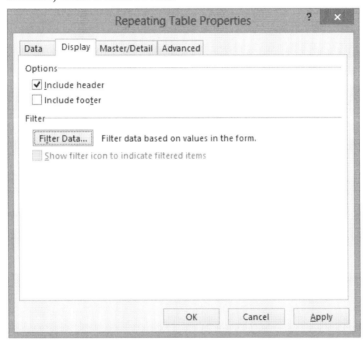

Figure 208. Repeating Table Properties dialog box of the master.

Note that the filter options on the **Display** tab are not available for repeating tables or repeating sections that are bound to repeating groups in a Secondary data source. To filter data in a Secondary data source, you must use conditional formatting.

4. On the **Filter Data** dialog box, click **Add**.

5. On the **Specify Filter Conditions** dialog box, select **The expression** from the first drop-down list box, and then enter an expression such as the following into the text box:

```
contains(translate(@BrandName, "abcdefghijklmnopqrstuvwxyz",
"ABCDEFGHIJKLMNOPQRSTUVWXYZ"), translate(../../my:filterOn,
"abcdefghijklmnopqrstuvwxyz", "ABCDEFGHIJKLMNOPQRSTUVWXYZ"))
```

Note that you must combine several techniques that have been discussed in this book to construct the filter expression. This filter expression checks whether the **BrandName** field under the **Brand** repeating group under the **dataFields** group contains the text that was entered into the **filterOn** text box and compares the two after having capitalized both strings so that the comparison is not case-sensitive.

6. Click **OK** when closing all dialog boxes.

7. Preview the form.

When the form opens, click the **Run Query** button to display all of the data from the **Brand** database table. Then enter a piece of text (for example "broo") into the **filterOn** text box and click away from the text box. The master repeating table should be filtered and only two rows containing "Brooks" as the brand name should appear in the master repeating table, since the **Brand** database table contains two records for "Brooks". Now you can click on each row to display their corresponding detail.

Important:

> To be able to use a **Master/Detail** control on an InfoPath form you must: 1. Create an InfoPath Filler Form, because the **Master/Detail** control is not available for Web Browser Forms, and 2. Bind the **Master/Detail** control to a structure that is located in the Main data source of the form.

Bonus Recipes

This chapter is a last-minute addition to the book and contains recipes that did not make it into the main selection of recipes, but which I still did not want to omit because of their usefulness.

Display only the last 10 rows of a repeating table

Problem

You have a repeating table on an InfoPath form and want to display only the last 10 rows of the repeating table.

Solution

You can use conditional formatting on rows of a repeating table to hide all of the rows that appear before the last 10 rows of the repeating table.

To display only the last 10 rows of a repeating table:

1. In InfoPath, create a new **Blank Form** template.

2. Add a **Repeating Table** control to the view of the form template.

3. Select the repeating table and then click **Home ➤ Rules ➤ Manage Rules**.

4. On the **Rules** task pane, ensure that **group2** is listed below the title bar (if it is not, click the text "Repeating Table" on the repeating table to select it or click on **group2** in the Main data source). You want to add conditional formatting to the repeating group (so to rows in the table); not to an individual field within the repeating group.

5. On the **Rules** task pane, click **New ➤ Formatting**.

6. On the **Rules** task pane, select the **Hide this control** check box, and then under **Condition** click the text **None**.

7. On the **Condition** dialog box, select **The expression** from the first drop-down list box, and then type the following expression into the text box:

```
count(following-sibling::*) >= 10
```

8. On the **Condition** dialog box, click **OK**.

9. Preview the form.

When the form opens, add 10 rows to the repeating table and enter numbers in the first field of each row so that you can distinguish between the rows. When you click to add an 11th row, the first row should disappear.

Discussion

In the solution described above, rows of a repeating table are hidden and not deleted. So when you save or submit the form, the hidden rows will be present in the XML of the InfoPath form.

The **following-sibling** XPath axis works similar to the **preceding-sibling** XPath axis, which was first introduced in recipe *100 Count the number of rows in a repeating table – method 2*. So you can refer to the discussion sections of that recipe and recipe *112 Highlight the last row of a repeating table* to learn more about these XPath axes.

The solution described above is handy to use for example if you have limited space on a form or do not want a repeating table to grow beyond a certain height.

Limit the amount of lines in a multi-line text box

Problem

You have a multi-line text box control on an InfoPath form and want users to be able to enter a maximum of 4 lines in the text box.

Solution

You can use data validation to limit the amount of lines in a multi-line text box.

To limit the amount of lines in a multi-line text box:

1. In InfoPath, create a new **Blank Form** template.

2. Add a data connection to an XML file (see recipe *33 Get data from an XML file*) that has the following contents:

```
<break>
  <value>&#xD;</value>
</break>
```

and name the data connection **LineBreak**.

3. Add a data connection to an XML file that has the following contents:

```
<helper>
  <helperField></helperField>
  <isLoading>0</isLoading>
</helper>
```

and name the data connection **HelperField**.

4. Add a **Text Box** control to the view of the form template, name it **maxLines**, and select its **Multi-line** property (see recipe *9 Make a text box multi-line*).

5. Add a second **Text Box** control to the view of the form template, name it **lineCount**, and select its **Read-Only** property. Alternatively, you could change the text box into a **Calculated Value** control.

6. Add a **Validation** rule to the **maxLines** text box with a **Condition** that says:

```
lineCount > 4
```

and that has a **ScreenTip** that says: "Only 4 lines max allowed".

7. Add an **Action** rule to the **maxLines** text box that has an action that says:

```
Set a field's value: helperField = .
```

where **helperField** is a field that is located in the **HelperField**

Secondary data source and where the dot (.) represents the field bound to the **maxLines** text box.

8. On the **Fields** task pane, select **HelperField (Secondary)** from the drop-down list box, click the **helperField** field to select it, and then on the **Rules** task pane, add an **Action** rule to the **helperField** field in the **HelperField** Secondary data source with a **Condition** that says:

```
isLoading = "0"
```

and that has an action that says:

```
Set a field's value: lineCount = string-length(maxLines) -
string-length(translate(., value, "")) + 1
```

where **isLoading** is a field that is located in the **HelperField** Secondary data source, **lineCount** is the field that is bound to the **lineCount** text box (or calculated value control), **maxLines** is the field that is bound to the multi-line text box, the dot (.) represents the **helperField** field in the **HelperField** Secondary data source, and **value** is the **value** field that is located in the **LineBreak** Secondary data source. The formula for the action looks like the following on the **Insert Formula** dialog box when you have the **Edit XPath (advanced)** check box selected:

```
string-length(xdXDocument:get-DOM()/my:myFields/my:maxLines) -
string-length(translate(.,
xdXDocument:GetDOM("LineBreak")/break/value, "")) + 1
```

This formula counts the amount of characters entered into the **maxLines** text box by using the **string-length** function:

```
string-length(maxLines)
```

Then it removes any line breaks from the text in the **helperField** field by using the **translate** function:

```
translate(., value, "")
```

and counts the amount of characters that are then left in the
helperField field by using the **string-length** function:

```
string-length(translate(., value, ""))
```

And finally, it subtracts the two amounts of characters from each other.
This should leave you with the amount of line breaks that are present in
the **maxLines** text box. The formula then corrects this amount by
adding a **1** to the result:

```
string-length(maxLines) - string-length(translate(., value,
"")) + 1
```

which then gives you the amount of lines in the **maxLines** text box.
Note that this rule only runs when a form is not loading, so only when
a form is open and a user is changing text in the **maxLines** text box.

9. Click **Data ➤ Rules ➤ Form Load**.

10. On the **Rules** task pane, add an **Action** rule to the **Form Load** event
    with 3 actions that say:

```
Set a field's value: isLoading = "1"
Set a field's value: helperField = maxLines
Set a field's value: isLoading = "0"
```

where **isLoading** and **helperField** are fields that are located in the
HelperField Secondary data source, and **maxLines** is the field that is
bound to the multi-line text box. This rule ensures that whenever the
form is opened, the **helperField** field in the **HelperField** Secondary
data source is initialized and set to have the same contents as the multi-
line text box.

11. Preview the form.

When the form opens, enter lines of text in the multi-line text box. As soon
as you go over 4 lines, you should see the validation error appear when you
click away from the text box.

Display the first of next month in a date picker

Problem

You have a date picker control on an InfoPath form and whenever a new form is opened, you want the date picker to automatically display the first of the month following the month of the current date.

Solution

You can use **Action** rules in the **Form Load** event to automatically set a date in a date picker to be the first of the month following the month of the current system date.

To display the first of next month in a date picker:

1. In InfoPath, create a new **Blank Form** template.

2. Add a **Date Picker** control to the view of the form template and name it **myDate**.

3. Click **Data ➤ Rules ➤ Form Load**.

4. On the **Rules** task pane, add an **Action** rule to the **Form Load** event that has a **Condition** that says:

```
myDate is blank

and

number(substring(xdDate:Today(), 6, 2)) < 9
```

and an action that says:

```
Set a field's value: myDate = concat(substring(today(), 1, 4),
"-0", string(number(substring(today(), 6, 2)) + 1), "-01")
```

Note that you must select **The expression** from the first drop-down list box on the **Condition** dialog box to enter the second expression for the condition or use the **Use a formula** option in the third drop-down list box to construct the expression (also see recipe *31 Set a maximum* *length on text in a text box* where this technique was explained for the first time). This rule sets the value of the **myDate** date picker when the month of the current date falls before September. Note that the resulting date must always have a format of **yyyy-MM-dd** for the date picker to accept it. And because all months before October have one number, you must prepend a "0" to the month number for the date to be valid.

5. Add a second **Action** rule to the **Form Load** event that has a **Condition** that says:

```
myDate is blank

and

number(substring(xdDate:Today(), 6, 2)) >= 9

and

number(substring(xdDate:Today(), 6, 2)) <= 11
```

and an action that says:

```
Set a field's value: myDate = concat(substring(today(), 1, 4),
"-", string(number(substring(today(), 6, 2)) + 1), "-01")
```

Note that you must select **The expression** from the first drop-down list box on the **Condition** dialog box to enter the second and third expressions for the condition. This rule sets the value of the **myDate** date picker when the month of the current date falls between September and November (inclusive).

6. Add a third **Action** rule to the **Form Load** event that has a **Condition** that says:

```
myDate is blank

and

number(substring(xdDate:Today(), 6, 2)) = 12
```

and an action that says:

```
Set a field's value: myDate =
concat(string(number(substring(today(), 1, 4)) + 1), "-01-01")
```

Note that you must select **The expression** from the first drop-down list box on the **Condition** dialog box to enter the second expression for the condition. This rule sets the value of the **myDate** date picker when the month of the current date is December.

7. Preview the form.

When the form opens, the first of the month that comes after the month of the current system date should appear in the date picker.

Discussion

The logic used in the solution above can be broken down in 3 month zones:

1. If the month following the current month consists of one number, the first rule must be applied. This rule should run if the current month falls between January and August (inclusive).

2. If the month following the current month consists of two numbers, the second rule must be applied. This rule should run if the current month falls between September and November (inclusive).

3. If the current month is December, the year must be increased by one and the next month should be January.

Populate a drop-down list box with dates excluding weekends

Problem

You have a drop-down list box control on an InfoPath form, which you want to automatically populate with dates that exclude weekends.

Solution

You can use the technique described in recipe *106 Auto-populate a drop-down list box with past and future dates* to populate a drop-down list box with dates that exclude weekends.

To populate a drop-down list box with dates excluding weekends:

1. In InfoPath, create a new **Blank Form** template.

2. Add a data connection to an XML file (see recipe *33 Get data from an XML file*) that has the following contents thereby ensuring that the file contains a total of 15 **dateRow** elements:

```
<dateData>
  <dateRow>
    <dateValue/>
    <dateDisplay/>
    <currentDate/>
    <calculatedDate/>
    <calculatedDayNo/>
    <calculatedDayName/>
  </dateRow>
  <dateRow>
    <dateValue/>
    <dateDisplay/>
    <currentDate/>
    <calculatedDate/>
    <calculatedDayNo/>
    <calculatedDayName/>
  </dateRow>
</dateData>
```

and name the data connection **DateData**. Note that the XML shown above only contains 2 **dateRow** elements and that you will have to add 13 **dateRow** elements more to your own XML file.

3. Add a **Drop-Down List Box** control to the view of the form template, name it **selectedDate**, change its data type to **Date (date)**, and change its font to **Courier New**.

4. Add an **Action** rule to the **selectedDate** drop-down list box that has a **Condition** that says:

```
selectedDate is blank
```

```
and
```

```
(substring(xdDate:Today(), 9, 2) +
number(substring(xdDate:Today(), 1, 4) - floor((14 -
substring(xdDate:Today(), 6, 2)) div 12)) +
floor(number(substring(xdDate:Today(), 1, 4) - floor((14 -
substring(xdDate:Today(), 6, 2)) div 12)) div 4) -
floor(number(substring(xdDate:Today(), 1, 4) - floor((14 -
substring(xdDate:Today(), 6, 2)) div 12)) div 100) +
floor(number(substring(xdDate:Today(), 1, 4) - floor((14 -
substring(xdDate:Today(), 6, 2)) div 12)) div 400) + floor(31 *
number(substring(xdDate:Today(), 6, 2) + 12 * floor((14 -
substring(xdDate:Today(), 6, 2)) div 12) - 2) div 12)) mod 7 =
6
```

and an action that says:

```
Set a field's value: . = addDays(today(), 2)
```

where the dot (.) represents the **selectedDate** field that is bound to the drop-down list box. Note that you must select **The expression** from the first drop-down list box on the **Condition** dialog box to enter the second expression for the condition or use the **Use a formula** option in the third drop-down list box to construct the expression (also see recipe *31 Set a maximum length on text in a text box* where this technique was explained for the first time). Note that the formula for the second expression is the same formula that was used in recipe *67 Display the name of the day for a selected date*. This rule ensures that whenever a user selects the blank item from the drop-down list box, the Monday following the current date is displayed if the current date falls on a Saturday.

5. Add a second **Action** rule to the **selectedDate** drop-down list box that has a **Condition** that says:

```
selectedDate is blank
```

```
and
```

```
(substring(xdDate:Today(), 9, 2) +
```

```
number(substring(xdDate:Today(), 1, 4) - floor((14 -
substring(xdDate:Today(), 6, 2)) div 12)) +
floor(number(substring(xdDate:Today(), 1, 4) - floor((14 -
substring(xdDate:Today(), 6, 2)) div 12)) div 4) -
floor(number(substring(xdDate:Today(), 1, 4) - floor((14 -
substring(xdDate:Today(), 6, 2)) div 12)) div 100) +
floor(number(substring(xdDate:Today(), 1, 4) - floor((14 -
substring(xdDate:Today(), 6, 2)) div 12)) div 400) + floor(31 *
number(substring(xdDate:Today(), 6, 2) + 12 * floor((14 -
substring(xdDate:Today(), 6, 2)) div 12) - 2) div 12)) mod 7 =
0
```

and an action that says:

```
Set a field's value: . = addDays(today(), 1)
```

Note that you must select **The expression** from the first drop-down list box on the **Condition** dialog box to enter the second expression for the condition. This rule ensures that whenever a user selects the blank item from the drop-down list box, the Monday following the current date is displayed if the current date falls on a Sunday.

6. Add a third **Action** rule to the **selectedDate** drop-down list box that has a **Condition** that says:

```
selectedDate is blank
```

and

```
(substring(xdDate:Today(), 9, 2) +
number(substring(xdDate:Today(), 1, 4) - floor((14 -
substring(xdDate:Today(), 6, 2)) div 12)) +
floor(number(substring(xdDate:Today(), 1, 4) - floor((14 -
substring(xdDate:Today(), 6, 2)) div 12)) div 4) -
floor(number(substring(xdDate:Today(), 1, 4) - floor((14 -
substring(xdDate:Today(), 6, 2)) div 12)) div 100) +
floor(number(substring(xdDate:Today(), 1, 4) - floor((14 -
substring(xdDate:Today(), 6, 2)) div 12)) div 400) + floor(31 *
number(substring(xdDate:Today(), 6, 2) + 12 * floor((14 -
substring(xdDate:Today(), 6, 2)) div 12) - 2) div 12)) mod 7 >
0
```

and

```
(substring(xdDate:Today(), 9, 2) +
number(substring(xdDate:Today(), 1, 4) - floor((14 -
substring(xdDate:Today(), 6, 2)) div 12)) +
floor(number(substring(xdDate:Today(), 1, 4) - floor((14 -
substring(xdDate:Today(), 6, 2)) div 12)) div 4) -
floor(number(substring(xdDate:Today(), 1, 4) - floor((14 -
substring(xdDate:Today(), 6, 2)) div 12)) div 100) +
floor(number(substring(xdDate:Today(), 1, 4) - floor((14 -
substring(xdDate:Today(), 6, 2)) div 12)) div 400) + floor(31 *
number(substring(xdDate:Today(), 6, 2) + 12 * floor((14 -
substring(xdDate:Today(), 6, 2)) div 12) - 2) div 12)) mod 7 <
6
```

and an action that says:

```
Set a field's value: . = today()
```

Note that you must select **The expression** from the first drop-down
list box on the **Condition** dialog box to enter the second and third
expressions for the condition. This rule ensures that whenever a user
selects the blank item from the drop-down list box, the current date is
displayed if the current date falls on or between Monday and Friday.

7. Add a fourth **Action** rule without a condition to the **selectedDate**
    drop-down list box that has an action that says:

```
Set a field's value: currentDate = .
```

where **currentDate** is a field that is located under the **dateRow**
repeating group under the **dateData** group in the **DateData** Secondary
data source and where the dot (.) represents the **selectedDate** field
that is bound to the drop-down list box. This rule ensures that
whenever a user selects a date from the drop-down list box, the values
of all of the **currentDate** fields in the Secondary data source are
initialized and the rules on those fields executed.

8. On the **Fields** task pane, select **DateData (Secondary)** from the drop-
    down list box, expand the **dateRow** repeating group, select the
    currentDate field, and then on the **Rules** task pane, add the following
    9 **Action** rules to the **currentDate** field:

a. Condition:

```
None - Rule runs when field changes
```

Actions:

```
Set a field's value: calculatedDate = addDays(.,
count(preceding-sibling::dateRow) - 7)

Set a field's value: calculatedDayNo =
(substring(calculatedDate, 9, 2) +
number(substring(calculatedDate, 1, 4) - floor((14 -
substring(calculatedDate, 6, 2)) / 12)) +
floor(number(substring(calculatedDate, 1, 4) - floor((14 -
substring(calculatedDate, 6, 2)) / 12)) / 4) -
floor(number(substring(calculatedDate, 1, 4) - floor((14 -
substring(calculatedDate, 6, 2)) / 12)) / 100) +
floor(number(substring(calculatedDate, 1, 4) - floor((14 -
substring(calculatedDate, 6, 2)) / 12)) / 400) + floor(31 *
number(substring(calculatedDate, 6, 2) + 12 * floor((14 -
substring(calculatedDate, 6, 2)) / 12) - 2) / 12)) mod 7
```

For the first action, you must enter the following formula on the **Insert Formula** dialog box:

```
addDays(., count(preceding-sibling::dateRow) - 7)
```

or

```
xdDate:AddDays(., count(../preceding-sibling::dateRow) - 7)
```

if you have the **Edit XPath (advanced)** check box selected on the **Insert Formula** dialog box. The second action uses the formula from recipe *67 Display the name of the day for a selected date* to calculate a day number for each **calculatedDate** field in the **DateData** Secondary data source.

b. Condition:

```
calculatedDayNo = "6"
```

Actions:

```
Set a field's value: dateValue = addDays(calculatedDate, 2)

Set a field's value: calculatedDayName = "Monday"
```

The first action ensures that if the calculated date falls on a Saturday, the **dateValue** field is set to be equal to the date of the Monday following the Saturday.

c. Condition:

```
calculatedDayNo = "0"
```

Actions:

```
Set a field's value: dateValue = addDays(calculatedDate, 1)

Set a field's value: calculatedDayName = "Monday"
```

The first action ensures that if the calculated date falls on a Sunday, the **dateValue** field is set to be equal to the date of the Monday following the Sunday.

d. Condition:

```
calculatedDayNo = "1"
```

Actions:

```
Set a field's value: dateValue = calculatedDate

Set a field's value: calculatedDayName = "Monday"
```

e. Condition:

```
calculatedDayNo = "2"
```

Actions:

```
Set a field's value: dateValue = calculatedDate
```

```
Set a field's value: calculatedDayName = "Tuesday"
```

f. Condition:

```
calculatedDayNo = "3"
```

Actions:

```
Set a field's value: dateValue = calculatedDate
```

```
Set a field's value: calculatedDayName = "Wednesday"
```

g. Condition:

```
calculatedDayNo = "4"
```

Actions:

```
Set a field's value: dateValue = calculatedDate
```

```
Set a field's value: calculatedDayName = "Thursday"
```

h. Condition:

```
calculatedDayNo = "5"
```

Actions:

```
Set a field's value: dateValue = calculatedDate
```

```
Set a field's value: calculatedDayName = "Friday"
```

i. Condition:

```
None - Rule runs when field changes
```

Action:

```
Set a field's value: dateDisplay =
concat(substring(calculatedDayName, 1, 3), ": ",
substring(dateValue, 9, 2), "/", substring(dateValue, 6, 2),
"/", substring(dateValue, 1, 4))
```

Note that the **substring** function is used to extract the first 3 characters from the **calculatedDayName** field and that the **concat** function is then used to prepend the shortened day name to the date.

9. Click **Data ➤ Rules ➤ Form Load**.

10. On the **Rules** task pane, add an **Action** rule to the **Form Load** event that has a **Condition** that says:

```
selectedDate is blank

and

(substring(xdDate:Today(), 9, 2) +
number(substring(xdDate:Today(), 1, 4) - floor((14 -
substring(xdDate:Today(), 6, 2)) div 12)) +
floor(number(substring(xdDate:Today(), 1, 4) - floor((14 -
substring(xdDate:Today(), 6, 2)) div 12)) div 4) -
floor(number(substring(xdDate:Today(), 1, 4) - floor((14 -
substring(xdDate:Today(), 6, 2)) div 12)) div 100) +
floor(number(substring(xdDate:Today(), 1, 4) - floor((14 -
substring(xdDate:Today(), 6, 2)) div 12)) div 400) + floor(31 *
number(substring(xdDate:Today(), 6, 2) + 12 * floor((14 -
substring(xdDate:Today(), 6, 2)) div 12) - 2) div 12)) mod 7 >
0

and

(substring(xdDate:Today(), 9, 2) +
number(substring(xdDate:Today(), 1, 4) - floor((14 -
substring(xdDate:Today(), 6, 2)) div 12)) +
floor(number(substring(xdDate:Today(), 1, 4) - floor((14 -
substring(xdDate:Today(), 6, 2)) div 12)) div 4) -
floor(number(substring(xdDate:Today(), 1, 4) - floor((14 -
substring(xdDate:Today(), 6, 2)) div 12)) div 100) +
floor(number(substring(xdDate:Today(), 1, 4) - floor((14 -
substring(xdDate:Today(), 6, 2)) div 12)) div 400) + floor(31 *
number(substring(xdDate:Today(), 6, 2) + 12 * floor((14 -
substring(xdDate:Today(), 6, 2)) div 12) - 2) div 12)) mod 7 <
6
```

and an action that says:

```
Set a field's value: selectedDate = today()
```

Note that you must select **The expression** from the first drop-down list box on the **Condition** dialog box to enter the second and third expressions for the condition. This rule ensures that if the current date falls on or between Monday and Friday, the value of the drop-down list box is set to be equal to the current date when a new form is opened.

11. Add a second **Action** rule to the **Form Load** event that has a **Condition** that says:

```
selectedDate is blank

and

(substring(xdDate:Today(), 9, 2) +
number(substring(xdDate:Today(), 1, 4) - floor((14 -
substring(xdDate:Today(), 6, 2)) div 12)) +
floor(number(substring(xdDate:Today(), 1, 4) - floor((14 -
substring(xdDate:Today(), 6, 2)) div 12)) div 4) -
floor(number(substring(xdDate:Today(), 1, 4) - floor((14 -
substring(xdDate:Today(), 6, 2)) div 12)) div 100) +
floor(number(substring(xdDate:Today(), 1, 4) - floor((14 -
substring(xdDate:Today(), 6, 2)) div 12)) div 400) + floor(31 *
number(substring(xdDate:Today(), 6, 2) + 12 * floor((14 -
substring(xdDate:Today(), 6, 2)) div 12) - 2) div 12)) mod 7 =
6
```

and an action that says:

```
Set a field's value: selectedDate = addDays(today(), 2)
```

Note that you must select **The expression** from the first drop-down list box on the **Condition** dialog box to enter the second expression for the condition. This rule ensures that if the current date falls on a Saturday, the value of the drop-down list box is set to be equal to the date of the Monday following the Saturday when a new form is opened.

12. Add a third **Action** rule to the **Form Load** event that has a **Condition** that says:

```
selectedDate is blank
```

```
and
```

```
(substring(xdDate:Today(), 9, 2) +
number(substring(xdDate:Today(), 1, 4) - floor((14 -
substring(xdDate:Today(), 6, 2)) div 12)) +
floor(number(substring(xdDate:Today(), 1, 4) - floor((14 -
substring(xdDate:Today(), 6, 2)) div 12)) div 4) -
floor(number(substring(xdDate:Today(), 1, 4) - floor((14 -
substring(xdDate:Today(), 6, 2)) div 12)) div 100) +
floor(number(substring(xdDate:Today(), 1, 4) - floor((14 -
substring(xdDate:Today(), 6, 2)) div 12)) div 400) + floor(31 *
number(substring(xdDate:Today(), 6, 2) + 12 * floor((14 -
substring(xdDate:Today(), 6, 2)) div 12) - 2) div 12)) mod 7 =
0
```

and an action that says:

```
Set a field's value: selectedDate = addDays(today(), 1)
```

Note that you must select **The expression** from the first drop-down list box on the **Condition** dialog box to enter the second expression for the condition. This rule ensures that if the current date falls on a Sunday, the value of the drop-down list box is set to be equal to the date of the Monday following the Sunday when a new form is opened.

13. Add a fourth **Action** rule to the **Form Load** event that has a **Condition** that says:

```
selectedDate is not blank
```

```
and
```

```
(substring(my:selectedDate, 9, 2) +
number(substring(my:selectedDate, 1, 4) - floor((14 -
substring(my:selectedDate, 6, 2)) div 12)) +
floor(number(substring(my:selectedDate, 1, 4) - floor((14 -
substring(my:selectedDate, 6, 2)) div 12)) div 4) -
floor(number(substring(my:selectedDate, 1, 4) - floor((14 -
```

```
substring(my:selectedDate, 6, 2)) div 12)) div 100) +
floor(number(substring(my:selectedDate, 1, 4) - floor((14 -
substring(my:selectedDate, 6, 2)) div 12)) div 400) + floor(31
* number(substring(my:selectedDate, 6, 2) + 12 * floor((14 -
substring(my:selectedDate, 6, 2)) div 12) - 2) div 12)) mod 7 =
6
```

and an action that says:

```
Set a field's value: selectedDate = addDays(selectedDate, 2)
```

Note that you must select **The expression** from the first drop-down list box on the **Condition** dialog box to enter the second expression for the condition. This rule ensures that if the selected date falls on a Saturday, the value of the drop-down list box is set to be equal to the date of the Monday following the Saturday when an existing form in which a date was stored is opened.

14. Add a fifth **Action** rule to the **Form Load** event that has a **Condition** that says:

```
selectedDate is not blank
```

and

```
(substring(my:selectedDate, 9, 2) +
number(substring(my:selectedDate, 1, 4) - floor((14 -
substring(my:selectedDate, 6, 2)) div 12)) +
floor(number(substring(my:selectedDate, 1, 4) - floor((14 -
substring(my:selectedDate, 6, 2)) div 12)) div 4) -
floor(number(substring(my:selectedDate, 1, 4) - floor((14 -
substring(my:selectedDate, 6, 2)) div 12)) div 100) +
floor(number(substring(my:selectedDate, 1, 4) - floor((14 -
substring(my:selectedDate, 6, 2)) div 12)) div 400) + floor(31
* number(substring(my:selectedDate, 6, 2) + 12 * floor((14 -
substring(my:selectedDate, 6, 2)) div 12) - 2) div 12)) mod 7 =
0
```

and an action that says:

```
Set a field's value: selectedDate = addDays(selectedDate, 1)
```

Note that you must select **The expression** from the first drop-down list box on the **Condition** dialog box to enter the second expression for the condition. This rule ensures that if the selected date falls on a Sunday, the value of the drop-down list box is set to be equal to the date of the Monday following the Sunday when an existing form in which a date was stored is opened.

15. Add a sixth **Action** rule without a condition to the **Form Load** event that has an action that says:

```
Set a field's value: currentDate = selectedDate
```

where **currentDate** is a field that is located under the **dateRow** repeating group under the **dateData** group in the **DateData** Secondary data source and where **selectedDate** is the field that is bound to the drop-down list box. This rule ensures that whenever you open a form in which a date has been saved in the **selectedDate** field, the values of the **currentDate** fields in the **DateData** Secondary data source are set, so that the rules on the **currentDate** fields can run to populate all of the **dateValue**, **dateDisplay**, **calculatedDate**, **calculatedDayNo**, and **calculatedDayName** fields in the **DateData** Secondary data source.

16. Open the **Drop-Down List Box Properties** dialog box and configure the drop-down list box to get its choices from the **DateData** Secondary data source, its **Entries** from the **dateRow** repeating group, and set its **Value** property to the **dateValue** field and its **Display name** property to the **dateDisplay** field. In addition, select the **Show only entries with unique display names** check box, since Monday will be appearing multiple times in the drop-down list box and you only want it to appear once for a particular date.

17. On the **Drop-Down List Box Properties** dialog box, click **OK**.

18. Preview the form.

When the form opens, the current date should appear in the drop-down list box. And when you expand the drop-down list box, you should see dates listed with the name of the day in front of each date and the dates excluding weekends.

```
Fri: 26/07/2013
Mon: 29/07/2013
Tue: 30/07/2013
Wed: 31/07/2013
Thu: 01/08/2013
Fri: 02/08/2013
Mon: 05/08/2013
Tue: 06/08/2013
Wed: 07/08/2013
Thu: 08/08/2013
Fri: 09/08/2013
```

Figure 209. Expanded drop-down list box displaying dates excluding weekends.

Discussion

In the solution described above, you not only used the technique from recipe *106 Auto-populate a drop-down list box with past and future dates*, but you also used the technique described in recipe *67 Display the name of the day for a selected date* to be able to display the name of the day in front of each date based on a day number.

Note that if you want to debug the functionality of the date calculations or see how all of the values of the fields in the **DateData** Secondary data source change as you select a date from the drop-down list box, you can drag-and-drop the **dateRow** repeating group from the **Fields** task pane onto the view of the form template and temporarily bind it to a repeating table control to make the calculations visible. Also remember that you can use the **Rule Inspector**, which you can open via **Data ➤ Rules ➤ Rule Inspector**, to see and double-check all of the rules you defined on the fields.

Appendix

Answers to questions

The following answers pertain to questions asked throughout this book. The first number in the numbering scheme refers to the recipe number, and the second number refers to the question number. For example, 1-2 refers to recipe number 1 and question number 2, while 2-1 refers to recipe number 2 and question number 1.

1-1   InfoPath form templates.

1-2   InfoPath forms.

1-3   InfoPath Filler Forms can be filled out only through InfoPath Filler 2013, while Web Browser Forms can be filled out using either a browser or InfoPath Filler 2013. In addition, InfoPath Filler Forms support all of the controls that are available in InfoPath while Web Browser Forms support only a subset of those controls.

2-1   You can use the **Preview** command in InfoPath Designer 2013 or you can first save a form template locally on disk and then double-click the form template to open and preview a form in InfoPath Filler 2013.

3-1   No, you can only add page breaks directly on a view. So to be able to add a page break between the custom tables, you would have to place the custom tables directly on the view instead of within a page layout. Another option would be to place each custom table in its own page layout on the view and then add a page break between the page layouts that contain the custom tables.

4-1   Fields allow data to be stored in an InfoPath form, while controls are visual elements that are bound to and allow access to fields. Fields are part of a data source (Main or Secondary) of a form, while controls are part of a view of a form template.

9-1   The **Properties** dialog box for a control.

InfoPath 2013 Cookbook

9-2   (Blank), TRUE, FALSE, 1, 0.

9-3   No, the **Read-Only** property is disabled on the **Properties** tab on the Ribbon and there is no **Read-Only** property on the **Properties** dialog box for a check box control.

12-1   Five commands.

12-2   No. The **Quick Publish** command becomes available after you have published an InfoPath form template. This command can be used as a quick one-click way to republish a previously published form template.

14-1   The first view that is shown when a form opens.

14-2   Only one default view.

14-3   By removing it from the **Current View** drop-down list box via the **Properties** dialog box for the view.

14-4   No. An InfoPath form must always have and be able to display at least one view.

14-5   An InfoPath form must always have and be able to display at least one view (there must be one default view present), so **View 1** will automatically become the default view when you delete **View 2**.

15-1   The function of a button is to perform an action, not to enter data. So the term "read-only" does not really apply to buttons. Therefore, buttons are not disabled when they are placed on a read-only view. In addition, because you may want to allow a user to for example switch to another view by clicking on a button, it is rather a good thing that they are not disabled when placed on read-only views.

18-1   The **now** function returns the current system date and time.

18-2   The **now** function returns the current system date and time, while the **today** function returns the current system date without the time.

18-3   The **Math** category.

18-4   `translate(., " ", "")`

19-1   The **Text** category.

19-2   `concat(field2, ", ", field1)`

20-1 `normalize-space(concat(`<u>`firstName`</u>`, " ", translate(`<u>`lastName`</u>`,`
`"abcdefghijklmnopqrstuvwxyz", "ABCDEFGHIJKLMNOPQRSTUVWXYZ")))`

21-1 **Action**, **Validation**, **Formatting**, and **Default Value**.

21-2 **Formatting** rule (in the main solution) and **Validation** rule (in the exercise).

26-1 Yes.

26-2 No.

26-3 You can make a group of controls read-only by making an entire view read-only and then using a rule that switches to the read-only view based on a condition.

28-1 You can place the repeating table control on a read-only view to make the control read-only. Another option would be to apply the technique(s) described in recipe *97 Make an entire repeating table read-only*.

31-1 `string-length(translate(`<u>`.`</u>`, " ", ""))`

34-1 Microsoft SQL Server only.

34-2 Microsoft SQL Server or Microsoft Access only.

34-3 Only Microsoft SQL Server or Microsoft Access. No, InfoPath does not support data connections to Oracle databases out-of-the-box. To connect an InfoPath form to an Oracle database, you must go through a web service that connects to the Oracle database.

42-1 No, you cannot. You can only add **Action** rules to the **Form Submit** event.

47-1 You can select the **Cannot Be Blank** property of a check box to make it required. However, because you wanted to make the check box conditionally required in this recipe, you had to use a **Validation** rule instead of the **Cannot Be Blank** property.

65-1 `concat(substring(`<u>`completionDate`</u>`, 9, 2), " ", `<u>`name[number =`</u>`
`<u>`substring(`</u>`<u>`completionDate`</u>`, 6, 2)], " ",`
`substring(`<u>`completionDate`</u>`, 1, 4))`

or

```
concat(substring(my:completionDate, 9, 2), " ",
xdXDocument:GetDOM("MonthNames")/months/month/name[../number
= substring(xdXDocument:get-
DOM()/my:myFields/my:completionDate, 6, 2)], " ",
substring(my:completionDate, 1, 4))
```

if you have the **Edit XPath (advanced)** check box selected on the
Insert Formula dialog box.

71-1 -1

InfoPath functions used in recipes

The following table displays a list of InfoPath functions with the
corresponding recipes in which they have been used, so that you can easily
find examples of how to use InfoPath functions.

Function	Recipe(s)
addDays	70, 72, 105, 106
addSeconds	70
avg	109
ceiling	74, 75, 76
concat	19, 20, 37, 38, 64, 66, 69, 81, 84, 101, 106, 119
contains	102, 121
count	58, 59, 77, 79, 80, 99, 100, 101, 102, 103, 106, 109, 110, 112, 113, 114, 115, 116
eval	81, 118, 119
false	101

Function	Recipe(s)
floor	67, 68
normalize-space	20, 101, 119
not	116
now	19, 38, 45
number	66, 67, 68, 73, 74, 75, 76
string	66, 101
string-length	31
substring	45, 63, 65, 66, 67, 68, 69, 73, 74, 75, 76, 106
substring-after	45
substring-before	69
sum	107, 108, 109
today	62, 66, 67, 68, 73, 74, 106
translate	18, 59, 102, 121
true	27, 44, 79, 97, 101
userName	38

Index

A

Access database, 133

Accessing data across domains is not supported for forms opened from the Internet, 164

Action rules, 79, 86–97, 89, 275

Close the form, 94

Query for data, 132

Set a field's value, 90, 157, 176, 258, 337

Submit data, 152, 174, 176, 179

Switch views, 96, 142, 157, 174, 177

vs. default values, 80, 89, 217

add

attachment, 333

control, 20

days to a date, 268

field to repeating table, 358

multiple files as attachments, 346

multiple Formatting rules, 98

relationship, 170

rule, 80, 82, 270

Add Field or Group dialog box, 24, 26, 35, 41, 359

Add Table or Query dialog box, 169

Add View dialog box, 48, 53, 55

addDays function, 269, 273, 393, 397

addSeconds function, 269

After submit, 141, 156, 164, 173

allow overwrite if file exists, 151

Allow the user to attach only the following file types, 335

Allow the user to browse, delete, and replace files, 335, 339, 343

allow users to insert and delete rows, 367, 371

Allow users to submit this form, 140, 147, 151, 156, 173, 176, 178

and, 123

Attach the form template to ensure users can open the form, 146, 176, 179

attribute, 26, 211, 253

Automatically create data source, 28, 34, 42, 357, 359

Automatically detect intranet network, 165

Automatically determine security level, 165

Automatically retrieve data when form is opened, 129, 132, 134, 138, 210

average, 406–9

avg function, 408

B

background image, 58

base64 encoded, 334

begins with, 214

best practice, 24, 262, 321

bind control, 22, 35

Binding dialog box, 35

Blank Form (InfoPath Filler) template, 133, 443

Blank Form template, 3, 5

Borders and Shading dialog box, 59, 120, 199

bulleted list, 444

button, 90, 94, 96, 103, 106, 143, 153, 193, 199, 218, 291, 310, 319–33, 336, 337, 343

Button Properties dialog box, 322, 325, 332

By position in the data source, 445

C

calculate

age from date of birth, 274

average, 406–9

date difference, 276–83

holidays, 290–94

sum, 186–88, 399–405

calculated value, 57, 61, 109, 184, 249, 315–19, 350, 381, 387

Calculated Value Properties dialog box, 62, 185, 316

calendar, 236

cannot be blank, 40, 195, 335

carriage-return, 326

cascading drop-down list boxes, 231, 430

case-sensitive, 387

ceiling function, 279, 282, 289

change binding, 34

change control, 31, 358, 387, 424

check box, 101, 108, 155, 189, 190, 193, 194, 196, 338, 372, 379, 411

Check Box Properties dialog box, 191, 372, 380

check formula, 68

choice group, 351

choice section, 351

Choose a data connection for submit, 147

clear

drop-down list box selection, 218

file attachment, 337

close the form, 94

Columns to the Left, 11, 15

Columns to the Right, 11, 15, 359

compare strings or dates, 271

compatibility, 5, 136

concat function, 74, 76, 146, 151, 241, 249, 260, 313, 325, 383, 397, 438

Condition

and, 122, 123

begins with, 214

contains, 215

does not match pattern, 113

is blank, 80, 111, 121, 195, 259, 336, 352, 396

is equal to, 101, 104, 121, 156, 177, 223, 229, 233, 243, 305, 412, 425, 441

is greater than, 117, 273

is greater than or equal to, 291

is less than, 420

is less than or equal to, 292, 423

is not blank, 111, 190, 196, 258, 270, 272, 282, 284, 300, 336, 349

is not equal to, 199

is present, 352

multiple, 119

not, 124

or, 122, 124

Select a field or group, 223, 229, 232, 291, 305, 327, 352, 431, 441

The expression, 107, 118, 122, 224, 247, 248, 271, 275, 300, 306, 370, 410, 413, 416, 419, 422, 425, 432, 454

Use a formula, 118, 214, 223, 243, 248, 273, 299, 305, 385, 419, 422, 425, 432

Condition dialog box, 101, 104, 106, 111, 113, 116, 121, 122, 123, 156, 177, 199, 223, 248, 273, 299, 305, 370, 410, 412, 413, 416, 419, 422

conditional formatting, 100

containers, 17

contains function, 386, 454

context menu

Attach, 333

Borders and Shading, 59

Change Control, 31, 358, 387, 424

Columns to the Left, 11

Columns to the Right, 11, 359

Delete Columns, 172

Design, 8

Merge Cells, 15

Open, 8

Properties, 38

Rows Above, 11

Rows Below, 11

Split Cells, 15

Table Properties, 15

context node, 252, 287, 313, 318, 375, 377, 388–89, 391, 402–5, 410, 414, 438

Control cannot repeat here, 362

Control cannot store data correctly, 361

Control cannot store this data type, 358
Control Properties, 20
Control stores duplicate data, 339, 418, 427
Control Tools, 37
  Control Properties, 37
  Field Properties, 40
  Properties, 37
Controls, 17–36, 18, 22
  add, 20
  bind, 22, 35
  bulleted list, 444
  button, 90, 94, 96, 103, 106, 143, 153, 193, 199, 218, 291, 310, 319–33, 336, 337, 343
  calculated value, 57, 61, 109, 184, 249, 315–19, 350, 381, 387
  cannot be blank, 40, 195, 335
  change binding, 34
  check box, 101, 108, 155, 189, 190, 193, 194, 196, 338, 372, 379, 411
  choice group, 351
  choice section, 351
  container controls, 17, 347
  copy, 54, 330
  date and time picker, 235, 237, 257, 269
  date picker, 31, 58, 103, 108, 194, 235–94, 393
  delete, 33
  disable control, 104, 106, 108, 109, 178, 259, 327, 370, 372
  drop-down list box, 111, 120, 201–35, 240, 259, 424, 430, 440
  field, 20
  file attachment, 109, 333–46
  focus, 332
  hide control, 101, 121, 156, 199, 223, 299, 305, 339, 349, 409, 411, 419, 422, 428
  input controls, 17, 109, 181
  invisible, 41
  make required, 39
  margins, 62

master/detail, 439–54
move, 339
multiple-selection list box, 294–314
objects, 17, 315
open controls task pane, 109
option button, 189, 198, 317
paddings, 62
picture button, 131, 143, 153, 319
read-only, 178
read-only based on condition, 103
repeating section, 27, 163, 171, 346
repeating section with controls, 304, 444
repeating table, 27, 101, 171, 205, 284, 346, 355–454
rich text box, 32, 358, 359, 362
section, 101, 120, 155, 222, 299, 338, 347–55, 418, 427
task pane, 17, 20, 28, 34, 66, 109, 357, 358, 359
text box, 20, 22, 24, 27, 31, 34, 36, 37, 42, 57, 58, 69, 73, 76, 80, 90, 111, 113, 115, 145, 178, 181–88, 190, 196, 198, 213, 219, 222, 228, 238, 274, 277, 280, 291, 310, 318, 336, 349, 352, 373, 384, 400, 406, 435, 436
unbound, 23, 33, 34
copy
  a rule, 84, 332, 370, 414, 419, 423
  all controls, 54, 330
  all rules, 85, 332, 381
  attachment, 335
  view, 54, 330
Copy XPath, 432
count function, 220, 223, 293, 299, 305, 373–84, 374, 375, 383, 385, 389, 397, 408, 410, 414, 416, 420, 428
count repeating table rows, 373–84
Create labels for controls automatically, 28
Current View menu, 49
  remove view, 50
current(), 432

custom submit button, 143
custom table, 11
customize commands, 354, 368, 418, 428

D

Data, 21
   Data Connections, 129
   Form Data, 21
   Form Load, 177, 246, 261, 319, 331, 398
   From Database, 133
   From Other Sources, 128
   From SharePoint List, 137
   From XML File, 128
   Get External Data, 128
   Resource Files, 131, 320
   Rule Inspector, 83
   Show Fields, 21
   Submit Options, 147, 151, 156
   To E-mail, 145
   To SharePoint Library, 150
data connection
   Receive data, 127, 130, 209, 310
   Submit as an e-mail message, 145–49
   Submit data, 130, 147
   submit to SharePoint Library, 150
Data Connection Wizard, 128, 134, 137,
   147, 150, 161, 169, 170, 176, 209
   Automatically retrieve data when form
     is opened, 129, 132, 134, 138, 210
   Include the data as a resource file in the
     form template, 131
   Resource Files, 132
   Send only the active view of the form
     and no attachment, 146
   Set as the default submit connection,
     149
   Store a copy of the data in the form
     template, 134
Data Connections dialog box, 130
data entry, 22
Data Entry Pattern dialog box, 113
data filtering, 213, 235, 417–26
Data Format, 182, 188

data from
   database, 133
   SharePoint list, 136
   XML file, 128
data source
   external, 126–38, 209, 213, 232, 425
   Main, 21, 350
   Secondary, 127, 130, 132, 135, 138,
     215, 220, 231, 259, 262, 348, 350
   XPath reference, 231
data type, 29
   Date (date), 31, 191, 276, 396
   Decimal (double), 114, 186, 400, 406
   Rich Text (XHTML), 358, 362
   Text (string), 31, 35, 114, 187, 276, 280,
     322, 400, 407, 444, 452
   Time (time), 182
   True/False (boolean), 24, 178, 191, 372,
     380
   Whole Number (integer), 114, 187, 249,
     254, 274, 277, 281, 301, 406
Database form template, 161, 169
   dataFields, 163
   Drag data fields here, 163
   Drag query fields here, 164
   New Record, 162, 170
   queryFields, 163, 171
   Run Query, 162, 170
database not supported, 135
database submit, 160–72
dataFields, 163
Date (date), 29, 31, 191, 276, 396
date and time picker, 235, 237, 257, 269
   format, 183, 239, 241, 260, 262
date difference calculation, 276–83
Date Format dialog box, 63
date picker, 31, 58, 103, 108, 194, 235–94,
   393
   format, 239, 241, 244, 247, 258
   year, 238
Date Picker Properties dialog box, 237,
   268
date range, 272
date validation, 254

Decimal (double), 29, 114, 186, 400, 406

Decimal Format dialog box, 114, 188, 400

decimal places, 400

default items in multiple-selection list box, 296–98

Default Value, 69, 73, 76, 80, 89, 182, 186, 216, 219, 237, 246, 249, 254, 268, 276, 281, 311, 319, 322, 373, 375, 385, 387, 390, 393, 401, 403, 407, 435, 437, 440

default view, 9, 47

delete

    a rule, 82

    attachment, 334, 337

    field or group, 33

dependent drop-down list boxes, 231, 430

Design

    add a control, 20

    borders and shading, 59

    layout table, 12

    page layouts, 12

    presets, 59

    themes, 11

    view, 12, 47

design a form template, 2

Design context menu, 8

Design Form button, 3, 6

Designate print view, 56

dialog box

    Add Field or Group, 24, 26, 35, 41, 359

    Add Table or Query, 169

    Add View, 48, 53, 55

    Binding, 35

    Borders and Shading, 59, 120, 199

    Button Properties, 322, 325, 332

    Calculated Value Properties, 62, 185, 316

    Check Box Properties, 191, 372, 380

    Condition, 101, 104, 106, 111, 113, 116, 121, 122, 123, 156, 177, 199, 223, 248, 273, 299, 305, 370, 410, 412, 413, 416, 419, 422

    Data Connection Wizard, 128, 134, 137, 147, 150, 161, 169, 170, 176, 209

    Data Connections, 130

Data Entry Pattern, 113

Date Format, 63

Date Picker Properties, 237, 268

Decimal Format, 114, 188, 400

Drop-Down List Box Properties, 111, 120, 203, 205, 209, 213, 241, 259, 398, 425, 430

Edit Default Values, 297–98, 308, 354, 364, 366

Edit Relationship, 169

Field or Group Properties, 25, 31, 73, 216, 250, 254, 277, 281, 311, 358, 373, 375, 387, 394, 437, 441

File Attachment Properties, 335, 339, 343

Form Options, 5, 19, 136, 144, 164, 166

InfoPath Options, 28, 165

Insert Calculated Value, 185, 243, 315

Insert Formula, 67, 69, 73, 76, 92, 116, 146, 150, 184, 214, 216, 219, 223, 229, 243, 270, 299, 305, 322, 385, 388

Insert Function, 69, 70, 73, 116, 385

Internet Properties, 165

Local intranet, 165

Master/Detail Binding, 452

Move Field or Group, 360

Multiple-Selection List Box Properties, 296

Option Button Properties, 198, 317

Options, 28, 64, 165

Picture Button Properties, 320

Print Multiple Views, 57

Properties, 37

Publishing Wizard, 44, 46, 152

Repeating Section Properties, 445

Repeating Table Properties, 367, 400, 406, 418, 428, 443, 453

Resource Files, 131, 321

Rule Details, 90, 95, 96, 103, 157, 174, 176, 179, 229, 258, 270, 337

Rule Inspector, 84, 263

Section Commands, 355

Select a Field or Group, 70, 73, 90, 103, 116, 146, 158, 176, 206, 210, 214, 216, 220, 223, 229, 232, 243, 258, 270, 291, 299, 305, 311, 322, 327, 338, 352, 382, 385, 398, 425, 430, 441

Select Table, 134, 161, 169

Specify Filter Conditions, 214, 223, 229, 232, 243, 300, 305, 385, 425, 431, 441, 454

Split Cells, 61

Submit Options, 140, 147, 151, 156, 173, 176, 178

Table Commands, 368, 418

Table Properties, 16, 60

Text Box Properties, 37, 66, 69, 182, 188, 219, 400, 436

Time Format, 183, 185

View Properties, 51

disable

a rule, 87

control, 104, 106, 108, 109, 178, 259, 327, 370, 372

display error messages, 348

Display the time like this, 182

does not match pattern, 113

domain security, 165

don't run remaining rules, 88, 157, 193, 247, 252

Drag data fields here, 163, 171

Drag query fields here, 164

drop-down list box, 111, 120, 201–35, 240, 259, 424, 430, 440

disappearing items in repeating table, 417–26

populate, 202–12, 395

Drop-Down List Box Properties dialog box, 111, 120, 203, 205, 209, 213, 241, 259, 398, 425, 430

dynamic label

for control, 317

on button, 322

E

Edit Default Values dialog box, 297–98, 308, 354, 364, 366

Edit Relationship dialog box, 169

Edit XPath (advanced), 68, 216, 226, 230, 300, 306, 388

electronic forms, vii

element, 26, 212, 253

E-mail form template, 6

enable printing background images, 64

enable submit, 142

Enable submit for this connection, 161, 170

Enter choices manually, 111, 120, 203, 241

errors in formula, 92

eval function, 312, 435, 437

event

Form Load, 177, 246, 261, 319, 331, 398

Form Submit, 141, 151, 156, 174, 176, 179

Exclude this group from the initial form, 364

Export Source Files, 221

external data source, 126–38, 209, 213, 232, 425

extract day, 250, 254

extract month, 250, 255

extract year, 238, 250, 255

F

false function, 191, 381

field, 20

Field (attribute), 26, 249, 253, 254, 276, 280

Field (element), 26, 35, 253, 276, 281, 444, 452

Field or Group Properties dialog box, 25, 31, 73, 216, 250, 254, 277, 281, 311, 358, 373, 375, 387, 394, 437, 441

Field Properties, 20, 40, 358

field type, 29

Fields

bind, 35
cannot be blank, 40, 195, 335
control, 20
data type, 114
dataFields, 163, 171
delete, 33
field, 20
Field (attribute), 26, 249, 253, 254, 276, 280
Field (element), 26, 35, 253, 276, 281, 444, 452
hidden, 41
make required, 39
move, 360
move down, 363
move up, 363
name, 25
numeric, 114
queryFields, 163, 171
repeating, 26
task pane, 21, 22, 24, 40, 129, 295, 356
type, 29, 253
unbind, 34
File
    New, 3
    Print, 56
    Publish, 44
file attachment, 109, 333–46
    add, 333
    add multiple files, 346
    clear via rule, 337
    copy, 335
    delete, 334
    menu items of control, 335, 345
    paste, 335
    read-only, 338–46
File Attachment Properties dialog box, 335, 339, 343
fill a drop-down list box, 202–12, 395
filter
    a drop-down list box, 213, 235, 417–26
    a secondary data source, 215, 229, 440
    in XPath, 218, 312, 386, 391

Filter Data, 215, 223, 229, 232, 243, 293, 299, 305, 357, 382, 385, 425, 430, 441, 452
floor function, 250, 255
focus, 332
following-sibling, 377, 414
form, 1
    InfoPath Filler form, 4
    preview, 8
    template, 1
    web browser form, 4
    XSN, 1
Form Load event, 177, 246, 261, 319, 331, 398
Form Options
    Security and Trust, 164
Form Options dialog box, 5, 19, 136, 144, 164, 166
form security, 165
Form Submit event, 141, 151, 156, 174, 176, 179
form template
    add a control, 20
    Blank Form (InfoPath Filler), 133, 443
    Database, 161, 169
    open, 8
form type, 5, 136
format
    calculated value result, 63
    date, 397
    text, 61
Format as, 185
Formatting rules, 79, 97–109
    add multiple, 98
    Disable this control, 104, 106, 108, 178, 259, 327, 370, 372
    Hide this control, 101, 121, 156, 199, 223, 299, 305, 339, 349, 409, 411, 419, 422, 428
formulas, 67–78
    resolving errors in, 92
from XML file, 128
full trust security, 165
Functions

addDays, 269, 273, 393, 397

addSeconds, 269

avg, 408

ceiling, 279, 282, 289

concat, 74, 76, 146, 151, 241, 249, 260, 313, 325, 383, 397, 438

contains, 386, 454

count, 220, 223, 293, 299, 305, 373–84, 374, 375, 383, 385, 389, 397, 408, 410, 414, 416, 420, 428

eval, 312, 435, 437

false, 191, 381

floor, 250, 255

normalize-space, 77, 380, 438

not, 425

now, 75, 150, 183, 237, 269

number, 246, 248, 250, 254, 274, 278, 282, 284

string, 249, 381

string-compare, 271, 292

string-length, 117

substring, 77, 183, 239, 242, 244, 249, 253, 254, 260, 274, 278, 282, 284, 397

substring-after, 182

substring-before, 258

sum, 187, 401, 404, 408

today, 237, 246, 249, 254, 274, 276, 396

translate, 71, 225, 386, 454

true, 107, 180, 191, 301, 370, 380

userName, 151

G

Get choices from an external data source, 209, 213, 232, 398, 425

Get choices from fields in this form, 205

Get data

  from database, 133

  from SharePoint list, 136

  from XML file, 128

Get External Data, 128

get-DOM, 224, 231, 244, 292, 306, 425

GetDOM, 216, 220, 224, 231, 244, 292, 428

group conditions, 124

H

hidden field, 41, 103, 155, 176, 178, 322, 382

hide

  control, 101, 121, 156, 199, 223, 299, 305, 339, 349, 409, 411, 419, 422, 428

  rows of repeating table, 409–12

holidays calculation, 290–94

Home, 3

  Add Rule, 80

  Controls, 17

  Current View, 49

  Format Text, 61

  Manage Rules, 82

  Page Views, 49

  Preview, 8

horizontal alignment, 60

Hover Picture, 320

Hyperlink (anyURI), 29

I

Include all network paths, 165

include data as a resource file, 131

Include footer, 400, 406

InfoPath 2003, 6

InfoPath 2007, 6

InfoPath 2010, 6

InfoPath benefits, vii

InfoPath cannot submit the form, 112, 172

InfoPath cannot submit the form because it contains validation errors, 303

InfoPath Designer 2013, vii

InfoPath Filler 2013, vii, 8

InfoPath Filler form, 4

InfoPath Options dialog box, 28, 165

input controls, 17, 109, 181

Insert

Custom Table, 11

Tables, 10

Insert Calculated Value dialog box, 185, 243, 315

Insert Field or Group, 67

Insert Formula dialog box, 67, 69, 73, 76, 92, 116, 146, 150, 184, 214, 216, 219, 223, 229, 243, 270, 299, 305, 322, 385, 388

Insert Function, 67

Insert Function dialog box, 69, 70, 73, 116, 385

Internet Explorer, 65, 165

Internet Properties dialog box, 165

Internet Security, 165

Invalid number of arguments, 74

invisible field, 41

Is After, 271

Is Before, 271

is blank, 80, 111, 121, 195, 259, 336, 352, 396

is equal to, 101, 104, 121, 156, 177, 223, 229, 233, 243, 305, 412, 425, 441

is greater than, 117, 273

is greater than or equal to, 291

is less than, 420

is less than or equal to, 292, 423

is not blank, 111, 190, 196, 258, 270, 272, 282, 284, 300, 336, 349

is not equal to, 199

is present, 352

J

Julian Day, 276–83

L

label, 14, 322

    dynamic for control, 317

    dynamic on button, 322

Layout

    layout table, 12, 14

    page layout, 12, 14

themes, 11

view, 12

Leave the form open, 141, 156, 164, 173

Limit text box to, 115

line break, 311, 325, 436

List box choices, 111, 203, 205, 209, 213, 241, 259, 425

Local intranet dialog box, 165

long load time, 132

M

Main data source, 21, 350

    automatically create fields or groups, 28, 34, 42, 357, 359

    bind to a different field, 34

    fields, 21

    groups, 21

    myFields, 22

main data source XPath reference, 231

make a field required based on a condition, 194

make control read-only, 104, 106, 108, 259, 327, 370, 372

    after submit, 178

mandatory field, 39, 110–12, 194–95, 303, 351–55

margin, 62

master/detail, 439–54

Master/Detail Binding dialog box, 452

merge cells, 15

Microsoft Office has identified a potential security concern, 163

mod, 417

month name, 242

move a control, 339

move a field, 360

Move Field or Group dialog box, 360

move text, 196

multi-line text box, 37, 115, 310, 436

multiple conditions, 119

multiple views, 49

multiple-selection list box, 294–314

    check if item has been selected, 308

default items, 296–98
Multiple-Selection List Box Properties
   dialog box, 296
myFields, 22

N

NaN, 408
network location, 44
new record, 162, 170
node-set, 292, 377, 383
normalize-space function, 77, 380, 438
not
   function, 425
   operator, 124
now function, 75, 150, 183, 237, 269
number function, 246, 248, 250, 254, 274,
   278, 282, 284
number of occurrences, 419, 423
numeric data type, 114, 187

O

objects, 17, 315
offline, 167
one-to-many, 168
open
   controls task pane, 109
   form template, 8
   InfoPath via command prompt, 3
Open context menu, 8
option button, 189, 198, 317
Option Button Properties dialog box, 198,
   317
Options dialog box, 28, 64, 165
or, 124
order of rules, 87

P

padding, 62
page break, 13
Page Design, 9
   New View, 48

Page Layout Templates, 10
   Themes, 11
   View, 9
   View Properties, 51
   Views, 47
page layout, 9, 12, 14
Page Views, 49
Paste All Rules, 85, 381
paste attachment, 335
Paste Rule, 84, 370, 415, 419, 423
pattern, 113
Perform custom action using Rules, 141,
   151, 156, 173, 176, 178
persist data, 262
Picture, 320
picture button, 131, 143, 153, 319
Picture Button Properties dialog box, 320
plus operator, 186, 401
populate a drop-down list box, 202–12,
   395
preceding, 404
preceding-sibling, 377, 389, 390, 394, 397,
   410, 417
presets, 59
prevent form submit, 154
previous month, 246
Print background colors and pictures, 64
Print Multiple Views dialog box, 57
print settings, 56
print view, 55
Printing, 13
   page break, 13
   Print Preview, 14, 56, 63
processing instruction, 43
Properties, 20
   Control Properties, 20, 37
   Data Format, 182, 188
   Default Value, 69, 73, 76, 80, 89, 182,
      186, 216, 219, 237, 246, 249, 254,
      268, 276, 281, 311, 319, 322, 373,
      375, 385, 387, 390, 393, 401, 403,
      407, 435, 437, 440
   Field Properties, 20, 40, 358
   Hover Picture, 320

Picture, 320
Shading, 199
Submit Actions, 144
Properties dialog box, 37
Publish, 43, 152, 221
Export Source Files, 221
Network Location, 44
Publishing Wizard, 44, 46, 152
Quick Publish, 45
SharePoint Server, 152
publishing a form template, 43
Publishing Wizard dialog box, 44, 46, 152

Q

queryFields, 163, 171
Quick Publish, 45

R

radio button, 189
read-only
after submit, 173–80
control, 103, 178
file attachment, 338–46
repeating table, 371
text box, 38, 371
view, 53, 96, 106, 173–77
Receive data connection, 127, 130, 209,
246, 310
Reconnect, 167
Refresh value when formula is
recalculated, 74, 186, 220, 250, 254,
311, 373, 379, 389, 390, 393, 401, 403,
407, 435, 437, 440
regular expression, 113
remove
attachment, 334, 337
relationship, 170
repeating field, 27, 187, 204, 206, 219,
295, 308, 310, 402, 408
repeating group, 27, 206, 220, 310, 356,
359, 373, 420, 435, 448
repeating section, 27, 163, 171, 346

Set as detail, 445
Repeating Section Properties dialog box,
445
repeating section with controls, 304, 444
repeating table, 27, 101, 171, 205, 284,
346, 355–454
add field to, 358
auto-number rows, 387–89
Include footer, 400, 406
remove first empty row, 363
Set as master, 443
Repeating Table Properties dialog box,
367, 400, 406, 418, 428, 443, 453
required field, 39, 110–12, 194–95, 303,
351–55
resolve errors in formula, 92
resource file, 320
Resource Files dialog box, 131, 321
retrieve data
from database, 133
from SharePoint list, 136
from XML file, 128
Rich Text (XHTML), 29, 358, 362
rich text box, 32, 358, 359, 362
Rows Above, 15
Rows Below, 15
Rule Details dialog box, 90, 95, 96, 103,
157, 174, 176, 179, 229, 258, 270, 337
Rule Inspector, 84, 263
Rules, 79–125
action, 86–97, 89
add a rule, 82
close form, 94
copy a rule, 84, 332, 370, 414, 419, 423
copy all rules, 85, 332, 381
Default Value, 89
delete a rule, 82
disable a rule, 87
Don't run remaining rules, 88, 157, 193,
247, 252
formatting, 97–109
manage rules, 82
multiple conditions, 119
order of, 87, 275, 279

paste a rule, 84, 370, 415, 419, 423
paste all rules, 85, 381
Rule Inspector, 83
switch views, 96
task pane, 81, 82
validation, 109–19
run query, 162, 170

S

save data, 262
save vs. publish, 43
saving a form template, 42
schema, 21
Secondary data source, 127, 130, 132, 135, 138, 215, 220, 231, 259, 262, 348, 350
secondary data source XPath reference, 231
section, 101, 120, 155, 222, 299, 338, 347–55, 418, 427
Section Commands dialog box, 355
security, 165
    Full Trust, 165
    Internet, 165
    message, 163
Select a field or group, 223, 229, 232, 291, 305, 327, 352, 431, 441
Select a Field or Group dialog box, 70, 73, 90, 103, 116, 146, 158, 176, 206, 210, 214, 216, 220, 223, 229, 232, 243, 258, 270, 291, 299, 305, 311, 322, 327, 338, 352, 382, 385, 398, 425, 430, 441
select first item in drop-down list box, 216
Select Table dialog box, 134, 161, 169
selected items in multiple-selection list box, 296–98
Send form data to a single destination, 147
Send only the active view of the form and no attachment, 146
Send the form data as an attachment, 146, 176, 179
set a field's value, 90, 157, 176, 258, 337

Set as default view, 51
Set as detail, 445
Set as master, 443
Set as the default submit connection, 149
set date and time picker date, 242
set date picker date, 241, 246, 268
SharePoint Server, 4
Show file placeholder, 334
Show insert button and hint text, 369, 428
Show on the View menu when filling out this form, 50, 55
Show only entries with unique display names, 211
show read-only view after submit, 173–77
show validation error, 270
Specify default file, 334
Specify Filter Conditions dialog box, 214, 223, 229, 232, 243, 300, 305, 385, 425, 431, 441, 454
speed up initial load time, 132
split cells, 15
Split Cells dialog box, 61
stop rules from running, 88, 157, 193, 247, 252
store a copy of the data in the form template, 134
store data, 262
string function, 249, 381
string-compare function, 271, 292
string-length function, 117
submit a form, 139–80
    As an e-mail message, 145–49
    Set as the default submit connection, 149
    to a database, 160–72
    to multiple destinations, 150
    To SharePoint Library, 150
submit data, 152, 174, 176, 179
Submit data connection, 130, 147
Submit Options dialog box, 140, 147, 151, 156, 173, 176, 178
    Send form data to a single destination, 147

substring function, 77, 183, 239, 242, 244, 249, 253, 254, 260, 274, 278, 282, 284, 397

substring-after function, 182

substring-before function, 258

sum, 186–88, 399–405

sum function, 187, 401, 404, 408

switch from offline to online, 167

switch views, 96, 142, 157, 174, 177

T

Tab index, 332

tab stop, 326

Table Commands dialog box, 368, 418

Table Properties dialog box, 16, 60

Table Tools, 172

    Layout, 172

Tables

    add columns, 15

    add rows, 15

    apply theme, 15

    custom table, 11

    layout table, 12

    merge cells, 15

    split cells, 15

task pane

    Controls, 17, 20, 28, 34, 66, 109, 357, 358, 359

    Fields, 21, 22, 24, 40, 129, 295, 356

    Rules, 81, 82

Text (string), 24, 27, 29, 31, 35, 114, 187, 276, 280, 322, 400, 407, 444, 452

text box, 20, 22, 24, 27, 31, 34, 36, 37, 42, 57, 58, 69, 73, 76, 80, 90, 111, 113, 115, 145, 178, 181–88, 190, 196, 198, 213, 219, 222, 228, 238, 274, 277, 280, 291, 310, 318, 336, 349, 352, 373, 384, 400, 406, 435, 436

    limit amount of characters in, 115

    Multi-line, 37, 115, 310, 436

    Read-only, 38, 371

Text Box Properties dialog box, 37, 66, 69, 182, 188, 219, 400, 436

The expression, 107, 118, 122, 224, 247, 248, 271, 275, 300, 306, 370, 410, 413, 416, 419, 422, 425, 432, 454

The form cannot be submitted because of an error, 172

The form does not contain any new data to submit to the data source, 172

The formula contains one or more errors, 92

The master that you just picked is in an incorrect context, 448

The selected database is not supported in Web browser forms, 135

themes, 11

This form contains validation errors, 302

Time (time), 29, 182

Time Format dialog box, 183, 185

today function, 237, 246, 249, 254, 274, 276, 396

toggle a check box, 192

translate function, 71, 225, 386, 454

trim text, 77

true function, 107, 180, 191, 301, 370, 380

True/False (boolean), 24, 29, 178, 191, 372, 380

U

Unbound (Control cannot store data), 36

unbound control, 23, 34

UNC, 165

Use a formula, 118, 214, 223, 243, 248, 273, 299, 305, 385, 419, 422, 425, 432

userName function, 151

V

validate

    a check box, 190

    a date, 254

    numbers, 114

validation errors, 112, 303

Validation rules, 79, 109–19

Value when checked, 191, 372, 380

Value when cleared, 191, 372, 380
value when selected, 198, 317
Verify Formula, 68
View Properties dialog box, 51
Views, 12, 47–66
    add a second view, 48–52
    background image, 58
    copy all controls, 54, 330
    copy view, 54, 330
    current view, 49
    default view, 9, 47, 51
    delete a view, 50
    delete last view, 47
    New View, 48
    Print Multiple Views, 56
    Print Preview, 56
    print settings, 56
    print view, 55
    properties, 51
    read-only view, 53, 173–77
    remove a view from the Current View
      menu, 50
    Set as default view, 51
    Show on the View menu when filling
      out this form, 50, 55
    switch, 96, 142, 157, 174, 177

W

web browser form, 4
week, 268, 393
what is InfoPath, vii–viii
Whole Number (integer), 29, 114, 187,
    249, 254, 274, 277, 281, 301, 406
working offline, 167

X

xdXDocument, 231
    get-DOM, 224, 231, 244, 292, 306, 425
    GetDOM, 216, 220, 224, 231, 244, 292,
      428
XML, 1, 8, 9, 21
    attribute, 26, 211, 253
    element, 26, 212, 253
    processing instruction, 43
    schema, 21
XPath, 67
    ancestor, 378
    ancestor-or-self, 378
    axes, 378
    child, 378
    context node, 252, 287, 313, 318, 375,
      377, 388–89, 391, 402–5, 410, 414,
      438
    copy expression for field, 432
    current(), 432
    descendant, 378
    descendant-or-self, 378
    filter, 218, 312, 386, 391
    following-sibling, 377, 414
    parent, 379
    preceding, 379, 404
    preceding-sibling, 377, 389, 390, 394,
      397, 410, 417
    self, 379
XSN, 1, 8

Y

year, 238
You are working offline, 167

16869674R00288

Made in the USA
Middletown, DE
23 December 2014